Woman, Ma

Asian Voices
Series Editor: Mark Selden

Woman, Man, Bangkok

Love, Sex, and Popular Culture in Thailand

Scot Barmé

ROWMAN & LITTLEFIELD PUBLISHERS, INC.
Lanham • Boulder • New York • Oxford

ROWMAN & LITTLEFIELD PUBLISHERS, INC.

Published in the United States of America
by Rowman & Littlefield Publishers, Inc.
An Imprint of the Rowman & Littlefield Publishing Group
4720 Boston Way, Lanham, Maryland 20706
www.rowmanlittlefield.com

12 Hid's Copse Road, Cumnor Hill, Oxford OX2 9JJ, England

British Library Cataloguing in Publication Information Available

Library of Congress Cataloging-in-Publication Data

Barmé, Scot.
   Woman, man, Bangkok : love, sex, and popular culture in Thailand / Scot Barmé.
      p.   cm. — (Asian voices)
   Includes bibliographical references and index.
   ISBN 0-7425-0156-6 (cloth : alk. paper) — ISBN 0-7425-0157-4 (pbk. : alk. paper)
      1. Man-woman relationships—Thailand—Bangkok.   2. Sex role—Thailand—
Bangkok.   3. Sex customs—Thailand—Bangkok.   4. Sex in popular culture—
Thailand—Bangkok.   5. Sex in literature.   6. Love in motion pictures.
   7. Bangkok (Thailand)—Social life and customs.   I. Title.   II. Asian voices
(Rowman and Littlefield, inc.)
   HQ801.A3 B37   2002
   306.7'09593—dc21   2001058739

Printed in the United States of America

∞ ™ The paper used in this publication meets the minimum requirements of American
National Standard for Information Sciences—Permanence of Paper for Printed Library
Materials, ANSI/NISO Z39.48-1992.

Contents

Acknowledgments

I am greatly indebted to Mark Selden, editor extraordinaire, for his ever-thoughtful comments and advice, not to mention providing me with the encouragement and inspiration to complete this book. At the same time, I offer my heartfelt thanks to my brother, Geremie Barmé, and Miriam Lang for invaluable suggestions that enabled me to transform a somewhat wooden academic thesis into the present, hopefully more readable, work.

Every book needs a cover and in this respect I was particularly fortunate in securing the creative talents of Emily Brissenden, a gifted graphic artist from the Cartography Section of the Research School at the Australian National University (ANU). My thanks also go to Jude Shanahan from the Division of Pacific and Asian History, ANU, for her assistance in dealing with various technical matters. Finally I would like to express my gratitude to the Division of Pacific and Asian History, RSPAS, ANU for providing me with the resources, the facilities, and (no exaggeration here) a perfect working environment to bring this project to fruition.

Introduction

C onsider the following comic exchange that appeared in the humor page of Siam's first movie magazine, *Phaphayon sayam* (Siam Cinema) in mid-1922. A teacher in a boy's school is addressing his class:

Teacher: Students, I hope you can all remember what I told you about the duty of each and every young man. That duty is to give one's unswerving loyalty to the Nation, the Religion [Buddhism], and the King.

Now, I'd like to pose a question. Imagine enemy forces are attacking Paknam [at the mouth of the Chaophraya River as it flows into the gulf of Thailand]. At this very moment I learn that someone is in my home fooling around with my wife. Class, tell me: what should I do?

The students rose to their feet as a group and, with a single voice, replied "Sir, go home."

Teacher: That's right! That's it! That's exactly what I was thinking.[1]

On one level, the joke may seem to be little more than ephemera from the realm of popular culture. On another level, however, it is of particular interest for the way it pokes fun at the type of self-serving, royal-centered nationalist rhetoric espoused, ad nauseam, by the Thai monarch, King Vajiravudh (r. 1910–1925).[2] Simply put, we find the humorist turning the monarch's conception of duty on its head by insisting that one's greatest loyalty was not so much to "Nation, Religion, and King" but rather to one's kin, with the writer suggesting that, in the overall scheme of things, the intimate, intensely personal sphere was what really mattered. More generally the joke, with its mockery of official nationalist discourse was, in its own small way, indicative of the changing tenor of public life in Bangkok during the early 1920s.

By this time the Siamese capital, which was becoming ever more closely inte-

1

grated into the nascent global capitalist economy, had developed an increasingly cosmopolitan, outward-looking character. To a large degree this process was shaped by the spread of new mass media technologies. With the advent of the popular press in its various guises (daily newspapers, magazines, comic books, and translated works of both fiction and nonfiction) and the expansion of the cinema business (which screened a variety of imported Western and, from the late 1920s, locally made films), the urban populace was exposed to a ceaseless flow of information, ideas, and images from both home and abroad. The development of print media and film during the early decades of the twentieth century marked the beginning of a new era in Siam's history. At one and the same time these mass technologies allowed for new popular forms of cultural expression and representation while providing members of the public with an enhanced awareness, if not always a thorough understanding, of a wider, largely Western-dominated, world. New conceptual horizons unfolded through both print and film, while audiences could adopt new points of reference and comparison, not only in terms of lifestyles, fashion, and habits of consumption but also with regard to social practices and forms of governance and administration.

Yet despite the growing cosmopolitanism of the capital, Siam remained one of the world's last surviving absolute monarchies, a country ruled by a small royal-aristocratic class and possessed of a strongly hierarchical social order in which distinctions based on rank, privilege, and wealth were paramount. From the latter nineteenth to the early part of the twentieth centuries, the monarchy and members of the princely elite were at the forefront of a complex and far-reaching process whereby Siam began modernizing and developing closer relations with the major foreign powers (notably Britain, France, the United States, and, to a lesser extent, Japan), a process which contributed to maintaining its political if not economic sovereignty. By the time the humorist writing for *Sayam phaphayon* penned the comic sketch cited above, however, the zeal for reform which characterized the reign of King Mongkut (r.1851–1868), and more particularly that of his son Chulalongkorn (r.1868–1910), had long since run its course. Rather than being an enlightened, benevolent force for change, the absolute monarchy came to be regarded by growing numbers of politically aware commoners as an archaic, repressive institution which impeded Siam's progress, while the social order fostered by absolutism was seen as moribund and profoundly corrupt. With the birth of the popular press such views were given free rein and elite authority came to be questioned and challenged to an unprecedented degree.

The press served as the primary forum for wide-ranging public debates that encompassed not only politics but also the economy, questions of social equality and justice, morality, the status of women, and relations between the sexes as well as consumerism, dress, and so on. These debates, which intensified from the early 1920s onward, are perhaps best seen as the most telling manifestation of an emergent Thai "imagined community," to invoke that simple yet incisive concept formulated by Benedict Anderson to refer to the nation.[3] Unlike the monarch Vajiravudh's view of the nation, which in essence was embodied by the throne, this broader community (albeit overwhelmingly Bangkok-centric in character) was a far more inclusive entity, representing popular interests rather than simply those of the ruling house. At the same time, and in a somewhat more diffuse manner, the idea of an imagined community was also being fostered by the development of indigenous prose fiction writing and local filmmaking, two areas of cultural production dominated by members of the rising middle class.

Significantly, both Thai and foreign historical writing on the transformations in early-twentieth-century Siam has, for the most part, generally little to say about commoners being the harbingers of political and social change and renewal. Instead one finds a singular emphasis given to the role played by the royal elite in the creation of the modern nation.[4] This is typified in the work of such Western scholars as Benjamin Batson, Walter Vella, and David Wyatt whose writings—underpinned by the "Great Man" theory of history—on King Prajadhipok (Rama 7), King Vajiravudh (Rama 6), and King Chulalongkorn (Rama 5) have provided strong academic endorsement for official Thai national-ist discourse.[5] In essence this discourse reduces Thai history to a hagiographic narrative that extols the munificence and sagacity of the house of Cakri through the ages up to the present. In contemporary Thailand this narrative, deployed and constantly reiterated through the education system and the media, remains virtually unimpeachable.[6] As a consequence, while there is a keen historical awareness about the activities of kings and princes, far less is known about the people they ruled over.

Recently, however, studies by Nakkharin Mektrairat and Matthew Copeland, both of which deal with the overthrow of the monarchy in 1932, have chal-lenged conventional interpretations of this key event in modern Thai history by examining aspects of growing popular resentment toward absolutism in the dec-ades prior to 1932.[7] These works argue that the overthrow of the monarchy was not simply the seizure of power by a small group of disaffected military officers and their civilian allies, as the dominant historiography would have it, but rather a response on the part of these individuals to a deep-seated malaise that had infected Siamese society and the body politic over a period of many years. The present work builds on and extends these pathbreaking studies in the sense that it seeks, among other things, to develop a fuller understanding of the social and intellectual context in which the breakdown of absolute rule took place. While the writings of Nakkharin and Copeland are primarily concerned with the politi-cal realm, this study examines aspects of the changing sociocultural landscape in Bangkok during roughly the same period (from around the turn of the twentieth century to the overthrow of the monarchy in June 1932), and traces this change into the early years of the constitutional era. In doing this I principally focus on questions relating to gender, class, and popular culture and the intersections between these particular domains.

GENDER AND GENDER RELATIONS
IN SIAMESE HISTORIOGRAPHY

In a number of his writings, Craig Reynolds, arguably the most influential contemporary Western historian of Thailand, has referred to the lack of research on Siamese social history. The most recent of these is an essay entitled "Predicaments of Modern Thai History."[8] Open to and informed by the impact of contemporary feminist theory within the Western academy, Reynolds addresses the issue of gender relations in Thai studies, noting the paucity of *historical* research in this area (there is, by contrast, a growing body of research on contemporary gender issues).[9] Indeed, it should be emphasized that with few exceptions,[10] the small corpus of Thai and English language scholarship on gender does not so much deal with relations between the sexes as concentrate squarely on the historical experience of Siamese women.[11] And while such women's history may provide a useful corrective to dominant male-centered representations of the past, it has not had any fundamental impact on the way Thai historiography is practiced or thought about. As such, questions relating to gender have tended to remain on the margins of historical inquiry.

In order to move ahead, a broader approach to the study of gender is in order—one in which the complex exchanges and mutual relationships *between* the sexes is given greater attention and recognition. Here Reynolds's argument is of fundamental import. He writes that we should not treat gender as "a subfield in Thai historiography, a specialized compartment of Thai history," but regard it as being "really central to the history of the Thai/Tai people."[12] The reason for this, he adds, is that by doing so it "could help us untangle nationalist historiography which reads the past in the image of the nation-state. And it could help us better understand power relations in Thai social formations."[13] This latter notion converges with ideas articulated by the feminist historian Joan Scott, who has argued that gender is "a primary way of signifying relationships of power," and that it can become "implicated in the conception and construction of power itself."[14]

As we shall see, questions relating to gender were integral to the broader transformation of power relations in Siam during the transition from royal absolutism to the new post-1932 polity. Throughout the last decade of absolute rule the issue of social equality, in a general sense, was much debated in the press. The subject of equality between the sexes featured prominently in this discussion, with the views and ideas expressed by educated young men and women providing what was in effect an unparalleled commentary on the relationship between gender and power in early-twentieth-century Siam. It was frequently argued that if the country was to progress and join the world of modern civilized nations females needed to be given greater social recognition and afforded the same educational opportunities as males, although at this point there was little discussion about equal opportunity with regard to employment. Meanwhile growing numbers of women (and some men) availed themselves of the press to argue for equality in marriage. The centuries-old practice of polygamy (closely associated with the male elite) was bitterly condemned, with its critics demanding that the state, in the interests of justice and fairness, introduce new legislation instituting monogamy.

In addition to questions of gender equality with respect to education and marriage, the issue of prostitution—which rapidly developed into a burgeoning industry from the early twentieth century and represented perhaps the most striking expression of differences and tensions in male/female power—stimulated a great deal of debate and criticism among those opposed to the absolutist social order. This historical reality has been scarcely recognized, however. While there exists a large body of academic research on various aspects of prostitution in modern-day Thailand,[15] the earlier history of the commercial trade in sex has not received much scholarly attention. Indeed, to my knowledge the only in-depth primary-source based historical study of prostitution in Siam is an unpublished Thai language master's thesis and a related (published) article—also in Thai—by Dararat Mettarikanon.[16] And while Dararat's study ostensibly covers the period up until 1960, when the Sarit regime (1957–1963) enacted more rigorous legislation that did away with the existing, and largely ignored, system of registering brothels and prostitutes, it primarily focuses on the nineteenth century into the early 1900s and has very little to say about what transpired in the subsequent decades. The present study examines developments in the 1920s and 1930s when prostitution became part and parcel of Bangkok public life. Here one may add that—in light of the controversy that erupted in mid-1993 when the British Longman Group published its *Dictionary of English Language and Culture*—there is a certain irony about this aspect of the Thai past. The Longman book, in which Bangkok was described as "famous for its temples . . . and a place where there are a lot of prostitutes" was roundly condemned by many Thais who were, understandably, enraged by such a glib characterization of their city.[17] Yet by the 1920s this was precisely the way that numerous contributors to the Thai popular press had come to see Bangkok.

Of course prostitution was nothing new to Siam, the existence of the trade being documented back into the Ayuthayan period (1350–1767).[18] From the latter nineteenth century, however, the scale of the practice grew dramatically. This development was part of a broader regional phenomenon stimulated by the spread of imperialism and the concomitant growth of the international market economy. Indeed, to a significant degree the intensification of prostitution in Bangkok during the late nineteenth century paralleled developments in the burgeoning colonial port cities of Singapore and Hong Kong. Following the opening of the Treaty ports in China during the 1840s and the subsequent relaxation of the Middle Kingdom's emigration policy, millions of poor but determined Chinese from the southeastern provinces Fukien and Kwangtung left their homeland in the hope of improving their fortunes overseas.[19] In Southeast Asia the British, eager to develop their colonial empire, encouraged this development. Nowhere was this more dramatic than in Singapore, where an immense force of young immigrant Chinese males were employed in transforming Singapore into a major international trade center. The sexual needs of these men were largely met by women brought to the colony specifically for this purpose from China and, to a lesser extent, from impoverished regions of southern Japan.[20] Meanwhile there was a similar inflow of Chinese coolie laborers into Siam to work on various large-scale infrastructure projects that were undertaken as the kingdom became drawn into the international economy. Unlike the case in Singapore, however, the prostitutes who serviced these men were primarily local (Siamese) women. At the same time some Chinese women also came into the country to work in the sex trade, together with a handful of prostitutes from Japan as well a small number from various European countries (in particular Russia), who, for the most part, plied their trade with Western seamen and other travelers who frequented the Bangkok port. Apart from the immigrant Chinese workforce and foreign male visitors, an expanding Siamese clientele for prostitution also began developing from around the early 1900s in the wake of major reforms to the administration of the country that saw the creation of a "modern"-style salaried bureaucracy. Growing male demand and increasing monetarization of the economy, together with various sociocultural factors discussed later in this work, helped create the conditions under which prostitution was to flourish in Bangkok to an unprecedented extent.

As mentioned earlier, the period covered by this study ranges from the beginning of the twentieth century until the early years of the constitutional era. This period marks the onset of what we may think of as modern Thai life, a time when a whole host of issues, concerns, practices, and cultural forms that appear as wholly contemporary first came into focus. Like many other terms commonly employed in scholarly discourse, the word "modern" is problematic in the sense that it has no immutable, universally agreed upon meaning (as if this were ever possible!). More than half a century ago, for example, Walter Benjamin remarked that "no epoch has existed that did not feel itself . . . to be 'modern,' "[21] while more recently leading Thai historian Thongchai Winichakul has made a similar observation, arguing that it is a "misleading" term, both "vague and relative [and one] which hardly signifies any specific historical character."[22] Bearing this in mind my use of word "modern" needs some clarification.

Broadly speaking I regard "modern," in the present context, to refer to the growth of the Siamese market economy from the latter nineteenth century and certain related transformations. In particular I am concerned with a fundamental change in the Thai social formation that saw the appearance of new social classes and the related development of mass commercial culture through which growing numbers of the populace were exposed to a myriad of ideas and influences. It was in this context that a Thai imagined community (alluded to above) emerged, and individuals personally unknown to one another began to engage in print-mediated public debate and discussion about "national" issues and concerns.

The spread of market relations as the kingdom opened up to the forces of international capitalism led to the gradual freeing up of the population, unsettling and transforming the premodern bonds of dependency and servitude, not to mention relations between the sexes. This was a complex, uneven, and drawn-out process, a transition from a social formation with a marked hierarchy of status and power based on a range of patron-client, legal-coercive relations, to one increasingly shaped by the market. As this took place, however, forms of patronage did not cease to exist, but rather became imbricated with those of class in dynamic and complex ways.[23]

BANGKOK SOCIETY IN THE EARLY TWENTIETH CENTURY

As indicated earlier, the geographical focus of this study is limited to the Thai capital, Bangkok, the epicenter of the country's socioeconomic transformation. In his study, Nakkharin sees Bangkok society during the early twentieth century as consisting of five distinct social groups or classes, largely based on occupational categories. These groups or classes were: royalty (*klum chao-nai*), the bureaucracy (*klum kha-ratchakan*), the middle class outside the bureaucracy (*klum khon chan-klang n'ok rab'op ratchakan*), the mass of common folk (*klum ratsad'on samanchon*), and a class or strata of literati or intellectuals (*klum panyachon*)— "the leading thinkers of the age."[24]

Given the unattributed nature of much of the available source material (editorials, articles, and so on in various newspapers, magazines, and journals), however, it is difficult to develop a nuanced analysis of the social tensions, conflicts, and dynamics of this period in terms of such discrete categories. In this regard, for example, we may briefly consider the critical assault on the upper echelons of society featured in the popular press from the early 1920s. This criticism was mounted by educated commoners from *both* within and outside the bureaucracy. Some of the latter were professional journalists who may be classified as part of an incipient literati, but many others—public-spirited nonprofessional observers and commentators—also sought to express their views in print. Similarly, elements from the middle and lower levels of the bureaucracy, writing anonymously, used the press to voice criticisms of their superiors. These critical voices can perhaps best be seen as coming from the ranks of a disenfranchised middle stratum as a whole. Given this, I propose a somewhat simpler model than Nak-kharin's by suggesting that early-twentieth-century Bangkok should be seen to have, in broad structural terms, three social groupings or classes.

At one end of the social spectrum was the ruling elite consisting of members of the upper levels of royalty and the nobility who dominated the state adminis-tration, together with powerful ethnic Chinese and Sino-Thai entrepreneurs who were often closely allied with various Western business interests. This repre-sented the male component of the ruling class. As for women from the elite stratum they inhabited a parallel world of comfort and ease. With the exception of a small number working in the field of education and health care, high-born women generally confined their activities to domestic matters and socializing with one another, although some also had a significant involvement in various rentier and money-lending activities.[25]

At the opposite social pole, a diverse urban proletariat of wage laborers had emerged, primarily composed of male Chinese immigrants but, from the latter nineteenth century onward, also comprising a growing Thai element, most nota-bly in the key transport sector (that is, the Bangkok tramways and the Siamese State Railway). In addition, numbers of lower-class women began working as wage laborers in Bangkok's small, though gradually expanding, industrial sector. For the most part, the majority of lower-class women did not work for a fixed, regular wage but earned a living through various marketing activities, or as inde-pendent providers of urban services (washerwomen, cleaners, and seamstresses) and, increasingly in the case of the young, as prostitutes. At this lower social level there were also substantial numbers of domestic servants, both female and male, who either worked for their board and lodgings in a more traditional man-ner or also received supplementary monetary payments.[26] Furthermore, there was a pool of unemployed and underemployed males from whose ranks came the "foot soldiers" of an expanding urban criminal milieu that had various linkages with elements in the upper sections of society.[27]

Located in between the small, elite capitalist class and the mass of uneducated urban workers emerged a growing but diffuse intermediate social stratum, or "middle class," composed of young, literate commoner men and women, created through the processes of economic change and administrative and educational reform. Indeed, many of these young folk came to Bangkok from the provinces to further their schooling and subsequently stayed on to seek paid employment.[28]

As Pamela Pilbeam points out in her work on a similar but earlier develop-ment in Europe, conceptualizing the "middle class" is deeply problematic. According to her the term "middle class" represents "a chameleon among defi-nitions, whether flopped down vaguely to cover multifarious ignorance, used with attempted precision by social scientists searching for rigor and objectivity, or employed by political commentators as a term of praise or a weapon in an ideological armory."[29]

In Siam during the period under discussion this new social stratum is similarly difficult to conceptualize with precision. As such, it must be thought of in broad, fairly general terms. I would suggest that the emergent Siamese middle class, which numbered many thousands by the early 1920s, was heterogeneous in terms of ethnic makeup, educational achievement, and income levels. Roughly speaking, it was composed of both Thai and Chinese elements, with the male component of the former group drawn largely from the lower and middle ranks of the newly restructured bureaucracy, while the latter were to be found working in the private sector as lesser merchants and entrepreneurs, skilled artisans, and the like. There was also a less-easily categorized Sino-Thai element (of mixed Thai-Chinese parentage), which was to be found in both the public and the private sectors. In addition, from the early twentieth century there were growing numbers of educated Siamese commoners working outside the state bureaucracy.

And what can be said of the women from the middle classes? At the beginning of the 1920s employment opportunities for such women—as was the case for their upper-class counterparts—were very limited, the areas of teaching and health care similarly being the main socially recognized avenues for paid work. More often than not women from the middle as well as the upper classes continued to be found in the domestic sphere, although this situation was not static and, as we shall see, began to change significantly as the decade wore on.

THE MIDDLE CLASS AS A CULTURAL AND SOCIAL FORCE

From the beginning of the 1920s, if not somewhat earlier, the emergent middle stratum began to assume an increasingly powerful influence in Siamese cultural life, which had previously been dominated by the princely elite. Middle-class entrepreneurs became deeply involved in various forms of commercial publishing as well as filmmaking, while other members of the middle class produced the material used in these enterprises, fusing both imported and local elements to create a new hybrid form of mass culture.

Broadly speaking, the spread of print and film—of both foreign and local varieties—helped establish the grounds for what amounted to a new "social theory," a term I use in the sense articulated by Fred Inglis in his work on popular culture. For Inglis, social theory does not mean a totalizing discourse or abstraction, but is rather conceived in terms of a narrative, for the simple but compelling reason that "stories are our essential instruments for turning the intense inanity of events into intelligible experience. . . . [These] stories are shaped out of the facts of life as well as out of the stories we contingently listen to. From these we construct a library of templates which we bring to the events as they trundle massively towards us."[30]

With the diffusion of commercial publishing and film, readers and cinema audiences were exposed to a plethora of new narratives from which they could shape, inform, or enrich their lives. In effect, then, the quintessentially modern technologies of mechanized print and film were integral to the process of constructing and deploying new social meanings in Siam, and to the creation of national narratives—that is, stories framed in terms of the nation.

From within the ranks of the expanding middle class emerged the leading proponents of notions integral to the idea of modernity itself, that is, the belief in such things as human equality, individual freedom, and female emancipation.[31] As bearers of modernity, elements of the middle class were involved in two broad, interrelated, transformative processes: the articulation and development of new ideas for the betterment and progress of the Siamese nation, on the one hand, and the questioning of absolutist social, economic, and political power on the other. Central to this study is an examination of these twin processes of social definition, or redefinition, and the popular critique of authority with specific reference to questions concerning the changing status of women and relations between the sexes. As I have already noted, transformations in these areas were emblematic of changing power relations in society more generally.

A useful point of reference for much of the discussion to be taken up in the following chapters is George Mosse's work on European social history.[32] Mosse argues that from the late eighteenth to the early nineteenth century notions of respectability and propriety espoused by the rising bourgeoisie in various European states became closely bound up with the discourse on nationalism.

> Through respectability, [the middle classes] sought to maintain their status and self-respect against both the lower classes and the aristocracy.[33]

> [Nationalism] absorbed and sanctioned middle-class manners and morals and played a crucial part in spreading respectability to all classes of the population, however much these classes hated and despised one another.[34]

Respectability, seen by Mosse as a touchstone of middle-class identity, was a wide-ranging concept embracing distinctive attitudes and behaviors in areas as diverse as table manners and relations between the sexes. It was a way for defining what was appropriate and worthy and what was not.

Two aspects of Mosse's discussion are of particular interest, those concerning sexual behavior and the notion of chivalry. With regard to the former, Mosse notes that members of the middle classes came to see sexual license in various forms as a significant threat to the social and moral order underpinning the state. In this context he suggests that nationalism and respectability "joined hands," as the former served as a countervailing force to uncontrolled sexuality by functioning to "redirect . . . [human] passions to a higher purpose."[35]

The notion of chivalry, which reinforced the idea of respectability, represented the polar opposite of self-indulgence and sexual excess. Born of the romantic tradition, chivalry, as conceived of by Sir Walter Scott, stood for "individual freedom in the service of the social order." It was that which "distinguishe[d] the gentle knight from the churl or the savage."[36] This notion of chivalry, embodied in the independent yet considerate and dedicated individual, was central to the ideal of romantic love which came to be represented endlessly in the literary form most closely identified with the ascendant bourgeoisie, the novel.

Returning to the Siamese case, it was during the last decade of absolute rule that various middle-class writers and commentators sought to define and delineate what they considered to be the appropriate relations between men and women. Something akin to Mosse's notions of respectability and chivalry were central to this process. These notions, for example, informed the conception of what it was to be a "gentleman" (*suphap-burut*) (that of the "gentlewoman" [*suphap-satri*] came to be based on a combination of "traditional" domestic skills and "modern" learning and sociability) as well as the idea of romantic love with its emphasis on independence, mutual fidelity, understanding and the family as a stable social unit. As we shall see, the expression of these new social meanings—through the new mass cultural forms of print and film—were often at odds with prevailing values and modes of social life, and developed within and against an environment in which gender relations, and social relations more generally, were in an unprecedented state of flux. Among other things, this sociological process of redefinition sought to establish order through the creation of a new contemporary morality that was seen as fundamental to the nation's progress and prosperity.

This study covers a good deal of territory incorporating a variety of interrelated topics. Chapter 1 looks at Siamese women's magazines from the early 1900s and the emergence of what may be described as a protofeminist discourse. Chapter 2 deals with the opening up of cultural space by the rising middle class in the first three decades of the twentieth century, focusing on the development of the cinema, prose fiction writing, and filmmaking during this period. In chapter 3 I look at the cinema as a social institution, suggesting that it represented a microcosm of Bangkok urban life during the 1920s. Chapter 4 is structured around a series of satirical newspaper cartoons that convey a sense of the popular anger and resentment directed toward the royal-noble ruling elite at the time. Chapters 5 and 6 look in detail at debates in the popular press concerned with the issues of female education and employment, polygamy, and prostitution during the last decade of absolutism. In chapter 7 the discussion moves from the critical to the prescriptive domain with an examination of new middle-class notions of sexual morality and propriety. Chapter 8 looks at a range of fictional and cinematic representations of contemporary womanhood as well as those concerned with male behavior in relation to women. The final chapter is concerned with a number of developments in the years following the overthrow of the absolute monarchy, in particular the last flourish of the Thai feminist press, and the way in which Siam's post-1932 rulers sought to incorporate women and romance into a new vision of the nation.

NOTE ON SOURCE MATERIALS
AND TRANSLITERATION

This book is largely based on materials from the National Library of Thailand in Bangkok, including Thai-language newspapers, newspaper cartoons, and magazines together with the English-language *Bangkok Times Weekly Mail* (for full details of the press and magazine materials consulted, see the bibliography). I also availed myself of a small number of official government documents from the National Archives of Thailand. In addition, I was fortunate enough to gain access to a number of rare film booklets, 1920s Thai novelettes, short stories, and other difficult to come by texts through the good graces of Dome Sukwongse from the National Film Archive of Thailand. Furthermore, I obtained copies of a number of useful Thai-language M.A. theses held at the libraries of Chulalongkorn and Thammasat Universities.

While conducting preliminary research in Canberra I made use of the extensive microfilm holdings of the *Bangkok Times* at the National Library of Australia. For the most part material incorporated in this study is drawn from the English-language section of the *Times*, although in one or two instances I also made use of the Thai-language section of the paper.

As for transliteration I employ a slightly modified form of the Thai Royal Institute system of Romanization in the case of certain vowels and diphthongs (all Thai words are written in italics). The differences are as follows:

Royal Institute	My system
ua	*'ua*
uai	*'uay*
iu	*iw*
eo	*ew*
aeo	*aew*
ieo	*iaw*
ru	*r'u*

As for initial and final consonants I use the Royal Institute system without modification. Compound nouns are hyphenated (e.g., *khwam-rak* [love]), while proper names (e.g., *thai* [Thai], *sayam* [Siam]) are not capitalized unless they come at the beginning of a transliterated phrase or happen to be the first word in the title of a particular text.

NOTES

1. *Phaphayon sayam*, 10 July 1922.
2. Scot Barmé, *Luang Wichit Wathakan and the Creation of a Thai National Identity* (Singapore: Institute of Southeast Asian Studies, 1993), 28–29.
3. Benedict R. O'G. Anderson, *Imagined Communities: Reflections on the Origin and Spread of Nationalism* (London: Verso, 1991).
4. See, for example, Nuttanee Ratanapat, "King Vajiravudh's Nationalism and Its Impact on Political Development in Thailand," Ph.D. diss., Northern Illinois University, 1990, Ann Arbor, Mich.: University Microfilms; Benjamin A. Batson, *The End of the Absolute Monarchy in Siam* (Singapore: Oxford University Press, 1984); J. C. Ingram, *Economic Change in Thailand, 1850–1970* (Stanford, Calif.: Stanford University Press, 1971); Ian Brown, *The Elite and the Economy in Siam, 1890–1920* (Singapore: Oxford University Press, 1988).
5. Batson, *End of the Absolute Monarchy*; Walter F. Vella, *Chaiyo! King Vajiravudh and the Development of Thai Nationalism* (Honolulu: University of Hawaii Press, 1978); David K. Wyatt, *The Politics of Reform in Thailand: Education in the Reign of King Chulalongkorn* (New Haven, Conn.: Yale University Press, 1969).
6. At times this reality is not fully appreciated by those unfamiliar with the mind-set of Thai officialdom. A recent case in point concerns Twentieth Century Fox when it sought permission to film the historical romance *Anna and the King*, an updated nonmusical version of its 1956 production *The King and I* (starring Yul Bryner and Deborah Kerr), in Thailand. As the company learnt to its cost, seeking to portray the monarchy at odds with this narrative proved totally unacceptable, with the National Film Board denying the company's request and subsequently banning the completed film (eventually made on location in Malaysia) from being shown in Thailand. See *Bangkok Post* 10, 14 November 1998.
7. Matthew P. Copeland, "Contested Nationalism and the 1932 Overthrow of the Absolute Monarchy in Siam," Ph.D. diss., Australian National University, Canberra, 1993; Nakkharin Mektrairat, *Kan-patiwat sayam ph'o s'o 2475* [The Siamese Revolution of 1932] (Bangkok: Foundation for the Social Sciences and Humanities [*Mulaniti sangkhomsat lae manutsat*], 1992).
8. Craig J. Reynolds, "Predicaments of Modern Thai History," *Southeast Asian Research* 12, no. 1 (March 1994): 64–90.
9. For example, see Peter A. Jackson and Nerida M. Cook, *Genders and Sexualities in Modern Thailand* (Chiang Mai: Silkworm Books, 1999).
10. Craig J. Reynolds, "A Nineteenth-Century Thai Buddhist Defense of Polygamy and Some Remarks on the Social History of Women in Thailand," paper presented at the Seventh Conference, International Association of Historians of Asia, Chulalongkorn University, Bangkok, August 22–26, 1977; William A. Callahan, "The Ideology of Miss

Thailand in National, Consumerist, and Transnational Space," *Alternatives* 23 (1998): 29–61.

11. For example, see Darunee Tantiwiramanond and Shashi Pandey, "The Status and Role of Thai Women in the Pre-modern Period: A Historical and Cultural Perspective," *Sojourn* 2, no.1 (February 1987): 125–49; Suwadee Tanaprasitpatana, "Thai Society's Expectations of Women, 1851–1935," Ph.D. diss., Sydney University, 1989; Siriphorn Sakhrobanek, "Kan riak-r'ong sithi-satri kh'ong ying thai (2398–2475)" [Thai Women Call for Their Rights, 1855–1932], *Satrithat* (August–October 1983), 28–35; Yuphaphorn Chaengchemchit, "Kan-s'uksa kh'ong satri thai: s'uksa korani chaph'o kh'ong rong-rian rachini 2447–250" [Thai Women's Education: The Case of the Rachini School, 1904–60], M.A. thesis, Thammasat University, Bangkok, 1987; Hong Lysa, "Palace Women at the Margins of Social Change: An Aspect of the Politics of Social History in the Reign of King Chulalongkorn," *Journal of Southeast Asian Studies* 30, no. 20 (September 1999): 310–24.

12. Reynolds, "Predicaments," 64–65.

13. Reynolds, "Predicaments," 64–65.

14. Joan W. Scott, *Gender and the Politics of History* (New York: Columbia University Press, 1988), 44–45.

15. For example, see Pasuk Phongphaichit, *From Peasant Girls to Bangkok Masseuses* (Geneva: International Labor Organization 1982); Wathinee Boonchalaksi and Philip Guest, *Prostitution in Thailand* (Salaya, Nakhon Pathom: Institute for Population and Social Research, Mahidol University, 1994); Jeremy Seabrook, *Travels in the Skin Trade: Tourism and the Sex Industry* (London: Pluto Press, 1996); Ryan Bishop and Lillian S. Robinson, *Night Market: Sexual Cultures and the Thai Economic Miracle* (New York: Routledge, 1998).

16. Dararat Mettarikanon, "Sopheni kap naiyobai rathaban thai ph'o s'o 2411–2503" [Prostitution and Thai Government Policy, 1868–1960], M.A. thesis, Chulalongkorn University, Bangkok, 1983. A condensed overview of her thesis was published in *Silapa-watthanatham* [Arts and Culture] 5, 1984.

17. *The Nation*, July 4, 1993.

18. Simon de la Loubere, *The Kingdom of Siam* (Singapore: Oxford University Press, 1969).

19. James Francis Warren, *Ah Ku and Karayuki-san: Prostitution in Singapore 1870–1940* (Singapore: Oxford University Press, 1993), 9.

20. Warren, *Ah Ku and Karayuki-san*, 3–5, 25–28.

21. Cited in David Frisby, *Fragments of Modernity: Theories of Modernity in the Work of Simmel, Kracauer, and Benjamin* (Cambridge: Polity Press, 1985), 266.

22. Thongchai Winichakul, *Siam Mapped: A History of the Geo-Body of a Nation* (Honolulu: University of Hawaii Press, 1994), 19.

23. The early careers of educated commoners such as Luang Wichit Wathakan and Kulap Saipradit are instructive with regard to the question of patronage. Wichit's rise in the bureaucracy was facilitated by patrons in high places while Kulap Saipradit's attempts at pursuing a similar career path were thwarted by a singular lack of patronage. See Scot Barmé, *Luang Wichit Wathakan*, 57; Scot Barmé, *Kulap in Oz: A Thai View of Australian Life and Society in the Late 1940s* (Melbourne: Monash Asia Institute, 1995), xvi.

24. Nakkharin, *The Siamese Revolution of 1932*, 13.

25. Suwadee, "Thai Society's Expectations of Women," 163–66.

26. Suwadee, "Thai Society's Expectations of Women," 170–72, 185.

27. Thepchu Thaptho'ng, "Nakleng to nakleng khon keng" [Bigtime Gangsters] in *Lao ru'ang thai-thai* [Thai Stories] vol. 1 (Bangkok: S'ong rao, 1992), 189–95.

28. Copeland, "Contested Nationalism," 54–55.

29. Pamela M. Pilbeam, *The Middle Classes in Europe, 1789–1914: France, Germany, Italy, and Russia* (London: Macmillan, 1990), 1.

30. Fred Inglis, *Popular Culture and Political Power* (New York: Harvester-Wheatsheaf, 1988), 14–15.

31. Terry Eagleton, *The Illusions of Postmodernism* (Oxford: Blackwell Publishers, 1996), 43.

32. George L. Mosse, *Nationalism and Sexuality: Respectability and Abnormal Sexuality in Modern Europe* (New York: Howard Fertig, 1985). I am grateful to Matthew Copeland for drawing my attention to Mosse's work.

33. Mosse, *Nationalism and Sexuality*, 5.

34. Mosse, *Nationalism and Sexuality*, 9.

35. Mosse, *Nationalism and Sexuality*, 11.

36. Mosse, *Nationalism and Sexuality*, 12.

1

❧

Protofeminist Discourses in Early-Twentieth-Century Siam

[In] the past, Siamese women were like dolls kept in a cupboard . . . cut off from the outside world. They were strictly controlled and not allowed to go anywhere. . . . Nowadays the position of women is greatly improved however; they are coming out of the dark.[1]

The above passage, written in 1914, appeared in an article published in one of Siam's earliest women's magazines, *Satri niphon* (Women's Writing). According to the author the position of women in Siam was undergoing a fundamental change. And while the change referred to here was conceived of purely in relation to the relatively small number of educated women, most of whom came from the elite strata of Bangkok society, it signaled the beginning of a new era marked by a growing female assertiveness—a desire for greater recognition and acceptance by the male populace.

To get an idea of this particular phenomenon, the present chapter looks at ideas on the position of women advanced by the commoner-intellectual Thianwan (T. W. S. Wannapho, 1842–1915) during the early 1900s, together with a series of articles from Siam's first two commercial women's magazines, *Kunlasatri* (which dates from 1906) and the aforementioned *Satri niphon* (from 1914).[2] Thianwan's views, part of a wide-ranging analysis he made of the contemporary Siamese sociopolitical world, represented an early (if not the earliest) attempt to argue that the position of women in society had a fundamental bearing on the well-being and progress of the nation. The material from the latter two publications, while sharing various similarities, is somewhat less easily classified. Written by various authors (whose identities unfortunately remain unknown to us), these texts provide a range of perspectives on Siamese women that reflect tensions and changes in relations between the sexes. Among these writings one can discern the earliest tangible expression of an indigenous feminism, a type of "protofeminism" as it were, in which women, largely from elite strata, began to develop a consciousness of themselves as a social group.

Elsewhere in Southeast Asia similar developments were unfolding, most notably in the Philippines. During the early 1900s two formal women's organizations were established in Manila and questions concerned with the equality of the sexes and gender roles began to be publicly debated. In 1909 Constancia Poblete launched a feminist magazine entitled *Filipina* whose objectives included the promotion of women's rights. During this period links were also established with women's movements in the West, with two noted suffragists, Carie Chapman Catt of the United States and Aleta Jacobs from the Netherlands, visiting the Philippines in 1912. As a result of this visit an organization known as the Society for the Advancement of Women was founded with the ultimate goal of achieving women's suffrage.[3] As far as can be determined there were no such interchanges between local women and European feminists in Siam (perhaps related to linguistic factors and a lack of colonial connections), nor were there any formal women's organizations established at this time. Nonetheless, with the growth of female education and literacy and the intensification of communications with the wider world, basic feminist ideas regarding equality and social justice began to take root among the more informed sections of the younger generation of Siamese women.

It almost goes without saying that the term "feminism," like much of the vocabulary found in the contemporary social sciences, has been used in many different and even contradictory ways with the result that it resists any singular, universally agreed upon definition. We have, for example, feminism being conceived of as a form of "advocacy of equal rights for women coupled with organized and sustained action for the purpose of achieving them."[4] Feminism in this sense suggests the type of political "first wave" women's movements which developed in Europe, Great Britain, North America, and subsequently in such non-Western countries as India and China. According to Siriphorn Sakhrobanek, the appearance of the two women's magazines referred to above represent the emergence of a "feminist movement" in Siam.[5] However, I would suggest that the publication of these magazines should not be taken as a sign of the existence of a formal movement comparable, or even remotely similar, to those found in the West. Indeed, there was none, at least during the period discussed in this chapter. Another view holds feminism to be a "self-defining process" in which the emphasis is not so much on "rights" per se, but rather on women seeking the "freedom to discover [their] own 'sphere' or 'destiny.' "[6] As we shall see, this particular conception of feminism as a somewhat diffuse self-defining process can be used to characterize the early development of women's consciousness in Siam—a phenomenon that was closely associated with the educated classes.

PREMODERN MEN AND WOMEN

Chilla Bulbeck has observed that "there is no hard, unarguable evidence that any known society has exhibited the reverse of patriarchy: [the] subjugation and economic oppression of men by women."[7] During the Early Bangkok era (late eighteenth through early nineteenth centuries), for example, Siam exhibited a marked degree of patriarchy, although not to the same degree as found in such countries as China, Vietnam, and India. Siamese society or, more specifically, the upper echelons of the society, was dominated by men whose positions were buttressed by both religious ideology and legal sanction. Admittedly, at times, there were women from the elite such as Queen Saowapha, one of Chulalongkorn's principal wives, who exercised considerable power, but such individuals were exceptional.

As for the population at large, the situation was markedly different, with non-slave, commoner women enjoying considerably greater autonomy and freedom in their daily lives than their counterparts living within the palace walls.[8] Even so, the partial, fragmentary nature of the available historical materials makes it difficult to develop a thorough picture of relations between commoner men and women.

The most comprehensive source on the position of women and relations between the sexes in premodern Siam is a section of the 1805 *Law of the Three Seals* (*Kot-mai tra sam duang*) concerned with questions pertaining to marriage (*Phra aiyakan laksana phua mia*).[9] This particular text, it should be emphasized, was primarily concerned with elite Siamese society. Furthermore, in referring to this document, a specific caveat needs to be added to the effect that, while the text gives us an idea of the nature of relations between well-born men and women from across the social spectrum in a formal sense, the actual historical reality and peculiar dynamics of such relationships are another matter altogether and remain largely unknowable.

According to the law, the most fundamental distinction with regard to gender relations in premodern Siam was the notion of "ownership" or control over women by parents or husbands. An unmarried female, regardless of age, was regarded as the possession of her family, of whom the father was the head. Similarly, married women were also deemed to be the exclusive property of their husbands, who had the right to discipline (that is, beat or otherwise abuse) their spouses should they misbehave. Wives, by contrast, had no corresponding right to use physical force against their spouses in case of violence.[10]

Broadly speaking, fathers and husbands were vested with the power to control their daughters' and wives' bodies.[11] This legally sanctioned form of control, as Suwadee points out, was geared to "confine [a woman's] reproductive roles within the [male-defined] social order."[12] At the same time, men had the right to sell a daughter or wife, or to transfer control to another man "with or without her consent."[13] In a crude sense, then, women were regarded as objects, not unlike a man's buffaloes or horses, which could be traded or exchanged for financial or other gain.

Apart from the question of physical ownership, another major distinction between men and women pertained to marriage: men were entitled to have numerous wives while women were strictly limited to one husband. Thus while male sexual license was legally validated through the institution of polygamy, autonomous female sexuality, with the exception of those women who were prostitutes, was tightly circumscribed.[14]

Under the law there were, in descending order of status, three general categories of wife: the major wife (*mia klang m'uang* or *mia luang*), the minor wife (*mia klang n'ok* or *mia noi*), and the slave wife (*mia klang that*).[15] As Adun Wichiencharoen and Chamroon Netisastra point out:

> The legal distinction between the different classes of wives had two functions. First, it served the purpose of determining the amount of compensation which [an] adulterer was made to pay [a] husband. The higher the class of wife, the greater the amount of compensation the adulterer had to pay. Secondly, wives of higher classes were entitled to larger shares of the husband's estate after he died.[16]

Just as the law prescribed a finely differentiated range of penalties for adultery, so it did also in cases where an unmarried woman was discovered in the company of a man outside her immediate family (penalties were imposed for various breaches, from a man touching the woman or going into her sleeping quarters to the act of copulation itself).[17] Matters of face and personal honor were central to the punishments meted out for sexual transgressions involving married and unmarried females. Men and women found to have engaged in some form of illicit relationship were commonly sentenced to public humiliation (*prachan*); for example, they were paraded around the city streets in addition to being whipped or flogged. Furthermore, a woman's punishment could also include being sold into bondage, while male offenders were required to pay a specific sum of money, this payment not representing a fine as such but rather a form of compensation to the woman's father or husband for the affront caused to their honor and dignity. This ancient practice of linking monetary compensation to unsanctioned sexual contact involving women, a phenomenon that Lyttleton notes continues to this day in northeastern Thailand,[18] may well have been a key cultural factor in naturalizing the idea of prostitution in Siamese society over the long term.

According to the *Law of the Three Seals*, an adulteress was little different from a prostitute (*ying phaetsaya*), a category of women defined as such on the basis of having sex with more than one man in the course of a day.[19] In contrast to "respectable" females, whose movement and freedom to associate with males outside the confines of family or harem was strictly limited, prostitutes (female slaves under the control of a bond or money master [*nai ngoen*])[20] were "public women" whose bodies were available to any man who could pay the asking price.[21] Prostitutes worked in state-taxed brothels that had been a part of Siamese urban life since Ayuthayan times. Some of these women served a foreign, non-Siamese clientele (trader-adventurers from China and elsewhere in Asia as well as those from various European countries). At the same time, brothel prostitution of a somewhat different character was also to be found. Elite women deemed to have committed some form of sexual transgression were, if not sentenced to death, sold as slaves to a special type of brothel reserved for upper-class men.[22] Although this may seem implausible given the fact that polygamy was a common practice among the well-to-do, such brothels, it may be imagined, had a particular social function, serving perhaps as a type of safety valve for married and unmarried nobles, or as some kind of school in the art of lovemaking for inexperienced, young unmarried upper-class men.

With the kingdom's increasing openness to the West from the mid-nineteenth century, however, questions relating to indigenous marriage practices and the position of women began to be discussed and debated among the elite. Chaophraya Thiphak'orawong (Kham Bunnag), one of the leading ministers of state, framed a Buddhist defense of polygamy in response to European critiques of the practice,[23] while King Mongkut cautiously moved to amend a number of regulations affecting women. Perhaps the king's most significant intervention in this regard came in 1867 when he decreed that a woman could not be sold to another party without her formal consent.[24] Even so, such changes as there were could hardly be considered to have been of a radical nature. Indeed, traditional notions about women remained largely unaltered, a situation that began to be contested at the beginning of the twentieth century with the growth of female education and the development of a print-mediated public sphere.

FEMALE EDUCATION

Prior to the twentieth century, access to formal education was largely, although not exclusively, confined to the male population. The kingdom's Buddhist monasteries were the principal centers of study and learning. As a passage from a 1926 English-language government pamphlet notes, "in those days education was in the hands of the priests, who received boys from various homes as their pupils. These pupils were taught reading, writing, arithmetic, and morality. . . . The teaching was done in their cells, each priest instructing his own boys during his spare time."[25]

Females were rigorously excluded from this monastic learning by religious injunctions that forbade close association with monks. It was only at the elite level that girls had the opportunity to gain an education similar to that of boys.

In the early Bangkok period this type of education was restricted to women from
the Inner Palace (*fai nai*) who, on completing their studies, either became tutors
themselves or were employed as clerks in the royal service.[26] In contrast, girls
from the population at large remained illiterate, their education being confined
to learning various domestic skills from their mothers or other female relatives.

The earliest initiatives to provide girls with some type of modern formal education came from Protestant missionaries during the nineteenth century. It was
in the mid-century, for example, that King Mongkut engaged a number of Western missionary women to teach ladies from the Inner Palace. This program continued for three years before it was terminated largely as a result, it seems, of the
missionaries' critical views on polygamy.[27] While missionaries were permitted to
teach in Siam shortly afterward, concern about foreign influences on local
women did much to stimulate direct Siamese involvement in female education.

The most prominent figure in this development during its initial stages was
Queen Saowapha, the most influential of King Chulalongkorn's wives and the
mother of his successor, Vajiravudh. At the queen's behest a number of girls'
schools were set up in the capital toward the end of the nineteenth century and
somewhat later in various provincial centers.[28] These initiatives in the field of
education, together with her elevation to regent during the king's first visit to
Europe in 1897, made Saowapha a role model and inspiration for many Siamese
women of the day.

For his part Chulalongkorn showed little interest in his wife's enthusiasm for
female education and was loath to allocate government funding to support it.
The king's disdain, it seems, was influenced by his own experiences with the
controversial English governess-teacher Anna Leonowens who had tutored him
as a young man and apparently voiced strong criticism of polygamy. Writing in
1898 Chulalongkorn candidly admitted, "I cannot bring myself to think about
my daughters' education. I have never endorsed it . . . , because it reminds me of
my own teacher who authored a book which many believe. So whenever the
suggestion is made that a girls' school be founded, I am quite annoyed."[29] Later,
in 1901, after two government schools for lower-class girls were established, the
king went on to caution the minister of education that "The government's revenue had better be used for boy's education. Do not promote girls' education too
much."[30]

Apart from state involvement in female education it was reported in 1902 that
four fee-paying day schools for girls had been set up in the capital by private
interests.[31] Clearly, a growing number of well-to-do Bangkok families had come
to see the benefit of female education and were willing to pay for the privilege
of sending their daughters to school. Here it is worth noting that, in some
instances, school fees were largely used to defray the cost of English lessons.[32]
Considering that elite women were not expected to seek paid employment, the
study of English was regarded as something of a status symbol and a means to

develop a broader cosmopolitan awareness. Furthermore, within the carefully calculated system of arranged marriages among the Siamese elite, familiarity with the English language enhanced the marital prospects of an educated young woman to a Siamese or Chinese man of substance whose work involved contact with Europeans. At the same time, and most crucially, the study of English also enabled such young women to extend their knowledge and experience of things beyond the confines of Siamese society.

As for the number of girls receiving a formal education during the first decade of the twentieth century it is difficult to give a precise figure. The available sources suggest there were anywhere between four and six hundred such students in 1905 and slightly in excess of one thousand by 1910. Four years later, a writer for *Satri niphon* stated that there were approximately 1,400 girls in school in the Bangkok *Monthon*, that is, the area comprising the Bangkok metropolitan region and the six surrounding provinces.[33] At the same time, official—albeit not wholly reliable—statistics give a total of 5,239 girls, and some 114,000 boys, attending schools throughout the kingdom.[34] Whatever the true figure for girls in school was in 1914, the number had increased considerably since the turn of the century. And although we do not have a clear idea as to the particular type of education many of these girls were receiving or how long they spent in school, rising female literacy (elementary as this undoubtedly was in many cases) provided the basis for a new generation of better informed and more assertive women than in the past. It is in this context that the work of Thianwan concerning the position of women in society becomes relevant.

THIANWAN'S WRITINGS ON WOMEN

Thianwan, one of the pivotal figures in the development of publishing beyond the confines of the Siamese nobility, has generally been portrayed as an isolated, iconoclastic thinker on the margins of society. In fact Thianwan's views were not his alone but rather, as Copeland notes, were "shared by a number of his contemporaries," and some of the ideas associated with him "had been discussed and debated within the capital for decades."[35] The importance of Thianwan then was not so much the perceived originality of his thought, but rather that, through the medium of print, he was able to bring such ideas to the attention of a broader public.

In his writings Thianwan articulated a reformist perspective largely informed by a keen awareness of Siam's lack of "progress" in relation to European nations. He repeatedly emphasized the need for greater justice and advocated a comprehensive transformation of Siam's political, economic, and social system in order to make it a modern, respected power on the world stage. Some of the changes he thought necessary included the establishment of a parliamentary system of government, the prohibition of gambling and opium smoking, the creation of industrial enterprises, and the abolition of slavery.[36] Thianwan also expressed a keen interest in improving the position of women in contemporary society, a topic he wrote about at length in newspaper articles and in a series of booklets published in 1907 entitled *Bamrung nari* (For the Advancement of Women).[37] I will concentrate on one of Thianwan's articles concerning women as representative of his thinking.

In this article, published in his newspaper *Tulawiphak phochanakit* (Critical Reflections) in June 1905, Thianwan outlined what amounted to a basic theory about women.[38] He claimed that women were important because they had the power to influence men and the nation in either a positive or a negative way. For example, whether a child became a "good" or "bad" adult was directly related to the quality of its mother. Similarly, he claimed a woman could play an important role as a wife. In developing this theme Thianwan pointed to what he saw as a major social problem in Siam, that of rootless, wayward men becoming addicted to drink or opium and descending into a life of misery and suffering. Nevertheless, he was of the view that women could redress this problem. A wife, Thianwan said, could be compared to a ship's anchor, a source of stability: "when a man has a loving, caring woman to share his life she will be able to exert a powerful and beneficial influence on him and prevent him from going to ruin."[39]

Having said this, Thianwan claimed that the situation in Siam was such that it inhibited the realization of this positive, supportive function of womanhood. He considered the position of women in general to be base and mean. For example, he pointed to his experiences of wandering around Bangkok where he had observed

> five times as many women in the gambling dens as there were men. And what is more, I've seen depressingly large numbers of our women working as prostitutes, parading up and down the streets at night. Even during the day I've seen respectable looking women going out to illicit places where, so I've heard, they sell their bodies. This distresses me enormously.[40]

Here Thianwan's observations about street prostitution highlight the dramatic socioeconomic changes that had been taking place in Siam. Prior to the latter nineteenth and early twentieth centuries, prostitution was, as mentioned earlier, confined to brothels staffed by female slaves. These women had no freedom of movement and lived in the brothels where they worked; anything they needed from the outside world was procured by their bond masters through intermediaries.[41] With the development of the market economy, however, the Siamese system of slavery and bonded labor broke down, the population was gradually emancipated, and money and commercial exchange increasingly came to define and order social life. In this process growing numbers of "free" lower-class women took to the streets of Bangkok in search of a livelihood in the emergent, cash-based consumer economy as prostitutes; this development was paralleled by frequent and widely reported urban crime, primarily hold-ups and burglaries committed by gangs of armed and desperate men.[42] At the same time, more well-to-do women took advantage of the increasingly liberal economic climate by participating in money-lending and rentier activities.[43]

Prostitution, Thianwan suggested, was bound up with long-standing social values which held that the role of women, apart from being responsible for domestic duties, was simply to make themselves look attractive—to function, he said, as "mere adornments." In the context of a lessening of traditional constraints within society and a growing importance of individual self-reliance in the labor market, female beauty and youthfulness became readily saleable commodities, particularly in the absence of other, nonsexual occupations. Given this, Thianwan, reiterating an idea expressed by the renowned nineteenth-century poet Sunthorn Phu in his epic *Phra Aphaimani*, argued that "an obsession with beauty at the expense of learning was sheer folly." He was of the view that the time had come when women needed to receive an education "equal to that of men in every way . . . including [the study] of law and politics." Thianwan's emphasis on the importance of law and politics was significant in that these two interrelated domains underpinned the elite male realm of power and authority. In his opinion, "a country whose women lack an education and an awareness, who don't know how to teach their children, and who don't know the difference between good and bad, is a country with a limited capacity for progress."[44]

While Thianwan made mention of the various girls' schools which had been established in Siam, he was scornful of their achievements, claiming that they were (as yet) insufficiently developed to be of any real benefit to the country. He was particularly critical of upper-class women "who go to school and study a range of subjects and languages, but then keep to themselves and do nothing to help the nation."[45] This, he noted, was in marked contrast to foreign countries where educated women had played a far more active role in national life. On the latter he cited with approval the example of the women's temperance movement in the United States and the financial support Japanese women had given their country in its war against Russia. Thianwan said he hoped that one day Siamese women would participate in national life to the same extent, and urged the upper classes to work together and become actively involved in promoting female education. "If this should come to pass," he wrote, "the name of the King and the progressive women in Siam will go down in the annals of history for their intelligence and foresight."[46]

Finally, Thianwan's views on marriage should briefly be considered. For one thing he was resolutely opposed to polygamy. His criticism of the practice, however, was not made with the female subject in mind, but rather was cast in economic and male-centered terms. In his view, polygamous marriage was a wasteful, costly practice diverting valuable economic resources away from more productive activities. Furthermore, he argued that a man's ready access to the physical gratification that polygamy allowed for was harmful to his health and well-being (and by inference a threat to economic and political well-being as well).[47] In place of polygamy Thianwan advocated monogamous marriage. He suggested that in such a union a wife should not only have the role of a home-maker but should also act as her husband's companion and intellectual help-mate. In advocating such ideas, which would not have been out of place amongst the bourgeoisie in Victorian England, Thianwan was, in effect, advancing a view supportive of the market-oriented socioeconomic development that was begin-ning to unfold in Siam, and it was against this backdrop that the country's two earliest commercial women's magazines emerged.

KUNLASATRI

In March 1906, a short article entitled "Feminism in Siam" appeared in the English-language newspaper Bangkok Times. It read:

> Siam is getting on. A magazine for ladies is to appear next month. The "Kul-satri" [sic] is to be published monthly, and is to deal with all matters of interest to ladies. The promoters promise that it will provide better reading for families than the sto-ries that are usually read by women and [which] are often harmful in their tenden-cies. Luang Chan and Luang Wikhanet are the promoters.[48]

The following month the first issue of Kunlasatri (Ladies of Good Birth and Breeding) was published. As the title of the magazine suggests, it was intended for elite women and girls (those from prosperous families, including royal prin-cesses together with the daughters of noble state officials and members of the expanding Chinese and Sino-Thai business-merchant class) who had received, or were in the process of receiving, an education. This readership was estimated by the promoters to be in the vicinity of 360 to 600 people.

The magazine provided no details about Luang Chan and Luang Wikhanet, but as the official title of each (Luang) indicates, they were both male middle-level state officials. That the backers of a magazine aimed at a specifically female audience were men is intriguing. And the reason for launching Kunlasatri was even more so given that the report in the Bangkok Times referred to the "harmful tendencies" of the materials being read by educated Siamese women at the time. While the precise nature of these "tendencies" is neither alluded to nor dis-cussed in the first issue of the magazine, an article on ancient Siamese customs and beliefs (prapheni boran), which appeared in the second issue of Kunlasatri, gives us a fairly clear idea. "In the past," wrote Mae (Mother) Chae,[49] the author of the article,

> if a woman learned how to read and write, complaints would be made and she would be condemned as a man hunter [nakleng chao chu]. Fathers were extremely concerned

about their daughters, for they had frequently seen instances in which women who had learned how to read and write became skilled in the art of *phleng yao* [a versified form of love song].[50]

The inference here was that in earlier times, female literacy was perceived by fathers (and husbands) to have the potential to undermine their authority and, in turn, threaten the existing gender order based on polygamy and strict injunctions against adultery and premarital sexual relations. When translations of Western romantic novels and short stories became available in Siam around the turn of the century this perception or fear appears to have been heightened.[51] In addition to romantic fiction, female readers were also exposed to news of the female suffrage movement in the West, not to mention Thianwan's ideas on the need to improve the status of Siamese women. Thus by means of the printed word, literate females were being presented with new ideas and models of behavior. For their part, the promoters of *Kunlasatri* appeared to be hopeful of channeling or directing female literacy in ways that were not "harmful," that is, in ways that affirmed male dominance.

In the introductory section to the first issue of *Kunlasatri* the author, possibly *Luang* Chan himself (writing under the name Chantharamat), told readers that the viability of the magazine was in their hands: "[*Kunlasatri*] will flourish and progress if you have an interest in progress and a willingness to provide financial support [i.e., subscribe to the magazine]. In turn, you'll have the opportunity to exchange ideas and knowledge."[52]

Here we find an appeal to readers that sought to identify them with the idea of being progressive or modern. Yet at the same time some of the material to appear in *Kunlasatri* was not exactly modern in nature. As Chantharamat made clear,

> Some of the stories that we will publish have been specifically written for this magazine while some pieces will come from other sources but have yet to be circulated. In addition, stories from the past will be featured together with old proverbs as well as translations of various [foreign] materials that suit the circumstances in our country.[53]

While this emphasis on the traditional and the "socially appropriate" intimated something of a conservative outlook *Kunlasatri* did incorporate "progressive" elements. Indeed, this is reflected if we consider the graphic used on the cover of the first issue of the magazine, together with the related discussion in the introduction.

As we learn in the introduction, the cover image (fig. 1.1) shows *Nang* Rewadi taking *Nang* Nophamat, her seventeen-year-old daughter, to be presented to *Phra* Ruang, the king of Sukhothai. The young woman had been eulogized in a popular folk song sung by female entertainers (*nang bamroe*) at court and the king was

Fig. 1.1.

desirous of meeting her. Born into a Brahmin family and given a comprehensive education by her learned father, Chottarat, *Nang* Nophamat was said to be possessed of a rare combination of qualities: an agreeable disposition, a lustrous golden complexion (to which her name Nophamat literally refers), and above all a keen intelligence and an outstanding ability as both a scholar and a poet. According to her admirers *Nang* Nophamat represented nothing less than a *y'ot ying* or "the epitome of womanhood." Consequently when *Phra* Ruang heard his entertainers sing her praises, he issued a command requesting that she be brought to his palace and become one of his royal consorts.

Readers were told that the story of *Phra* Ruang and *Nang* Nophamat was contained in the northern chronicles, but that it remained "shrouded in mystery" and was "not widely known." *Nang* Nophamat was, in fact, a fictional character, the subject of an eponymous literary work produced by a number of authors, including King Rama II, during the first half of the nineteenth century.[54] Be that as it may, *Nang* Nophamat was presented in the pages of *Kunlansatri* as a genuine, credible person who was ahead of her time, embodying qualities worthy of emulation by contemporary Siamese women.

The introduction also included short passages on other notable Siamese women from the past: Queen Suriyothai of the Ayuthayan era and the sisters *Thao* Thepsatri and *Thao* Sisunth'on of the early Bangkok period. These women were renowned for their valor in battle; the queen had fought and died in a war against the Burmese during the sixteenth century, while the two sisters had led a successful defense of Thalang (Phuket in southern Siam) against a Burmese attack in the late eighteenth century. Notably, although these "warrior" figures were duly recognized for their valor, far greater emphasis was given to *Nang* Nophamat. In early-twentieth-century Siam, erudition, dignity, and subservience were portrayed as being more desirable qualities for women than heroics, daring, and personal sacrifice. In Chantharamat's view, these former qualities were considered to be essential for a *mae r'uan* or housewife—the only role, it was implied, that an educated woman should aspire to. The association between learning and the role of a *mae r'uan* signified a distinct change from the early Bangkok period when the idea of the educated woman, while not entirely absent, was confined to a small number of court ladies.[55]

The emphasis given to *Nang* Nophamat rather than the female "warriors" in this text may be seen to underscore a significant difference between the historical experience of the Siamese and that of the peoples in neighboring and nearby states. Whereas the Burmese, Lao, Khmer, Malays, Vietnamese, Javanese, and various other ethnic groups experienced major social disruptions as a result of colonization, the Siamese social order was spared the same type of dislocation. Instead, through a process of accommodation with the Western powers by means of gradualist reform and the granting of economic and territorial concessions, the traditional ruling elite was able to maintain its preeminent sociopolitical position into the early twentieth century. A fundamental aspect of this process of change and adaptation was the diffusion of Western-derived notions of "civilization" and "progress" among the educated populace.[56] It is in this particular sociohistorical context that the emphasis on *Nang* Nophamat as an ideal for contemporary elite Siamese women rather than the warrior queen or the valiant sisters is to be understood. As an educated, graceful woman, *Nang* Nophamat was presented as an indigenous exemplar embodying "civilization." Thus, despite her reputed antiquity, she could be regarded as being modern and in tune with the changing socioeconomic environment; nonetheless, at the same time, she was also portrayed as an icon of submissive womanhood who posed no threat to male power.

The fundamentally moderate, traditionalist tone of the magazine was further reflected in an article entitled "A Woman's Duty" (*na-thi kh'ong ying*) written by a woman (as indicated by the use of the feminine first person pronoun, *dichan*) under the pseudonym Sangwanphet. The author begins her account with the following characterization of gender roles:

> Men are the ones who find the means to support a family. In this they are similar to the male bird that brings food to the nest. The female bird, on the other hand, tends the nest and looks after the young. Consequently it is the duty of a woman to look after the home while a man has the responsibility of providing the sustenance. Since ancient times and almost everywhere in the world it has been customary for men to live and sleep in the home while the duty of women has been to maintain it. However, if a woman is ignorant and lacks the appropriate knowledge to carry out this important task, how can a man go on and have the energy and confidence to do his duty?[57]

In order for a woman to carry out this prescribed role, Sangwanphet argued that female education was essential and urged men to be supportive of the idea, claiming that it was in their own interests to do so. According to her, girls should begin their education by studying the same subjects as boys and then go on to acquire other skills including sewing, embroidery, poetry, drawing, and home science. They should also be taught about the law as it related to women, as well as the religions, customs, and geography of other parts of the world. Furthermore, girls should be trained in the requisite social skills for coping with public occasions and, if they had the time, be given the opportunity to study foreign languages. In effect what Sangwanphet was proposing was a particular educational ideal for women from the elite informed by the type of socioeconomic changes that were taking place in Siam at the time. Thus education was envisaged not only as preparing such women to run a household but also to equip them for an increased public role. With the growth of urban life, the expansion of commerce and increasing foreign contacts the wife, or prospective wife, of a member of the elite was no longer isolated from the male world as had traditionally been the case. Now a wife was expected to be able to interact and converse with her husband's associates and acquaintances.[58]

In Sangwanphet's article there were what may be termed progressive elements, in particular, her interest in having girls learn about the law and how it related to them. Like Thianwan, she recognized the law as a key social determinant, a realm in which individual rights, obligations, and power relations were defined. Yet she also sought to articulate traditional verities. For example, she conceptualized the relationship between men and women by invoking a metaphor said to date from the early Bangkok period: "A man is like the front legs of an elephant while a woman is like its hind legs. When the front legs move forward the hind legs must follow. If one takes a false step, both will suffer, but if they are both in step things will work well."[59] This metaphor, referring to women as the "elephant's hind legs" (chang thao lang), continues to be widely used in contemporary society as an invocation justifying the "secondary" position of Thai women.

However, while talking about and supporting the subordinate role of women, Sangwanphet also argued that a man's success or progress in the public domain was dependent on his wife's support in the private sphere of the home. In her view, a woman, or more correctly an educated woman, was not conceived of as being incidental to the life of her husband, but was rather of fundamental importance to his advancement in the world.[60]

This type of bourgeois notion, so redolent of the Victorian era, reflects something of the education young Siamese women commonly received while at school. For example, in the mid-nineteenth century when Mongkut invited missionary women to provide palace ladies with a modern education, their instruction included the teaching of Western customs and social behavior. Subsequently, with the establishment of various girls' schools in the capital from the second half of the nineteenth century, the study of occidental sociocultural values and practices (thamniam kan-samakhom baep tawan-tok) became an integral part of many young women's formal learning, including such subjects as Thai and English language, geography, mathematics, domestic skills, and sports ranging from badminton and tennis to croquet.[61]

Clearly, what Sangwanphet had to say in regard to women's roles was very similar to views expressed by Thianwan. Yet there was a crucial difference between the two that underlines the changing social dynamics of the period. While Sangwanphet argued for education for women from the elite, Thianwan advocated education for all women, regardless of class. The difference in outlook is stark. On the one hand we find Sangwanphet articulating a discourse on women from a "progressive" elitist social perspective, oblivious to the needs of the broader society, while Thianwan presents a more comprehensive vision encompassing an emergent public community.

The second issue of Kunlasatri featured an article entitled "Ancient Customs" (prapheni boran) by Mae Chae, a female author who was critical of the contemporary status of women (noted above).[62] The emphasis here was somewhat different from that of Sangwanphet in that Mae Chae concentrated her discussion on the position of ordinary women rather than on members of the educated elite. Mae Chae claimed that ordinary women and girls in traditional Siamese society were at a disadvantage in terms of the work they did in comparison to that required of their male counterparts. Her argument can be summarized as follows: Whereas female work (which encompassed tending and rearing children as well as maintaining a household) was constant, male work (consisting primarily of corvée service, herding buffalo, and planting rice) was irregular. Furthermore, males spent varying lengths of time in the monkhood where they were not required to work. In the present era, the situation was little different from that in the past. Commoner males were now subject to military service which, in Mae Chae's view, was a form of "learning" or "study." When a man completed military service it was common for him to become a monk, and only when he disrobed would he take a wife and start a family.

Like Sangwanphet, Mae Chae recognized the male as the head of the contemporary household, but she chose a different metaphor to make her point. Rather than an "elephant's front legs," she compared a husband to a "victory flag" (thong chai) who "led his family to a livelihood." Similarly, like Sangwanphet, she also conceived of masculine and feminine genders as existing in a complementary relationship, suggesting that "a woman and a man depend on each other like a cart and horse." However, Mae Chae took a more forthright position by asserting that men and women were "equal in weight" (ying kap chai y'om mi nam-nak thao kan), the only difference between them being that each had distinct "duties." Failing to recognize this equality between men and women, she insisted, would prove disastrous. She warned men that if they continued to look down on women and did not seek to improve their position, "suffering and confusion will grow in your hearts"; while at the same time warning women that if they did not respect men or give them their support they would be subject to "unceasing evil and degradation."[63]

A number of things are particularly striking about this article. For example, at one point, Mae Chae refers to the "many ways in which a man could avoid the persistent demands of work." Military conscription, conceived of as "study," not "work," was one such avenue. However, the easiest route for a man to avoid work, she maintained, was to "escape into a temple [and become a monk]." In making these observations, Mae Chae suggested that the military and Buddhist monkhood served the interests of men in general at the expense of women. This is underlined by the fact that the military and the sangha were wholly male institutions which, together with the monarchy, served as pillars underpinning the patriarchal nature of Siamese society. Interestingly, Mae Chae made no mention of traditional Buddhist notions of karma that were customarily asserted to underpin the inequities between men and women, but rather posited a rational, secular concept of male and female equality. Furthermore, this concept, at least the way it is expressed in the article, is not explicitly argued as following from any precedent found in the "civilized," "progressive" West, as was often the case at a time when authors sought to legitimize an argument in this way, but is instead related to the indigenous experience of work and duty. These are original and perceptive observations, and although Mae Chae did not elaborate upon them, they are significant in that they represent perhaps the earliest written female critique of male domination in Siam.

While Kunlasatri was a pioneering venture it failed to prosper and ceased publication during the latter part of 1906. It was another eight years before Siam's next commercial women's magazine, Satri niphon, appeared in October 1914. During this eight-year period a number of important changes had taken place: the French and English colonial threats to Siamese dynastic authority receded, the country's contemporary boundaries were formally established by international agreement, and, following the death of his father, Chulalongkorn, Crown Prince Vajiravudh became king in 1910. With the question of territorial sovereignty vis-à-vis the colonial powers more or less resolved, press discussion about Siam's future increased and the status of the absolute monarchy began to come under scrutiny.

At the same time as ultimate power and authority was vested in the king and a handful of senior officials, the urban populace was increasingly exposed to ideas and developments from abroad through both print and film. For example, news of the republican movement in China and the success of the revolution in 1911 were followed with great interest by many members of the public, who took a growing interest in international affairs. Such developments, transmitted by the fledgling mass media, helped raise local awareness about new sociopolitical possibilities while helping to galvanize and focus popular dissatisfaction with the existing order. The king, for his part, became extremely anxious about his own position and sought to shore up the legitimacy of the throne by articulating and deploying ideas about the "nation" in which he identified the absolute monarchy as the central and most fundamental element of Siamese national life.

Although he can in no way be considered "the founder of modern nationalism in [Siam]," as claimed by Vella,[64] Vajiravudh's intervention helped stimulate an unprecedented degree of public discussion about concepts of the "nation" and notions of "freedom" and "independence" embodied in the word "Thai." Significantly, once this process had begun, it could neither be contained nor controlled and differing views on various national issues found expression in the expanding public sphere of print.

Copeland describes the evolution of this public form in the following way:

> By the early years of the Sixth Reign, a schism between "the government" and "the people" was firmly embedded in the conventions and language of newspaper publishing. In common parlance, a newspaper was a "voice" (*pak-siang*) which spoke on behalf of a specific *khana*—the "party" or "faction" of writers affiliated with the owner of a given printing press. In common practice, however, the "voices" of the capital were generally divided into two broad camps: publications of the government-subsidized press (*nangs'u-phim rathaban*) which were insulated from the market and relatively free from the threat of prosecution, and the independent or "popular newspapers" (*nangs'u-phim ratsadon*) which ran the risk of having their "mouths shut" (*pit pak nangs'u-phim*) by the court. Not surprisingly, the former were generally supportive of the government, carrying an authoritative commentary in defense of its various policies and plans, while the latter frequently served as a forum for the government's critics, many of whom claimed to be writing on behalf of the people of the kingdom as a whole.[65]

It was within this restive, increasingly complex political environment that *Satri niphon* made its appearance. As we will see, the views expressed in the magazine were, for the most part, critical of the contemporary status of women and, as such, echoed or paralleled the debate over power at the state level.

SATRI NIPHON

Regrettably, we do not know the identity of those responsible for producing *Satri niphon*. However, the female writer of the introduction to the inaugural issue of the magazine made it clear that the days of unquestioned male dominance were coming to an end.[66] She announced that the purpose of *Satri niphon* was essentially twofold. First, it was hoped it would serve as a means of raising the honor of Siamese women. Second, the aim of the magazine was to make men realize that old values and attitudes were obsolete, in particular the view that men alone were truly human while women were regarded as little different from buffaloes.[67]

One writer referred to these undercurrents of change in a short article entitled "Siamese Women Are Becoming Civilized" (*Satri sayam doen su khwam-siwilai*).

Way back in the past, Siamese women were like dolls kept in a cupboard . . . cut off
from the outside world. They were strictly controlled and not allowed to go anywhere. They had no books to read or study because their parents or guardians
thought that they would learn about men from such things. . . . And when a woman
married a man, it wasn't necessary for them to know each other or love each other
at all. These days, however, the position of women is much improved, they study
the same things as men and most of them are educated. They are coming out of the
dark.[68]

Here it should be mentioned that, like Sangwanphet in *Kunlasatri*, this author
used the term "women" (*satri*) to refer to elite women, not the mass of the female
population of Siam who were implicitly overlooked.

While *Satri niphon* adopted a similar elitist stance to that of *Kunlasatri*, it was
markedly different in the pronounced emphasis that it gave to women in
national affairs. In one notable article entitled "Do Not Underestimate Women"
(*Ya pramat satri*), readers were reminded of the contributions of women to the
nation in the past.[69] Women such as Queen Suriyothai, *Thao* Thepsatri, and
Thao Srisunthorn (all of whom, it will be recalled, were referred to in the first
issue of *Kunlasatri*) as well as *Than phu-ying* Mo, the wife of the lord of Nakon
Ratchasima (Khorat) in northeastern Siam, were discussed in this context.[70] The
central figure in the article, however, was Queen Suriyothai, whose life was the
subject of a short account based on material drawn from the royal chronicles.

Briefly, the story of the queen as related in the magazine was as follows: In
A.D. 1543, the Burmese, led by King Hongsawadi, invaded Thai territory and
established a series of military camps outside the then capital, Ayuthaya. In
response, a Thai force led by the monarch, King Chakraphan, his wife, Queen
Suriyothai, and their two sons went out to engage the invaders on elephants.
During the course of the ensuing battle, Chakraphan was outmaneuvered and
menaced by the Burmese king. Seeing that her husband's life was in peril, Queen
Suriyothai came to his aid but was killed in the encounter. The king, however,
survived and the Burmese were defeated. On the cessation of hostilities, the
fallen queen was given an elaborate cremation ceremony and a monastery, *Wat
sop suwan* (literally, "Temple of the Heavenly Corpse"), was built in her honor.[71]

Significantly, in contrast to the introductory section of *Kunlasatri*, we find no
mention of the genteel, learned *Nang* Nophamat. Instead, the focus is on heroic
figures and martial endeavor. One may ask what this particular emphasis signifies, and how it relates to the broader social environment of the time? For one
thing it would seem to indicate a growing sense of frustration and assertiveness
among sections of the female population toward men who were contemptuous
of women. It can also be seen as reflecting the author's recognition and appropri-
ation of the way that the dominant discourse of nation had been framed and
shaped by historical accounts of Siam's armed struggles with her neighbors. In
this connection, it should be remembered that since early in the reign of King

Vajiravudh the public had been exposed to an insistent linking of nation with a martial ethos, as evidenced in the following excerpt from a speech the monarch gave to his newly established paramilitary force, the "Wild Tigers," in 1911: "Soldiers are part of the Thai people as are civilians. How can they be separate groups? Every soldier is also a civilian. Every civilian likewise ought to be a soldier."[72]

Given an environment in which ideas of this sort were circulating, it is perhaps hardly surprising that the author of "Do Not Underestimate Women" sought to invoke the heroic exploits of female warriors in the Thai past in order to claim a space of significance for women and to seek to mobilize them. This theme of a female role in a martial context was further underscored by various accounts in *Satri niphon* detailing the exploits of foreign women in the Great War, which had just broken out in Europe. One report referred to a seventy-year-old Prussian woman who had climbed a church tower and shot at Russian soldiers with a machine gun, killing and wounding fifteen of them. Yet another account mentioned the numerous female students in Serbia who had volunteered to fight against Austria. In conclusion to this piece the writer remarked, "if it became necessary, you could be assured that the female students in our country would compare well with these foreigners and do exactly the same thing."[73]

This process of locating and emphasizing female involvement in what was hitherto considered the masculine domain of warfare can be seen as an attempt by various writers to challenge widely held traditional assumptions about women and about the special powers of men. Indeed, the presentation of the "woman as warrior" was not only a counterpoint to the view that linked female activity to the domestic sphere but also suggested the idea of some sort of parity or equality between women and men.

Elsewhere in the magazine a notion of equality in relation to the interpersonal realm was alluded to in a short polemical article, entitled "Het-rai satri sayam ch'ung pen khon khi-h'ung chat" (Why are Siamese Women so Jealous?), which raised the subject of polygamy and the Siamese law on marriage.[74] This article is of particular interest in that it appears to represent the earliest extant written critique of polygamy by a Thai woman. As mentioned earlier, polygamous marriage had become a sensitive issue among members of the male elite during the second half of the nineteenth century as Siam was drawn into closer contact with the West. It was also at this time that Mongkut had made an oblique reference to female opposition to polygamy in a royal decree when he noted that a group of unnamed "belligerent women" (*ying phan-phan*) had criticized the law which allowed for the practice.[75] Somewhat later, in the period from 1908 into the first few years of Vajiravudh's reign, wide-ranging discussions concerning reform of Siam's ancient marriage laws were carried out at the highest levels of government (see chapter 6). In the course of this debate, it was proposed that monogamous marriage should be introduced, an idea firmly opposed by the new king.[76]

According to the author of "Why are Siamese Women so Jealous?" relations between men and women in European countries were far more equitable than those in Siam. This, she argued, was due to the nature of the marriage laws in the West where a couple "had to take marriage vows before witnesses . . . in doing so the man had to promise not to have any secondary or minor wives (*mia n'oi*). Furthermore if he marries a second time, without first obtaining a divorce from his original wife, he is considered to have broken the law and is subject to punishment."[77]

The situation in Siam, she noted, was very different indeed: "There are no laws governing the behavior of men. A man can marry as many times as he likes or have as many minor wives as he chooses. This is not considered wrong in any way. And if he wants to abandon any of these women there is nothing to prevent him, for he can do as he likes."[78]

In her opinion, the fact that men were permitted to have numerous wives was the root cause of the jealousy that was endemic among Siamese women. She advocated the introduction of "a law like that in the West" as a means of overcoming the problem. Emotional dissonance, it seems, was not regarded as a peripheral or unimportant matter, but rather something that the author suggested had a detrimental effect on Siam's hopes of becoming an advanced country on a par with the European powers. As we shall see, the question of polygamy and the law on marriage was to assume a growing significance in the following decade when it became an issue of much public debate. Here it should be mentioned that a similar debate on marriage and other issues pertaining to the status of women unfolded in Republican China from the latter 1910s through much of the 1920s. During this time issues relating to women were vigorously discussed in the context of a wide-ranging national debate on virtually all aspects of contemporary life ignited by the Fourth of May Movement of 1919.[79] In China, as in Siam, practices such as polygamy and the system of arranged marriages came to be seen by reformist critics as an anathema, impediments to the emergence of a truly modern, progressive nation-state.

Finally, before leaving the discussion of *Satri niphon*, a short, but intriguing article featured in the magazine should be noted since it touched directly on the complex issue of the position and honor of Siamese women in explicitly stratified terms. The article, written in the form of a dialogue between two old friends, Si and Anong, was entitled "A Conversation between Ladies" (*sonthana rawang satri*).[80] As they talk to one another, Si tells Anong she is involved in the production of *Satri niphon*, "a magazine which is designed to improve the position of women." The two friends then move on to discuss the central theme of the "conversation": the way in which women were perceived, that is, the female public persona. Si refers to women (*phu-ying*) in Bangkok riding around in cars with their husbands. She says she finds this offensive, claiming such behavior "is far too Western for Thai women." Anong agrees, suggesting women should be careful not to do anything that might be subject to criticism in the press, her comment indicating the perceived influence of the print media. She then says,

> Above all else we must maintain the honor of [Siamese] women as there are so many evildoers around the place who damage the name of respectable women. Those whores [kin'on], those creatures from hell [phuak narok]. It makes one furious. I wish there was a regulation in force preventing them going out and about as they do.[81]

Si responds by saying she is in complete agreement. What is of particular interest in Si's response is the language used. In agreeing with Anong's comments, Si uses the term phuak rao, literally "our group," to refer to both herself and Anong and, implicitly like-minded others. This signifies a specific form of solidarity or class-consciousness, identifying both of them as members of the same (presumably well-to-do) social stratum. At the same time, it is clearly implied that women who worked as prostitutes (kin'on, phuak narok) were of another, clearly "inferior" social class. Here we find women such as Si and Anong in something of a paradoxical situation. On the one hand, their conversation highlights a desire to improve the status and position of women, while on the other it advocates the suppression of another category of women who are characterized contemptuously in subhuman terms. In its own way, this contradiction suggests that while gender was becoming an issue of public debate, as manifest in the discussion of social advancement and equality for women, it was class that functioned as a more profound category in terms of social definition and power.

Satri niphon, like its predecessor Kunlasatri, proved to be a short-lived publication that appears to have gone out of business after only one issue. Exactly why both magazines failed is unknown, although one would have to assume that the lack of a sufficiently developed or committed readership in the early 1900s would have seriously hampered their commercial viability. Indeed, even during the 1920s, when a Siamese reading public had become well established and the nation's publishing industry was growing rapidly—a development which saw a whole host of new women's newspapers and magazines appear on the market—commercial success remained elusive, with many publications having a brief, tenuous existence before ceasing operations.

The various texts discussed here provide us with a sense of new class and gender dynamics emerging in Siam during the early 1900s. In the following decades this social dynamism intensified and found expression in a wide-ranging popular debate about the future of the nation. This will be examined in due course. First, however, it is useful to get a clearer idea of the changing sociocultural landscape in the Siamese capital beginning with an examination of the development of popular mass culture (in particular the cinema).

NOTES

A shorter version of the present chapter, "Protofeminist Discourses in Early-Twentieth-Century Siam," was published in *Genders and Sexualities in Modern Thailand*, eds. Peter A. Jackson and Nerida M. Cook (Chiang Mai: Silkworm Books, 1999), 134–53.

1. *Satri niphon*, 15 October 1914, 23.

2. There were two earlier magazines for females, *Narirom*, a fortnightly magazine that came out in 1888, and *Maekasin watthana witthaya*, which was produced by the Watthana School for girls in 1892 (Suwadee, "Thai Society's Expectations," Ph.D. diss., Sydney University, 1989, 209–10). The former, which appeared in verse form, had little to say about women; indeed, its main function appears to have been to publish palace news and report on the activities of royalty. Manun Wathanakomen, "Narirom: manda haeng nangs'u-phim phuying" [Narirom: The Mother of Women's Newspapers], *D'ok nangs'u* 22, 1996, 43–54. As for *Maekasin watthana witthaya*, virtually nothing is known about the circumstances of the publication of this magazine.

3. Lilia Quindoza Santiago, "Rebirthing Babaye: The Women's Movement in the Philippines," in *The Challenge of Local Feminisms: Women's Movements in Global Perspective*, ed. Amrita Basu (Boulder, Colo.: Westview, 1995), 118–19.

4. Marilyn J. Boxer, " 'First Wave' Feminism in Nineteenth-Century France: Class, Family, and Religion" in *Reassessments of 'First Wave' Feminism*, ed. Elizabeth Sarah (Oxford: Pergamon Press, 1982), 552.

5. Siriphorn Sakhrobanek, "Kan riak-r'ong sithi-satri kh'ong ying thai (2398–2475)" [Thai Women Call for Their Rights (1855–1932)], *Satrithat* (August–October 1983): 28–29.

6. Michele Wender Zak and Patricia A. Moots, *Women and the Politics of Culture* (New York: Longman, 1983), 301.

7. Chilla Bulbeck, *One World Women's Movement* (London: Pluto Press, 1988), 13.

8. See Anthony Reid, *Southeast Asia in the Age of Commerce, 1450–1680* (New Haven, Conn.: Yale University Press, 1988), 146–72; Simon de la Loubere, *The Kingdom of Siam* (Singapore: Oxford University Press, 1969), 73.

9. *Phra aiyakan laksana phua mia* [The Royal Code Concerning Husbands and Wives] in *Kot-mai tra sam duang* [Law of the Three Seals], vol. 2 (Bangkok: Khurusapha, 1962). The Law of the Three Seals, codified in 1805 under King Rama I, drew heavily on laws from the earlier Ayuthayan period, although it should be noted that certain provisions were modified or excluded altogether from the new legislation. Suwadee, "Thai Society's Expectations," 37.

10. Suwadee, "Thai Society's Expectations," 38.

11. In this regard, a third category of ownership may also be mentioned, that of the prostitute slave-woman whose body and sexuality was controlled by her master.

12. Suwadee, "Thai Society's Expectations," 39.

13. Suwadee, "Thai Society's Expectations," 38.

14. In addition to the law the sexual double standard was reaffirmed in classical literature perhaps nowhere more powerfully than in the epic *Khun Chang Khun Phaen*. In this text the young and handsome *Khun* Phaen, a renowned fighter and womanizer, was celebrated as hero while the central female character, Phim (also known as Wan Th'ong), who had sexual relationships with both *Khun* Phaen and a *Khun* Chang (an aging, balding

man of great wealth), was portrayed as the most loathsome of creatures for her infidelity. She was ultimately put to death on the king's orders after being unable to decide which of the two men she would take as her husband. Suwadee, "Thai Society's Expectations," 53–54.

15. In addition there was a fourth, less common category of wife known as *mia phrarat-chathan* of an even higher status than a *mia luang*. This particular type of woman was "given by the King to a nobleman as a reward for meritorious service to the country." Adul Wichiencharoen and *Luang* Chamroon Netisastra, "Some Main Features of Modernization of Ancient Family Law in Thailand," in *Family Law and Customary Law in Asia: A Contemporary Legal Perspective*, ed. David C. Buxbaum (The Hague: Martinus Nijhoff, 1968), 91.

16. Adul Wichiencharoen and *Luang* Chamroon Netisastra, "Some Main Features," 91.

17. *Phra aiyakan laksana phua mia* [The Royal Code Concerning Husbands and Wives], 252.

18. Chris Lyttleton, "Changing the Rules: Shifting Bounds of Adolescent Sexuality in Northeastern Thailand," in *Genders and Sexualities in Modern Thailand*, eds. Peter A. Jackson and Nerida M. Cook (Chiang Mai: Silkworm Books, 1999), 37–38.

19. *Phra aiyakan laksana phua mia* [The Royal Code Concerning Husbands and Wives], 1962, 210.

20. Dararat Mettarikanon. "Sopheni kap nayobai ratthaban thai ph'o s'o 2411–2503" [Prostitution and Thai Government Policy 1868–1960], M.A. thesis, Chulalongkorn University, Bangkok, 1983, 14.

21. This notion of the prostitute as a "public woman" was suggested by the terms commonly used to refer to them, such as *ying ngam m'uang* (beautiful woman of the town/city) and *ying nakh'on sopheni*, which means much the same thing.

22. Thanh-Dam Truong, *Sex, Money and Morality: Prostitution and Tourism in Southeast Asia* (London: Zed Books, 1990), 148.

23. See Reynolds, "A Nineteenth-Century Thai Buddhist Defense of Polygamy," 1977.

24. Suwadee, "Thai Society's Expectations," 89–90.

25. *Siam—Education*. Ministry of Education pamphlet, printed by *Bangkok Times* Press Limited, September 1926, 1.

26. Suwadee, "Thai Society's Expectations," 66.

27. Yuphaphorn Chaengchemchit, "Kans'uksa kh'ong satri thai: s'uksa korani chaph'o kh'ong rong-rian rachini (ph'o s'o 2447–2503)" [Thai Women's Education: The Case of the Rachini School, 1904–1960], M.A. thesis, Thammasat University, Bangkok, 1987, 17–18.

28. The Sunanthalai Girls' School was founded on the queen's initiative in January 1893 followed by the establishment of the Ratchakumari School in May of the same year. David, K. Wyatt, *The Politics of Reform in Thailand: Education in the Reign of King Chulalongkorn* (New Haven, Conn.: Yale University Press, 1969), 163–66. While the latter institution was a stopgap measure to provide an education for a limited numbers of royal princesses, the Sunanthalai School, originally patronized by daughters of the nobility, has been described as "a significant experiment . . . and an example for later girls' schools." Suwadee, "Thai Society's Expectations," 107.

In the following years Saowapha was instrumental in the creation of the School of Obstetrics and Nursing at Siriraj Hospital in 1896 and the Rachini School (the Queen's School), which opened in 1904 (Suwadee, "Thai Society's Expectations," 134). A prestigious, exclusive institution, Rachini School had an enrollment of approximately one hundred students by 1907, the year in which it became the first girls' school to become a part of the education system proper, administered and funded by the state. *Bangkok Times* (hereafter B. T.), 25 March 1907, 19 January 1907.

In 1914 Saowapha, who was now officially known as the Queen Mother, donated 50,000 baht to the Ministry of the Interior in order to establish three girls' schools: one in Ayuthaya, one in Ratburi, and one in Nakhon Pathom. B. T., 25 May 1914.

29. Quoted in Suwadee, "Thai Society's Expectations," 106.

30. Suwadee, "Thai Society's Expectations," 140.

31. B. T., 9 July 1902. Over the next few years, a number of other girls' schools were set up in Bangkok while formal schooling was also made available to girls in various provincial centers for the first time. Schools were established in Paknam at the mouth of the Chaophraya River (1905), Songkhla in the south (1905), and Phimai in the northeast (1907). These developments, it should be emphasized, were (like those in the capital) private initiatives, financed by members of the local elite (officials and well-to-do merchants) who were intent on providing some type of formal education for their daughters. B. T., 26 August 1905, 25 November 1905, 17 May 1907. In 1908, a number of girls were also reported to be attending a boys' elementary school in Rayong to the southeast of Bangkok. B. T., 21 January 1908.

32. English language instruction at two private girls' schools established in June 1901 was reported to cost two baht per month. B. T., 22 August 1901.

33. *Satri niphon*, 15 October 1914.

34. *Siam—Education*. Ministry of Education pamphlet, September 1926, 8.

35. Copeland, "Contested Nationalism and the 1932 Overthrow of the Absolute Monarchy in Siam," Ph.D. diss., Australian National University, Canberra, 1993, 26n43.

36. Chai-anan Samudavanija, *Chiwit lae ngan kh'ong thianwan lae k'o s'o r'o kulap* [The Life and Work of Thianwan and K. S. R. Kulap] (Bangkok: Bannakit, 1981), 98–107.

37. Some one thousand copies of this work were published.

38. *Tulawiphak phochanakit*, 27 June 1905.

39. *Tulawiphak phochanakit*, 27 June 1905.

40. *Tulawiphak phochanakit*, 27 June 1905.

41. Dararat, "Prostitution, and Thai Government Policy 1868–1960," M.A. thesis, Chulalongkorn University, Bangkok, 1983, 45–51.

42. For instance, on 31 January 1901, the editor of the *Bangkok Times* wrote: "The subject of crime in Bangkok is exercising the attention of our contemporaries . . . and is likely to be for some time yet, a perennial subject of discussion. It is easy to exaggerate our ills. . . . But no-one can fairly deny that robberies and violent assaults are much more common occurrences than they ought to be, or need be. The *farang* [European] is indeed fortunate who has not suffered from the visits of burglars; he is the exception, not the rule; while the ordinary Siamese householder lives in greater dread of the *kamoi* [thief] and *nakleng* [hoodlum] than should be the case in a thoroughly well-governed town. . . . Every dangerous character in the place is armed as a matter of right, and crimes of violence are a natural consequence."

43. Suwadee, "Thai Society's Expectations," 194.

44. *Tulawiphak phochanakit*, 27 June 1905.

45. *Tulawiphak phochanakit*, 27 June 1905.

46. *Tulawiphak phochanakit*, 27 June 1905.

47. Suwadee, "Thai Society's Expectations," 200.

48. *B. T.*, 13 March 1906.

49. Although the pseudonym *Mae* Chae was used by a female writer in this case (the gender of the writer indicated by the use of the first person pronoun *dichan* throughout the text), it was also a common practice during the early decades of the twentieth century for male writers to employ pen names which incorporated the word *mae* (mother) as the root. For example, *Phraya* Surintharacha, who translated Marie Corelli's *Vendetta* into Thai (*Khwam-phayabat*) in 1902, wrote under the pseudonym *Mae* Wan (see n. 51).

50. *Kunlasatri*, May 1906, 71.

51. For example, *Khwam-phayabat*, the Thai version of Marie Corelli's *Vendetta*, and generally considered to be the first English novel translated into Thai, dealt with the issue of female infidelity in upper-class (Italian) society. Thamkiat Kanari, "Mae wan kap khwam-phayabat" [*Mae* Wan and the Novel "Vendetta"] *Sinlapawathanatham* 5, no. 9 (July 1984): 102–105.

52. *Kunlasatri*, April 1906, 4.

53. *Kunlasatri*, April 1906, 5.

54. For a detailed analysis of the historical processes which helped shape and inform the story of *Nang* Nophamat, see Nithi Aeusrivongse, "Lok kh'ong nang nophamat" [The World of *Nang* Nophamat] in *Pak kai lae bai r'ua* [Pen and Sail] (Bangkok: Amarin, 1984), 336–72.

55. Suwadee, "Thai Society's Expectations," 66–68.

56. See Barmé, *Luang Wichit Wathakan*, 17–21.

57. *Kunlasatri*, April 1906, 12.

58. From the mid-nineteenth century, elite Siamese women were encouraged to play a part in the reception of Western guests at court. Yet, as Suwadee points out, this did not represent a substantive social change, but was simply a calculated attempt to impress foreign visitors. By the turn of the century, however, with increasing social intercourse between Siamese and Europeans, such women "were expected to know English and Western social etiquette as well as to have some basic knowledge about European countries. . . . In addition, . . . upper class men of this period began to expect their wives to share their interest in modern affairs." Suwadee, "Thai Society's Expectations," 93–94, 98–99.

59. *Kunlasatri*, April 1906, 13.

60. *Kunlasatri*, April 1906, 13.

61. Yuphaphorn, "Thai Women's Education," 24–25, 34–36.

62. *Kunlasatri*, May 1906.

63. *Kunlasatri*, May 1906.

64. Walter F. Vella, *Chaiyo! King Vajiravudh and the Development of Thai Nationalism* (Honolulu: University of Hawaii Press, 1978), ix (preface).

65. Copeland, "Contested Nationalism," 55–56.

66. The gender of the author is indicated by the use of the first person feminine pronoun, *dichan*.

67. *Satri niphon*, 15 October 1914, n. p.

68. *Satri niphon*, 15 October 1914, 23.

69. *Satri niphon*, 15 October 1914, 6.

70. *Than phu-ying* Mo (also known as *Thao* Suranari) is said to have led other local women in a successful uprising against Lao invaders in the nineteenth century (also see chapter 9).

71. Following the description of Queen Suriyothai's sacrificing her life on the battlefield, the account concludes with a short section that refers to her qualities in times of peace. Not only had she acted in an assured "regal" manner and raised her children successfully, she was also said to have won the "respect and praise of officials together with that of the populace at large" when she was installed as regent while her husband spent time in the monkhood. *Satri niphon*, 15 October 1914, 7.

72. Vella, *Chaiyo!*, 31.

73. *Satri niphon*, 15 October 1914, 137.

74. *Satri niphon*, 15 October 1914, 30–31.

75. Suwadee, "Thai Society's Expectations," 87.

76. Reynolds, "A Nineteenth-Century Thai Buddhist Defense of Polgamy." National Archives of Thailand R.6 Y, Krasuang Yuthitham (Ministry of Justice), 2/2 [*r'uang kot-mai laksana phua-mia*: About the Law on Marriage].

77. *Satri niphon*, 15 October 1914, 30.

78. *Satri niphon*, 15 October 1914, 30.

79. Hua R. Lan and Vanessa L Fong, eds., *Women in Republican China: A Sourcebook*, (New York: M. E. Sharpe, 1999), ix–xix.

80. *Satri niphon*, 15 October 1914, 42.

81. *Satri niphon*, 15 October 1914, 42.

2

❧

Cinema, Film, and the Growth of National Culture under Absolutism

H istorical studies on early-twentieth-century Siam have tended, as mentioned earlier, to place great emphasis on the world of the ruling elite while providing us with little sense of what was taking place elsewhere in the society.[1] Indeed, the sociocultural dynamism that characterized Bangkok life as the market economy developed is largely absent from these works. In an attempt to redress this lacuna, the present chapter is concerned with cultural and social change during the latter period of absolutist rule. As a point of departure and theme for much of what is to follow, I look at the emergence of that quintessentially modern cultural form, the cinema. The development of the cinema, together with that of indigenous filmmaking, was closely associated with the growth of the local newspaper industry and heralded the beginning of a new era in which members of the rising middle class contested the long-standing dominance of the royal-noble elite in Siamese cultural life. This was not a case of one elite displacing another, however, but a rather more complex process marked not only by competition, but also a significant degree of ambiguity, accommodation, and cooperation. Members of the royal elite, for example, played a key initiating role in the creation of the local film industry and, at various points, were actively involved in the running of the cinema business itself. At the same time, the enormous popularity of the cinema fostered the growth of indigenous prose fiction writing, a development that gave members of the middle class new opportunities to earn a living and define and articulate their sensibilities.

THE CINEMA COMES TO SIAM

During the late nineteenth century, a small number of commercially-oriented playhouses were established in Bangkok by members of the Siamese elite who

43

sought to profit from staging performances of various forms of dance drama (*lak-h'on*).² It was at one such playhouse, owned by M'*om Chao* (Prince) Alangkan, that Siam's first cinema showing took place in June 1897, just eighteen months after Louis Lumière publicly unveiled the new medium to Parisian audiences.³ The premier Bangkok cinema screening was mounted by S. G. Marchovsky, a traveling showman of unknown origins, who showed two films: one of an undersea diver and the second of a boxing match, together with a series of magic performances. The program was widely publicized, with the premiere attracting an audience of approximately 600 patrons from a cross-section of Bangkok society.⁴

When referred to in the Thai-language press, the films shown by Marchovsky were immediately dubbed *nang farang*, or European shadow theater.⁵ This particular choice of terminology was based on indigenous perceptions; the experience of seeing a film projected onto a screen was not dissimilar to watching the older traditional forms of shadow theater such as the *nang yai*, an elite cultural form, or the more "popular" *nang tal'ung* from southern Siam (itself closely related to the shadow theater of Java). The *nang tal'ung* performance, for example, features two-dimensional puppets, made from leather (*nang*), which are manipulated against an illuminated screen and appear to the audience as moving shadows.⁶

Following Marchovsky's departure, film was seen only intermittently by the Thai public over the next few years, and then usually only in conjunction with some other form of amusement. Although a regional entertainment circuit had become reasonably well developed in Southeast and East Asia by the turn of the century (featuring circuses and various types of professional stage acts from Europe, Great Britain, the United States, and Australia), Siam remained somewhat of a backwater. Writing early in 1903, for example, an English resident of the Siamese capital said that in comparison to "Hong Kong and Singapore (which have a plethora of entertainment), Bangkok pursues its solemn leaden course content to be neglected by the whirligig of amusements."⁷

It was not long, however, before foreign cinema entrepreneurs began to see Siam as a market with a good deal of potential. While a growing number of Western concerns (including the British Imperial Bioscope and the American Edison Cinematograph Company) came to Bangkok to screen their films,⁸ it was a Japanese promoter by the name of Watanabe Tomoyori who pioneered the early development of a local cinema industry.⁹ Arriving in October 1904, Watanabe secured the right to set up a large tent (capable of accommodating up to 1,000 people) in the Nakhorn Kasem area of central Bangkok where he put on a show of Japanese documentary-type films.¹⁰ His three-hour program was an immediate success; indeed it proved to be so popular with local audiences that he was asked to extend his season repeatedly and did not leave the city until the end of the year.¹¹

Watanabe's program included a series of films with boldly stated martial themes celebrating Japan's recent successes in its war against Russia. Footage of

Japanese troops on parade and marching on Port Arthur were shown together with film of a wrestling match between soldiers relaxing after a battle, and a cinematic representation of combat between warriors in the feudal era. Juxtaposed with this martial imagery were films depicting a more serene, settled world featuring elements of indigenous cultural life, a dance performed by geishas, a garden party in Tokyo, and a game of football played by Japanese nobles in traditional costume. The nature of Watanabe's cinematic offerings served to project a vision of Japan not only as a modern military power but also as a civilized, cultured nation. Indeed, it may well be imagined that the films provided a good deal of inspiration for budding Siamese nationalists by projecting potent images of a "progressive" Asian nation defeating a European power in war and forcefully asserting its own independence.

In an effort to capitalize on the strong demand for cinematic entertainment among the Bangkok public Watanabe returned to Siam in 1905, purchased the piece of land on which he had originally screened his films, and set about establishing the first permanent cinema theater in the kingdom. The theater, a barn-like structure made from timber and corrugated iron, opened in November 1905. Unlike his initial foray into the business, however, Watanabe screened popular Western films, in particular those from the French Pathé Frères Company, such as "Ali Baba and the Forty Thieves" and "The Hooligans of Paris."[12] As before, he succeeded in drawing large audiences on a regular basis and the business prospered.

Unsurprisingly, the commercial success of Watanabe's cinema did not go unnoticed and other foreign promoters (both European and Chinese, but no Siamese at this stage) soon followed his lead and established permanent cinemas of their own.[13] Apart from these enterprises, which were the best-known establishments in town, Bangkok also saw the appearance of numerous other smaller operations.[14] These included film screenings in general merchandise stores (much like the nickelodeon phenomenon in the United States), warehouses, and in tents set up on open land. Meanwhile, a number of the city's playhouses began including film shows with their usual theatrical programs as a means of increasing their takings.[15]

In 1907 the lucrative nature, not to mention the great popularity, of the cinema was highlighted when the *Bangkok Times*, reporting on the sale of Watanabe's theater (to another Japanese), noted that he had "cleared a sum of considerably over 100,000 baht from the show."[16] This figure, a substantial amount of money at the time (equivalent to more than £10,000 sterling), referred to the profit Watanabe had made from his business since establishing it less than two years earlier. The rewards of the cinema business were further underlined in 1909 when the rival Krungthep Cinematograph Company announced a similar level of profit after its first year in operation.[17]

While the Japanese Cinema continued as a leading force in the local industry, over time it went into gradual decline as growing numbers of entrepreneurs and investors entered the field eager to tap the strong public demand for moving pictures.[18] Perhaps the most significant development at this point was the formation, in 1910, of the Phathanakorn Film Company, a business set up by Low Pength'ong, the owner of a general merchandise store in Phahurat Road, in concert with a number of other Chinese merchants from the Siam-Chinangkun Association.[19] The company, with its flagship theater the Phathanakorn Cinema, was to be enormously successful.

The ascendancy of the Phathanakorn group was largely due to the efforts of a middle-class Sino-Thai, Siaw S'onguan Sibunr'uang, arguably the most important figure in the early history of the Thai cinema. The third son of a Chinese father from Malacca (*Nai* [Mr.] Siaw Hutin [Siow Hoot Tin]) and a Siamese mother (*Nang* [Mrs.] Dam), Siaw was born in Thonburi in 1878.[20] He began his education across the Chaophraya River in Bangkok and then went to Malacca for further study. During this time the linguistically gifted Siaw developed fluency in English, Malay, and Hokkien. Following his return to Bangkok, he worked in a number of clerical and accounting jobs, first at the Hong-Li Rice Mill, then the Oriental Store, the Chartered Bank, and later the Siam Electricity Company. In 1911, after eight years as an accountant for Siam Electric, Siaw moved on to take up a managerial position at the recently formed Phathanakorn Film Company. His educational background and his work experience provided him not only with a cosmopolitan outlook but also an extensive network of business contacts. Through these channels he was able to secure the agency rights from a number of Western film companies in both Europe and the United States. In addition to signing with Pathé Frères he also entered into contracts with Éclair, Vitagraph, and Selig.[21] Access to the catalogs of these and, later, other companies, made the Phathanakorn group a very powerful force in the local industry;[22] moreover, the company may be seen, in its own way, as contributing toward the increasingly cosmopolitan atmosphere of the capital through the eclectic range of films it screened.

Throughout the 1910s Siaw's company became locked in fierce competition with its major business rival, the Krung Thep Cinematograph.[23] However, when another well-financed competitor, the Nakhorn Kasem Cinema Company,[24] entered the field in 1919 Siaw was able to broker a merger between the Phathanakorn group and the Krung Thep Cinematograph creating a single entity under his management, the Siam Cinema Company.[25] As it turned out the competition provided by the Nakhorn Kasem Cinema Company was short-lived. Within a year it had gone out of business and was forced to sell off its original two theaters as well as a number of others it had subsequently acquired.[26]

Some of these theaters became independent operations, while the remainder were purchased by the Siam Cinema group that then came into competition with yet another new cinema business, the Siam Niramai Company. Secretly financed by King Vajiravudh, this enterprise was operated by the Wasuwat family (owners of the Sikrung publishing company), who subsequently played a central role in the development of indigenous Thai film (see below).[27] However, for reasons that are not entirely clear, the Siam Niramai Company, like the Nakhorn Kasem Company before it, was ultimately unable to provide long-term competition to Siaw's business. Indeed, the royal-sponsored enterprise seems to have gone out of business within a year or so of its establishment. This left the Siam Cinema Company as the dominant force in bringing film to the Thai public, a position it maintained for many years. By 1923, for example, the company was operating twenty theaters in Bangkok (by contrast its main competitors, such as the Capital Company and the Tang Hua Company, had only one or two cinemas apiece), reportedly drawing audiences well in excess of 30,000 people a week. At the same time, the company also operated a string of successful movie houses in various provincial centers throughout the country.[28]

As it turned out, however, the fortunes of the Siam Cinema Company were to change dramatically during the latter 1920s. In 1927 differences at the managerial level resulted in the long-term alliance between Siaw's Phathanakorn Group and the Krung Thep Cinematograph being dissolved, with the former (which had a majority shareholding in the business) continuing to trade alone under the name of the Phathanakorn Company. Siaw's sudden death the following year compounded the difficulties soon faced by the new scaled-down company. With a reduced capital base, the onset of the Great Depression at the end of the decade and the introduction of costly new sound technology, the Phathanakorn Company went into sharp decline and was ultimately taken over by the United Cinematograph Company (*Borisat saha sinema*). This new enterprise was established by King Prajadhipok, an avid cinemagoer and dedicated film enthusiast (see below) shortly after the fall of the absolute monarchy in 1932. The king's direct involvement in the cinema business had begun a few years earlier when he set aside 300,000 baht of state funds for the construction of a modern state-of-the-art theater to commemorate the 150th anniversary of the Cakri dynasty in 1932.[29] This new structure, the Sala Chalerm Krung Cinema, was eventually completed in July 1933 and became, so to speak, the "jewel in the crown" of the United Cinematograph Company's operations. Like the Siam Cinema Company before it, the royal-financed venture came to exercise an almost monopolistic position in the local cinema industry. As things eventuated, however, royal control of the United Cinematograph Company was short-lived. Anxious to reduce royal influence and expenditure, the constitutional administration transformed the palace ministry into a bureau and restructured the finances of the throne more generally. In the process, the operations of the United Cinematograph Company came under government control, a situation which, given the market dominance of the company, ensured that the state could readily determine the type of films shown to the Thai public.[30]

At the same time as the Siamese cinema business proper represented a domain in which the fortunes of older and newer elites fluctuated wildly, it also provided a powerful stimulus for the development of indigenous prose fiction writing among members of the emergent middle class.

FILM AND FICTION WRITING

Of the thousands of films shown in Siam during early decades of the century, the overwhelming majority came from the West: prior to World War I European (primarily French and Italian) films predominated, while in the postwar era American serials and features came to the fore as Hollywood emerged as the filmmaking capital of the world.[31] Audiences were exposed to an extraordinary array of material: documentary newsreels of contemporary political and social developments around the globe, historical epics, slapstick comedies, science fiction, detective and cowboy films, as well as romantic confections replete with graphic expressions of passion and desire. Cinemagoers became familiar not only with a host of screen heroes including Tarzan, Robin Hood, and Sherlock Holmes, but also with a range of heroines in such action adventure serials as *The Exploits of Elaine* with Pearl White, *The Wildcat of Paris* featuring Priscilla Dean, and *Madcap Madge* starring Olive Thomas.[32] To what extent these plucky, self-assured female screen characters fired the imagination of young Siamese women, or young men for that matter, is difficult to say, although it is hard to imagine that these figures had no effect on audiences at all. If nothing else these films, together with those of a more romantic nature, had a powerful influence on the types of fashion and hairstyles adopted by contemporary Siamese youth. This filmic influence was complemented and reinforced by images that appeared in the press, such as the advertisement for Golden Dragon cigarettes featuring two modish young women smokers (fig. 2.1). Here the parallel between this particular form of advertising (utilizing comely young females) and that found in other Asian countries such as China is unmistakable, reflecting, as it does, the spread of Western-style mass marketing in the promotion of modern commodities among the growing body of urban consumers.[33]

The period under discussion here was, of course, the age of the silent film. While many films were rudimentary in terms of plot and therefore easy enough to follow, many others had more complex narrative structures, not to mention intertitles in foreign languages incomprehensible to all but a tiny minority of Thai cinema patrons. As a means of addressing the problem of comprehension, at least as far as literate viewers were concerned, a new commodity appeared on the market: the film booklet. These booklets provided details of a film's plot and dialogue in Thai, allowing patrons to gain a greater appreciation of what they saw on the screen. Although information about these works is rather scarce, it is clear that by 1918 they had become widely available and were enormously popu-

lar. According to a report in the
Bangkok Times of that year, the
booklets were actually translations
of Western language materials—
perhaps promotional literature used
to advertise films, or synopses from
foreign film magazines—and "sold
cheaply as programs" at the
cinema.[34]

Up to this time, the translation of
Western language materials had
largely been the preserve of members of the royal and aristocratic
elite well versed in European
tongues.[35] However, with the spread
of modern secular education,
increasing numbers of young middle-class men and women also
became familiar with foreign languages (primarily English and, to a

Fig. 2.1. *Bangkok kan-m'uang,* 4 March 1924

lesser extent, French). It was from among their ranks that a new wave of transla-
tors emerged, using their talents to produce film booklets as well as adapting
what have been described as "indifferent [foreign] novels" for the stage.[36] Popular
demand for such works was enormous and writers were said to earn between 40
and 50 baht for producing a couple of hundred pages of translated text, a tidy
sum of money equivalent to the monthly salary of a middle-level government
administrator.[37]

For his part, the author of the *Bangkok Times* account mentioned above brand-
ed the middle-class creators of these works as "a crowd of nobodies."[38] The dismissive tone of the *Times's* journalist is revealing. For one thing it reflected the
patrician outlook of the paper. More generally it embodied the type of contemptuous attitude held by many members of the Siamese elite toward ordinary citizens at the time, particularly toward those with a modicum of learning who were
in a better position to question authority than their illiterate brethren.

The cinema, and by extension the printed materials it inspired, was disparaged
by certain members of the elite as "an eighth grade art form."[39] According to
such critics the film booklets were not only badly written but their authors were
incapable of rendering English words in Thai properly, a sure sign of a lack of
education. This view did not go unchallenged, however. As one commentator
working for the film magazine *Phaphayon sayam* (Siam Cinema) wrote:

> There are some people the same age as me who are given the [exalted] official rank
> of *Chao phraya* by royal command. They live in unimaginable comfort, waited on by

slaves [*that*] of both sexes. At the same time one finds people who only possess a single piece of cloth to cover their nakedness. They live precariously and are forced to beg for food. Sometimes they go hungry. Of the eight million people living in Siam there is just one king, and out of every one hundred thousand people there is but one government minister. So when someone has the good fortune to be able to write to earn a living they should be left alone and allowed to get on with what they do best.[40]

In making these observations the writer was giving voice to the simmering resentment and anger among ordinary people toward their social superiors during the last decade of absolutist rule (see chapter 4). The piece also reflects, in its own way, the burgeoning populism that characterized Bangkok life in the 1920s. In arguing against elite criticisms of popular writing, the author sought to validate this type of work as a legitimate and valid cultural form.

At the beginning of 1922 the popular low-cost film booklets referred to above were joined on the market by *Phaphayon sayam*, a weekly magazine put out by Siaw's Siam Cinema Company. The first magazine of its type in the country, *Phaphayon sayam* was a substantial publication averaging fifty pages per issue with a print run of 3,000 copies.[41] *Phaphayon sayam* featured the latest movie news from Hollywood, publicity stills from the various American studios which provided the company with its films, a regular column featuring indigenous and translated humor, and a column entitled *Sayam palimen* (Siamese Parliament), a type of public forum which gave readers the opportunity to express their opinions on matters related to the cinema (see below). The bulk of the magazine, however, was given over to serialized film stories based on the most popular features shown in the company's theaters.

In addition to the stories in *Phaphayon sayam*, the Siam Cinema Company, following the lead of the film booklet producers, also began publishing a line of cheap (15 satang) film-based books of its own.[42] Significantly, while some of these works, as well as some of the stories serialized in *Phaphayon sayam*, were translations or adaptations of foreign language materials, others were of an entirely different order altogether. As *Khun* Chim, a regular columnist for the magazine, noted,

> The writers of these stories do not translate them from English sources. Rather they go along to the cinema and watch a film. Then they write up an account of what they've seen. They have little time to think about what they're doing, at most four or five days, often much less. Sometimes the work must be done within a day so they don't have the luxury of writing in a complex refined manner.[43]

The emergence of these film booklets and books marked a decisive step beyond translation or simple adaptation. Indeed, it signaled the beginning of a more creative phase of Thai prose writing, although admittedly one in which action, movement, and dialogue, the most fundamental elements of film, were emphasized at the expense of detailed representations of character, setting, and mood. Popular demand for film-based texts, and the money that could be made from churning out this type of material, was such that from the early 1920s increasing numbers of young middle-class Siamese were drawn into the world of commercial writing. It is no exaggeration to say that this period marked the efflorescence of Siamese "print capitalism" with some ninety-nine privately owned printing presses operating in Bangkok by 1924, "a number which rose to one hundred and twenty-seven over the next three years." Moreover, in one month alone during this period it was recorded that "fourteen of the capital's publishing houses produced some 40,000 copies of thirty-nine titles," the majority of which were fictional works (r'uang an len) with many of these undoubtedly based on film.[44] Over time the cinema-publishing nexus proved to be a particularly fertile training ground for aspiring young middle-class writer-journalists, many of whom, such as Kulap Saipradit and Op Chaiwasu,[45] went on to become well-known novelists and short story writers in their own right.

We will return to examine some of this early prose fiction writing at a later stage (see chapter 8). For the moment, however, let us move on to take a look at another key aspect of cultural production at this time—the development of the indigenous film industry.

MAKING MOVIES

The history of filmmaking in Siam is generally agreed to have begun with Prince Sanphasat Suphakit, a younger brother of King Chulalongkorn. Both the prince and the king had been introduced to photography and filmmaking during Chulalongkorn's first visit to Europe in 1897.[46] As a result the king developed a passion for photography and provided the inspiration for many of his peers amongst the royal-noble elite to take up the hobby. While the prince also took a keen interest in photography he was far more enamored with the possibilities of filmmaking, and, having acquired a cine camera, film stock, processing equipment, and chemicals from Europe, he made the first of a series of short documentary-style films in 1900. Most of these recorded the public activities of the king as well as major royal ceremonies. Apart from being an avid filmmaker the prince was also a frequent exhibitor who charged audiences a fee to see his productions when they were screened at the larger temple festivals and other venues in the capital.[47]

Watanabe, the Japanese Cinema entrepreneur mentioned above, together with his fellow compatriot, projectionist Kayama Komakichi, was also involved in filmmaking. When the pair came to Siam they brought their own moviemaking equipment with them and produced a number of short documentary-style films. These productions included Chulalongkorn's funeral procession in 1910, the lavish coronation ceremony of Vajiravudh, his son and successor, and a boxing match.[48] In addition, Watanabe and his cohort also made some rudimentary narrative-style films. According to the archivist and film historian Dome Suk-wong, one of these productions was entitled *Muak pliw* (Hat in the Breeze); in it, a well-dressed man boards a tram, has his hat blown off by the wind, and chases after it along the street, barely avoiding all sorts of mishaps in the process. Although a precise date for this film cannot be ascertained with certainty, Dome believes that it may have been a 1905 film advertised in English as *Misadventures of a Hat*.[49]

Seven years later a somewhat more complex film was made in the Thai capital, although by whom is not known. While the existing scholarship credits the 1923 film *Nangsao suwan* (literally, *Miss Heaven* or *Survarna of Siam*, as it was generally known in English) as Siam's first commercial, narrative motion picture[50] (that is, a film with an unmistakably Thai theme), an obscure 1912 production, adver-tised in English as *A Siamese Elopement*, actually deserves the honor.[51] Set in Bangkok, the film starred local theatrical performers and featured "vocal and instrumental accompaniment." As for the plot, the *Bangkok Times* offered the following brief synopsis: "[it shows] the elopement of the loving couple in a gharry, the pursuit of the infuriated father along local streets, and the final chase by water which ends in the capsizing of the father, his rescue by the gallant young man and the reconciliation."[52]

This telegraphic summary is the only record we have of the content of Siam's earliest narrative film. Even so, despite its brevity, this account hints at the new social landscape of early-twentieth-century urban Thai society as the film cele-brates the triumph of romantic love, a decidedly modern notion, over familial obligation.

Following the appearance of *A Siamese Elopement*, two other local produc-tions, presumably made by the same anonymous filmmakers, were screened at the Japanese Cinema in rapid succession. The first of these was *The Burglar and the Chloroform*, a work for which there are no details regarding the plot, although the title suggests a European influence. The second work, *The Flirt and the Croco-dile*, by contrast, had an overt Thai flavor as evidenced by the accompanying advertising copy that simply read, "a new amusing and interesting film depicting a story of Siamese life—with a moral."[53]

From this point in early 1912 there is no record of further filmmaking activity in Siam until 1922. It was in this year that the Royal Siamese Railway Film Unit was established on the initiative of Prince Purachatra (Prince Kamphaengphet) who, like his brother, the future king Prajadhipok (see below), had a lifelong fascination with filmmaking. Over the following years the Royal Siamese Rail-way Film Unit was to play an important role in the development of the local film industry. Until it was disbanded in the wake of the 1932 overthrow of the abso-lute monarchy, it produced numerous newsreels and documentary films on the activities of the king and his government as well as travelogue-type footage from various provincial areas. Shortly after it was established, for example, a camera crew traveled along the newly opened northern rail line to film the visit of Prince Boriphat to Lampang and Chiang Mai, together with footage of the local people and their customs.[54] These documentaries were screened in conjunction with imported foreign films in the Bangkok cinemas as well as those in regional centers. The appearance of these locally made films was of particular significance in that it represented the dawning of a new era in which the Thai state began to utilize moving images to broaden and extend its nation-building project. Through the medium of film, growing numbers of Siamese developed a heightened awareness of their rulers, their fellow compatriots, and the territory they inhabited. In effect the Film Unit helped to shape and define the growth of a Thai national consciousness, a process that complemented the work of the Railway Department as it sought to draw the nation together physically through the extension of the rail network into different parts of the country.

In addition to producing documentary-type material, the Film Unit was also involved in providing technical assistance for the production of the aforementioned *Nangsao suwan* (also see chapter 8). This film, which starred an all-Thai cast, was made by Henry Macrae and a small team of his associates from the Hollywood-based American Motion Picture Company.[55] Approximately one and a half hours long (eight 12–15-minute reels), *Nangsao suwan* was filmed in and around Bangkok with additional footage shot in Hua Hin and Chiang Mai. It opened simultaneously in a number of Bangkok theaters in June 1923 and featured a new innovation for Siam: Thai-language intertitles between scenes that were used to enhance narrative continuity and coherence. Not surprisingly, given the enormous popularity of the cinema, *Nangsao suwan* was enthusiastically received by local audiences, while columnists for *Phaphayon sayam* portrayed the release of the film as an event of major significance and a cause for national pride and celebration. As one writer was moved to observe in a mood that reflected equally a jingoistic spirit and his lack of awareness of foreign involvement in the project,

> It is a Thai story filmed in Siam featuring Thai performers. There has never been any other picture that we have seen that is as beautiful, as entertaining, or as good as *Nangsao suwan*. All of the Chinese, Burmese and Indian films that have been shown here pale in comparison, not only in terms of acting skills, but also in terms of amusement and coherence of plot.[56]

Meanwhile another commentator portrayed the significance of the film in a broader context.

> Most of the people I've met from different Asian countries are greatly surprised and somewhat puzzled when I tell them I am Thai. Some Japanese have asked me, "Siam is near to Sweden and Norway, isn't it?" while many people from Hong Kong have told me the only countries in Asia they've ever heard of are India and Burma, both

British colonies, and Vietnam, a French colony. As for Siam, an independent nation in this very region, they don't know a thing! And when I go to Shanghai, Formosa or Manila people are under the impression I come from Vietnam or Japan. When those in nearby countries don't know anything about Siam there is no point in talking about what they think of us in more distant lands.

However, after seeing *Nangsao suwan*, the first Thai film, I'm ecstatic. It shows various regions of the country, temples, palaces, rivers and canals, rice paddies and beautiful forests, not to mention our beloved ancient sites that look so dignified. And it's wonderful to see a cast composed entirely of fellow Thais whose acting ability loses nothing in comparison to the stars of American films. When the images in this film are seen around the world it will be immensely gratifying for not only will other peoples learn who the Thai are, but they will also see that Siam, like other countries, has its own precious treasures.[57]

In addition to Macrae and his team from Hollywood, the Wasuwat family (owners of the Srikrung printing house which published the popular daily newspaper *Sayam rat*) also played a role in the film's production.[58] The Wasuwats' interest in moviemaking had begun the previous year (1922) when they produced an experimental film, a single-reel documentary about floods ravaging Shantou in southern China, created by filming a large number of still photographs obtained from mainland sources. The finished product was shown at a Bangkok cinema and reportedly drew large numbers of Chinese patrons. Further short films of a more conventional nature followed, including footage of a trip to Saiyok waterfall in Kanchanaburi province and of King Vajiravudh playing golf at Hua Hin, south of Bangkok.[59] Over the following years the family's interest continued to develop and in 1926 Phao Wasuwat (*Luang* Konkan Chenchit, previously an official in the Royal Siamese Maritime Service), and one of his brothers, Kasian Wasuwat, were employed for a time by the Railway Film Unit. Here they gained further valuable experience which, together with that acquired working with members of Fox Movietone who had come to Siam at the end of 1929 to make sound documentaries, was put to use when the family became involved in the production of commercial feature films in the 1930s.[60]

Meanwhile the introduction of 16mm movie cameras together with film and processing facilities during the early 1920s stimulated a keen interest in filmmaking—of the "home movie" variety—among members of the upper class. The most prominent figure in this movement was King Prajadhipok, whose major and abiding cultural interest was the cinema. This interest dates from the time when he was still a prince. In 1924, on the return trip to Siam following the completion of his studies in England, Prajadhipok made it a point to visit Hollywood with his wife. Not only did the couple get to look at the film industry firsthand but they also had the opportunity to socialize with some of the leading stars of the age, including Douglas Fairbanks and his wife, Mary Pickford. During his stay Prajadhipok procured some of the most modern cinematic equipment avail-

able and started making 16mm films back in Siam where he was frequently photographed with a movie camera in his hands (much like the present royal
incumbent who, until quite recently, was often photographed with a Canon SLR
dangling from his neck). The extent of Prajadhipok's fascination with film was
reflected not only in his extensive collection of moviemaking equipment, which
included over ten different cine cameras, but also in the processing laboratory
and the private cinema that he had built at Sukhothai Palace, his principal residence. Throughout the 1920s and early 1930s he made numerous films ranging
from documentary-style works to experimental films and short features, one of
which, *Waen wiset* (The Magic Ring), a forty-minute silent production shot on
the southern Thai island of K'o Phang-ngan in 1929, is the earliest complete
Thai film known to exist.[61] However, as far as can be determined, none of the
king's works were ever exhibited in the Bangkok cinemas, perhaps out of fear
that they would be publicly criticized by discerning viewers for their lack of
sophistication in comparison with the productions of other, more skilfull filmmakers.

That is not to say that the king's films were only for his own personal enjoy-
ment. They were also shown to his peers at one of the regular monthly meetings
of the Amateur Film Makers Association of Siam, a body that had been set up
under his patronage in 1930. This appears to have been an outgrowth of a similar
but earlier organization, the Amateur Film Association that had been formed in
1926 with his brother, and fellow film enthusiast, Prince Purachatra as presi-
dent.[62] The Amateur Film Makers Association of Siam had a membership of
more than one hundred people drawn from the Bangkok elite, including a number of "high-born ladies," businessmen, and members of the local European community. Apart from providing an opportunity for its members to exhibit their
work, the association also set up a shop that sold film equipment and offered
processing services. It also held formal lectures on various technical and creative
aspects of filmmaking and in doing so played a contributing role to local film
production during the 1930s.

The Siamese film industry proper, that is the making of commercial feature
films by Thais rather than foreign nationals, can be said to begin in 1927. This
development was related, in part, to a marked contraction of the public sector
the previous year. Approximately ten thousand officials had been retrenched at
the beginning of King Prajadhipok's reign in an attempt to reduce the high level
of state spending and debt that his administration had inherited from its predecessor.[63] As a consequence of the new government's actions, opportunities for
employment in the bureaucracy, which up to this time had absorbed much of
Siam's educated middle-class male population, were sharply reduced. This, in
turn, forced increasing numbers of educated men to look for opportunities in the
private sector. Early in 1927, for example, a group of retrenched officials established the Central Electric Company to provide electricity in provincial areas.
Meanwhile another group of former officials formed the Thai Film Company.[64]

The company, headed by the recently retrenched *Luang* Sunth'on Atsawarat (Chamrat S'onwisut), announced ambitious plans to "produce Siamese films . . . with Siamese actors and actresses in Siamese stories and to market these worldwide."[65] However, *Luang* Sunth'on's new company did not have the field to itself. Shortly afterward Siaw S'onguan Sibunr'uang, the canny manager of the Siam Cinema Company, members of the Wasuwat family, together with some associates from their newspaper publishing business, and a number of government officials formed a rival firm of their own, the Bangkok Film Company. According to the daily *Pakka thai* (Thai Pen), news of these developments "inspired a great hunger in members of all classes and both sexes to appear in the movies."[66] Indeed, when the Bangkok Film Company placed advertisements in the press seeking fifty people to appear in its first production, more than 1,200 applications from eager young men and women were received.[67]

From this point the two rival companies vied with one another to be the first to get a film onto the market. Better organized and possessing far greater expertise, the Bangkok Film Company won the race, as it were, with its initial offering, *Chok s'ong chan* (Double Luck), a contemporary romance, premiering at the Phathanakorn Cinema on 30 July 1927.[68] Public interest in the film was intense and a crowd of almost 7,000 people was said to have gathered outside the 3,000-seat capacity theater on the opening night. Over the next four days, more than 12,000 people went to see *Chok s'ong chan*; food shops and stalls in the vicinity of the cinema reported unprecedented business, and nearly 4,000 copies of a specially prepared booklet about the film were bought up by patrons.[69]

Less than a month later, the Thai Film Company brought its first film to the public. This production, *Mai khit loei* (Well, I Never Imagined), another contemporary romance, was based on a script by *Luang* Sunth'on and filmed by *Khun* Pathiphak Phimlikhit (Pleng Traipin), the former head-cameraman at the Railway Film Unit.[70] Again there was great public interest in the film, leading one journalist to write, "at the present time most people are talking about the cinema. In fact, it seems as though every young man and woman is living and breathing the idea of being in the movies."[71]

Buoyed by their initial success the two companies quickly made plans to produce other films. In what proved to be a serious miscalculation, however, *Luang* Sunth'on's Thai Film Company went ahead and made a work entitled *Amnat m'ut* (Dark Forces) about the seamier side of Bangkok life that dealt with prostitution, opium smoking, and secret society activity. At this time a formal film censorship law had yet to be introduced (stringent, wide-ranging legislation was finally enacted in 1930 and remains in force, largely unaltered, to this day); instead, a practice had developed during Vajiravudh's reign, in which all films, both imported and locally made, were to be shown to the monarch and his close associates for their authorization before being released for general exhibition. While it appears that there were very few (if any) films that did not meet with royal approval up to this time, *Luang* Sunth'on's second cinematic production was a notable exception. The film's depiction of the Bangkok demimonde was offensive to King Prajadhipok, who saw it as presenting a negative, damaging image of Siam to the outside world. Nevertheless, the king decided to give *Luang* Sunth'on permission to screen the film briefly so as to enable those who had put money into the venture to recoup their investment. When this was accomplished the film was to be withdrawn from circulation and all copies destroyed. However, before any screenings could be arranged, the police department insisted on viewing the film and banned it from being shown. In response *Luang* Sunth'on edited out the film's most contentious scenes, renamed it *Chana phan* (Defeat of the Hooligans) and was granted permission by the police to have it shown to the public. But as things transpired, news of the official controversy surrounding the film leaked out and no large cinema operators dared to show it. Instead an increasingly desperate *Luang* Sunth'on organized screenings of the work in various small venues in Bangkok and different regional centers. Yet for all his efforts the returns were meager and the Thai Film Company, for want of capital, went out of business.[72]

Here it may be added that official concern and anxiety about how Siamese society appeared to foreigners, specifically Europeans, was intense. In 1921, for example, when a Captain Harold Holland arrived in Bangkok "for the purpose of taking photographs and preparing scenarios in connection with an important cinematograph film production," Prince Dhani, one of King Chulalongkorn's younger brothers, wrote to other high-ranking state officials saying that precautions needed to be taken to ensure that he did not film anything that would reflect badly on the country. In particular he did not want Holland, or any other foreigners for that matter, to have the opportunity to film anything of a "sexual nature" such as the "harems" of influential men.[73] Later such concerns over the kingdom's international reputation influenced the decision of Vajiravudh to allow Macrae unprecedented access to royal resources and personnel in the making of *Nangsao suwan*. It was envisaged that by engaging in close cooperation with the American the project could be "properly controlled and supervised."[74] Even so, when Macrae visited Chiang Mai he evaded such controls and was able to take footage of a public execution and smuggle it out of the country. However, the Siamese government learned of the film and, when an attempt was made to exhibit it back in the United States, successfully lobbied the State Department to have the screening blocked.[75]

As for *Luang* Sunth'on's rival, the Bangkok Film Company, it came out with *Khrai di khrai dai* (known in English as None but the Brave), an uncontroversial contemporary tale, described at the time as being designed "to impart values and exert a positive influence on the negative side of the human character."[76] This film, like its predecessor, was a great public success and was soon followed by the release of yet another film, a comedy feature entitled *Khrai pen ba* (Who's Crazy?). At this point in early 1928, however, Siaw Songuan Sibunr'uang, the guiding force behind both the Bangkok Film Company and the Phathanakorn

Cinema Company, passed away. Without his drive and leadership both operations faltered, and the former, faced with a shortage of capital and lacking any
clear plans for the future, soon went out of business.[77]

Following Siaw's unexpected death Manit Wasuwat, who had been involved
in the business side of Bangkok Film, teamed up with his brothers to launch a
new cinematic enterprise, the Sikrung Film Company.[78] Using profits from his
highly successful publishing business Manit spared little expense in acquiring the
most up-to-date filmmaking equipment from the United States for the new company. In 1930 the Wasuwats began conducting tests with imported sound technology and produced a series of short experimental films. The fruits of their
labors were subsequently realized in early 1932 when the Sikrung Company
released *Long thang* (Gone Astray), Siam's first "talkie" (for further details, see
chapter 8). A dramatic work incorporating contemporary music and song, *Gone
Astray* was also notable for the controversy (and hence publicity) it generated:
critics claimed that a number of sexually suggestive scenes contained in the film
were obscene, charges which led to a drawn-out court case ultimately decided in
the company's favor.[79]

During the late 1920s and throughout the 1930s a number of other filmmaking companies were also established, although none of these businesses ever
really threatened the position of the Sikrung Film Company, which, in the
period prior to the outbreak of the Pacific War, came to represent the very acme
of the Siamese film industry.[80] Following its construction of the country's first
sound film studio complex at Bangkapi on the outskirts of Bangkok in the early
1930s (dubbed as Siam's own Hollywood), Sikrung produced the vast majority
of Thai-language feature films in the prewar era, many of which were to help
define the taste and style of the postabsolutist elite.[81] Regrettably there are no
extant copies of any of these films or, for that matter, any of the other productions referred to earlier. Indeed, with the exception of a handful of movies, most
notably Pridi Phanomyong's 1941 epic *Phrachao chang ph'uak* (Land of the White
Elephant) (see chapter 9 for further discussion of this work) and King Prajadhipok's *Waen wiset* (The Magic Ring) referred to above, virtually no pre–World
War II Thai films have survived. For students of the early history of Thai film
interested in other productions from this era, all that remains are a number of
exceedingly rare booklets containing film plot outlines and still photographs
taken on set.

The establishment of cinema theaters and the making of films were, of course,
activities that required significant capital investment only available to very few
Siamese, such as members of the royal-noble elite and entrepreneurs from the
upper echelons of the emergent middle class. In the development of the cinema
industry and the filmmaking business during the first decades of the twentieth
century, these two elites were engaged in something of a symbiotic relationship
marked by varying degrees of competition and cooperation. Overall, however,

whatever ideological differences may have existed between these groups was largely of secondary importance to that of market-driven imperatives. Accommodation rather than confrontation was the hallmark of their relationship.

More generally it may be added that royal interest and involvement in the cinema and filmmaking business from its earliest days has had a continuing impact on the sociocultural landscape of modern Thailand. As we have seen, the throne played a crucial role in determining what type of films the Thai public could see, originally through the process in which films required royal approval before being released for general exhibition, and subsequently by means of the rigorous film censorship law enacted by the absolutist regime in 1930 which, as previously noted, is still in force to this day and continues to limit the type of films available to contemporary cinemagoers. A second enduring feature of royal involvement is the legacy of the Railway Film Unit. In producing newsreel-type works about the activities of the king for general release, it played a crucial role in placing the monarch at the forefront of the public imagination. As such it paved the way for the development of the modern public relations machine associated with the palace through which footage of the activities of the king and other members of the royal family are broadcast nationwide daily by all of the country's free-to-air television networks.

Let us now turn to look at the cinema as a social institution, an institution intimately bound up with Bangkok life. As such the capital's movie houses represent a unique arena from which to develop a feel for class and gender relations within the rapidly changing urban landscape.

NOTES

A part of the section on the history of the cinema and filmmaking was previously published under the title "Early Thai Cinema and Filmmaking," in *Film History* 11, no. 3 (1999): 308–18.

1. For example, see D. K. Wyatt, *The Politics of Reform in Thailand: Education in the Reign of King Chulalongkorn* (New Haven, Conn.: Yale University Press, 1969); Walter F. Vella, *Chaiyo! King Vajiravudh and the Development of Thai Nationalism* (Honolulu: University of Hawaii Press, 1978); Benjamin A. Batson, *The End of the Absolute Monarchy in Siam* (Singapore: Oxford University Press, 1984).

2. Dome Sukwong, "85 pi phaphayon nai prathet thai" [85 Years of Cinema in Thailand], *Silapa-wathanatham* 3, no. 8 (June 1982): 12.

3. Members of the public had already become familiar with simple moving images in shows such as the Chrono and Chronophone bioscopes brought to Bangkok by traveling showmen in 1891. *Bangkok Times Weekly Mail*, 29 January 1927.

4. *Bangkok Times*, 11 June 1897. The admission prices charged varied widely. At one end of the scale a complement of chairs in a theater box cost 10 baht (approximately £1 or US $5 at the exchange rate of the time), first-class chairs cost three baht each, while second class chairs cost two baht. For the less well-heeled, there were benches in the

gallery where a seat was priced at two saleung (equivalent to 50 satang or half a baht), a fee that was just within reach for a member of the urban working class in full-time employment. *Bangkok Times*, 9 June 1897.

5. Dome, "85 Years of Cinema," 18.

6. For more on Thai shadow theater, see "Shadow Puppet Theater in Northeast Thailand," *Theater Journal* (31 October 1979): 293–311.

7. *Bangkok Times*, 3 February 1903, 18 February 1903.

8. *Bangkok Times*, 12 February 1903, 27 November 1903.

9. Watanabe, who was involved in the rubber plantation business in the Straits Settlements, briefly returned home in the latter half of 1904 where he witnessed the huge popular success of films about the war then being fought between Japan and Russia. Inspired by what he saw, Watanabe purchased copies of this material together with a number of documentary-style films and the projection equipment for showing them. Accompanied by Kayama Komakichi, an experienced film projectionist, Watanabe traveled back to the Southeast Asian region, making Bangkok his first port of call. See Yoneo Ishii and Toshiharu Yoshikawa, *Khwam samphan thai-yipun 600 pi* [600 Years of Thai-Japanese Relations] (Bangkok: Mulanithi khr'ong-kan tam-ra sangkhomsat lae manutsat, 1987), 186–87. It has been suggested that Watanabe was well known in the city and may have actually worked in some capacity for the Japanese legation. See Dome Sukwong, "R'uang kh'ong rong yipun" [The Japanese Cinema in Bangkok], *Silapak'on* no. 28 (5 May 1984): 73–74.

10. Watanabe's film program consisted of twenty-one films. *Bangkok Times*, 9 December 1904.

11. *Bangkok Times*, 8 December 1904. Following his stint in Siam, Watanabe took his show south to the Straits Settlements, Borneo, and Sarawak, then returned to Bangkok for further screenings before finally making his way back to Japan. Yoneo Ishi and Toshiharu Yoshikawa, *600 Years of Thai-Japanese Relations*, 188.

According to Dome, the exhibition of films mounted by Watanabe followed the example of the cinema in Japan, where a narrator or commentator (*benchi*) stood in front of the audience near the screen and provided dialogue to accompany the particular film being shown. This assumption is based on the fact that the notice Watanabe placed in the *Bangkok Times* announcing the film exhibition also included an advertisement for a "Siamese interpreter who speaks English." Presumably the Japanese were to communicate in English with the interpreter who, in turn, was to translate this into Thai for the benefit of the audience. Dome, "The Japanese Cinema," 74.

12. *Bangkok Times*, 24 May 1906.

13. Only three months after Watanabe had established his business, a Frenchman opened another cinema near the Oriental Store featuring the added attraction of European women in Siamese dress performing during breaks between the films. Although this venture soon collapsed, another new cinema was opened in October 1906. Set up on the grounds of Prince Prida's palace in New Road, the Royal Vitascope Theater, operated by a Mr. Faulkner Wilkes, was a large weatherproof building equipped with electric lights and fans, and capable of seating an audience of 3,000 patrons.

During the following year (1906), the cinema business continued to expand. This was made possible, in part, by the establishment of a branch office in Singapore by the Pathé Frères Company as it sought to extend its worldwide distribution network. At least one new theater was established at this time when *Nai* Seng Huat, a Chinese merchant from Singapore, founded the Samyaek Cinema, a development that appears to have been related to the greater availability of film with the arrival of the Pathé Company in the region. *Chum-num phaphayon*, 9 October 1941.

The Royal Vitascope (referred to above) changed hands toward the end of 1907 when it was taken over by a consortium of Siamese and Italian interests headed by Sunchai Khutrakun, the owner of the Ratamala Store, and reopened as the Krung Thep Cinematograph. *Bangkok Times*, 18 December, 1907. The growth of the industry continued in 1908 with the addition of another new theater, the Bangrak Cinema, set up by another Frenchman in the grounds of the home of *Phraya* Surasak Montri on Silom Road. *Bangkok Times*, 14 February 1908.

14. *Bangkok Times*, 15 January 1908. As one observer noted, "there are far more cinematographic shows flourishing in this town than the average foreign resident has any idea of."

15. Bangkok's playhouses, it should be mentioned, had an important role in the development of the local acting and writing professions.

16. *Bangkok Times*, 19 April 1907.

17. The Krung Thep Cinematograph was formed as a limited liability company in October 1909 with a paid-up capital of 100,000 baht divided into shares of 100 baht each. In addition to the original cinema in front of Prince Prida's palace, the company also took over the management of the old French-run theater on *Phraya* Surasak Montri's land.

It was reported that in the period from August 1908 to August 1909, before the company was established, the former venue, the Krung Thep Cinematograph theater, had a gross income of 92,101 baht with working expenses totaling 32,077 baht, leaving a gross profit of 60,024 baht. When additional costs such as management fees and depreciation of buildings, plant, furnishings, and films were deducted, a net annual profit of 42,334 baht was realized. *Bangkok Times*, 7 October 1909.

18. New movie houses established at this time included the Ratana Cinema and the Sayam Phaphayon Cinema; the latter, owned by *Luang* Prasan Aksonphan, was the first wholly Thai financed and managed theater in Bangkok. It remained in business for just one year. *Bangkok Times*, 28 August 1909.

As for the Ratana Cinema, it was badly damaged by fire on its opening night when one of the volatile nitrate films caught alight. According to the *Bangkok Times* (3 May 1909), the resulting fire caused a stampede among the audience of 2,000 in which "a number of persons were concussed." The theater was subsequently refurbished and opened for business.

Meanwhile, outside the capital, traveling cinematographic shows had been staged at the annual temple festival at Paknam in Samut Songkhram since at least 1908. *Bangkok Times*, 19 October 1908. The following year the Siam Coast Biograph operated by three Danes, was reported to be screening films in the southern town of Songkhla. *Bangkok Times*, 21 May 1909.

19. Siaw (Sieow) S'onguan Sibunr'uang, *Cremation Volume* (Bangkok: Phathanakorn Printery, 1928), 3. *Bangkok Times*, 5 January 1910.

20. Siaw, *Cremation Volume*, 1.

21. Siaw, *Cremation Volume*, 4. In newspaper advertisements it ran in 1912, the Phathanakorn Cinema boasted that it was "the only cinema in town which receives new supplies of film each week." *Bangkok Times*, 17 October 1912.

22. Siaw, a model capitalist entrepreneur, was committed to expanding his business operations. Apart from his work with the cinema he was also involved in electrification and road concession projects in rural areas. During his travels out of the city he came to see how successful traveling film showmen had become in the provinces (a number of these individuals had previously worked in the Bangkok cinema business, but as the competition grew were forced to quit the capital and seek opportunities elsewhere). This provided Siaw with the inspiration for the Phathanakorn Film Company to mount traveling film shows in a number of provinces in the central region, including Ratburi, Phetburi, and Nakhorn Chaisi, all of which were conveniently located along the southern railway line to the Malay States. Siaw, *Cremation Volume*, 4–5.

However, the first permanent cinemas in provincial centers were not established until World War I. In 1916, for example, it was reported that two regional cinema halls had been opened, one in the southern coastal town of Chumporn and another in Nakhorn Pathom, to the west of Bangkok. *Bangkok Times*, 30 May 1916, 6 June 1916, 2 November 1916. Yet another theater was established in Ayuthaya the following year. *Bangkok Times*, 1 August 1917. Although there is little available information about links between these enterprises and the cinema business in Bangkok, newspaper accounts indicate that the Phathanakorn Film Company was supplying if not actually operating these provincial theaters. *Bangkok Times*, 15 March 1920.

23. One observer with firsthand experience of this rivalry noted that the advertising leaflets put out by one company would regularly include scathing denunciations of its competitors. At other times, he said, there were often violent incidents involving razors and knives when the staff of competing firms met while out distributing leaflets. *Chumnum phaphayon*, 9 October 1941.

24. The company, founded by a Chinese merchant, Low Peng Ngee, began by establishing two cinemas, the first of which, the Nakhorn Kasem, was erected on the site of the old Japanese Cinema which it had purchased from the Phathanakorn Film Company. This new theater, described as "the pioneer in ferro-concrete cinema buildings in Siam," was reported to have cost in excess of 220,000 baht. A newspaper correspondent provided the following account of the new theater:

> For the painting of the walls and stage scenery the services of prominent members of the Fine Arts Department have been secured. . . . The ornamentation of the screen was designed by HRH Prince Nares [Naret]. The theater is able to accommodate comfortably 1,500 persons, with still plenty of room available before the stage of crowding is reached. The main seating accommodation is on the second floor with a raised platform at the rear for boxes and first and second-class seats. There is a balcony right around the hall and tables placed at convenient distances so as to allow those who wish to enjoy both drinks and cinema pictures at one and the same time to have their privilege.
>
> In all there are about 600 electric lamps which illuminate the interior and exterior of the hall. There are two electric dynamos which are worked by the Siam Electricity Company's current . . . there are six approaches to the hall and each gateway is brightly illuminated. Cars need not line up on either New Road, Chakravadi Road or Yawarad Road because there is quite ample room for vehicles to safely line up in the roadways around the hall. There are some three stairways leading [into the theater]—two to the one-saleung and two-saleung seats, and one to the first, second

and third class seats. Besides the bar there is a billiards room and there is going to be a sort of cave in the center of the hall, illuminated with electric bulbs, where girls will sell refreshments.

By contrast the company's second cinema was somewhat more modest in scale. Occupying a converted Chinese theatrical hall, it was located near a tram crossing at the entrance of Plabplajai Road. In addition to this the company also announced ambitious plans to set up a number of other theaters through the city. *Bangkok Times*, 10 October 1919.

25. Dome, "The Japanese Cinema," 93–94.

26. In July 1920, the Nakhorn Kasem Cinema Company was purchased for 125,000 baht by a newly floated import-export business, the Nakhorn Kasem Company. This enterprise was formed by a cartel of Siamese, Chinese, and European investors with a paid-up capital of 500,000 baht. Almost immediately, however, problems emerged, financial irregularities were discovered, and certain members of the group were accused of embezzling company funds. By the end of September, a meeting of shareholders in the faltering concern decided that it should cease operations and its assets be liquidated. *Bangkok Times*, 7 August 1920, 1 October 1920.

27. The background to the formation of this company is unusual, to say the least. The Siam Cinema Company had received a print of an Indian-made film of the classical tale *Sakuntala*, a work that was of particular interest to King Vajiravudh since he had once produced a Thai version for the stage. Over the years a practice had developed in which exhibitors took their films to the palace where they were screened for the king before being released for general public exhibition. However, for reasons that are unclear, the Siam Cinema Company did not put on a private screening of *Sakuntala* for the king. Vajiravudh was apparently enraged by this incident, which he took as a deep personal slight. As a result he told his intimate associate *Chao Phraya* Ram Rakhop that he would start up a "Thai" cinema group to compete with the "Chinese-run" Siam Cinema Company. Interview with Dome Sukwong, Thai National Film Archives, Bangkok, 28 May 1993.

28. Cinemas operated by the company in Bangkok included the Hong Kong, the Penang, the Sathorn, the Phathanakorn, the Phathanarom, the Singapore, the Java, the Banglamphu, the Nakhorn Kasem, and the Nang Lerng. *Phaphayon Sayam*, 23 January 1923.

29. A second, and much larger, project to commemorate the 150th anniversary of the founding of the Cakri dynasty was the construction of the Phuthayotfa Bridge across the Chao Phraya River, linking Bangkok with Thonburi.

30. Dome Sukwong, "Phrabat somdet phra pok klao kap phaphayon" [King Pradjadhipok and Film], unpublished paper, Bangkok, 1993, 32–37.

31. From time to time, cinema audiences also had the opportunity to see films from China and India. *Bangkok Times*, 20 January 1917, 21 June 1922, 26 July 1922.

32. For example, see cinema advertisements in *Bangkok Times*, 25 February 1916, 11 May 1918, 6 March 1920, 19 August 1920.

33. See Francesca Dal Lago, "Crossed Legs in 1930s Shanghai: How 'Modern' the Modern Woman?" *East Asian History*, no.19 (June 2000): 103–44.

34. *Bangkok Times*, 9 August 1918. Cinema magazines had been produced in the United States since at least 1912. Eric Rhode, *A History of the Cinema from Its Origins to 1970* (Great Britain: Pelican Books, 1978), 72.

35. Wipha Senanan, *The Genesis of the Novel in Thailand* (Bangkok: Thai Watana Pan-ich Press, 1975), 38–39, 64.

36. *Bangkok Times*, 9 August 1918.

37. *Bangkok Times*, 9 August 1918.

38. *Bangkok Times*, 9 August 1918.

39. *Phaphayon sayam*, 26 June 1922.

40. *Phaphayon sayam*, 26 June 1922.

41. Priced at thirty satang a copy, it was not cheap; daily newspapers of the time cost anywhere between three and ten satang while the most inexpensive cinema seats went for between ten and fifteen satang.

By the standards of the day, when the longevity of many publications was measured in months, *Phaphayon sayam*, which remained on the market for over two and a half years, was an undoubted success. Admittedly, some changes were made in order for it to survive. Shortly after the magazine first appeared, readers began calling for a reduction in its price. Some months later, in an attempt to oblige these requests, the company started producing a budget version printed on cheaper paper for the price of 20 satang a copy while continu-ing to publish a better quality version at the original cost of 30 satang an issue. In addition it was announced that anyone who bought a ticket at one of the company's cinemas could also purchase the magazine at the reduced price of 10 satang a copy. Ultimately, however, the company made a commercial decision and stopped publishing the magazine, replacing it with a far more modest newspaper called *Khaw phaphayon* (Movie News). *Phaphayon sayam*, 28 November 1924. Like its predecessor, *Khaw phaphayon* featured short reports about the goings-on in Hollywood as well as one or two serialized film stories. Published twice weekly, with a print run of two thousand copies, the paper was distributed free of charge. With no revenue from sales, commercial interest came to the fore with at least half of its twelve pages being filled with advertisements for various pharmaceutical prod-ucts, cigarettes, shoes, hair oil, perfume, tennis racquets, and sewing machines. Sponsors, it seems, were not difficult to find and *Movie News* became the leading, and for much of the time the only, newspaper devoted to film in Siam during the mid-1920s. It continued to be published over the next four years until the death of Siaw So'nguan Sibunr'uang in June 1928.

42. The number of works put out by the company was extensive and included such titles as *Invisible Ray* (*Ratsami wiset*), *The Soul of a Woman* (*Long rit sane nai*), *Peril of the Yukon* (*khumsap nai alaska*), and *The Adventures of Robinson Crusoe* (*R'obinsankhruso*). *Pha-phayon sayam*, 24 August 1923. It should be noted that in some cases the film titles were translated rather freely. For example, *The Soul of a Woman* or *Long rit sane nai* would be more accurately rendered as "Falling for [the Charms of] the Mistress."

43. *Phaphayon sayam*, 10 January 1923.

44. Matthew P. Copeland, "Contested Nationalism and the 1932 Overthrow of the Absolute Monarchy in Siam," Ph.D. diss., Australian National University, Canberra, 1993, 54.

45. Wipha, *The Genesis of the Thai Novel*, 68.

46. Chulalongkorn was actually filmed on a number of occasions by cameramen work-ing for the Lumière Company.

47. Dome Sukwong, *Prawat phaphayon thai* [The History of Thai Film] (Bangkok: Ong-kan kha kh'ong khurusapha, 1990), 8. In November 1903, for example, he showed a film

of the celebrations of the thirtieth anniversary of the coronation of Chulalongkorn at the Oriental Hotel as a part of a film program mounted by the Edison Cinematograph Company. *Bangkok Times*, 27 November 1903. Another somewhat less well-known filmmaker, who began working shortly after the prince, was *Phra* Sathaphong (Tuay), owner of the Ratana Cinema. Dome, *The History of Thai Film*, 9. One of *Phra* Sathaphong's films shown at the Ratana was "a view of Bangkok streets taken from a moving cart." *Bangkok Times*, 23 October 1909.

48. Dome Sukwong, "85 Years of Cinema in Thailand," *Sinlapawatthanatham* 3, no. 8 (June 1982): 18.

49. Dome, "The Japanese Cinema," 88.

50. For example, see Dome, *The History of Thai Film*, 12; John A. Lent, *The Asian Film Industry* (London: Christopher Helm, 1990), 213; and Sakdina Chatrakul na Ayudhya, "Direction Unknown," in *Cinema* (summer 1989): 58.

51. I have been unable to locate any vernacular sources that refer to the film using its Thai name.

52. *Bangkok Times*, 29 February 1912.

53. *Bangkok Times*, 20 and 25 March 1912.

54. Sakdina Chatakul na Ayuthaya, "Phaphayon kap kan t'o-su chon chan nai huang wela haeng dan phlat phaendin" [Film and Class Struggle in a Time of Political Change], *Sethasat kanm'uang* 7 (January–June 1989): 1–2, 19–20; *Bangkok Times*, 4 September 1922.

55. In addition to Macrae, the film's director, the team was made up of Robert Kerr (assistant director), Dale Clawson (cameraman), and production assistant Gordon Sutherland Moss. The group arrived in Bangkok in January 1923. National Archives, *Krasuang tang-prathet* [Ministry of Foreign Affairs], 84/1; Letter from Eldon R. James, the Office of the Advisor in Foreign Affairs, to Prince Devawongse, 16 March 1923. Macrae had it in mind to "produce a play of modern Siam" and, apparently well briefed as to the most effective way of achieving his aim, he sought and obtained the permission and support of King Vajiravudh.

In a rather self-congratulatory account published on his return to the United States, Macrae wrote, "His Majesty the King is a graduate of Oxford, England, and believes he is a second Shakespeare, that he is the Shakespeare of Siam. He spends a great amount of his time translating Shakespeare into Siamese and producing these dramas and comedies with his own people—actors from what they call the Royal Entertainment Company. . . . I felt that His Majesty would be interested in moving pictures, and after considerable maneuvering I finally secured an audience which resulted in securing the entire company's assistance together with the free use of the King's 52 automobiles, His Majesty's 600 race horses, the free use of the navy, the Royal Palaces, the railways, the rice mills, . . . klongs and elephants, and white elephants at that." Henry Macrae, *Film Daily Yearbook* (New York and Hollywood, 1924).

56. *Phaphayon sayam*, 29 June 1923.

57. *Phaphayon sayam*, 29 June 1923.

58. "Khun Wichit Matra kap wongkan nang thai" [*Khun* Wichit Matra and the World of Thai Film], *Siam nik'on* 4, no. 166 (1980): 34.

59. Dome Sukwong, "Manit Wasuwat kap phaphayon siang sikrung" [Manit Wasuwat and the Sikrung Talkies], *Sinlapawathanatham* 4, no. 7 (May 1983): 91.

60. Dome, "Manit Wasuwat," 92; Dome, *The History of Thai Film*, 21; the creation of the Sikrung Film Company by members of the Wasuwat family is further discussed in the latter part of this chapter.

61. Department of Fine Arts, *Nithan kh'ong lung r'uang "waen wiset" phaphayon fi phrahat phrabat somdet phra pokklao chao yu hae lae phaphayon phuthaprawat "burapha prathip"* [Uncle's Folk Tale "The Magic Ring": A Film by His Majesty King Prajadhipok, and an Historical Film on Buddhism, "The Light of Asia"] (Bangkok: Department of Fine Arts, The Thai Film Foundation, and the National Film Archives, 1987).

62. The prince, like the king, shot enormous amounts of film including scenes from his domestic life. One of his more interesting home movies included rather erotic footage of two of his barely teenage wives frolicking together naked and hosing themselves with water as well as sequences showing some of his slightly older wives bathing. More mature wives were filmed with their clothes on.

63. Batson, *The End of the Absolute Monarchy*, 34.

64. *Bangkok Times Weekly Mail*, 31 January 1927.

65. *Bangkok Times Weekly Mail*, 31 January 1927. Following the announcement, the company advertised for people interested in appearing in film and was immediately inundated with applications. Months passed, however, before anything further was done since the members of the company could not agree among themselves as to what type of film they should make. Dome, *The History of Thai Film*, 16.

66. *Pakka thai*, June 1927.

67. *Sikrung*, July 1927.

68. Dome, "Manit Wasuwat," 93.

69. *Khao phaphayon*, 5 August 1927.

70. Dome, *The History of Thai Film*, 18–19.

71. *Pakka thai*, 5 August 1927. The writer then went on to add that a film did more than simply help the production company make a profit but also "benefited the nation." Given this he believed that the government should assist the development of the fledgling industry by helping filmmakers to obtain up-to-date equipment and find suitable locations for their work. At the same time, he suggested that Siam follow the example of the United States:

> Hollywood is a name that filmmakers and film stars are well acquainted with. The film capital is indeed a beautiful city. As yet we still don't have a film center in Siam but I certainly believe we will have one in the future. Does anyone think that Lumphini Park could become the film center of Siam during this progressive era? I personally believe that Lumphini Park would be a most suitable site for such a development. The air is clear, and what is more, it is frequented by foreign residents and tourists. If the local film industry was located in the park the prestige of Thai film would be raised in the eyes of visitors and, in my opinion, draw increasing numbers of tourists to the country.

However, he then concluded the piece on the following note, "this is probably an impossible dream for there is news that the park has already been made a royal gift to a high ranking noble."

72. Dome, "King Pradjadhipok and Film," 45–56; Sakdina Chatrakul na Ayudhya, "Film and Class Struggle," 19–20.

73. Letter dated 1 September 1921, National Archives, R6, B'o 14/1.

74. Letter dated 16 March 1923, National Archives, Ministry of Foreign Affairs 84/1, box 1.

75. Letter dated 23 June 1926, National Archives, Ministry of Foreign Affairs 84/1, box 1.

76. *Sikrung*, October 1927. *None but the Brave* was notable not only for its combination of melodrama, humor, and violence, the hallmark of hundreds of subsequent Thai films, but also for showcasing the products of local businesses: furniture from the Bangkok House Furnishing Company (which provided tables, chairs, and household goods) and clothing from the Suphorn Phanit Company (which supplied the cast with fashions "of a pleasing design").

77. Dome, "Manit Wasuwat," 93.

78. Manit Wasuwat was born in Bangkok on 12 May 1897. His father was *Phraya* Suthorn Phimon (Phle Wasuwat) and his mother was *Khunying* Thim. He had four brothers— Sukri, his senior, and three younger brothers, Phao (*Luang* Konkan Chenchit), Krasian, and Krasae. All of them were mechanically minded and became interested in photography and filmmaking from a young age.

On completion of his schooling at the Royal Pages' College (*Rong rian ratchawithayalai*), Manit began his career as an official in the Finance Ministry and later went to work at the Samsen Electric Company. Following the death of Sukri in 1922, however, Manit left this job and took over the Sikrung Publishing House, which his elder brother had established in the mid-1910s. Under Manit's management, the company prospered and developed into one of Siam's most successful publishing enterprises in the pre–World War II period. Dome, "Manit Wasuwat," 90–92.

79. See Dome Sukwong, *Long thang lae khadi long thang* [Gone Astray, the Film: *Gone Astray*, the Legal Case], (Bangkok: Film House, 1996).

80. Other companies included Si Sayam Films, Sayam Pictures, the S'ong Sahai Company, Asiatic Productions, and Hatsadin Films. For the most part, these companies were family-run enterprises, hampered by either limited capital or a lack of expertise. As a result they often produced one or two features and then disappeared from the scene. Dome, "85 Years of Cinema," 20.

81. Sikrung also accepted commissions from outside interests to make films. In 1933, for example, the company was employed by local Chinese merchants to make a film in Cantonese entitled in Thai *Khwam-rak nai m'uang thai* (literally, Love in Siam, although it was advertised in English under the title *Honor Redeemed*). *Chalerm prathet*, 1 August 1933. Later, in 1935, it was engaged by the Ministry of Defense to produce a big-budget propaganda film, *L'uat thahan thai* (Blood of the Thai Military) (also see chapter 9). Although the Sikrung Company was not formally allied to the state, Manit Wasuwat enjoyed good relations with various members of the post-1932 government. Such connections led to his appointment as one of the seventy members in Siam's original National Assembly. Dome, "Manit Wasuwat," 94.

3

✣

In and around the Cinema: Romance and Sex in the City

A part from screening films and providing an impetus to the development of prose fiction writing, the cinema was a key social institution intimately bound up with Bangkok life, and represented something of a microcosm of Siam's "city of dreadful delight."[1] What we will see is that the cinema was more than simply a place of entertainment but also a site of class tension, violence, crime, romance, sexual harassment, and solicitation. Indeed, in a sense, it was an intermediate zone between "polite society" and the demimonde. As such, an examination of the cinema as a public space allows us to develop some sense of Bangkok's changing class and gender dynamics, including those related to prostitution and erotic entertainment.

THE CINEMA-GOING PUBLIC

Following the establishment of the first permanent theater by Watanabe in 1905, the cinema rapidly became an integral part of urban life. It was, in a sense, an extension of the playhouses and the *likay* (Thai folk opera) and *ngiw* (Chinese folk opera) halls that had been established in Bangkok during the latter part of the nineteenth century. Yet the playhouses, set up by princes or members of the aristocracy, were essentially the domains of the capital's elite, while the *likay* and *ngiw* theaters drew their patrons from among the ranks of Siamese and Chinese commoners.[2] The cinema, on the other hand, was not burdened by a particular history or identified with a specific class or group. As an imported modern technological form it embodied the notions of "civilization" and "progress" that made it attractive to the elite and the educated, while its cost was within reach of all but the most impoverished members of society. As such, the early history

69

of the cinema in Siam was rather different from that in such countries as Britain and the United States, where it was primarily associated with the working classes.[3] Even so it would be mistaken to place too much emphasis on the idea of the Siamese cinema as a truly egalitarian, democratic institution since the difference in seating prices and seating arrangements tended to preclude intimate contact between the wealthy and privileged in their private boxes, and the remainder of the audience sitting in separate sections of the theater. This latter group represented a cross-section of ordinary society ranging from middle- and low-level government officials, clerks, and sales staff in the private sector to wage laborers, rickshaw men, washerwomen, street vendors, prostitutes, and petty criminals.

THE CINEMA AS PUBLIC SPACE

The most detailed and comprehensive information about Bangkok's cinemas during the 1920s comes from *Sayam palimen* (Siamese Parliament), a column that appeared in the weekly film magazine *Phaphayon sayam*. As mentioned above, the column allowed members of the public, almost invariably from the middle class, to express opinions on matters related to the cinema.[4] Although this correspondence deals specifically with particular writers' experiences in the capital's cinemas, it also provides us with a good deal of insight into the life of the city more generally.

Broadly speaking, the image of the Bangkok movie houses that emerges from these accounts is one of rampant squalor and anarchic, disorderly behavior. Sanitary conditions and the comfort of patrons were apparently not of prime consideration for cinema owners. Numerous letters appeared in the column complaining about the vermin that infested most theaters. The Nang Lerng Cinema, owned and operated by Siaw's Siam Cinema Company, was particularly notorious in this respect. As one writer complained after a visit, "you could see people refusing to sit down on their seats because of the filth, while some of those who did sit down soon began scratching themselves."[5] In the Banglamphu cinema, another one of the company's theaters, urine flowed freely across the floor and the pungent odor of excrement wafted through the air.[6] This situation was apparently widespread since a number of writers called on the Siam Cinema management to install toilets and rest rooms in their theaters for the benefit of patrons.[7]

A number of correspondents voiced their grievances about the condition of the Phathanakorn Cinema, the largest and most prestigious theater in the capital. According to one critic, "the floor is filthy; indeed, it is absolutely disgusting. Some people squirt betel juice all over the place; it bounces off the ground and sprays over the clothing of other patrons. I'm continually hearing complaints about this. Should you go to the movies barefoot and tread in this goo you'll be doubly revolted."[8]

One regular patron of the Phathanakorn Cinema writing to the opinion column in *Phaphayon sayam* magazine said that he was appalled by the "rough boys" who worked as vendors selling drinks and peanuts inside the theater, claiming that "they smell so bad you can't go near them."[9] Another correspondent expressed concern about the image of Siam which the Phathanakorn presented to outsiders, noting that it was the theater of choice among foreigners.[10] As a consequence he urged the house's management to stop allowing children and adolescents "dressed in filthy clothes," to beg inside the cinema and annoy members of the audience.

This situation was common throughout much of Bangkok, with throngs of young boys and youths to be found loitering outside most movie houses as well as up and down any number of the city's streets. Some were neglected by their parents while in other cases they had been abandoned altogether. As a result many resorted to begging or turned to crime, with cinema patrons and passers-by regularly being targeted by pickpockets and snatch-and-grab robbers.[11]

Low-class women who brought their babies and young children into the cinema were also the subject of readers' complaints. As one aggrieved theatergoer wrote,

> Some of these women have no interest in maintaining their appearance or attending to their personal hygiene. They chew betel and spit it onto the floor fouling the clothing of other people in the audience. In the 25 satang seat section some of them pull the benches close together and set out makeshift hammocks for their babies to lie on, obstructing the passage of other patrons.[12]

Yet as another correspondent made clear, resentment toward the poor or disadvantaged was only part of the picture. When "high-class" people went to the Banglamphu, the Nang Lerng, and the Java cinemas (all operated by the Siam Cinema Company) they were frequently heckled by ordinary folk in the audience. In response some anxious upper-class patrons apparently took to wearing disguises to avoid harassment and abuse.[13]

Such tensions were exacerbated by the problem of overcrowding, which was endemic to most Bangkok cinemas. The Siam Cinema Company, for example, did not limit the number of people permitted to enter a theater to the actual number of seats available. Even when all the seating was filled tickets continued to be sold, with the result that those who had seats often had their view blocked by crowds of people standing in front of them. This, together with instances in which seated patrons refused to remove their hats, frequently led to heated arguments, scuffles, and sometimes even violent fights.[14] Throughout the 1920s the rowdiness and disorderly behavior that characterized the cinema continued unabated, a fact that greatly disconcerted state officials. It was only belatedly in 1930 that the authorities finally made some attempt to curtail such activity.

> Owing to the failure of the public in general to give proper attention and due respect to His Majesty the King when the Siamese National Anthem is being played after performances in the local entertainment halls, H.R.H the Minister of the Interior has issued an order to the police authorities to remedy the situation. It has been noticed that when the band strikes up the National Anthem some persons seem to pay little attention to it, while others walk out of the hall, quite oblivious to the patriotic custom. The police on duty have been instructed to remind the public when the tune is being played, and to take down the names of the offenders in the case of government officials or military men.[15]

To what degree these orders were enforced or effective is impossible to gauge. However, if nothing else, their introduction highlights the indifference if not outright contempt felt by certain sections of the populace toward their social superiors.

Another dimension of class difference was manifest within the educated middle stratum itself and was reflected in an exchange of views between a number of contributors to the "Siamese Parliament" column. One of these correspondents who used the pseudonym "Golden Dragon" (*Mangk'on th'ong*) was an unabashed critic of the poor. He claimed that it was "impossible to find any pleasure going to the movies sitting near someone in tattered smelly clothes," and called on the Siam Cinema Company to enforce a dress code to ensure that patrons were well presented and clean before being allowed entry. Referring to these less-privileged members of the audience as "the stench" (*phuak men sap*), he suggested that the theater management only tolerated them because they had paid the price of admission. He admonished the company for being "unconcerned with the annoyance suffered by the public" and urged other readers who agreed with him to register their disapproval.[16] While some writers endorsed his views, others did not. One correspondent, calling himself "Silver Dragon" (*Mangk'on ngoen*), suggested that Golden Dragon and those who held similar views were overreacting. He felt that the most offensive people in the cinema were "not beggars and the unwashed" but rather those who sat in the audience reeking of perfume. The cinema company, he argued, should take pity on the poor; he advised Golden Dragon and his supporters that "if they can't take it they should move to the West, because this is the way things are in Siam."[17] Another contributor, calling himself Not Amused at All (*mai kham loei*), wrote to the magazine endorsing Silver Dragon's views.

> The Siam Cinema Company has indeed progressed, but have you ever thought about how it has done so? Isn't it as a result of the support of the Thai people? And for the most part who are these people? Aren't they what "Golden Dragon" refers to as "the stench," or whatever? If he goes into a cinema on any day other than his

usual Saturday and Wednesday visits who, pray tell, will he come across apart from "the stench"? Again let me ask who is responsible for helping the Siam Cinema Company progress? If the company brings in regulations as suggested by "Golden Dragon" what will be its fate? . . . Sir, remember the people you complain about are human beings just like you. You should have sympathy for them.[18]

This exchange of opposing viewpoints, as suggested above, provides us with a glimpse of some of the tensions within the Siamese middle class itself. Here one finds a marked contrast in social outlook: on the one hand, a conservative, exclusivist perspective voiced by Golden Dragon and on the other, a rather more egalitarian, democratic view articulated by his critics. This particular divergence of opinion is of interest in that it not only reflected a degree of friction and tension within the rising middle class but also prefigured, in its own small way, the broader democratic-authoritarian struggles which have characterized Siamese politics in much of the post-1932 period.

THE CINEMA AND RELATIONS
BETWEEN THE SEXES

Up until the latter nineteenth century, young women from wealthy Bangkok families were strictly supervised and their activities carefully monitored by their parents or guardians. Often they were confined to the home and had few opportunities to meet young men. One of the only public places they were permitted to go, and which offered them the chance of coming into contact with men, was the annual temple fairs or festivals held in the city. Even so, these events were few in number and ran for just a matter of days, factors which limited the possibilities for young well-to-do women to fraternize with members of the opposite sex.

With the advent of playhouses and cinemas, however, elite women as well as those from the emergent middle class and working classes gained new opportunities for social interaction.[19] Indeed, notwithstanding the often chaotic and rambunctious atmosphere of the Bangkok movie houses, going to see a film became a socially acceptable pastime and the cinema emerged as a site of romance. In fact it was one of the only places where a young man and woman could go out together, generally in the company of relatives or friends, or with a chaperone. Unlike cinemas in southern Siam where Islamic practice enforced a rigid separation of the sexes,[20] the Bangkok theaters were not segregated and men and women sat alongside one another. This meant that when women went to the movies either alone or in groups they came into close contact with men.

This new social reality also soon featured in popular literature. In a number of serialized novels and short stories from the late 1920s and early 1930s we often find the central female character, either of elite or middle-class origins, going to

the cinema on a date. A good example of this can be found in the work of D'ok-
mai Sot, one of Siam's best-known early female authors. In *Sattru kh'ong chao
l'on* (Her Foe), her first novel (published in 1929), the female protagonist Mayuri
is taken to the Phathanakorn Cinema by a suitor, while in *Kam kao* (Past
Karma), another of the author's works (from 1932), the heroine, Nuch, is invited
to the cinema by Phong, a man she eventually marries.[21] Similarly Raphin, the
principal male character in Kulap Saipradit's 1932 novel *Songkhram chiwit* (The
War of Life), takes Phloen, the woman he loves, on a date to the cinema.[22] And
in an intriguing 1933 "autobiographical" novella entitled *Dichan chua phr'o chai*
(Men Made Me Bad), the author, *Nangsao L'oi Lom* (Miss Floating on the
Breeze), relates her experience of being courted in a movie house by an employee
of the Siam Cinema Company with whom she subsequently elopes (for further
details of this work see chapter 9).[23]

While the cinema provided new opportunities for women and men to mingle
and meet one another, it was also a place where women were exposed to the
unwanted attentions of unruly, aggressive males. Public space and sexual harassment were closely intertwined. Take, for example, the following incident
reported at length in the *Krungthep Daily Mail*. Three young women had gone to
the Singapore Cinema for an evening's entertainment. As they sat in their seats,
two men, referred to as *chao-chu* (womanizers), began to flick watermelon seeds
at them in a rather puerile attempt to attract their attention. The women, however, were unamused. Shrieking in disgust they quickly moved to vacant seats in
another part of the cinema. Undaunted the men pursued them and continued
to shoot watermelon seeds in their direction. Unable to endure such behavior
any longer, the women made a hurried exit from the theater. The men then
pursued them along a nearby street and began menacing one of the women who,
in self-defense, struck one of her would-be assailants across the face with a shoe.
An all-out fracas ensued but was quickly broken up by the police, who arrested
the men and laid assault charges against both of them.[24]

Harassment of a more intimate nature was also commonplace in the city's
crowded cinemas. A typical example of this was reported in the Thai-language
section of the *Bangkok Times*. The story concerns a fifteen-year-old girl,
described as having a "shapely figure" (*rup rang sa-suay ph'o chai*), who had gone
to the movies with her mother at the Japanese Cinema. As they sat watching
the show, "a short, light-skinned man wearing a shirt, trousers and a hat"
reached into the young woman's blouse and tried to fondle her breasts.[25] Curiously, although this incident was presented as a factual account, it was written
in a rather jocular tone, suggesting a complacent and indulgent attitude toward
this type of behavior. The extent to which young women were subject to such
harassment in public is further highlighted in the newspaper cartoon shown in
figure 3.1.[26]

The graphic comprises a number of scenes from the annual festival at the

Temple of the Golden Mount (*Wat Saket*).[27] These images are fascinating in that they graphically convey a sense of the raw bustle and menace endemic to Bangkok public life during the 1920s, which is lacking in most other sources. Significantly, the issue of male harassment is featured in the scene at the center of the cartoon. A semicircle of mature, stoutly built matrons surround a young woman, shielding her from the advances of a swarm of men. A similar theme is also addressed in the picture in the top right-hand corner of the cartoon which shows two female figures disguised as men, one armed with an axe, the other with a lance. The adoption of such disguises and the bearing of arms

Fig. 3.1. *Sikrung*, 27 November 1926

serve to emphasize the potential dangers women faced when going out in public.

At the same time the scene at the bottom left-hand corner of the graphic depicts another rather different form of public danger. Here a woman, dressed in contemporary garb, is being sized up by two men who stare at her in an uncertain, somewhat disapproving fashion. The woman's modish clothing and the fact that she is on her own indicates she is a streetwalker, and the men's proximity to her suggests sexual interest, while their cautious looks convey a sense of anxiety about the possibility of contracting venereal disease which was rampant in the city at the time (see chapter 6). We also find a more general sense of menace and danger evoked by the image immediately above in which gangs of Chinese and Siamese men, armed with pikes and axes, are shown marching about. The caption below the picture simply reads "frightening."

The disorderly conduct and rowdy behavior which often characterized the public realm is further conveyed by two other images—the first on the far right, opposite the parading gangs, shows a man, most likely a pickpocket or bag snatcher, eluding the gendarmerie, and the second, at the top of the picture in the center, depicts two inebriated men who are described as "enjoying themselves to the hilt."[28] Finally, beneath the central image of the young woman and her sturdy female guardians, the edge of a stage and a crowd can be dimly seen. The accompanying caption says, "This is a stall with beautiful *things*," a subtle reference to some type of erotic performance staged by attractive young women.

From the world of the *Wat* Saket annual fair, let us return to the cinema and the issue of prostitution. As was the case during the early period of cinema in Great Britain it was not unusual for low-class prostitutes or their pimps to solicit for clients inside Bangkok movie houses.[29] One particularly lurid example of this was the subject of a 1921 press report: a man by the name of *Nai* Hui was arrested for taking a girl, described as under the age of twelve (the legal age of consent at the time), to a number of the capital's theaters and forcing her to have intercourse there with paying customers.[30] Meanwhile prostitutes were said to congregate "in droves" outside cinemas in the hope of snaring customers.[31] Indeed, for many men a night at the movies was not complete without some form of sexual encounter. As *Khun* Wichit Matra (a well-known author and writer of film screenplays) noted in his memoirs, for young men of his day the cinema experience was often followed by a visit to a brothel.[32]

As mentioned earlier, while prostitution is a much-debated issue in contemporary Thailand, not to mention the subject of a great amount of international media interest, the historical antecedents of the present-day sex industry are not well known.[33] The following section is an attempt to extend our understanding of this phenomenon by considering the growth and changing nature of prostitution in Bangkok during the latter period of absolutist rule. This examination, I hasten to add, deals exclusively with heterosexual prostitution; the subject of homosexual, lesbian, and transgender commercial sex is beyond the scope of this book and awaits further historical study.[34]

SEX IN THE CITY

It will be recalled that in the Ayuthayan period, prostitution was an activity confined to brothels staffed by female slaves. These houses, owned and operated by bond masters, were legally sanctioned and subject to taxation by the state. This form of prostitution appears to have continued largely unchanged well into the Bangkok era, when it was seen as an unrivalled source of financial opportunity and gain. As the wife of a brothel-keeper writing to government officials in the mid-nineteenth century noted, "My husband has run a brothel for twenty-five years. Presently we have sixteen female slaves working for us. . . . Both of us agree that there is no better form of business than obtaining beautiful young [slave] girls and having them work as prostitutes. They earn you a living in the most comfortable way."[35]

At this time the attractions of operating a house of prostitution (and reaping the profits) were closely related to the increasing numbers of single, young male Chinese immigrants coming into the country to meet a growing demand for labor as the Siamese market economy developed.[36] This movement of coolie laborers was part of a broader regional process related to harsh conditions in China, new economic opportunities presented by the development of the colonial states, and the improvement and expansion of international shipping between Chinese ports and those in Southeast Asia.[37] For the most part these men inhabited the Sampheng area of Bangkok that had been established during the reign of Rama I (1782–1809), and it was at Sampheng, the major commercial center in the capital, that most of the brothels were located.[38] These establishments and the mostly local women who worked in them provided the immigrant labor force with a source of pleasure and relief from their arduous work and as such should be seen as playing a vital role in the development of the capital. Indeed, as noted earlier, there was a close parallel in this regard between Bangkok and Singapore, with the British colony's growth into a major port city similarly based on coolie labor and the Chinese and Japanese prostitutes who serviced them.

A part of the broad process of economic transformation that saw the arrival of increasing numbers of Chinese immigrants in Siam included the freeing up of the indigenous population through the abolition of slavery and the replacement of *corvée* service obligations with a system of cash payments. Over time these changes, together with the growing monetarization of the economy, served to enlarge the domain of commercial sexual activity, stimulating local male demand for sexual services on the one hand and increasing the supply of prostitutes on the other.

The creation of the functional bureaucracy during Chulalongkorn's reign was of fundamental importance in creating this demand which, in turn, was underpinned by the long-standing sexual double standard condoning male license while demanding that "good" women be chaste and monogamous. Administrative reform saw the appearance of a new social type: the salaried bureaucrat. By the early twentieth century their numbers were already in excess of 25,000, a figure that rose to almost 80,000 in less than two decades (the vast majority of these officials were located in Bangkok).[39] Educated Siamese men working in professions outside the bureaucracy as well as the growing class of indigenous wage laborers also joined the ranks of potential sexual consumers.

In contrast to men, Siamese women had fewer choices or opportunities to earn a living in an increasingly monetarized environment. For those from more well-to-do families, this was not a significant issue. As for those from the general commoner population, many worked as market vendors, washerwomen, and servants. But these were not lucrative occupations. Given that the market economy spawned a growing taste for luxury and consumerism among the urban population at large, that social values stressed the idea of daughters helping their families, that the lax state of the country's marriage laws readily allowed for husbands to abandon their wives, and that the prevailing sexual double standard discriminated against women who were no longer virgins, the conditions were such that increasing numbers of young women, either voluntarily or through some form of coercion, turned to prostitution.

The most public and obvious manifestation of change in the world of prostitution was the emergence of the streetwalker, whose appearance was duly remarked upon by Thianwan in the early 1900s. This development was facilitated, in part, by the appearance of numerous small hotels and traveler's rest houses that were established as commercial activity and communications networks expanded. Prostitutes working on the street commonly took their clients to these establishments or otherwise solicited customers directly on the premises themselves.[40] While some streetwalkers appear to have plied their trade independently, others worked in conjunction with "agents" from among the ranks of the city's hire-car operators, or were controlled or organized by pimps who inhabited Bangkok's extensive criminal milieu.[41] The realm of street prostitution was characterized by intimidation and acts of violence, with press accounts frequently reporting cases in which customers were bashed or robbed by pimps or even by the women themselves.[42] At other times, newspapers told of customers who fought each other over the affections of a particular prostitute. Similarly, there were regular reports about madams and pimps fighting among themselves, robbing and bashing customers, terrorizing local residents, and beating the women who worked for them.[43]

In addition to the proliferation of streetwalkers, brothel prostitution also grew in scale. As a part of Chulalongkorn's administrative reforms, the state, keen to extend its revenue base, sought to re-exert a degree of control over the brothel trade, control which had been on the wane since the 1890s.[44] The government attempted to accomplish this through the promulgation, in 1908, of a law that provided for the registration of brothels and brothel workers in the Bangkok metropolitan area. This legislation, which developed out of an 1899 draft law known as the "Municipal Law on Prostitution" (*Phrarachabanyat khanikaphiban*), was inspired to some extent by a legal code in Singapore designed to control the rampant spread of venereal disease in the colony. The Siamese draft law, which referred to prostitution as a social evil that had to be regulated, was vigorously debated among members of the ruling elite who decided to rename it the "Law for the Prevention of Venereal Disease" (*Phrarachabanyat p'ongkan sanch'onrok*). However, for reasons that are not entirely clear, almost nine years elapsed before a revised version of the legislation was finally enacted in Bangkok. It was subsequently extended to the rest of Siam in 1913.[45]

Under this new legislation, brothel keepers were required to make a quarterly payment of 30 baht to register their premises, maintain a list of all their workers for official inspection, and display a green lantern (*khom khiaw*) outside the brothel bearing the house's registration number. Furthermore, it was stipulated that no one under the age of fifteen was to be employed as a prostitute, a provision that suggests it was not unusual for younger females to be found working in brothels at the time. As for the prostitutes themselves, the law provided that all brothel workers were to pay a registration fee of 12 baht for a three-month permit. Each woman was also required to undergo regular medical check-ups and, should any sign of disease be detected, her permit was to be revoked until she could demonstrate that she had been cured. However, the idea of being subjected to a vaginal examination by a male doctor or medical worker, not to mention the high cost of the registration fee, proved to be highly unpopular. Indeed, almost immediately after the law was introduced, two Chinese brothels were forced to shut down when their inmates decided to flee, too embarrassed to face such an examination and, no doubt, reluctant to part with their hard-earned money.[46]

During the first year under the new law (1908–1909), the government netted some 40,000 baht in revenue from the eighty or so registered brothels operating at the time, together with fees paid by registered prostitutes working in these establishments (their numbers ranging from a low of 574 to a high of 690 in this particular year).[47] The type of brothels within this legal category varied considerably and catered to a diverse clientele from across the social spectrum. At the lower end of the market, for example, there were crudely appointed wooden row houses staffed by two or three women which serviced members of the working class, while at the other there were far more substantial establishments such as the famed "Yellow Rose" (*kulap l'uang*), a two-story stone building whose customers included well-to-do middle-class men and "playboys from the elite."[48]

In his memoirs, *Khun* Wichit Matra provides the following description of the Yellow Rose during the 1910s:

> In front of the building, located off a laneway, was a big open space that led onto a flight of stairs that took you up to the top floor. Inside there was a very large, spacious room surrounded by smaller adjoining rooms. In the middle of the large room was a big cloth-covered table surrounded by five or six chairs. On the table there were plates of fruit and a jumble of bottles, glasses and cups. Inside some of the small adjoining rooms one could see good-looking women with fleshy, shapely figures combing their hair or putting on makeup. Typically a room had an iron-framed bed with a mattress, pillows and a mosquito net; there was also a cupboard for clothing, a spittoon and a water bowl. The floor was covered with linoleum and a mirror draped with garlands of fragrant jasmine flowers hung on the wall. All of the rooms were, without exception, immaculately clean and tidy.[49]

According to Wichit, the Yellow Rose had a long pedigree as a high-class bordello dating well back into the nineteenth century, when it operated under another name that he does not mention. Although we cannot be sure of its origins, the predecessor to the Yellow Rose may well have been a Siamese version of the *geguan* (sing-song houses) and *chafang* (tea houses) found in China which were frequented by members of the literati and high officialdom. These establishments usually contained many rooms on a single floor, with separate chambers arranged around a common room that was luxuriously decorated. In Canton, they often had two stories, with the individual rooms around a salon on the upper floor.[50]

Institutions such as the Yellow Rose were known in Thai as *khlap*, or "club," a linguistic innovation that was inspired by the growing familiarity and fascination among members of the Siamese elite with English, the major language of international "civilization." In contrast with *s'ong*, the common Thai word for brothel, which signified a decidedly low-class enterprise, *khlap* implied an exclusive, rarefied zone of carnality. This distinction was underlined by the fact that the proprietors of these "clubs" were referred to as *khun nai*, a term of respect used to refer to individuals of high social standing. According to Wichit, the halcyon days for these elite houses of prostitution were the latter years of the nineteenth century. By the time he came of age, early in the reign of King Vajiravudh, the prestige and dignified aura once associated with these establishments had largely evaporated and the word *khlap* had fallen out of usage, to be replaced by the less salubrious *s'ong*.[51]

The reason for this terminological shift is not entirely clear, but it may well have been related to the changing nature of Siamese society and social attitudes. As we have seen, around the turn of the century the creation of a new salaried bureaucracy composed of young Thai men contributed to a growing demand for commercial sex. With an increasing number of Thai commoners in a position to avail themselves of the services of prostitutes, the social exclusivity previously enjoyed by the clubs was eroded as owners sought to maximize profits from this new enlarged market. A second possible factor in the demise of these clubs may have been a reaction on the part of those upper-class Siamese associated with the operations of such establishments to European sensitivities regarding prostitution and public morality, one which led these individuals to abandon their overt involvement in what were increasingly seen as houses of ill repute. In any event, high-class prostitution did not disappear; rather, it seems to have become somewhat less dignified or respectable than it had been in the late nineteenth century.[52]

In the decade following the introduction of the "Law for the Prevention of Venereal Disease," the number of registered houses and prostitutes remained virtually static, paling almost into insignificance when compared to the booming illegal brothel trade.[53] Among the most notable of these illicit venues were the tea houses (*rong nam-cha*) that sprang up around the city. Although these establishments did serve tea and refreshments, this was little more than a cover; their primary business was to provide customers with prostitutes, opium, and the opportunity to gamble.[54] Similarly, many retail stores ostensibly trading in con-sumer goods were in fact clandestine brothels, while growing numbers of illicit opium dens took to employing young women as masseuse-prostitutes to provide a range of services to smokers.[55] This burgeoning trade reflected, in its own way, increasing economic self-determination on the part of various sectors of the soci-ety, not to mention the impotence of state legislation and the police, who were often directly involved in the business themselves.

By the 1920s it was no exaggeration to say that, in one form or another, prosti-tution was one of the most ubiquitous features of the urban landscape. As one newspaper correspondent in 1923 wrote, "no matter where you go in Bangkok you can not avoid coming across these women."[56] This is exemplified in a car-toon (fig. 3.2) that shows well-to-do men openly cavorting with prostitutes under a tree at night, perhaps in Lumpini Park, one of the major public spaces in the capital.

Writing about Bangkok in 1926, another observer complained that "at pres-ent it appears that about only one out of ten neighborhoods, districts, lanes, or streets is free of prostitutes. These women are even found along the entire length of Ratchadamnoen Road [the main ceremonial thoroughfare in the city]."[57] Indeed, the very ordinariness of the phenomenon was such that it was commonly discussed in a simple, matter-of-fact manner as in the following pas-sage from a journalist's report on the annual kite flying season at *Sanam l'uang*,

ภาพ กลางคืน บาง แห่ง ในพระนคร

Fig. 3.2. *Bangkok kan-m'uang,* 10 June 1925

the city's major public recreation area: "In the evening one finds members of the nobility and aristocracy, businessmen, modern young women, older ladies and widows, prostitutes, soldiers. In short, people of both sexes and every type."[58]

Notwithstanding these observations, the extent of the commercial sex trade during this period is difficult to quantify. According to one 1927 newspaper account, however, it was estimated that there were at least 30,000 women working as prostitutes in Siam, the overwhelming majority of whom did so illegally.[59] Another contemporary observer concurred with this figure and claimed that some 20,000 prostitutes were operating in Bangkok, while the remaining 10,000 worked in provincial centers throughout the country.[60] Exactly how these figures were derived is unclear and the very general way in which the category of "prostitute" was constituted is open to question. For example, did this figure take into account those women who worked as dancers, singers, and other types of entertainers who provided sexual services? Unfortunately, it is impossible to say.

Bearing in mind the unverifiable nature of these sources, it is nonetheless of interest to attempt to make a rough estimate as to how much money the sex industry in Bangkok might have generated during the later 1920s. According to contemporary newspaper accounts and other documentary materials, the price of intercourse with a prostitute in the capital during the first three decades of the twentieth century varied greatly. It ranged from a low of 50 satang for a ragged streetwalker up to between 5 and 7 baht for a young, attractive woman in a well-appointed brothel.[61] Even higher prices of between 10 and 20 baht, the monthly salary of a junior government clerk, were reportedly charged by madams who arranged for high school girls, working as part-time prostitutes, to sleep with wealthy male customers.[62] In general, however, the most commonly quoted price for sex (calculated as a single ejaculation) was between 1 and 2 baht. While we do not know how many clients the average prostitute serviced, a very conservative estimate would be in the vicinity of thirty men per month. If 50 satang (the lowest reported fee charged for sex) is taken as a baseline figure, such a prostitute would generate a gross monthly income (for herself, pimp, and/or brothel owner) of approximately 15 baht. This means that in Bangkok alone at least 300,000 baht a month, or 3,600,000 baht a year, was being spent on commercial sex, a sum in excess of the state's annual expenditure on education throughout the 1920s and into the 1930s.[63]

As for the women who worked in the capital's thriving sex industry, they came not only from Bangkok but also from other regions in the country and in some cases from farther afield. Procurers, most often women themselves, frequently traveled to nearby provincial capitals and rural areas in search of young new recruits, many of whom were sold into prostitution by their parents or relatives.

And with the opening of the rail line to Chiang Mai in 1922, increasing numbers of northern women were brought to the capital. The ease of travel provided
by rail also facilitated the movement of prostitutes out of the city, and many
women traveled to provincial centers to ply their trade during one of the periodic
crackdowns against vice mounted by the Bangkok police. At the same time,
female immigrants began to arrive from China (prior to the 1920s, immigration
to Siam from the mainland was almost exclusively male) and an increasing number of Chinese prostitutes could be found working in the capital and various provincial towns with a high concentration of coolie laborers. Meanwhile Bangkok
itself emerged as a center for the trafficking of Chinese, Siamese, and Lao women
elsewhere in the region, in particular to Singapore and the Straits Settlements.
With the increasing freedom of movement afforded by the growth of shipping
and rail services, prostitution in Siam became an ever more mobile, complex,
and diversified phenomenon, with local, national, and international dimen-
sions.[64]

EROTIC ENTERTAINMENT

Apart from prostitution in its most overt form, the sexual topography of Bangkok
also encompassed the more diffuse realm of erotic entertainment and dance—
cultural forms, it should be noted, which had existed in a close relationship with
prostitution since premodern times.[65]

One of the most intriguing facets of this eroticized sphere, and one often
assumed to be a relatively contemporary development related to the Vietnam
War and the growth of international tourism, was the "sex show." In fact this
type of entertainment had begun to emerge as a feature of Bangkok nightlife by
the early 1920s. According to a report in the popular daily newspaper *Sayam rat*,
employees from the Chai-oi *ngiw* (Chinese folk opera) theater walked around
the city streets carrying placards advertising performances of a "humorous tale
with interesting pornographic elements" (*r'uang nithan khop-khan lae mi kan-po
yang na-du*). In response the theater drew large crowds, primarily (although not
exclusively) from the Chinese community. The show itself featured young male
and female performers on stage who began their act by admiring scenery in a
garden, flirting with one another, and "falling in love." As this scenario unfolded
the performers stripped down, their nakedness covered only by "skimpy undergarments." They then proceeded to simulate copulation, in a "most realistic
fashion," before a packed audience that cheered them on enthusiastically.[66]

Another account, which provides us with a Western perspective on the Bangkok demimonde, is that of Hermann Norden, an American travel writer who
visited Siam in 1921 and wrote a book about his experiences.[67] In this work,

Norden talks of being taken to what he describes as "a theatre of the underworld," a wooden building set on a raft moored at the edge of the Chaophraya
River. His account of this visit is worth quoting at length.

> By the light of a kerosene lamp, we bought tickets at twenty satangs each (eight
> cents, United States money). Smoke obscured the view as I entered, but when my
> eyes grew accustomed, I thought I must have strayed by mistake into a public bath.
> I seemed to be surrounded by naked arms and legs, naked shoulders, naked bosoms,
> much jewelry and a few gay shawls.
>
> There was a stage, probably twelve by twenty feet, covered with a Brussels carpet.
> Whatever color it had once had was quite lost in dirt. At the edge of the carpet
> sat the orchestra—two boys that made a terrific noise by picking instruments that
> resembled banjos. A dozen players, men and women, were on the stage, but I did
> not linger long enough to find out what the play was about. The noise, smoke, and
> generally hideous atmosphere stifled any desire to extend my studies in the dramatic
> art among the cut-throat fraternity of Siam.[68]

What Norden would have seen had he stayed longer is difficult to ascertain.
However, given the fact that he evinced a keen interest in seeing some of the
raunchier aspects of Bangkok nightlife to his Siamese hosts, it is possible that
the performance in this seedy establishment was similar to that staged in the
ngiw theater referred to above.

In contrast to this visit, Norden was beguiled when he had the chance to
experience the somewhat more refined level of entertainment enjoyed by members of the male elite. This opportunity was made possible by a young upper-class
Siamese man, recently returned from studying in Europe, whom Norden had met
on a train while traveling from the Malay states to Bangkok. The well-connected
(but unnamed) young man was a member of a number of fashionable clubs in
the city and invited Norden to accompany him on his nocturnal wanderings. On
one such outing he was taken to a private party in the "Room of the Moon," a
"smart new Chinese restaurant."[69] The assembled male company, including various married men who, he noted, customarily left their wives at home, were
tended by a bevy of sophisticated Siamese, Chinese, Lao, and Malay courtesans.
He also observed that, apart from lounging around drinking tea and Scotch
before an elaborate banquet was served, some of the men smoked pipes of opium
prepared by Cantonese sing-song girls who, together with a number of dancers,
provided the party-goers with formal entertainment.

At another point in his account, Norden related a visit to the exclusive
"Siamo-Chinese Co-operative Club" to enjoy the pleasures of what he describes
as "Siamese dancing."

> Twenty of us sat around a big table. The scene was far more suggestive of a directors'
> meeting than one of festivity, and a solemn air of expectancy prevailed. . . . The
> program, arranged by an Arab impresario, had been lengthened for my entertain-

ment; besides a dance by a half-caste Laos [sic] and French girl, and another by a Malay girl, two Siamese Pavlovas had been engaged to do a historical dance of old Siam. They were very young; neither could have been more than fifteen. Their clothes were negligible, hardly enough of anything to make an impression.

They floated into that directors' meeting to the music of a luptima played by a bent, gray old man. . . . In the rhythm of this primitive instrument the girls knelt before us, folded and lifted their hands, and bowed low.

With the swelling of the music they began to circle, to sway, and then to bend like young trees. Their muscles quivered; they were alive from head to the tips of their beautiful, bare toes.[70]

More generally, public exhibitions of dance were becoming increasingly popular. In 1919, for example, as competition for patrons intensified between the Nakhorn Kasem Company and Siaw's Siam Cinema Company, the two rival groups introduced dance shows featuring young women performers to their film programs. For its part the Nakhorn Kasem group regularly staged performances by the "Nakhorn Bantherng" Siamese opera troupe, which, it proudly announced, was composed of "35 ladies." On other occasions it featured shows by the Lakhorn Kasem Naramit, a troupe of "50 ladies" who specialized in both Siamese and European dances.[71] Meanwhile, not to be outdone, the Sathorn Picture Palace, owned and operated by the Siam Cinema Company, staged twice-weekly performances by "beautiful Siamese girl-dancers" from the Pramodya Theatre Troupe. Patrons were enticed with the promise that the show "will surely make your heart pump and over fill you with a thrilling sensation of joy [sic]."[72] Although cinema audiences included many women, these performances were often of a titillating or suggestive nature and more obviously directed at the male spectator. A 1920 cartoon (fig. 3.3) makes a pointed commentary on this development noting an avid, indeed lascivious, male interest in Western-style dancing and total indifference to the rather more demure traditional Siamese variety.

Over time, as the Siam Cinema triumphed over its competitors, these types of dance performances were dropped from the film program and instead came to be staged in a range of hotels, restaurants, and other establishments. One of the better-known venues was the *Tu'k Damong Phanit*, Bangkok's tallest structure at the time, a seven-story building located on Yawarat Road in the heart of the Chinese quarter. In a newspaper advertisement for this establishment (fig. 3.4), patrons were urged to "come and relax, forget all your worries, our shapely, sweet-eyed performers will set your hearts aflutter with their costumes and provocative [yua-yuan] dances."

Another popular venue featuring scantily dressed young women in Western-style clothing was the Siam Hotel. The two women shown in figure 3.5, Pratum and King, were among the performers; erotic entertainers who may be said to be the forerunners of the go-go dancers found in the girlie bars of Patpong, Soi Cowboy, Nana Entertainment Plaza, and other locales in present-day Bangkok.

Fig. 3.3. *Sayam rat,* 7 August 1920

Apart from such attractions, a number of Bangkok hotels, such as the Phaya-thai, Oriental, and Trocadero, opened ballrooms to accommodate dance enthu-siasts from the European expatriate community as well as members of the for-eign-educated Siamese elite who had acquired a taste for the waltz and tango. In this physically intimate environment there emerged a new profession or calling: the dance partner, essentially a high-class prostitute, a somewhat ambiguous figure whose appearance in the city's opulent ballrooms served to blur the social distinction between respectable and disreputable women.[73] At the same time, however, Western-style dance was not confined to the upper echelons of society. In addition to the elite ballrooms in the city's better hotels, dance halls of a considerably less salubrious nature were also established throughout the capital, catering to a rough-and-ready clientele similar to that encountered by Norden on his nocturnal visit to the "theatre of the underworld." These elite and lower-class dance venues represented yet another aspect of the increasingly diverse world of entertainment, sexual services, and eroticism that came to characterize the Thai capital in the 1920s.

In many respects Bangkok of the 1920s would be recognizable or familiar to a contemporary observer in a way that would have not been the case thirty or forty years earlier. With the advent of cinemas, concrete buildings, western dress, and automobiles, the city took on an increasingly modern, frenetic feel. Indeed, as one learns from reading "Phua hai" (The Disappeared Husband), a 1929 short

Fig. 3.4. *Sikrung,* 27 October 1931

story by *Luang* Wichit Wathakan, Bangkok was already beginning to experience the type of traffic congestion for which it has become infamous in more recent times.[74] At the same time, the foundations for the modern sex industry were set in place and a vibrant, no-holds-barred newspaper industry emerged which anticipated the development of what is generally regarded as the freest, most liberal press in Southeast Asia. However, as we shall see in the following chapter, there was one aspect of the 1920s popular press that would seem quite unimaginable, even shocking, in the present age: namely, the way in which the Thai royal house was portrayed.

Fig. 3.5. *Ying thai,* 22 January 1933   *Ying thai,* 24 January 1933

NOTES

1. This evocative phrase is taken from the title of Judith R. Walkowitz's social history, *City of Dreadful Delight: Narratives of Sexual Danger in Late-Victorian London* (Chicago: University of Chicago Press, 1992).

2. The audiences for these popular forms of entertainment were largely, though not exclusively, differentiated along ethnic lines with *likay* being popular among Siamese commoners while *ngiw* tended to be favored by working-class Chinese.

3. Robert Sklar, *Movie-made America* (New York: Random House, 1971), 45.

4. Their class status can be ascertained by the fact that in going to the cinema the vast majority of those writing to *Sayam palimen* said they sat in the cheaper cinema seats (ranging in price from 20 to 50 satang), not the more expensive areas patronized by members of the elite.

5. *Phaphayon sayam,* 9 March 1923.

6. *Phaphayon sayam,* 9 March 1923.

7. *Phaphayon sayam,* 4 October 1922. These were not the only things that caused discomfort to patrons, however. For example, a woman, writing about the twenty-five-satang seats in the Singapore Cinema, said that she and many others sitting nearby got very annoyed when cigarette butts and water came falling from the roof onto their heads or clothing. "I can stand the heat," she wrote, "but then I have to put up with these irritating things as well, it nearly drives me out of my mind."

8. *Phaphayon sayam,* 13 July 1923.

9. *Phaphayon sayam*, 15 June 1923.

10. *Phaphayon sayam*, 2 March 1923.

11. *Chino sayam warasap*, 3 May 1918; *Krungthep Daily Mail*, 29 December 1919, 10 February 1922.

12. *Phaphayon sayam*, 1 February 1924.

13. *Phaphayon sayam*, 29 November 1922.

14. *Phaphayon sayam*, 26 September 1924. Further complaints were raised about care-less projectionists, described as "non-human," who regularly screened films upside down or from end to beginning. *Phaphayon sayam*, 6 July 1923.

15. *Bangkok Daily Mail*, 21 October 1930. Cited in H. G. Quaritch Wales, *Siamese State Ceremonies: Their History and Function* (London: Bernard Quaritch, 1931), 6. In fact the Thai national anthem (*phleng chat*) was not introduced until shortly after the overthrow of the absolute monarchy in 1932; the particular tune referred to here was actually the "King's Anthem" (*song soem phra barami*). It is interesting to note that in the late 1970s or early 1980s the playing of the national anthem was moved from the end of the film program to the beginning, apparently to ensure that each and every member of the audi-ence stood and paid their respects to the royal house.

16. *Phaphayon sayam*, 27 July 1923.

17. *Phaphayon sayam*, 7 September 1923.

18. *Phaphayon sayam*, 14 September 1923.

19. Indeed, the presence of elite women at the cinema during its early days was com-monly remarked upon in the press. In 1909, for example, the Krung Thep Cinematograph was reported to attract "a lot of fashionable ladies, Thai and foreign," while the Siam Phaphayon Cinema was described as being well attended with "the boxes largely occupied by Siamese ladies." *Bangkok Times*, 10, 12 July, 28 August 1909.

20. *Phaphayon sayam*, 13 July 1923, *Bangkok Times*, 7 May 1921.

21. D'ok-Mai Sot, *Sattru kh'ong chao l'on* [Her Foe] (Bangkok: Bannakan, 1971), 130; *Kam kao* [Past Karma] (Bangkok: Khlang Withaya, 1971), 23.

22. Kulap Saipradit [Siburapha], *Songkhram chiwit* [The War of Life] (Bangkok: K'o Phai, 1979), 153.

23. *Nangsao L'oi Lom*, *Dichan chua phr'o chai* [Men Made Me Bad], serialized in the daily newspaper *(10 thanwa) phanuak khaw rew* from 12 June 1933 to 30 July 1933 (for further details of this work, see chapter 8).

24. *Krungthep Daily Mail*, 7 June 1920.

25. *Bangkok Times*, 3 May 1910.

26. *Sikrung*, 27 November 1926.

27. Here it should be added that temples had long been places where young people flirted or courted one another.

28. Note the following 1915 account of the annual festival at the Paknam temple near the mouth of the Chaophraya River bemoaning what is perceived to be a trend toward growing social unruliness.

There is no doubt whatever that on occasions like this the consumption of strong liquors is greatly on the increase. Ten years ago or less it was not considered proper; now it is a common sight. . . . On the train [from] Bangkok it was not at all uncom-mon to see people solacing themselves against the rigors of an hour [long] journey by pulls from a bottle of beer and not over-clean conversation, whilst pilgrims of a decade ago were content with betel and lime and [discussing] . . . the prospects of the crop, etc.

The crowds on Saturday evening were fairly orderly. The tendency to jostle women, particularly young women, was at once checked when seen by the force of police present. The patrols of Wild Tigers and navy men all helped to control the rowdy element. . . .

Siamese crowds used to have a reputation for being the best ordered and sober. It is a disquieting feature that these habits, supported as they were by time-honored custom, are in some measure disappearing, and giving place to the demonstration of pleasure, induced in part by liquor, coupled with a general throwing off of the restraint which characterized the appearance at public festivals of the people a generation ago. (*Bangkok Times*, 2 November 1915)

29. By the end of the first decade of the twentieth century prostitutes regularly worked the cinemas in London. Previously they were found in music halls where "there had been a running battle to prevent [them] and drunks from spoiling the show." In the darkened cinema these women were able to carry on their business with less chance of being detected. Audrey Field, *Picture Palace: A Social History of the Cinema* (London: Gentry Books, 1974), 25.

30. As a result of his actions, *Nai* Hui was sentenced to eight years imprisonment. *Bangkok Times Weekly Mail*, 13 June 1921.

31. *Sayam rat*, 26 December 1923. Streetwalkers were also to be found milling around the entrances of various *ngiw* and *likay* theaters as well as those of Bangkok's numerous illegal gambling dens.

32. *Khun* Wichit Matra [Sa-nga Kanchanakhaphan], "80 pi nai chiwit khaphachao" [Eighty Years of My Life] (Bangkok: *Anus'on* [*Cremation Volume*], 1980), 181.

33. For example, see Wathinee Boonchalaksi and Philip Guest, *Prostitution in Thailand* (Bangkok: Institute for Population and Social Research, Mahidol University, 1994), 1.

34. A general lack of source material makes the historical study of the nonheterosexual domain problematic. During the first four decades of the twentieth century, for example, discussion of homosexuality was generally avoided in the popular press. A journalist writing on the problem of venereal disease in Siam made mention of homosexual prostitution in France but refrained from providing any details, claiming that "it is a topic too embarrassing to talk about." *Sikrung*, 19 July 1927.

However, there were rare exceptions to this. In a 1935 news story it was reported that the police in Bangkok had arrested a man by the name of Karun Phasuk. Karun, also known as *Thua dam* (black bean), a name that subsequently became a common slang term used to refer to sodomy, was investigated for running what was described as a "perverse illicit brothel" (*song sopheni th'uan yang witthan*). It was alleged that he seduced boys and adolescent males between the ages of ten- and sixteen-years-old and had them work for him as prostitutes servicing Indian and Chinese businessmen. *Sikrung*, 20 June 1935.

35. Quoted in Dararat Mettarikanon, "Sopheni kap naiyobai rathaban thai ph'o s'o 2411–2503" [Prostitution and Thai Government Policy, 1868–1960], M.A. thesis, Chulalongkorn University, Bangkok, 1983, 15.

36. G. W. Skinner, *Chinese Society in Thailand: An Analytical History* (Ithaca, N.Y.: Cornell University Press, 1957), 58–59, 109, 115.

37. Skinner, *Chinese Society in Thailand*, 45–53.

38. In fact the close association between Sampheng and the brothels was reflected in the terminology of the times, a prostitute commonly being referred to as a *ying sampheng* or a "Sampheng woman." Dararat, "Prostitution and Thai Government Policy," 17.

Another element of the commercial sex trade which should be mentioned here was that associated with Bangkok's foreign expatriate community. Toward the end of the nineteenth century a small number of brothels, hotels, and all-night bars were established in and around the Bangrak area adjacent to the Chaophraya River where most foreigners lived. Both European and Japanese interests were involved in this trade, operating venues such as the "International," the "Splendid Bar," the "Metropole," the "Star Hotel," "Madame Thasahi's," and "Khono Yipun." The Japanese businesses, of which there were four at the turn of the century, were staffed by Japanese women and in all likelihood were similar to the far more numerous Japanese brothels found in Singapore. At the same time, there were some eight European bar-cum-brothels, most of which were staffed by women of Russian origin although a few of these houses also had German and Italian women. Unfortunately little is known about this aspect of prostitution. While various sources, in particular the local press of the day, give us a relatively clear picture of the foreign community's public life in Siam, that of the expatriate demimonde appears to have gone unrecorded. Dararat, *Prostitution and Thai Government Policy*, 24–26. For further details about Japanese brothels in Singapore, see James F. Warren, *Ah Khu and Karayuki-san: Prostitution in Thailand* (Bangkok: Institute for Population and Social Research, Mahidol University, 1994), 81–87.

39. W. J. Siffin, *The Thai Bureaucracy: Institutional Change and Development* (Honolulu: East-West Center Press, 1966), 94.

40. *Krungthep Daily Mail*, 10 February 1922.

41. *Chino sayam warasap*, 10 July 1917; *Satri thai*, 28 June 1926.

42. *Chino sayam warasap*, 10 July 1917.

43. *Krungthep Daily Mail*, 22–23 February 1922, 20 March 1922; Wichit Matra, *Eighty Years of My Life*, 181.

44. During the early Bangkok period, the old Ayuthayan system in which brothel keepers paid a tax to the state apparently continued unchanged although it was plagued with problems. For example, bond masters regularly avoided making their stipulated payments to the state. They were also said to take unfair advantage of their slave workers by making exaggerated claims as to their value, thus denying them the possibility of escaping servitude.

At some time during the Fourth Reign the government made an attempt to redress these problems by demanding that the price of slaves be reduced. It also issued an injunction which proscribed bond masters from forcing women into prostitution. In addition, the state did away with the old system of payments and introduced an impost on brothels known as the Road Maintenance Tax (*phasi bamrung thanon*). Under the original provisions of this regulation it seems that tax collectors, many of whom were actually brothel keepers themselves, were required to provide the state with a certain quantity of sand or earth for construction and road-building purposes. Later, however, during the reign of Chulalongkorn, as the financial imperatives of the state intensified, this practice was abandoned and replaced by a system of cash payments. As a part of this new regime it was stipulated that the monthly income earned by a prostitute be divided into ten parts: of this sum the brothel owner took six parts, the woman received three parts, while the tax farmer was paid one part. Up until 1891, when legal changes were instituted, prostitutes were also formally required to pay between 1 and 2 baht of their monthly income to the owner of the brothel for water and lighting oil. At the same time, the state issued an injunction prohibiting brothel keepers from deducting money for food and rent from their employees or charging them excessive prices for goods purchased on their behalf. While such provisions may seem to suggest an official attempt to ameliorate the difficult circumstances of women working as brothel slaves, Dararat claims that the state was only really interested in obtaining revenue and did not hesitate to impose fines on brothel keepers and their workers if they tried to avoid making scheduled payments.

During Mongkut's reign (1851–1868), state income from the road maintenance tax in Bangkok (it was extended to the provinces in Chulalongkorn's reign, 1868–1910) amounted to 50,000 baht per annum, a sum equal to the total tax revenue obtained from the northern region of the kingdom. By the late nineteenth century, however, the amount of revenue the state derived from the road maintenance tax was in sharp decline. Tax farmers regularly sought to defraud authorities, withholding funds that should have been forwarded to the treasury while simultaneously attempting to establish new brothels in provincial areas so as to increase their income. Dararat, "Prostitution and Thai Government Policy," 50, 60–61, 72.

45. Dararat, "Prostitution and Thai Government Policy," 84.

46. Dararat, "Prostitution and Thai Government Policy," 84.

47. In Dararat's work there is some ambiguity as to the actual number of brothels and prostitutes registered during the first year of the new law. One set of her figures shows a total of 319 registered brothels and 2,500 registered prostitutes. Elsewhere official government figures are cited which give a quarterly breakdown of these annual totals. This set of figures indicates that for each three-month period there were between 77 and 84 registered brothels and between 574 and 690 registered prostitutes. It would appear that the figures for each of these quarterly statements actually refer to the same brothels and prostitutes being reregistered a number of times, with some minor variations, rather than referring to newly registered brothels and prostitutes.

Four "ethnic" categories of brothel and brothel workers are given in these more detailed statistics: Chinese, Thai, Vietnamese, and Lao (a general term used at the time to refer to the inhabitants of both the north and northeast regions of present-day Thailand). In each of these quarterly tables the number of Thai brothels is marginally greater than the number of Chinese brothels, while the number of Chinese prostitutes is significantly greater than the number of indigenous registered sex workers. For example, in the period from January to April 1909, there were thirty registered Chinese brothels with 389 workers, and forty-seven registered Siamese brothels with 260 Siamese prostitutes. By contrast, the number of registered Vietnamese and Lao brothels and prostitutes represented only a small percentage of the legally recognized trade. During the same period there were three Vietnamese brothels employing twenty-four women and three Lao brothels with a combined workforce of just sixteen women. There was also one registered Mon prostitute in one of the quarterly charts. Dararat, "Prostitution and Thai Government Policy," 80–83.

48. Wichit, Eighty Years of My Life, 181.

49. Wichit, Eighty Years of My Life, 181–82.

50. Sue Gronewold, Beautiful Merchandise: Prostitution in China 1860–1936 (New York: Haworth Press, 1982), 5.

51. Wichit, *Eighty Years of My Life*, 183.

52. It is interesting to note that the disappearance of the word *khlap* has proved temporary. Perhaps the most spectacular form of elite prostitution in contemporary Thailand is now carried on within lavishly appointed and extremely expensive establishments known as "Member Clubs" which have been a prominent feature of Bangkok yuppie nightlife since the 1980s.

53. In 1920, for example, it was reported that Bangkok had a total of seventy-seven registered brothels with some 616 workers; these totals were further categorized along ethnic lines with some thirty-six Siamese brothels containing 165 prostitutes and forty-one Chinese brothels with 451 women (the ethnicity of these women, however, was not recorded). Overall these sources provided the state with revenue of 38,808 baht for the year (*Krungthep Daily Mail*, 16 September 1920). It is worth noting that the level of the registration fees, particularly those applied to prostitutes, provided no incentive whatsoever to comply with the law. In fact it represented a marked form of exploitation of women by the state. At the rate of 48 baht per year, legally registered prostitutes paid significantly more tax than the vast bulk of the Siamese male population aged between eighteen and sixty, who were required to pay a poll tax that varied up to a maximum 6 baht per annum. For their part Chinese males paid a fixed triennial tax of 4.37 baht up until 1910 when they were taxed at the same rate as Siamese men. J. C. Ingram, *Economic Change in Thailand: 1850–1970* (Stanford, Calif.: Stanford University Press, 1971), 60.

54. *Krungthep Daily Mail*, 1 March 1922.

55. *Krungthep Daily Mail*, 3 March 1922, 19 July 1920.

56. *Sayam rat*, 26 December 1923.

57. *Satri thai*, 28 June 1926.

58. *Pakka thai*, 26 March 1926.

59. *Pakka thai*, 5 August 1927.

60. *Sikrung*, 3 August 1927. During the latter nineteenth century brothels opened in various provincial centers where the most significant concentrations of Chinese workers were to be found, in particular in Chantaburi, Trat, Nakhorn Chaisi, Samut Sakon, Chachoengsao, and Chonburi, as well as in the thriving tin-mining center of Phuket in the south (Dararat, "Prostitution and Thai Government Policy," 29). Subsequently, around the turn of the century, the greater freedom of movement ushered in by the process of social and economic reform allied with the expansion of Siam's internal communications contributed toward the intensification of prostitution in regional centers. In 1909, for example, the expansion of prostitution outside of the capital was remarked upon by the then crown prince Vajiravudh during a royal tour of the south of the country.

Ranong (on the west coast of peninsular Siam) has become quite civilized, as witnessed by various things. For example, in the market they have beautiful ladies on sale. Doesn't this indicate that Ranong is civilized? Maybe it not as civilized as Bangkok since the mansions of paradise [*wiman sawan*] down there are still not adorned by [green] lanterns hanging out the front. But then again, is this an indication that they are more civilized than in Bangkok? (Cited by Wichit, *Eighty Years of My Life*, 85)

This somewhat ironic notion of prostitution as an indicator of "civilization" was also used by a newspaper journalist who wrote a piece on the changing face of the provincial capital Ayuthaya in 1917. In his article entitled "Siwilai" (Civilization), the writer said that the town had changed greatly over the past ten years with the addition of new roads, bridges, and buildings, including a rebuilt prison. Apart from the transformation of the physical environment he mentioned other differences, pointing out that "the [local] people are going ahead in stages, bringing with them the progress of Bangkok, for example through the selling of sex." *Chino sayam warasap,* 14 July 1917.

By 1920, this had become one of the most prominent features of life in Ayuthaya, with one observer of the period writing, "at night the streets of the town are teeming with prostitutes." He also noted that two new brothels had recently been opened, one located opposite a military barracks and the other in front of a Buddhist temple. The former establishment was said to be doing rather well from "the friendship of the soldiers," while the latter was reported to draw large numbers of patrons from the local civil administration. *Krungthep Daily Mail,* 18 September 1920.

News stories on prostitution elsewhere in the country appeared regularly in the press. For example, a journalist visiting Surathani in southern Siam wrote that many prostitutes, both of the registered and unregistered variety, were to be found around the town's market area (*Krungthep Daily Mail,* 18 August 1919). Similarly, a 1920 newspaper account of the situation in Phitsanuloke, in the north-central region of Siam, noted the existence of numerous brothels (*Krungthep Daily Mail,* 3 February 1920). Meanwhile a correspondent writing from Lampang in the north of the country during the same period reported that the town had numerous prostitutes "who are available for sex at all hours of the day and night." Many of these women, he said, worked in one of Lampang's three illicit brothels which were frequented by a clientele of both young and old men. *Krungthep Daily Mail,* 10 June 1920.

61. *Sayam rat,* 21 April 1922, 9 February 1923; Wichit, *Eighty Years of My Life,* 182.

62. *Sayam saki,* 22 December 1922.

63. *Statistical Yearbook of Siam,* no. 17, 1931–33, 306. Some figures for government expenditure on education are as follows: 1920–21: 2,335,251 baht; 1924–25: 2,640,344 baht; 1929–30: 3,422,591 baht; 1932–33: 3,280,956 baht.

64. *Krungthep Daily Mail,* 18 September 1920; *Sayam rat,* 26 December 1923, 14 March 1925; *Pakka thai,* 16 June 1926, 6 August 1926; *Sikrung,* 2 September 1927.

65. This is indicated in a section of the ancient Law of the Three Seals concerning husbands and wives, where traveling female performers, singers, and dancers who "beg" for a living are equated with prostitutes. The realm of entertainment, with its implicit eroticism, and the world of prostitution, can be said to have existed in a symbiotic relation with one another. Together they represented a socially distinct domain, men being proscribed by law from living with or marrying women engaged in any of these pursuits. *Phra aiyakan laksana phua mia* [The Royal Code Concerning Husbands and Wives], 1962, 209; Dararat, "Prostitution and Thai Government Policy," 13.

66. *Sayam rat,* 12 July 1922.

67. Hermann Norden, *From Golden Gate to Golden Sun: A Record of Travel, Sport, and Observation in Siam and Malaya* (London: H. F. and G. Witherby, 1923).

68. Norden, *From Golden Gate to Golden Sun,* 130–31.

69. It may be that this was the renowned Hoi Thian Lao Restaurant established by the Lamsam family.

70. Norden, *From Golden Gate to Golden Sun,* 124–25.

71. *Bangkok Times*, 5 February 1920, 7 August 1920.

72. *Bangkok Times*, 28 July 1920. The Siam Cinema Company also engaged other types of entertainers, such as the black American performers Smith and Bella Jackson, who were billed as "Eccentric Singers and Dancers of the Latest Coon Songs and Dances, Buck Dancing and Wing Dancing." *Bangkok Times*, October 1920.

73. *Pakka thai*, 5 January 1926.

74. *Luang* Wichit Wathakan, "Phua hai" [The Disappeared Husband], *Ammata niyai chut phua hai* [Classic Stories, the "The Disappeared Husband" series] (Bangkok: Khlang-sam'ong- media fokat, 1992), 59–60.

4

꧁

Visually Challenged:
Graphic Critiques of the
Royal-Noble Elite

During the early 1920s the growth of the Bangkok reading public stimulated a rapid expansion of the local publishing industry. Above all this period marked the rise of the popular newspaper, and a rash of new publications appeared on the market, facilitating the development of an expanding forum for public debate and discussion.[1] In the process, existing forms of social power and privilege became subject to intense scrutiny and criticism from members of the educated populace who came to see themselves as citizens actively participating in the life of the nation. Deference and respect for authority, notions that are frequently held up as deep-rooted, quintessential elements of "Thai-ness" by official cultural brokers in modern-day Thailand were, for the most part, conspicuously absent from the pages of the popular press during the 1920s. Indeed, as we shall see, irreverent, contemptuous attitudes toward authority figures in general, including the monarch himself, were commonplace, particularly in the latter years of King Vajiravudh's reign. It was from this time that the sociopolitical dominance and legitimacy of the ancien régime began to weaken and falter, signaling the end of an era.

In order to get an idea of the way in which the absolutist order came under popular assault, the following discussion is structured around a range of critical newspaper cartoons drawn from the popular press during the 1920s, materials that convey an immediacy and power lacking in other available historical sources. At this time Siamese cartooning was still very much in its infancy, with the first recognized graphic work of political satire dating from 1915.[2] Western forms of pictorial representation had become increasingly popular among certain sections of the upper classes from the late nineteenth century, with King Chula-

longkorn in particular developing a keen interest in the visual arts, most notably
the work of various Italian painters and sculptors.[3] By the early 1910s Western
styles of drawing, painting, and decoration began to be taught in Bangkok at a
small number of newly established institutions such as the Arts and Crafts
School (*Rong-rian p'oh chang*), founded under royal patronage in 1913.[4] However,
it is doubtful that any of Siam's budding cartoonists received their training in
these elite institutions. Instead it appears that they were largely a self-taught
group of individuals who drew their inspiration from such works as the satirical
British magazine *Punch* and Thomas Wright's mid-nineteenth-century illustrated book A *History of Caricature and Grotesque in Literature and Art*.[5] At the
same time, the growth of visually oriented advertising in the press provided
ambitious young graphic artists with the opportunity to develop their craft and
earn an income.

The cartoons I have chosen are representative of the type of graphic satire
regularly featured in the capital's most popular daily newspapers, most of which
had print runs of between two and three thousand copies per issue. Regrettably,
there is little information about the actual nature and size of the readership of
these publications although it is reasonable to assume that it included low- and
middle-level government officials, salaried workers in the private sector, and literate members of the Thai working class, as well as educated middle-class women
who, for the most part, were not engaged in paid employment. It is even more
difficult to determine the scale of the readership although it may be imagined
that significantly larger numbers of people actually read newspapers than the
number of copies published per issue. Once read by the purchaser it was likely
that a newspaper would be passed on to other members of his or her family,
friends, acquaintances, or workmates (as is frequently the case in modern-day
Thailand). This being the case, a newspaper with a print run of three thousand
copies may have ultimately been read by six or seven thousand people or more.

The importance of graphic satire in 1920s Siam has been underlined by Matthew Copeland, who writes that "the press made increasing use of cartooning
and caricature, both as a supplement for written opinion and as a form of independent editorial comment in its own right."[6] This new phenomenon, he adds,
quickly became accepted as a "popular form of political communication [as a
result of] a growing disaffection for dynastic authority in society at large."[7] One
contemporary observer saw the purpose of the caricatures (*phap-l'o*) regularly
published in newspapers from the early 1920s onward in the following terms:

> Insomuch as our world is daily moving closer to an age of equality, it is essential
> that caricature capture the attention of those on high and make them less inclined
> to put on airs. While it's true that the rich, the titled, and the powerful should be
> free to do as they please within the confines of their own homes, they must also
> understand that their behavior is capable of hindering the prosperity of the home-

land and the development of its newly awakened citizens, who are just learning to be free [thai].[8]

More generally these graphics represent a tangible manifestation of an emergent struggle for social equality that pitted elements of the rising generation of disenfranchised middle-class commoners against established authority and tradition. In this context, questions of ethics and morality were central, with many cartoonists—whose identities, for the most part, unfortunately remain unknown—relentlessly portraying the elite as a degenerate and corrupt group of self-interested individuals obsessed with sex and money. In certain cases such criticism and that concerned with broader political and economic issues resulted in the closure of a number of newspapers, the impounding of printing presses, and the arrest of alleged offenders. Nonetheless the application of censorship, such as it existed, was carried on in a very uneven, unsystematic fashion. To a degree this was related to the very personal nature in the way that power was exercised under the absolute monarchy. As we have seen in the case of film there was no formal censorship legislation until 1930; what could or could not be shown depended on the assessment of the king and his closest advisers. By contrast the press was far more difficult to control, and owners of critical newspapers with powerful patrons could use their influence to avoid being prosecuted. Another crucial factor that limited the state's ability to silence its critics was a practice adopted by a number of publishers to register the ownership of their newspapers with foreign nationals.[9] Should the authorities attempt to prosecute such a "foreign-owned" publication, they were faced with myriad difficulties posed by the legal complexities inherent in extraterritoriality agreements Siam had entered into with foreign powers during the mid-nineteenth century. While this ruse was used successfully for a number of years, by the mid-1920s it was effectively neutralized by the government. Subsequently a comprehensive press law was introduced in 1927 superseding earlier, less stringent legislation. As a result the more libelous type of attacks on members of the elite that had been such a notable feature of the popular press during the early 1920s largely disappeared, and criticism of authority came to be expressed in broader, less personal terms.

In the work of the kingdom's first generation of cartoonists examined in this chapter, we get a vivid sense of the prevailing social attitudes, tensions, and conflicts found in Bangkok during the last decade of absolute rule. The investigation begins by looking at a number of cartoons concerned with social division, the increasing importance of money, and the indifference to the poor on the part of the well-to-do. This is followed by an examination of a series of cartoon images focusing on various social problems and the way in which graphic satirists, expressing more generalized popular feeling, ridiculed and demonized the ruling royal-noble elite. In the final and concluding section, gender and, to a lesser extent, class issues are further discussed, concentrating primarily on graphic and literary critiques of elite male behavior in relation to women.

BIG PEOPLE, LITTLE PEOPLE

Historically Thai society was characterized by a pronounced sense of hierarchy, embodied in what is known as the *sakdina* system.[10] In broad terms this ranked order has been seen by indigenous writers, including no less a figure than King Vajiravudh himself, as being composed of two social categories—*phu yai* and *phu n'oi*.[11] The *phu yai*, literally "big people," represented those possessed of power, status, and wealth, a relatively small group of individuals in the royal family and the aristocracy. By the early 1920s this elite stratum, including both men and women, would have numbered in the vicinity of a thousand members at most.[12] The remainder of Siam's population of approximately eight million was comprised of *phu n'oi*, or "little people." Some members of this disparate mass, most particularly elements within the state bureaucracy, were aligned in one way or other with a *phu yai* patron or protector. The vast majority, however, were not. Siamese absolutism was, above all, a sociopolitical system with a singularly personal character structured around the interests of the *phu yai* and those most closely associated with them.

We begin with a graphic from the early 1920s that satirizes the nature of *phu yai-phu n'oi* relationships within the bureaucracy. Figure 4.1 depicts a veritable giant of a man, clearly a *phu yai*, who stands cradling a horde of *phu n'oi* in his arms while supporting others on his shoulders. Meanwhile another group of "little people" swarm around his feet licking his shoes and legs. The caption reads roughly "Milord's relatives/family" (*Luk lan wan khr'ua kh'ong than*), referring to those whom the big man is supporting. As a whole, the cartoon conveys the singular message that personal connections with "big people" were of fundamental importance if one was to prosper and advance socially; for those *phu n'oi* keen to develop such a relationship, the cartoonist suggests there was but one way, shamelessly toadying to one's superiors.[13]

Another cartoonist represented the vast social chasm between the royal-noble elite and the commoner population in a more general way. In the upper left-hand corner of figure 4.2 there is a head of a man shown in profile, he has a grin on his face, the word for "person" (*khon*) is written beneath. To his right is another head in profile, in this instance adorned by a crown; the accompanying caption reads *thewada* or "heavenly being." Parity between the two figures is indicated by an equal (=) sign. Below there is a parallel representation; on the left a man's head in profile, similar, though slightly different to that shown above.[14] An equivalence is also drawn but in this case it is between the man and a buffalo.

What is the cartoonist telling the reader? Both of the figures on the left are

Fig. 4.1. *Sayam rat,* 15 September 1923

clearly human; indeed they could even be twins. Yet the upper head is labeled as that of a person and by extension, divine—an exalted member of the ruling elite. The head beneath bears no caption. It is equated with nonhuman life—a buffalo, an animal which in Siam symbolizes stupidity and ignorance. While *phu yai* and *phu n'oi* were held to be fundamentally different by some members of the elite—so much so, in fact, as to represent radically distinct species—the cartoonist ridicules such an assumption by indicating their essential sameness. This reading can be more fully appreciated if we realize that from the early 1920s onward, as Copeland puts it, "the idea of equality (*khwam-samoephak*)—a concept . . .

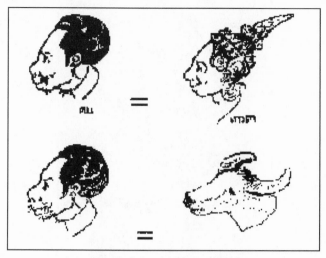

Fig. 4.2. *Sayam rat,* 22 May 1923

variously interpreted in terms of social standing, legal rights, and economic opportunity—was frequently used by members of the educated urban middle class to critique the nobility as an institution."[15]

The huge social gap between members of the elite and ordinary folk portrayed above is further underscored in the following cartoon. Figure 4.3 shows the same location but at two markedly different times. The image at the top (captioned "the usual state of affairs" [*tammada*]) depicts a typical inner Bangkok street scene in front of a general store; on the left a trishaw puller relaxes in his conveyance, and half-naked men and boys eat and loiter on the road strewn with refuse; in the background laundry is hung out to dry, while on the right a vendor squats on her haunches selling fruit. In essence we have a somewhat crude representation of the raw, earthy nature of urban life experienced by the general populace. The lower scene, however, shows a dramatic change. The crush of people and the signs of their presence, the garbage and drying clothing, have been cleared away, rendered invisible. The reason for this transformation is explained in the brief caption beneath which reads *cha sadet,* meaning that a royal entourage is about to proceed along the street. In juxtaposing these two scenes the cartoonist draws attention to the totally separate worlds inhabited by the upper and lower classes, suggesting that the former sought to deny the existence of the latter. Here it may be observed that this characterization of the "royal progress" would not be out of place in contemporary Thailand; whenever members of royalty visit local communities, either in the capital or the provinces, extraordinary measures are taken to ensure that they move within a sanitized, ordered, and controlled environment. However, for a modern-day cartoonist to comment on

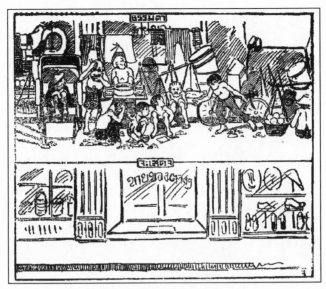

Fig. 4.3. *Sayam rat,* 11 July 1922

this in a manner similar to that of the *Sayam rat* artist is scarcely imaginable. Indeed, if a local newspaper were to publish this particular cartoon or a number of other more pointed images which appear later in this chapter it would almost certainly run afoul of the authorities.

Apart from rather generalized social observations of this type, discussed above, cartoonists also focused more specifically on the possession of wealth, or the lack thereof, as the key determinant underpinning the stark divisions found in Bangkok society of the time. As has been noted, with the development of the market economy from the latter nineteenth century onward, money came to play an increasingly important role in Siamese urban life. The growing pursuit of wealth and the passion for buying imported consumer goods that had became increasingly common in King Chulalongkorn's time further intensified during the reign of Vajiravudh. In commenting on this trend a 1912 *Bangkok Times* editorial entitled "The Growth of Luxury" observed, "the older generation can truly say that what in their younger days would have been luxuries, and indeed luxuries that offered but little temptation, are today regarded as necessities. [This is] not true [only] of the young; it applies to both old and young, to both rich and poor. The well-to-do man today spends enormously more than did his grandfather, or even his father."[16]

King Vajiravudh, whose ostentatious lifestyle and extravagant habits sometimes left European visitors dumbfounded,[17] served as a model for his peers and subordinates. It is in this context that figure 4.4 is to be understood.

Fig. 4.4. *Sayam rat,* 31 January 1923

A squat, rotund figure dressed in an official uniform stands holding aloft a large sack of marked money (*ngoen*), his jacket pockets bulging with cash. The caption, directed at an unseen interlocutor, reads, "Rest assured, everything's fine." Curiously, the uniformed, balding man bears an uncanny resemblance to King Vajiravudh himself. Here the cartoonist infers that money had become the measure of all things, the source of contentment, a means of calming the heart and securing obeisance, if not heartfelt loyalty, to the absolutist order.

The idea that money had become the standard for defining social worth and respectability was also at the heart of the following graphic (fig. 4.5) entitled "Our Custom of Crawling" (*thamniam khlan kh'ong rao*) from the early years of the reign of Vajiravudh's successor, King Prajadhipok.

A Siamese *phu yai* is shown seated at a table conversing with a European guest. The Westerner, pointing to three female servants crouching on the floor amid the master's hounds, says, "Aren't these [people] your fellow nationals?" To this the *phu yai* replies tartly "Yes, that's true, but they're poorer than me!" Thus the significance of wealth is baldly stated, with the possession of money linked directly to a person's social status. At the same time, the graphic is also notable for its none-too-subtle commentary on the position of lower-class women in Siamese society; the cartoonist intimates that their status is equivalent to that of dogs. This imagery represents a strong critique of contemporary class and gender relations and is given a particular edge by the fact that deep-seated concerns and anxieties in regard to the Siamese public persona vis-à-vis Westerners often expressed at the highest levels of society are inverted here with the *phu yai*, and by extension his peers, being portrayed by the cartoonist as lacking any real degree of national sensitivity.

At this point it is instructive to note the way in which less well-off members of the *phu n'oi* strata of society were represented by newspaper cartoonists of the day. Typically such cartoons depicted the harshness of life for the city's poor in highly sympathetic terms and served to draw attention to their plight, thereby helping turn it into a public issue. Cartoons like the two shown next seek to

Fig. 4.5. *Sayam riwiw,* 26 September 1926

convey the sense of despair and neglect experienced by members of the needy as they struggled to survive in the merciless, impersonal environment of the cash economy.

Figure 4.6 shows a destitute family, a glum-faced man and his wife sitting in his shadow tending their infant child. The caption beneath simply reads "I can't find any work." They must make do as best they can, like many other unemployed people, by begging on the streets. Figure 4.7 features three related images that act as a visual comment on the lot of the underprivileged. It suggests a particular progression in life, from lack of opportunity as a child to resorting to criminal activity at a later stage. On the left a young child sits on the ground crying. Above, the caption notes that the cost of education is high: free public schooling was virtually unheard of at this time with a government fee being levied on all students. In essence education, a prime means of social advancement and securing employment, was beyond the reach of the poor. The second image is that of a forlorn figure unable to obtain a job. On the right the consequence of this is spelled out. The same figure is shown stealthily tiptoeing along clutching various objects. Above, the caption reads, "I can't stand the hunger," implying that the man (the uneducated child now an unemployed adult) has taken to thieving in order to survive. Significantly, the cartoonist intimates that the man's criminal activity is not a result of moral failure or a weak disposition but rather the consequence of a lack of opportunity and indifference on the part of more powerful members of society toward their fellow citizens.

หางานทำไม่ได้

Fig. 4.6. *Sayam rat*, 26 June 1923

๒ หางานทำไม่ได้   ๓ ทนตรมหิวไม่ไหว

๑ ค่าเล่าเรียนแพง

Fig. 4.7. *Sayam rat*, 12 August 1922

In the following graphic (fig. 4.8) the cartoonist, again identifying with the urban poor, seeks to explain their plight in more specific terms.

A group of wretched figures are shown cowering on the ground; beneath, the caption reads, "When will justice be done and those on high make an example of those corrupt individuals who take bribes?" Here the impoverishment and suffering of ordinary folk is seen to be the result of bureaucratic corruption. The full weight of the artist's criticism, however, is not so much aimed at the bribe-takers themselves as at "those on high" (*than phu saksi*) for failing to take action and curb such practices.

We will take a closer look at a range of graphic critiques of the ruling elite shortly. Before doing so, it is useful to consider a number of cartoons that deal with some of the issues commonly seen by press commentators as inhibiting Siam's progress and prosperity.

THE NATION BEDEVILED: RECURRENT PROBLEMS

The growing importance of money as a factor in defining one's social worth has already been referred to. It was in this context that financial self-interest on the part of members of the elite and those under their patronage came to the fore, with the question of embezzling government funds emerging as one of the major issues of the time.[18] This practice is the subject of numerous cartoons such as the

เมื่อไหร่หนอ ? ท่านผู้ศักดิ์สิทธิ์ จะบันดาลให้พวกที่ถือ
สินบนเปนความยุติธรรม ให้เปนตัวอย่างแก่โลกบ้าง.

Fig. 4.8. *Sayam rat,* 27 May 1922

two shown below, the first from Vajiravudh's reign, and the second from that of his successor, Prajadhipok.

Figure 4.9 depicts a number of men, clearly government officials as indicated by their dress, reaching out to pick up bundles of money lying on the ground in front of them. A group of half-naked, ordinary Siamese look on passively in the background. The caption beneath says, "Those with the biggest hands haul it in," intimating that it was men like those on the ground, as opposed to less well-placed common folk, who had the ways and means of enriching themselves. A similar but rather more pointed commentary is presented in figure 4.10, which again features a number of state officials down on their haunches. As they reach out for bags of money, labeled "government funds," each intones his love of the nation (*chan rak chat*). Below, the cartoonist sarcastically remarks, "While your mouths may love the nation, what in the devil's name do your hands love?" In other words we find naked self-interest and hypocrisy presented as a defining characteristic of the absolutist administration.

At the same time, cartoonists frequently drew attention to a range of problems seen to be bedeviling the nation. Two examples of this type of work are featured below, the first from the reign of Vajiravudh the second from that of Prajadhipok.

In figure 4.11, from 1923, a policeman is shown wading through a swamp hacking away at the dense growth with a huge machete. Here the swamp and its seething foliage stand as a metaphor for some of the difficulties confronting the nation. These problems, inscribed on the vegetation around the policeman were

มือใครยาวสาวได้สาวเอา

Fig. 4.9. *Sayam rat,* 8 August 1922

Fig. 4.10. *Sayam riwiw*, 9 January 1927

Fig. 4.11. *Sayam rat*, 15 May 1923

(clockwise from the upper left-hand corner) gambling, contraband opium, illicit prostitution, and counterfeit money. Through the use of fecund jungle imagery, it is suggested that these were resilient, tenacious problems that would persist unless unyielding attempts were made to deal with them.

Figure 4.12, from the Prajadhipok era, shows a well-dressed young man asking a high-ranking police officer the question, "How do we get rid of these things?" The "things" he is referring to are, from the left: prostitution, gambling, and criminal gangs. The policeman stands by nonchalantly with his hands in his pockets, a noncommittal stance that seems to say, "Why ask me such a ridiculous question?"

Indeed, in regard to the question of prostitution one needs only to look at the way in which the police suppression of this booming illicit industry was commonly portrayed to understand their failure to respond. Consider, for example, the following image. Figure 4.13 shows an irate police officer ordering his men to arrest a group of women who, it seems, are prostitutes. Three policemen holding bunches of flowers move toward the women with grins on their faces. Clearly they have not the slightest intention of arresting the women, quite the opposite, it would seem. One may even go so far as to say that the officer's commands to *chap! chap!!* carry a double meaning, not only the literal one to "arrest them! arrest them!!," but also "grab them! grab them!!" which carries distinct sexual connotations. The leering look on the face of the young policeman glancing at his commander certainly lends some validity to such an interpretation.

Police inaction in dealing with illicit prostitution is also the topic of the cartoon featured in figure 4.14. A group of prostitutes lounge around waiting for customers at the front of a hotel or rest house. Two police officers blithely walk

Fig. 4.12. *Sikrung*, 20 July 1926

Fig. 4.13. *Sikrung*, 25 August 1926

Fig. 4.14. *Sayam rat*, 14 April 1925

past the women, showing not the slightest interest in the illegal activity obviously being carried out in the building. As newspaper columnists of the period commonly observed, the general lack of concern on the part of the police was best understood in light of the fact that they were often deeply implicated in the carnal trade themselves.[19] However, as we shall see, it was not only the police who were seen to sanction, or be involved with various illicit activities that were widely seen as inhibiting national progress.

Witness the graphic depicted in figure 4.15. An ordinary Siamese man is

Fig. 4.15. *Sayam rat,* 19 June 1923

shown peering through a hole in the wall of a house. The sign above his head tells us that this is the home of a member of the nobility (*ban chaokhun*). "Whoa!" the man exclaims, "This place is a big-time crim hangout. They got gambling, counterfeit money, and pros in there." The message presented is unambiguous—members of the supposedly "respectable" upper classes were seen as playing a central role in the world of criminality and vice.

We now turn to take a look at some of the more trenchant critiques of the ruling elite, and the king in particular—images which express the intensity of popular discontent and disaffection with the absolute monarchy.

DEMONIZING THE RULING CLASS

Hypocritical, self-aggrandizing behavior on the part of high-ranking officials was, as we have seen, the subject of a good deal of graphic satire and comment. This, in turn, was accompanied by an extraordinary amount of written criticism and condemnation in the press.[20] A striking graphic incorporating a range of this type of criticism is shown in figure 4.16.

The cartoon is titled "Duplicitous Beast from Hell" (*ai sat narok luang lok*). On the left a man is shown wearing a mask with a winsome, innocent-looking visage. Above, the caption reads, "Outwardly I'm an angel." In the adjacent pic-

Fig. 4.16. *Sayam rat,* 20 October 1923

ture, the mask is drawn back revealing the man's true self. A scowling demon-like face glowers menacingly; in each hand he grasps a bag full of money. The captions on the bags refer to various aspects of the man's character and the types of activity he is involved in. He is described as "oppressive," a "swindler of government revenue," an "exploiter of *phu n'oi*," a "criminal," and a "thug." In addition he is said to "beguile women" (to take advantage of them sexually), "solicit bribes," produce "counterfeit money," "run gaming houses and brothels," and promote "injustice."

The full import of the cartoon is to be understood by the artist's use of the mask, indeed, a particular type of mask. Masks were worn by performers in the dramatic arts, which, as most readers would have been well aware, were one of King Vajiravudh's greatest passions. The mask shown features a crown—an unambiguous symbol of royalty. Further, the reference to "angel" (*thewada*) above the masked head also refers to the throne that, it hardly needs stating, was commonly represented through the use of heavenly metaphors. Having said all of this, however, I would suggest that the cartoon be interpreted on two levels: as an unambiguous critique of the king personally and, at the same time, as an indictment of the absolutist political system more generally. In this regard the cartoonist asserted that although members of the royal-noble ruling elite presented themselves as dignified, honorable men, they were, in reality, nothing less than criminals, perpetrators of oppression and injustice.

Another graphic artist, similarly mindful of the monarch's thespian interests, invoked a classical literary reference in order to condemn the type of society that flourished under Vajiravudh's rule.

In this cartoon (fig. 4.17) the absolutist administration is portrayed in the form of Thotsian (also known as Thotsakan), the ten-headed demon king from

Fig. 4.17. *Sayam rat*, 2 May 1925

the Ramakian (Ramayana). All ten heads bear Vajiravudh's likeness, each with a different expression on its face, suggesting, it would seem, a particular attitude toward the type of activity or form of behavior referred to in each of the accompanying captions. I will concentrate on just three images. To begin with, the third head from the left depicts a laughing face, and the caption beneath reads "philanderer" (*chao-chu*). It appears that the message here is that although this sort of behavior was subject to much public criticism, including that by Varjiravudh himself, the king did not really consider it to be a serious matter (see below). Beneath the fifth head from the left, a hand is wrapped around the shoulder of a young woman, suggesting enslavement or exploitation. The caption below reads "prostitution" (*sanch'on*). Meanwhile the royal visage above winks, displaying a wry, knowing look as if to endorse or sanction the commercial trade in sex. Finally we may turn to the head immediately to the right with a hand beneath proffering playing cards in the direction of the young woman's outstretched arm. The caption simply says "gambling," an activity formally proscribed by the state yet, as we have already noted, immensely popular (also see below). A certain tension is suggested here through the artist's use of the card-dealing hand and his depiction of the face above which registers a degree of sorrow, even disapproval. What this is meant to convey is not entirely clear although it can be interpreted as another critique of official hypocrisy. Here it may be added that while Vajiravudh presented a sympathetic, seemingly progressive, enlightened attitude toward women in a number of his writings, the cartoonist offers a distinctly different view, intimating that the monarch's concerns in this area were not really genuine.[21]

An equally pointed, if somewhat more humorous, commentary on the nature of Vajiravudh's regime is presented in the following cartoon by Sem Sumanan, one of the few cartoonists of the period whose name we know. A native of northeast Siam, Sem emerged as one of the most provocative young graphic artists working for the Bangkok press during the early 1920s.[22]

The cartoon (fig. 4.18) shows an emaciated rickshaw puller representing morality (*thamma*) straining to drag his conveyance and its passenger (a smug-looking, obese, balding man wearing a crown—none other than the king himself) up a steep gradient. At the top of the incline is a small sign that reads "heaven" (*sukati*). Captioned "Morality will take us to a better place," the ironical intent of the cartoon is clear: the rickshaw's bloated passenger makes the advance of "morality" an exceedingly difficult if not impossible task. In other words, Vajiravudh's administration was seen to be anything but moral.

Sem also framed this perceived lack of morality on the part of the king in more direct personal terms. The graphic (fig. 4.19) carries no caption. It shows a set of scales, one side weighed down on the ground by a young man smoking a cigarette, while the other side, containing a large bag marked "treasury funds" (*ngoen khlang*), hovers in the air. Rays of light, symbolizing royalty, emanate from

Fig. 4.18. *Bangkok kan-m'uang,* 21 August 1923

Fig. 4.19. *Bangkok kan-m'uang,* 16 October 1923

the top of the stand from which the scales are suspended. The image is particularly notable in that it drew attention, albeit obliquely, to a relationship between Vajiravudh's intimate affairs and the financial state of the country. In effect what the cartoonist suggested was that the king carried out his homosexual lifestyle (patronizing and supporting male lovers) at the expense of the nation.[23] Here it may be added that while the degree to which the average person was aware of the monarch's love life is impossible to gauge, it seems there must have been a reasonable number of people in the know for Sem to have even drawn the cartoon in the first place.

Notwithstanding the boldness of this particular image, Sem's most confrontational and vitriolic work appeared toward the very end of Vajiravudh's reign. It was at this time that he produced a number of cartoons, articles, and poems on what Copeland refers to as "the *hia* trade."[24] In Siam the *hia*, or monitor lizard, is associated with great misfortune. It is also a highly pejorative term when applied to a person. Indeed, the word *hia* preceded by the derogatory particle *ai* (pronounced "eye") to form the expression *ai-hia* ranks as perhaps the strongest term of abuse in the Thai language. Copeland glosses *hia* in English as a "low-life bastard," a serviceable enough rendering although one that does not really give us a full sense of the loathing and disgust the expression *ai hia* conveys in Thai. Something along the lines of "you fuckin' low cunt" in contemporary Australian argot, however, would be close.

While the *hia* was used in cartoon graphics as a general symbol for the corrupt, embezzling official from at least 1923,[25] it does not appear to have been applied to specific individuals until Sem's fearless contribution in 1925. During this time he wrote at length about six different varieties of *hia* found in Siam and produced a related series of cartoons. In these Sem identified a number of the highest-placed men in the land as *hia*, including the powerful minister of the interior *Chaophraya* Yomarat, *Chaophraya* Ram Rakh'op (one of Vajiravudh's favorites), and Ram's brother, *Phraya* Aniruthewa. The sixth and final cartoon in the series—quite remarkable from a contemporary perspective given the irreproachable public standing which Thai royalty currently enjoys—is shown here.

The figure on the left in figure 4.20 is none other than Sem who refers to himself here, as elsewhere in his work, as *Kaen phet* (literally, "diamond core," suggesting the sharpest, most incisive of cutting tools). Pointing with his thumb he says, "Here it is, that red-tailed fucking bastard number six." The aggrieved-

Fig. 4.20. *Kr'o lek*, 22 November 1925

looking figure he points at looks suspiciously like the king—the "sixth" a reference, it would seem, to one of the ways in which Vajiravudh was referred to (*ratchakan thi hok*), the *sixth* monarch of the Chakri dynasty. He shakes his fist at the
artist and warns him, "Watch your head."

As it turned out this particular cartoon appeared on the cover of the newspaper *Kr'o lek* at virtually the same time as the king passed away after succumbing
to a host of ailments. While the authorities finally decided to act by ordering the
closure of the paper, no charges appear to have been laid against the publishers
or the cartoonist and, after a six-week hiatus, it was back on the market. This
particular turn of events, Copeland surmises, was because Sem enjoyed the protection of an "influential patron" who enabled him to continue working in the
print industry.[26]

Toward the end of 1925, following Vajiravudh's death, there was a certain
expectation among the public that the incoming administration would be more
responsive to calls for reform than its predecessor and would usher in a new era
of hope and prosperity.[27] But as things turned out, this optimism was sadly misplaced. It soon became apparent that King Prajadhipok's ascension to the throne
served the interests of the royal elite rather than those of the general populace.
Indeed, the new administration came to be seen as little different from that
which had gone before, based as it was on the old personalist formula of patronage and sycophancy. Consequently, after a brief respite, newspaper commentators and cartoonists began to direct their critiques and ridicule at elite power and
privilege once more. A fitting image to represent this new and final era of absolute rule, and one that concludes this section, is the following graphic (fig. 4.21)
by Sem Sumanan's alter-ego, *Kaen phet.*

Fig. 4.21. *Kr'o lek,* 9 May 1926

Here the monarch, the embodiment of the state, is portrayed as a fretful "monkey king" struggling to maintain his balance while trying to control a speeding chariot drawn by a pack of rampaging *hia* (representing the newly established Supreme Council of State composed of five senior princes).[28] The caption to the graphic, and one commonly used by Sem in his work, reads "Kaen phet's Dream," a somewhat ironic title suggesting not so much a dream as a national nightmare.

MEN BEHAVING BADLY

In addition to condemning the monarchy and mounting critiques of high-ranking officials during the 1920s, newspaper cartoonists and commentators frequently attacked male members of the elite for the way they used their positions of authority to gain sexual advantage.

Consider the cartoon depicted in figure 4.22, for example. On the left a lascivious old man, a *phu yai* government official, is shown standing behind his desk. Globules of saliva drip from his chin as he reaches out to accept a tasty offering—a tiny young woman—from an underling, most probably her father. The caption reads "M'Lord, here's a present for you," the idea of the woman being a "present" emphasized by the enormous bow in her hair. What we have here is a critique of exploitative class and gender relations. In accepting the gift, the *phu yai* is shown to be taking advantage of his vastly superior social position. At the same time the image highlights exploitative gender relations both between

Fig. 4.22. *Katun,* 18 February 1926

classes—the *phu yai* official in taking the *phu n'oi* woman for his pleasure—and within the *phu n'oi* strata itself, expressed through the subordination of the woman (a daughter) to the prostrating man (a father) who proffers her to his master.[29]

The propensity of elite men in positions of authority to use their influence for sexual ends is similarly emphasized in the next cartoon. This graphic (fig. 4.23) concerns the issue of finding work in government service, the most sought-after employment for educated Siamese males at the time. The man crouching at the left of the picture has come to apply for a bureaucratic position and says, "Sir, I have passed my high school exams and would like to apply for a job." However, the high-ranking official he has come to see rushes past him while flashing a card that reads "I'm busy." At the same time, the official is shaking the hand of a young woman who tells him that she has brought her younger brother along to apply for a job. The official tells her "You're guaranteed of that," drooling at the mouth in anticipation of getting sexual favors in return for his help. That the lecherous fellow was a member of the Siamese elite is indicated by his use of the English word "insure" (*inchua*) to vouchsafe the young woman's request, and the handshake, a European custom. The man's speech and form of greeting identify him as having had a Western education, which, at the time, was something only available to the wealthy or very well connected.

Such foreign-educated elite males were frequently the subject of criticism by cartoonists, press commentators, and even prose fiction writers (see below). The following cartoon (fig. 4.24), for example, offers a highly unflattering portrait of this type of individual, his Western education indicated by the words *hua n'ok*, meaning someone schooled abroad, inscribed on his upper chest.

In one hand the man tightly grasps a sack labeled his "forebears' money" while in the palm of his other hand he holds a prostitute, the type of woman men of

Fig. 4.23. *Sayam sakkhi*, 11 July 1922

Fig. 4.24. *Bangkok kan-m'uang,* 14 June 1923

his sort are said to associate with. The tiny figure raises her arms in supplication, her gesture and diminutive size signifying both dependency and the enormous difference in social status between herself and the man. In addition he is described as arrogant, a drinker of "every type of alcohol," one who worships gambling, and an individual who holds ordinary Thai people in contempt. In depicting a foreign-educated member of the Siamese elite as wholly self-interested and morally bankrupt, the cartoonist intimates that the man and his ilk were nothing less than enemies of the Siamese nation and its people.

At the same time, we also find particularly telling portrayals of the behavior of elite foreign-educated men in various literary works of the period. For exam-

ple, this is one of the main themes of *Ten-ram* (Dancing), a novel by Chamnong
Wongkhaluang serialized in the popular newspaper *Thai thae* from mid-1931.[30]

The beginning of each installment featured the graphic depicted in figure
4.25. Western-style dancing, involving close physical contact between men and
women, was closely associated with members of the foreign-educated elite, and
even King Vajiravudh was said to be "an enthusiastic devotee." Indeed, he took
lessons from Madame Sophia Belikovich, the premier dancer of the Warsaw
Opera Company, while she was in Bangkok. According to Madame Belikovich,
the king "made a splendid pupil . . . in the ballet, he was not so good, but in
your modern dances—your foxtrot—he was a royal success."[31] From the early
1920s, Western-style dancing was often the subject of discussion and debate in
the popular press. Many newspaper commentators viewed dance in a critical
light, raising concerns about its appropriateness for Siamese people, who, according to some observers, were a "hot-blooded" (*l'uat r'on*) and volatile race. More
specifically, concerns were voiced to the effect that the intimacy inherent in
Western dancing posed a threat to female virtue and thereby served as a contributing factor to the growth of prostitution.[32]

In the introductory section to the novel itself, Chamnong refers to dance as a
"new Asian art form" (*pen silapa samai mai kh'ong esia*) and then, echoing the
sentiments expressed in the press, poses the question, "Is Western-style dance
suited to Siam?" The debate on the appropriateness of dance, the central theme
of the novel, is taken up by three male characters: Wisit Pranit (a former foreign
student now unemployed), *Luang* Sanit Wannakhadi (who had studied abroad
with Wisit and now works in the bureaucracy), and the somewhat older *Phraya*
Intaramat (another former foreign student and currently a high-ranking government official). The unemployed Wisit, whose social status is considerably lower
than that of the other two, is firmly opposed to Western-style dancing in Siam
despite the fact that he had become an accomplished dancer during his studies
in England. At one point he tells *Phraya* Intaramat:

> It's not wise for a sport [*kila*] like this to be introduced into a country with a hot
> humid climate like ours. You know what a great evil communism is? In my opinion
> the doctrine of dance [*lathi ten-ram*] is equally menacing. It's a disgraceful and idiotic
> trend. Only when everybody in the world turns to communism will dancing become
> acceptable in Siam.[33]

In equating the dangers of dance to society with those posed by communism
(a radical comparison by any measure), Wisit is portrayed as a guardian of morality and protector of Siam's integrity in the face of imported foreign ideologies
and practices. By contrast, both *Luang* Sanit and *Phraya* Intaramat were avid proponents of dancing. For them dance in combination with drink presented opportunities for socializing with women and, more important, for reaching "heaven"
(*suwan*), a euphemism for having sex.[34] *Phraya* Intaramat in particular was an

unabashed hedonist. Although he had an attractive and modish young wife, he wanted more. One night, while fondling a young prostitute on a visit to the Sunli Bar, a tawdry low class dance hall, *Phraya* Intaramat candidly tells Wisit about his deepest desires.

> When you're born you should seek all the pleasure you can get. I've come to the conclusion that women are the only real source of a man's joy. I'm getting older by the minute, but before my body gives up I want to taste the "sweetness" of all the women I possibly can. After I die I don't want to regret missed opportunities, since I don't know if I'll get the chance to experience such pleasures again. . . .

> I've got wives in almost every street in the capital. . . . I use my money to lure them. . . . The law in Siam doesn't limit the number of wives a man can have. If you've got the money you can take as many as you like. . . . Go and visit the homes of *Chaokhun* [a title used to refer to a high-ranking man] so-and-so or *Khun Phra* [ditto] whoever, and you'll see it's no different from a Turkish harem: their houses are jam packed with women. Indeed, they're just like me, we're all of the view that it is better for the home to be filled up with people rather than be overgrown by grass. And when I say filled up, I mean filled up with females of every age from growing girls and young women, to mature and middle-aged ladies.[35]

For our present purposes further details about the novel need not concern us; suffice it to say that the work was representative of the type of titillating prose writing that began to appear in the popular press of the time.[36] The point to be emphasized here concerns male behavior and class. As we have noted, the unemployed Wisit was not the social equal of *Luang* Sanit and *Phraya* Intaramat, both officials in the absolutist regime. This social difference was expressed in stark moral terms: Wisit is depicted as an exemplar of virtue and restraint while *Luang* Sanit and *Phraya* Intaramat embody excess and debauchery. In juxtaposing these characters the author provides a blunt critique of upper-class male morality. The behavior of such men was seen to be at odds with the social good, the moral fitness of the upper class to rule called into question.

Elite male obsession with sensual pleasure was also a subject of particular interest to cartoonists who offered critical perspectives on such behavior that was condoned, if not encouraged, by the marriage laws of the day (see chapter 6). The cartoon below is a good example of the way in which an elite male at the head of a polygamous household was now portrayed.

In figure 4.26 a wealthy, pot-bellied noble is ensconced on a divan smoking a pipe; to his left stands a small table with a bottle of alcohol and two glasses. He is entertained by a bevy of young women playing musical instruments while another older woman sits nearby fanning him. The caption, expressed in verse rather than prose, reads something like "both night and day he but listens to music and indulges his lust." Here the cartoonist characterizes the elite male as

Fig. 4.25. *Thai thae*, 20 June 1931

Fig. 4.26. *Sayam rat*, 21 Dec 1920

living an idle, licentious existence, immersed in pleasure while contributing nothing to the wider community.

At the same time, other related aspects of the lives of upper-class males and their polygamous households were frequently satirized by cartoonists. The following graphic (fig. 4.27) is a representative example. Here an aggrieved-looking *phu yai* is shown at home sitting in an armchair besieged by a legion of wailing women, some with young children in tow. The caption below reads "A picture at the end of the month showing wife Number One to wife Number ? asking the master for their regular payments." As the cartoonist suggests, the man has so many wives he has lost count and has no idea of how many dependents he must support. His sexual peccadilloes are shown to have come back to haunt him, the implication being that polygamy was a financially ruinous practice.

As mentioned above, elite men were often portrayed by their critics as having insatiable desires and prodigious sex lives which saw them engaging in dalliances with prostitutes. The graphic shown in figure 4.28 provides a succinct commentary on this type of behavior. A wizened old man, again a high-ranking government official as indicated by his mode of dress, is shown fraternizing with some young prostitutes. In the background a Buddhist temple is visible, a question mark hovers in the sky, and the caption at the bottom of the scene simply states "You're an old man now!!" (*kae laew!!*). The cartoonist's meaning is clear enough: the man has reached an advanced age when he may be expected to be thinking about religion and coming to terms with the transitoriness of human existence. Instead he is shown to be driven by lust rather than a concern for his

ภาพสิ้นเดือน แสดงเมียที่ ๑ ถึงที่ ? มาขอเงินเดือนจากท่านจ๋าคุณ

Fig. 4.27. *Sayam rat,* 2 May 1922

Fig. 4.28. *Sayam riwiw*, 17 April 1927

spiritual well-being. Such an obsession with the pleasures of the flesh, the cartoonist implies, was typical of aging members of the male elite.

At the same time, the practice of government officials consorting with prostitutes also came under the critical gaze of fiction writers. This type of work is exemplified in a 1927 short story entitled "Mia klang wan" (Daytime Wife) by K'opkan Wisitthasi, a male author who wrote under the pseudonym "Kulap khao" (White Rose).[37]

A woman by the name of Prayong goes to a brothel in the Nang Lerng district of Bangkok during the middle of the day. She plans to confront her husband Prayun, a state official who regularly patronizes the house, believing that he is about to abandon her and their young child. Prayong pays the madam a bribe to stay in the brothel, disguises herself as a prostitute, and waits in hope that her husband will come on one of his visits. Shortly afterward Prayun appears and, as it happens, chooses Prayong, disguised with a scarf covering her head, as his consort. However when he moves to embrace her he is aghast to discover that the woman whose services he has paid for is, in fact, his own wife. Before she can utter a word he explodes in a fit of rage and abuses her for being "in this filthy place to be the wife of another man." She tells him he is completely mistaken and says that, contrary to what he thinks, she has come to the brothel in order to catch him red-handed, as it were. A heated exchange between the couple follows. Prayong says that she loves him dearly and implores him to consider the future of their young daughter. Prayun, for his part, says that her coming to the brothel will cause him a great loss of face among his peers, and adds that if he were to leave now "They'll say I'm afraid of my wife, everyone—even the owner of this place." She is unmoved and says, "Does that mean you're staying? You're going to let people say, 'Here he is, a public official in the service of the king, sneaking off from work to see his daytime wife,' are you? Oh, heaven help us. I say it's better for them to accuse you of fearing your wife than for you to treat me with contempt and do as you please."[38]

Caught off guard by her line of argument, Prayun concedes that she has a point, and the story ends with him sheepishly asking her if there is a back way out of the brothel so they can sneak off together without being noticed.

Here, as elsewhere in his writing, K'opkan evinced a strong empathy with women and the difficulties they experienced at the hands of men (also see chapter 6). That he portrayed Prayong as resorting to a radical form of direct action (going into a brothel and pretending to be a prostitute) in order to combat her husband's wanton behavior serves to underscore the degree of anger and bitterness women felt at being treated by men in such a cavalier fashion. In focusing on the arbitrary nature of the sexual double standard, the author intimated a need for equality between men and women in their personal relations. At the same time, in representing Prayun as a licentious fellow who spent time in a brothel while ostensibly at work, K'opkan provided a critique of officialdom more generally, questioning attitudes and forms of behavior common among members of the absolutist bureaucracy. In "Mia klang wan," then, we find an imaginative work that not only incorporates critical social commentary but also bears implicit political overtones.

Finally, in a brief addendum to conclude our discussion of the ways in which the absolute order and upper-class society were portrayed, it may be added that the behavior of elite women (i.e., the major wives of powerful men and their daughters) also came under the scrutiny of graphic satirists. Invariably such women were represented as leading idle, frivolous lives. Commonly they were seen as spending their time indulging in the illicit activity of gambling. The following two cartoons address this theme.

The first graphic (fig. 4.29), simply captioned "A Card-Playing Circle of Titled Ladies" (*phai wong khun-ying*), requires little comment. The second cartoon (fig. 4.30), which appeared on the cover the feminist newspaper *Satri thai* (see chapter 5), is somewhat more complex. It shows six women of different ages immersed in a game of chance. They represent a cross-section of upper-class society; one, for example, is married to a member of royalty, one to an aristocrat, and another to a merchant. As they sit playing cards, the women tell one another that their husbands have gone off to work or are out of the house (perhaps visiting a brothel up the road). Meanwhile, a policeman suspecting that the women are engaged in some form of illegal activity stands peering through a keyhole and says to himself, "Aha, I thought so!" Given the vast social gap between the women and the policeman, however, it is unlikely that he would intervene and make an arrest. As a news report from the period noted, elite

Fig. 4.29. *Sayam rat,* 17 June 1924

Fig. 4.30. *Satri thai,* 8 March 1926

women running gambling parlors such as this had little to fear since their social standing virtually guaranteed them complete immunity from police harassment or prosecution.[39] The cartoonist, who would have been all too well aware of this fact, could do little more than offer readers advice that "A good housewife shouldn't behave like this" while insinuating that these upper-class women, who presented themselves as dignified, honorable individuals, were in fact little different from their husbands and not nearly as virtuous and respectable as they might have outwardly seemed.

As mentioned above, cartooning was still very much a new expressive form in Siam during the 1920s. In comparison with the type of graphic art being created in the Philippines, for example, a good deal of the work produced in Siam at the time was rather amateurish and crudely executed.[40] Yet despite their relative lack of technical sophistication, early Thai cartoonists avidly embraced the medium and, in doing so, leveled a sustained attack on the hypocrisy and moral weaknesses of the ruling elite while relentlessly critiquing the corruption endemic to the prevailing sociopolitical order. Satirical cartoons were frequently published in conjunction with related pieces of editorial comment, adding an extra dimension to text-based criticism. Indeed, the cartoon, as a graphic form of mass communication, worked beyond the print environment which carried it, providing the less literate members of the reading public with an understanding of what was being "said." As such the satirical images that were regularly featured in the daily press represented a potent force that helped galvanize popular discontent toward princely authority.

NOTES

1. Matthew Copeland, "Contested Nationalism and the 1932 Overthrow of the Absolute Monarchy in Siam," Ph.D. diss., Australian National University, Canberra, 1992, 51–52.

2. Copeland, "Contested Nationalism," 78, n. 5.

3. Apinan Poshyananda, *Modern Art in Thailand: Nineteenth and Twentieth Centuries* (Singapore: Oxford University Press, 1992), 12–13.

4. Apinan Poshyananda, "Modern Art in Thailand in the Nineteenth and Twentieth Centuries," part 1, Ph.D. diss., Cornell University, 1990, 171.

5. Copeland, "Contested Nationalism," 79, n. 10.

6. Copeland, "Contested Nationalism," 77. My approach in emphasizing the visual element in this chapter has been inspired by Matthew Copeland's unpublished doctoral dissertation, which utilized previously neglected newspaper graphics to great effect.

7. Copeland, "Contested Nationalism," 77, 123.

8. Quote from *Bangkok kan-m'uang*, 4 October 1924, translated and cited by Copeland, "Contested Nationalism," 77.

9. Copeland, "Contested Nationalism," 69–71.

10. See, for example, Akin Rabibhadana, *The Organization of Thai Society in the Early*

Bangkok Period—1782–1873 (Ithaca, N.Y.: Southeast Asia Program, Cornell University, 1969).

11. Scot Barmé, *Luang Wichit Wathakan and the Creation of a Thai National Identity*, (Singapore: Institute of Southeast Asian Studies), 31.

12. At the beginning of Vajiravudh's reign, the royal family from the *M'om chao* (Prince of the Fourth Rank) level upward numbered just over 500 (Malcolm Smith, *A Physician at the Court of Siam* [Kuala Lumpur: Oxford University Press, 1982], 60). As for the upper levels of the nobility (i.e., those with the titles *Chaophraya, Phraya,* and *Phra*), this numbered perhaps one or two hundred men plus their wives and daughters.

13. In Siam, where various cultural taboos attach to the pointing and placement of the feet, this image serves as a powerful visual metaphor for obsequiousness and servility.

14. The difference being his sour expression, more facial hair, a slightly more sloping forehead, and a longer, curving side lever.

15. Copeland, "Contested Nationalism," 61.

16. *Bangkok Times,* 18 July 1912.

17. Barmé, *Luang Wichit Wathakan,* 36, n. 52.

18. Copeland, "Contested Nationalism," 58.

19. Copeland, "Contested Nationalism," 106, n. 19.

20. Copeland, "Contested Nationalism," 61.

21. See, for example, the king's articles, "Taeng-ngan chua khrao" [Part-time Marriage] and "Kan-kha ying sao" [The Trade in Young Women], from *Klon tit l'o* [Clogs on Our Wheels], originally published in the daily newspaper *Phim thai* in mid-1915. Reprinted in Cremation Volume for *Phraya* Athakariniphon [Sithi Chunyanon] (Bangkok, 1978), 44–47, 51–54. In addition, see "Khr'uang-mai haeng khwam rung-r'uang kh'u saphap haeng satri" [A Sign of Progress Is the Status of Women in Society], first published in 1918, reprinted *Satrithat* 1, 3 (August–October 1983): 46–51.

22. Copeland, "Contested Nationalism," 79.

23. Homosexuality was an issue that journalists of the period tended to avoid writing about. See chapter 3, endnote 34. With respect to modern-day Thailand, homosexuality does not appear to be an impediment to attaining high political office as it would, for example, in the United States. While a number of former Thai prime ministers were reputed to be gay, this did not hinder their political careers and their private lives were not subject to public scrutiny or criticism.

24. Copeland, "Contested Nationalism," 115.

25. For example, see *Sayam rat,* 8 May 1923.

26. Copeland, "Contested Nationalism," 118, 123.

27. Barmé, *Luang Wichit Wathakan,* 63–64.

28. Barmé, *Luang Wichit Wathakan,* 64.

29. The practice of using a daughter as a token of exchange for personal benefit was also underlined in some of M. C. (Prince) Akat Damkoeng's prose fiction writing. For example, in "Wai sawat" (Age of Romance), a short story about contemporary upper-class Siamese society, he refers to fathers selling off their daughters to other elite families, describing one such man in the following terms: "*Phra* Banchoet is an old-fashioned Thai who believes that having a beautiful daughter is like having a huge amount of money. When she grows up she can be sold just like we sell Siamese cats to the Americans, and better still if one has two beautiful daughters." M. C. Akat Damkoeng, "Wai sawat" in

Wiman thalai (Crumbling Mansion), a collection of short stories (Bangkok: Phrae Phi-thaya, 1972), 75.

30. The first installment of *Ten-ram* was published in *Thai thae*, 6 June 1931.

31. *Bangkok Times,* 14 September 1922.

32. *Bangkok Times,* 16 February 1920, 23 March 1921; *Satri thai,* 8 March 1926, 14 March 1927.

33. *Thai thae,* 6 June 1931.

34. The sexual aspect of dance was elaborated in the following terms:

All dancers know about the "Lumbar Spinal Chord," (original expression in English) it's a gland that stimulates the most delicate, exquisite sexual feelings. If it is caressed gently even a shy woman will lose all her inhibitions. Her dignity and gentility evaporate. Once she has been aroused the way is open for depravity to take hold. She forgets herself, forgets everything, forgets how to reason and think, forgets all sense of morality. [When stimulated] a young woman with a beautiful figure, wealth and an honored position in society will give her body over to the sexual desires of a man. The shadow of destruction is visited upon her, a shadow that has its roots in dance! dance! This "secret gland" is like an electric switch, a switch a man skilled in the devious tricks of dance can activate with the utmost precision. He'll use his fingers gently on this hidden "secret gland" and when he hits the mark there is no doubt, a bright light will begin to burn. (*Thai thae,* 17 June 1931)

35. *Thai thae,* 27 June 1931, 8 August 1931.

36. Somewhat more erotic writings became widely available during the 1920s, a phe-nomenon remarked upon in 1927 by a newspaper commentator: "Pornographic books are currently on sale in large numbers with titles such as . . . *Saep cing* [It Really Stings], *Th'ung chai khun nai* [Pleasing the Master], *Poet suwan* [Opening Heaven], and *Tal'ot kh'un* [All Night Long]. These books are readily available; ninety-year-old men and children as young as six are able to buy and read them at their leisure." The writer notes, however, that these works, while aimed at "sexually arousing the reader," were not as obscene as books that appeared on the market only a few years earlier, works employing the "most coarse language." The reason for the change in tone of such writings, he suggested, had come about as a result of a number of arrests and fines, a development that saw producers adopting more figurative language in the hope that they would avoid prosecution. *Sikrung,* 7 March 1927.

37. Published in the monthly magazine *Phaphayon* [Cinema], August 1927, 1401–15.

38. *Phaphayon,* August 1927, 1414.

39. *Krungthep Daily Mail* (in Thai), 16 June 1920.

40. Alfred McCoy and Alfredo Roces. *Philippine Cartoons: Political Caricature of the American Era, 1900–1941* (Quezon City, Philippines: Vera-Reyes, 1985).

รูปนางเขียม ใจเด็ด

อายุ ๒๒ ปี   ค้องหาของกรมอัยการว่าท่านายอะมาร์นาททหรือเอชบีฮาริชาติแจกมังคับอังกฤษ   ที่
ห้องชั้นบนของผู้ตาย   ตำบลถนนสุรวงศ์   จังเลยสารภาพโดยชื่นๆตา   ว่าคนเป็นผู้ฆ่าๆ เพื่อป้องกันการ
อนาจารอันทารุณของผู้ตาย   บัดนี้เป็นที่น่ายินดี   ซึ่งนางเขียมได้รับความอิศระภาพโดยชอบธรรมจากคำ
พิพากษาศาลต่างประเทศ   แต่เมื่อวันที่ ๑ เดือนนั้แล้ว

Fig. 5.1

5

❧

Evocations of Equality: Female Education and Employment

In March 1926 the photograph in figure 5.1 was featured on the cover of the feminist magazine *Satri thai*.[1] The caption immediately below reads, "A picture of the heroic *Nang* Yiam." In the brief passage that follows, we learn that *Nang* Yiam was a twenty-two-year-old woman who had killed an Indian man who tried to rape her. Judging by reports that appeared in the daily press, her experience was not an unusual one (although her emphatic response was quite out of the ordinary); girls and young women were frequently the victims of sexual harassment (see chapter 3), indecent assault, and rape (with incidents of gang rape not uncommon).[2] In this particular instance *Nang* Yiam had "proudly" confessed to her crime when arrested by police. Put on trial for the killing she was subsequently acquitted by the court and given her freedom. *Satri thai* warmly applauded this decision and honored *Nang* Yiam for what she had done. While this may appear as something of a radical gesture on the part of the magazine, it was, in its own way, indicative of a broader trend in which women began to assert themselves more forcefully in order to gain greater respect and recognition from their male peers.

Questions concerning the status and position of women were central to the popular debate on social equality that unfolded in Bangkok during the 1920s. Indeed, this period heralded something of a new phase for Siamese women, with the protofeminism of the early twentieth century giving way to a more robust, self-confident type of feminist consciousness. This development reflected the changing nature and structure of Bangkok society. Whereas the emergence of protofeminism discussed earlier was, by and large, an elite phenomenon, the debate on women in the 1920s was associated with the rise of the middle class and calls from within its ranks for a more just, egalitarian social order. A range of women's newspapers and magazines came on the market promoting the view that if Siam was to become a modern, "civilized" nation, the status of women needed to be improved. Similar questions concerned with women and the future of the nation were also being raised in nearby colonial Vietnam. However, there were significant differences. Vietnam, for example, lacked a women's press comparable to that found in Siam, a situation influenced by the fact that female education was still poorly developed (see below). Instead women's issues were taken up by newly created organizations such as the Nu Cong Hoc Hoi, or "Women's Labor Study Association," established in 1926.[3] At the same time, it should be noted that in the Vietnamese case male intellectuals and writers had originally initiated the discussion of women's issues in relation to the nation, and, notwithstanding the emergence of women's organizations, continued to play a leading role in this debate. A similar situation also prevailed in China from the late 1910s. Questions relating to the status of women were a fundamental element of the all-encompassing public debate on contemporary Chinese sociopolitical life generated by the May Fourth Movement. As Christina Gilmartin writes, "the broad-ranging literature on women's issues [that emerged as part of the May Fourth Movement] was largely a male discourse. Through the torrent of words that poured from their pens, May Fourth male intellectuals set the terms of radical discussion on women's issues and also assumed the right to speak on behalf of women."[4] Some of the central figures of the modern Chinese revolution, including Lu Xun, Chen Duxiu, Hu Shi, Li Dazhao, and Mao Zedong, were active participants in the debates with "the fierce passion displayed in much of their writings [revealing] the great personal significance they attached to this issue."[5] In Siam, by contrast, it was women who were at the forefront of the debate to improve their status, a project that found varying degrees of support—as well as opposition—from sections of the male populace. While the reasons for these historical differences are open to debate, it is clear that Siamese women were not subject to the same degree of social constraint as their Vietnamese and Chinese counterparts.

The present chapter examines the debate on equality for women in the Bangkok press concerned with education and, to a lesser extent, employment. As we shall see, discussion of these issues was not cast in simple male-female oppositions, but rather had a diffuse, multiaccented character. Broadly speaking, there were both men and women who held what may be termed socially "progressive" views, that is, views based on notions of equality between the sexes in which women would enjoy the same educational and employment opportunities as men. At the same time, other commentators (both men and women) expressed a rather more "conservative" or "traditionalist" outlook which stressed fundamentally different social roles for the sexes, men being regarded as providers or breadwinners while women were essentially seen as being responsible for domestic matters such as housekeeping and the raising of children.[6] Meanwhile other commentators voiced a combination of views by promoting the idea of equality of education between the sexes on the one hand while rejecting the notion of equal employment opportunities between men and women on the other.

As a preliminary to this discussion, it is useful to sketch out various changes and developments that occurred during the last decade of absolute rule, in particular the expansion in female education, the growth in women-oriented magazines and newspapers, and the growing discussion of issues related to women in the mainstream press and via the new medium of radio.

EDUCATION

In the decade from 1915 to 1925 the number of girls attending school in Siam increased significantly. While 5,396 girls were reported to be receiving a formal education of one sort or another in 1915, this number had grown to some 235,465 by 1925. The greatest increase in enrollments took place at the primary school level, rising from 4,907 students in 1915 to 232,120 in 1925. At the secondary level the number rose from 489 students in 1915 to 3,277 in 1925, the overwhelming majority of these being located in Bangkok. By 1925 there were also some 68 young women attending Chulalongkorn University, the only tertiary institution in the country. A handful of these undergraduates were enrolled in the Faculty of Medicine, although the available sources do not specify what courses of study the remainder of these students pursued.[7] In Vietnam, by contrast, female education was developed on a considerably more modest scale. Marr notes that by 1930 some "40,752 girls [were] undergoing public or private instruction [while] at least an equal number were probably being taught basic *quoc-ngu* [the Vietnamese writing system] at home, or at the informal study associations beginning to crop up in many localities."[8] These developments, it should be emphasized, were at the primary level with the colonial state making little or no effort to provide young women with secondary or tertiary education at the time.

As the above figures indicate, the number of literate females in Siam grew rapidly during the 1920s, with the levels of literacy and knowledge attained varying enormously. Nonetheless, by the middle of the decade there were thousands of females with well-developed reading and writing skills, the majority of whom lived in the Bangkok-Thonburi area where most of the secondary schools as well as Chulalongkorn University were located. These young women, together with a much larger number of educated young men,[9] formed the basis of an avid and growing reading public. At the same time, many young educated men and women also evinced a keen interest in becoming writers and journalists. As a result of these developments a host of intrepid entrepreneurs came to see the publishing industry as a potentially lucrative business proposition and an increasing number of new publications appeared on the market.[10]

WOMEN'S PUBLICATIONS

Following the demise of *Satri niphon* in 1915 and *Nari chaleng*, an obscure monthly that came out for a brief period the following year,[11] it seems that no other women's publications were launched until the 1920s. During the last decade of absolute rule, a rash of new women's papers and magazines were published, beginning with the short-lived biweekly *Satri sap* (Women's Words) in 1922. This was followed in 1926 by three new titles: the weekly *Satri thai* (Thai Woman); *Nari kasem* (The Complete Woman), published three times a month; and *Nari nithet* (Women's News), a fortnightly paper. In 1927 the daily *Ying sao* (Young Woman) came out, followed by the weekly *Sayam yuphadi* (Young Siamese Woman) in 1928. The year 1930 saw the appearance of three women's publications, the daily *Ying sayam* (Siamese Woman), the weekly *Suphap-nari* (Lady), and *Nari nat* (In Support of Women), published monthly. In 1931 another weekly, the *Sao samai* (Modern Young Woman) came onto the market, while the following year saw the publication of the daily *Ying thai* (Thai Woman) (for further details of *Ying thai*, see chapter 9).[12]

Largely owned and operated by women, these publications were diverse in outlook.[13] At one end of the spectrum there were politically oriented papers such as the daily *Ying sayam* and the weekly magazine-style *Satri thai*, both of which actively participated in the national debate on the position of women. The editor's preface to the first edition of the latter publication gives us a clear idea as to its aims and objectives.

> *Satri thai* has been established as a result of the collaborative efforts of women writers, students, and private-school teachers. Our purpose is to serve as the voice, eyes and ears of all women, regardless of class or status. We intend to be a genuine friend to Siamese women.
>
> The material we publish will be specifically for the benefit of women. Among other things we will discuss politics (*kan-m'uang*) as it relates to women at large.
>
> We encourage readers to contribute their own thoughts and ideas to *Satri thai*, not only for the good of other women but also for the nation more generally. In addition, we are more than happy to serve as a forum both to air your grievances and to push for rights and justice on your behalf.[14]

From the very beginning to its ultimate demise nearly two years later, *Satri thai* adhered closely to the founding principles laid down by its promoters. For example, the magazine provided readers with a comprehensive and intelligible overview of the contemporary laws on marriage, information that had previously been difficult to obtain and even more difficult to understand, couched as it was

in complex, archaic legalese.[15] It also launched various initiatives such as a public appeal to discover the identity of a young female murder victim and bring her
killer or killers to justice. On 28 June 1926, Satri thai published a picture of the
murdered woman (fig. 5.2), whose naked body had been stuffed in a sack and
thrown into a Bangkok waterway, and offered a substantial reward of 100 baht
(the equivalent of five months' salary of a junior official) for information leading
to the arrest and prosecution of the person or persons responsible for her death.
A further reward of 20 baht was offered to anyone who could identify her. In
launching the appeal, the editor of Satri thai wrote that she was appalled by the
"brutal killing of a fellow woman" and urged readers who could provide assistance to contact the offices of the magazine directly before going to the
police—a request that implied that without outside pressure the authorities
would not make a serious effort to solve this crime or other similar cases.

Like the vanguard critical magazines of the day such as Kr'o lek (Steel Armor)
and Katun (Cartoon), Satri thai also regularly featured pointed satirical cartoons
on its cover (see below). It may also be noted that the magazine had few advertis-
ers, and published very little serialized fiction—indeed, none of the Chinese-
style chronicle stories which accounted for the long-term success of mainstream
commercial newspapers such as the daily Sikrung. Given this, the relative longevity of Satri thai in the cut-and-thrust environment of the Bangkok publishing
world should be seen as quite an achievement, particularly in comparison with
other women's newspapers and magazines, all of which survived for considerably
shorter periods, and attests to the existence of a loyal and committed readership.

At the other end of the spectrum were publications such as Nari-nithet, Suphap-
nari, and Nari kasem, the latter owned and edited by M'om Luang-ying Wanida
Chumsai na Ayuthaya, a minor member of the royal family. Interestingly,
although Nari kasem proclaimed a firm commitment to the advancement of Siamese women, it evinced a strong apolitical stance. This was emphatically stated
by M'om Luang-ying Wanida in the premier issue when she wrote: "Nari-kasem
has absolutely no intention of including any political commentary in its pages
for we know that this is not a woman's business."[16] Indeed, Nari-kasem, like Nari-
nithet and Suphap-nari, was primarily concerned with the publication of translations of Western romantic fiction as well as original works by up-and-coming
young local women authors.

While these publications did not take on an overtly political role per se, social
commentary and criticism was not entirely absent from many of the fictional
writings they published (see chapter 8). In fact it may be said that despite the
marked differences between the various female-oriented publications that came
out during the 1920s, as a whole they represented a discernible intellectual
movement among the growing number of educated women. And while this was
not a formal, organized movement as such, it marked a clear advance beyond the
earlier stage of protofeminism. In the process, the elite focus of earlier women's

Fig. 5.2.

publications was largely, though not entirely, replaced by a more populist approach that catered to the tastes and interests of an expanding middle-class readership.

At the same time, questions regarding the social position of women were no longer seen as tangential matters confined to the pages of women's magazines. Indeed, with increasing public debate about the future of the nation, such questions were frequently discussed by male observers in the mainstream commercial press. Graphically, this development is nicely illustrated by the following cartoon (fig. 5.3) published by the popular daily *Bangkok kan-m'uang* in 1923.

The caption at the top of the image reads, "The prosperity of the nation

Fig. 5.3. Bangkok kan-m'uang, 4 September 1923

depends on four things." These were, from right to left, trade, manufacturing, agriculture, and patriotism. Each of these four elements was represented by a particular type of person: trade by a Chinese man, manufacturing by a somewhat ethnically ambiguous (Sino-Thai?) figure, agriculture by a Siamese peasant farmer, and patriotism by a fashionable young woman (as indicated by her contemporary mode of dress and hairstyle). The cartoonist's use of an alert modern woman as a symbol for patriotism (echoing the Western examples of Germanica and Britannia) is of particular interest. Indeed, this choice may be seen as an expression of an evolving social perspective among sections of the middle-class literati who were of the view that women must be recognized as an integral part of the broader community if Siam was to become a prosperous, civilized nation like those in the West.

This notion of increased social recognition for women was advanced by various male commentators, perhaps none more prominent than *Luang* Wichit Wathakan, a leading middle-class intellectual and popular historian who was to play a major role in formulating official notions of Thai identity in the following decades.[17] One of Wichit's earliest public broadcasts on Siam's fledgling radio network, made toward the end of 1930, was devoted to the subject of women. Wichit told his audience that although women were physically the "weaker sex" (*phet 'on ae*), he believed that they were just as capable as men and (although weaker) were tougher and had greater will power.

If we consider the historical record [*tha rao cha ral'uk th'ung phongsawadan*] and compare the qualities of kings and queens in the past, it will be seen that of ten kings
only six were truly resolute, while four of them were weak-willed. In contrast, out of
ten queens some eight were resolute, determined individuals, with only two lacking
such qualities.[18]

When Wichit cites the "historical record" here, it is not entirely clear if he
meant that concerning Siam, or if he was referring to a more generalized view of
the past which incorporated historical figures from a range of countries. Be that
as it may, the argument he advanced was unambiguous; in terms of resolve and
determination, women were seen as superior to men. Having made this point,
Wichit went on to assert that the degree to which a country could be considered
as "civilized" was directly related to the "rights" which women enjoyed. "A
country in which women have many rights" he said, "is a country that has
achieved significant progress." If, on the other hand, a country granted its wom-
enfolk few rights and treated them as if they were slaves, it was "immoral and
tainted with selfishness."[19] Without explicitly criticizing the situation in Siam
the subtext to Wichit's remarks was that for his homeland to progress and
become a civilized country it was necessary that women be accorded greater
rights and respect than was presently the case.

This notion of linking the position of women to broader developments in society was underscored in the following graphic (fig. 5.4) which appeared in 1927,
a time when public debate on the question of political reform had come to the
fore.[20]

A coy young woman sits on a bench chatting with a suitor. Her hat is
inscribed with the word "parliament/people's assembly" (*sapha ratsad'on*) while
the man's suit bears the label *phonlam'uang*, "Mr. Citizen" as it were. Their conversation goes as follows:

Man: I've tried speaking to your father (for permission to marry), but he
          didn't say a word, he just shook his head.
Woman: If that's so, haven't you given up hope of marrying me?

The cartoon is a political allegory. Here popular desire for a more representative,
egalitarian polity (embodied by "Miss Democracy") is thwarted. The problem
lies with the unseen father who represents the monopolization of power and
authority under the absolute monarchy. Conceived of more generally, the cartoon stands as a metaphor for the type of class and gender ferment of the period,
revolving around the expression of new sociopolitical aspirations. That a female
is used as a symbol for "democracy" (i.e., plurality, greater equality, and freedom)
is telling in that it reflects a point of connection, a relationship between the
struggle for popular sovereignty in political terms and a concern with transforming the place of Siamese women in national life.

Effecting such change, however, was fraught with great difficulty.

เขา ผู้ชาย " ฉันได้ตรอง พูด กับ คุณแม่ เรขแล้ว ไม่เห็น
ท่านว่ากระไร เปนแต่อั้น ศีรษะ "
เขา ผู้หญิง " ถ้าเช่นนั้น มิเปน อันว่า หมด หวังไซ รัว
กอัน หรือ ฉะ ? "

Fig. 5.4. Sayam riwiw, 4 July 1927

RESISTING WOMEN'S ADVANCES

While there was a growing recognition of the need to allow women greater freedom and opportunity among sections of the male population, there was also a
great deal of resistance to any changes to the status quo. In this regard we may
consider a few specific instances of the opposition women faced when they
attempted to extend their educational and employment aspirations into areas
dominated by men.

At the end of 1920 six young women applied to study at the Law College, an
all-male institution run under the auspices of the Ministry of Justice that provided training for most of the kingdom's leading officials and administrators. A
journalist, commenting on their applications in the popular daily *Sayam rat*,
wrote, "on the surface this is rather strange news [*khao plaek*]; however, if one
thinks carefully, it is not really so unusual. After all, the present era is one in
which the country is progressing and everyone, both men and women, has the
right to independence and equality [*mi sit thi cha dai rap khwam-itsaraphap samoe-
na kan thang burut lae satri*]."[21] The writer was strongly supportive of the initiative
and said that women were "by nature more eloquent, incisive and thorough than
men." Such qualities, he added, would make them "good legal advocates." Notwithstanding this assessment, the women's submission was rejected. The authori-

ties argued that it was morally inappropriate for young women students to fraternize with male students, and claimed that close proximity between the sexes posed a threat to the propriety of the institution. Shortly afterward a number of other women sought admission to the college but their applications were also turned down for the same reason.[22] This drew the ire of some observers, with one writer venting her outrage (something no doubt felt by many other educated women) by asserting that the authorities "do not want women to know about the law. Indeed, the government doesn't love its daughters at all; instead it prefers its sons to go on harassing and abusing them."[23]

That opposition to women studying the law was framed in moral terms is revealing. By attempting to expand their educational horizons to encompass the law, a domain that underpinned male power and privilege, women were portrayed as posing a danger to the existing order of things. In effect the authorities had acted to safeguard male dominance by reaffirming traditionalist, metaphysical conceptions of the world in which women, especially young sexually attractive women, were regarded as having the potential to undermine and threaten men's moral integrity.[24]

A similar form of moral censure was also applied to women seeking to enter male-dominated fields of employment. Male anxiety and concern about women wanting to do this was underscored in 1929, for example, when a woman by the name of Charuaywilawia Lilachat sought to obtain a taxi driver's license. As it turned out, however, her request was turned down by officials who refused to accept the idea of a female taxi driver. This decision was enthusiastically endorsed by a columnist for *Sikrung* who wrote, "It is not right that women, who serve the nation as mothers, should be allowed to drive taxis." According to him women were "easily flustered, nervous, and prone to accidents," factors that made them unsuited to such work. He also claimed that "womanizers would harass them, making it difficult to drive straight, other men would tease them and play practical jokes, and the threat of robbery would be an ever-present danger." Furthermore, he pointed out that the word "taxi" had highly negative connotations in the minds of many men who associated it with commercialized sexual activity. Indeed, the writer even went so far as to suggest that "if the government permitted women to drive taxis they would turn to prostitution, and life in Bangkok would become as evil and sordid as it was in the last days of Rome."[25]

Bizarre as this comment may seem, it exemplifies the type of hostility women commonly faced when they sought to enter male-dominated realms of activity. For a great many men, women's roles in society were conceived of in exceedingly narrow terms: positively on the one hand, as mothers and bearers of children, or negatively on the other as temptresses or objects of sexual desire. At the same time, those women who were determined to seek work were faced with a very limited choice of socially appropriate occupations. According to one writer the only acceptable jobs for women at the time were school teacher, nurse, telephone receptionist, or shop assistant in a store.[26] Of course what was meant here was that these were the only acceptable forms of work to be taken up by respectable, educated women. Meanwhile increasing numbers of lower-class women, who scarcely figured in the thinking of their social superiors, worked in Bangkok's small but growing industrial sector (which included match factories and dyeing shops), or were self-employed as seamstresses, street vendors, and various other occupations that required little or no schooling.

Against this background we may now move on to examine the debate on female education and employment carried out in the popular press.

DEBATING FEMALE EDUCATION
AND EMPLOYMENT

In 1915 the women's magazine *Satri niphon* published an article entitled "The Problem of Female Education." The article, which was almost entirely devoted to remarks made by Prince Chainat, noted that the question of female education was a continuing topic of discussion among sections of upper-class Bangkok society.[27] This discussion, however, did not take place in the public forum afforded by print but rather was carried on in private, at the personal level. Like a growing number of his peers the prince wrote that some form of female education was essential. In this regard he was supportive of the then dominant view that held that male and female education should be of a fundamentally different charac-ter—the former designed with a public, administrative role for graduates in mind with the latter purely conceived of in terms of teaching students some domestic skills. While he felt that there would be no need to change this approach for a "long time," he predicted, "At some point in the future problems with regard to differences between boys' and girls' education will most certainly arise."[28]

As it turned out, the prince's prediction came to pass, although perhaps some-what sooner than he may have anticipated. By the early 1920s female education had emerged as a frequent topic of debate in the press. In 1922, for example, it was the central theme in the editorial of the first issue of the women's magazine *Satri sap*. The editor of the magazine sharply criticized the government's han-dling of female education.[29] She said that as things stood girls and young women were at a clear disadvantage compared to their male counterparts. In particular she noted that the existing system provided girls with only three years of primary education compared to five years for boys. At the secondary level the situation was similarly inequitable; girls received six years of secondary schooling whereas boys' high school education continued for an additional two years.

In developing an argument against these educational disparities she reiterated the words of an unnamed official who had said: "Whatever boys are capable of studying, so are girls; this is a view held in all civilized countries." At the same time, she also pointed out that there were some men who held the view that "if girls received the same education as boys it would harm the nation." She dismissed this notion as absurd, citing the comments of another official who insisted that "the future strength and prosperity of any country is dependent on equality between men and women." Endorsing this view, the editor rounded off her discussion by posing the following questions: "Isn't it time that girls received the same schooling as boys? Moreover, without promoting education in this way, where will the nation's future vitality come from?"[30]

At roughly the same time, the theme of female education and the nation was taken up by Phramat, a commentator writing for the mainstream daily newspaper *Sayam sakkhi*. According to him, "the vigor and energy of a nation lies with its citizens [*phonlam'uang*], and by citizens here I mean both men and women. As yet, however, women are not really allowed to participate in national life even though their ability is clearly there for us to see."[31] He claimed that there were various reasons why women in Siam were not given the opportunity to participate in the public domain: fathers prevented their daughters from receiving an education, husbands did not allow their wives to study or work, teachers were opposed to girls studying the same subjects as boys, and there was a failure on the part of government to provide women with the same employment opportunities as men. Phramat said that women were only allowed to work in the home, a practice which, he said, impeded "the economic development of the nation." To overcome this problem, he argued that it was necessary for the economic power of women to be unleashed, and suggested that for this to happen the fundamental importance of female education had to be recognized. "If daughters and wives were allowed to study for a career they would, over a period of time, be able to increase household income and no longer be totally dependent on men."[32] While conceding that servants would need to be employed if wives and daughters were to work outside the home, he believed that the cost of hired help would be less than the salaries women earned. In his view the benefits in allowing women to study and pursue a career were twofold; not only would a family be better off financially, but this would also permit such women to acquire the same degree of formal knowledge and expertise as men.

Phramat's observations are of particular interest because of the way in which he develops a linkage between the loosening of male control over women, education, economic growth, and the idea of national progress. In essence he was espousing what may be seen as a bourgeois outlook informed not so much by ideals of equality and justice for women as by the growing importance of the market economy in national life. And when he refers to "women" here, it is clearly not *all* women, but rather specifically those from middle- and upper-class families. The assumption underpinning his argument was that these women could be liberated as long as lower-class women worked for them as servants.

A related argument concerned with female education and employment was the subject of a letter published in Thawat Ritthidet's newspaper *Kammak'on*

(Laborer) early in 1924. The letter, submitted by an anonymous body which referred to itself as the "Siamese Women's Group" (*Khana satri sayam*), criticized the government for its failure to provide educated women with the opportunity to work. The authors pointed out that many women (perhaps including themselves) had gone to school and trained to be nurses or teachers, and were now unemployed.

> When these women finished their studies they ended up stuck at home. "What's the point?" they ask themselves. Young men go to school with the expectation of getting a job, status, and money. But young women who entertain such hopes are badly disillusioned and feel bitter. As things stand a woman's education may be likened to an investment that yields little or no return. What use is this? It needs to be recognized that women, like men, can work for the good of the nation.
>
> The government needs to think about the number of educated women who lie around uselessly all day. What benefit is to be gained in allowing this to continue? The authorities ought to devise ways to utilize these women's talents and abilities for practical purposes; they should also increase the number of girls in school.[33]

In addition to this type of written commentary, cartoonists also addressed the issue in graphic form. In figure 5.5 the cartoonist employs a device with which we are already familiar, the depiction of two contrasting scenes. In scene one on the left, a young woman is shown during her school days proudly holding various objects bearing the names of the subjects she is studying: mathematics, physics, and languages. The second scene represents the woman's post-school experience. She sits on the ground with an abject look on her face; in the background a rat gnaws on her old mathematics bag. The caption beneath reads, "Girls' School

Fig. 5.5. Bangkok kan-m'uang, 20 November 1923

Curriculum," an ironical commentary on the fate of many young women—that at the end of their schooling, they were unable to put their knowledge to any practical use.

Another cartoon (fig. 5.6), which appeared on the cover of the feminist magazine *Satri thai* in 1926, takes up the same theme, albeit somewhat more bluntly. A young woman sits at home rocking a child's cradle. The text above the image reads "A female student after she's finished her studies. When will the government show some sympathy toward women like this who have no work? Why the hell study up to the seventh or eighth grade at high school?"[34]

The sense of frustration and anger conveyed by the graphic is clear: sections of the young educated female populace were dissatisfied with officialdom and not content to simply accept the traditional role of childbearing, as their mothers had done. Instead they wanted the opportunity to use their learning and ability to forge a career.

At the same time, however, there were educated young women, especially those from more well-to-do backgrounds, who had markedly different aspirations. As one commentator of the period somewhat cynically suggested in the cartoon depicted in figure 5.7, such women were not so much interested in pursuing a career as indulging in leisurely pursuits, such as getting dressed up, promenading about, or traveling around in automobiles or motorboats.

More generally there were a great many other women who did not see themselves either in terms of being salaried employees or as leading a carefree existence devoid of substance or responsibility. A typical counterargument against

Fig. 5.6. Satri thai, 5 July 1926

Fig. 5.7. Sayam rat, 1 December 1923

the idea of seeking paid employment was advanced by a reader, Pikunsot na Thonburi, in a letter published by *Satri thai*. She said that it was not necessary for women to have the same degree of schooling or knowledge as men. In her opinion the most important thing a woman could do was to be a "good house-wife."

> A housewife can be compared to food that nourishes the family. If the food is rotten it will poison whoever partakes of it. Conversely, whenever a family has a good and competent woman there will be happiness and joy. Indeed, such a woman would be lauded as "Queen of the Home" [*ratchini haeng ban*].
>
> These days, however, it is very difficult for women to become good housewives because most of them despise the very idea of housework. Instead they employ slaves and paid servants [*that lae luk-chang*] to take care of things.
>
> In the past they used to say "don't trust other people, depend on yourself." People in whom you place the greatest trust are those who are most liable to betray you later on. Therefore every Thai woman should try to be a good housewife before going on to do other things.[35]

In comparing a housewife with food, Miss Pikunsot echoed what Thianwan had said a quarter of a century earlier when he likened a wife to fertilizer that provided nourishment to her husband.[36] However, unlike Thianwan (who gave unqualified support for girls' schooling), she elided the significance of female education altogether by reaffirming the traditional view that a woman's place was in the home. Clearly, while the notion of a woman working and gaining greater independence was on the rise, it had yet to find general acceptance.

At this point it is instructive to look more closely at an extended debate concerned with female education and employment carried out in the mass-circulation daily *Sikrung* during the latter stages of absolutist rule. Although this retraces some of the same ground already covered, it is useful insofar as it provides us with a clear and succinct overview of the way these issues were commonly discussed.

THE *SIKRUNG* PRESS DEBATE
ON FEMALE EDUCATION

Early in 1930 the editor of *Sikrung* urged readers to write in and respond to the question "Should Thai women receive the same type of education as males?" (*ying thai khuan dai-rap kan-s'uksa thao chai r'u plao?*) According to one commentator this exercise was designed to remind "the government to pay greater attention to women and improve their honor and status."[37]

The first in a series of reader's letters to be published was by a woman writing under the pseudonym Arun. She began by hypothesizing that if the minister of education was asked about the current state of female education he would respond by saying that numerous advances were being made and insist that he was "very attentive to the issue of girls' schooling." However, as Arun wrote, "If this were true, women would be very fortunate indeed. Regrettably, the actual situation is very different."[38] She took particular exception to men who were of the opinion that Siamese women could not compete with their Western counterparts either as housewives or in their ability to socialize in public. Here it seems that she was referring primarily to well-to-do males with some experience of Europeans, although one can also imagine that other men may have formed such a view through exposure to Western films or reading translations of foreign prose fiction. While Arun conceded that Siamese women could be compared unfavorably with those in the West on these grounds, she argued that this was entirely due to the fact that "Siamese men did not give women the same degree of freedom [*seriphap*] as European men." She went on to say:

> When I talk of freedom here, I mean more than anything else the freedom to study. When women attempt to study law or medicine, try to learn how to drive a car or use machinery, men prevent them from doing so. In other words they won't give women the same degree of freedom to study as they allow themselves. Are men afraid that if women became more knowledgeable they would no longer be able to

control them? Or are they scared that an educated woman might cast aspersions on their abilities and thereby have a negative impact on the administration of the country?[39]

She accused men who failed to allow women the same educational opportunities as themselves of being "cowardly, selfish individuals." Siam, she wrote, "had reached a stage in which it was vitally important that women be given the same type of education as men. Indeed, the future of the country depends more on women than men, for women are the ones who will raise and instruct the up-coming generation."[40]

One response to Arun's contribution came from W'o Ch'o Yuwanatemi, a male correspondent who countered Arun's argument by posing the following questions: "If she received the same education as a man would the cost be worth it? Would she use the knowledge gained through study to pursue a career? And finally, does she have the strength and endurance to work like a man?"[41] "Absolutely not!" was his own emphatic response. Advancing an argument that was hardly unique to Siam, he asserted that women were by "nature" (*thammachat*) physically weak and possessed of unstable, capricious emotions. "Even if a woman did receive an education," he wrote, "her value as a worker would not be equal to that of a man." He also wondered if Arun had considered the problem of who would look after the children when a working woman married? "When would a working woman with children find the time to cope with this task?" he mused, suggesting that she would have her husband assume this duty: "Isn't it just delightful that *Mae* Arun would have us reverse men's and women's roles?" As an alternative, he said, servants might be employed to look after the children while the mother was off at work; this, however, was a prospect he viewed with alarm, claiming that such a development would have a detrimental effect on the psychological and attitudinal development of the child with potentially dire consequences in the future. Expressing what may be described as a form of patri-archal nationalism, W'o Ch'o Yuwanatemi wrote in conclusion:

> In my opinion the government should not allow women to receive an education equal to that of men. In addition to the negative consequences I have already men-tioned there are many other related problems that need not be discussed here. Ide-ally, female education should be limited to the study of morality, domestic skills, and first-aid. Furthermore they would require a rudimentary knowledge of reading and writing. Anything beyond this is absolutely superfluous.
>
> Women shouldn't try to imitate those in the West or Japan. These countries have already progressed. It would be more to the point if our women considered them-selves as Thai, not as foreigners. To slavishly follow in the path of other people would be a disaster both for our women and for the country at large.[42]

In sharp contrast to W'o Ch'o's views, another male contributor to the debate writing under the name Taphiangth'ong, supported Arun's position. Taphiangth'ong said that there were many different kinds of men who, largely out of fear, were opposed to improving the status of women. Some of them, he added, were actually "well-intentioned" but had a poor understanding of women and of their abilities.[43] He made the point that there had always been knowledgeable, accomplished women in society. "During the early Buddhist era, for example, women were ordained into the monkhood, the reason being that the Lord Buddha believed that they were capable of understanding the sacred *dhamma* [*Phra-phutthachao song hen wa phu-ying at ru tham wiset dai*]."[44] An awareness of this, Taphiangth'ong suggested, would serve not only to remind men as to the value of women but also to encourage them to cooperate with their female compatriots for the good of the nation.

Other male participants in the debate expressed a range of opinions which fell somewhere in between those voiced by W'o Ch'o Yuwanatemi and Taphiangth'ong. One such contributor, Worawan, agreed with the latter, saying that women should be provided with the same type of education as men "for the good of the nation."[45] However, his support was qualified in that he believed that the notion of "education" should not be conceived of in narrow terms and simply equated with formal schooling. According to him this type of learning alone was not sufficient. "We must also rely on the home to produce good children. Women play the most vital role in this process by instructing their children and teaching them appropriate forms of behavior. If women are not educated they will not be able to carry out this duty. And should that happen, how could the children possibly become good citizens?"[46]

A similar view was expressed by another contributor, Somphong. He said that education enhanced a woman's prospects of employment and noted, "If a married woman used her knowledge to get a job . . . it would benefit her family enormously. The most obvious examples of this are those women who work as midwives, merchants, and traders. In the future, however, I imagine there will also be women doctors and lawyers."[47] He also pointed out that an educated woman would be in the position to take up employment and support her family in the event that her husband fell ill or died. At the same time, he said that although women should have the same opportunities to study as men, it was essential that they also became well versed in domestic skills. In other words, the traditional role of a woman was to be preserved no matter what.

A somewhat more curious view on the issue of female education was expressed by S'o Sawatsawang. His contribution to the debate began with the following statement: "All people, regardless of who they are, or whether they are male or female, feel as though they have little worth or meaning if they do not receive an adequate education. The uneducated son or daughter of a millionaire, for example, is less of a human being than an ordinary person who has studied at school."[48]

He then moved on to the specific issue of female education. "Before marrying, women should not be allowed to fritter away their time, as is so often the case, on frivolous matters such as getting dressed up and putting on make-up. They should go to school and study whatever they like, whether this be basic, practical subjects or more advanced areas of learning such as medicine and law."[49]

After presenting this seemingly enlightened, liberal view, however, S'o came to the central thrust of his argument, which was that women's education should be seen as an end in itself. For a woman to receive an education was, in his view, akin to being awarded a badge of honor, something to be proud of and treasured, but little else.

> Those women who complete their studies should not expect to go off and compete with men. Thus if they happened to study law they should not expect to be judges or lawyers like men, as this sort of work is unsuited to their sex.
>
> Admittedly, it's true that people should work in an area that is related to what they have studied. But it is more appropriate if this prerogative is given to men. Siamese women should not think that they can do whatever men can do. Rather they should think about doing something that men can't do.[50]

And what couldn't men do? The answer was simple; they could not be house-wives, a role that S'o insisted was the most important duty of a woman. Indeed, he went so far as to say that the duties of a housewife were so many and varied that "even if you employed a well-educated man on a wage of two to three hun-dred baht a month he wouldn't be able to cope."[51] Given this, S'o argued that a woman's true place was in the home adding that, "if a woman was insufficiently schooled in the art of housekeeping . . . she would be useless."[52]

Unsurprisingly, most of the women who participated in the debate took a very different view of things. One correspondent, Ruchirek, advanced what may be described as a developmentalist position. She said that those countries which had already advanced had done so as a result of *both* their male and female popu-lations receiving a comprehensive education. In Siam, however, education was still primarily designed with males in mind, a fact which she claimed limited the extent to which the nation could progress. Ruchirek was of the opinion that for the situation to change it was necessary to impress upon men the vital national functions already being performed by women, functions which included produc-ing the nation's population, providing children (the nation's future citizens) with appropriate values and knowledge, and working in the bureaucracy as tele-phonists, teachers, nurses, and midwives.[53] Nonetheless, she saw this as just a beginning. Now it was time for the Ministry of Education to involve itself directly and ensure that girls received the same type of schooling as boys in order that "the vitality of the nation will grow without end."[54]

Yuwadi, another contributor to the discussion, also argued strongly in favor of equal educational opportunities for women. She began by acknowledging that some things had changed in this regard; for example, a recent decision by the Ministry of Education extended girls' high school education to eight years, the same length of time as that of boys. Yet despite this she stressed that girls' educational choices were still severely limited, restrictions which she said must be done away with. Like Arun, Yuwadi drew attention to what she perceived to be the major factor inhibiting change—men who believed that if women were given equal educational opportunities it "would diminish their [men's] honor and intellectual standing."[55] She said such men were seriously mistaken and claimed that they "just wanted to keep on taking advantage of women by denying them their freedom." To this she added: "Men need to realize that women, like themselves, can contribute toward the good of the nation both in normal times and during periods of crisis (at this point Siam was beginning to feel the effects of the Great Depression). So, isn't it time for the government to allow women to receive the same education as men?"[56]

Yuwadi, like Arun and Ruchirek, also drew attention to the issue of women studying the law. She was acutely aware that the law, which provided a formal framework delineating social and political rights, obligations, and privileges, was intimately bound up with the exercise of power (kan pok-khr'ong). As such she saw the law as one of the most important areas of higher learning and said that young women should be allowed to pursue legal studies. She sought to justify her argument by pointing out that women in Western countries were permitted to study the law, and she urged the government, in the interests of the nation, to adopt a similar approach. In advancing this view Yuwadi added yet another voice to the ongoing struggle by women to pursue legal studies which had been underway since 1920.

Discussion of the law here leads us to the subject of the next chapter. As will be recalled, the practice of polygamy, sanctioned by the kingdom's marriage laws, had come under criticism during the earlier protofeminist era. However, it was not until the 1920s that this issue really came to the fore. Indeed, as we shall see, it was at this time that the continuation of Siam's marriage laws emerged as the most hotly debated issue in the struggle for equality between men and women.

NOTES

1. *Satri thai*, 29 March 1926.
2. *Sayam rat*, 12 November 1920, 8 April 1922, 11 July 1922, 8 May 1923, 13 March 1924.
3. David Marr, *Vietnamese Tradition on Trial: 1920–1945* (Berkeley: University of California Press, 1981), 214.

4. Hua R. Lan and Vanessa Fong, eds., *Women in Republican China: A Sourcebook* (New York: M.E. Sharpe, 1999), xiv.

5. Lan and Fong, *Women in Republican China*, xiv. While men dominated much of the proceedings there were also significant contributions by women, both as writers and activists committed to practical change.

6. In Vietnam during the 1920s there was a similar broad distinction between those of a moderate feminist persuasion and those holding traditional views in the debate on women's issues. Marr, *Vietnamese Tradition*, 191.

7. *Sayam rat*, 16 December 1920; *Statistical Yearbook of Siam*, 1933–1935, 28–29.

8. Marr, *Vietnamese Tradition*, 206.

9. For the period from 1915 to 1925 the figures for male education were as follows: In 1915 there were 128,129 boys in school across the kingdom, this number growing to 385,808 boys and young men ten years later. At this time (1925), 19,835 young men were studying at the secondary level compared to the figure of 3,277 young women. In addition it was recorded that there were 318 male students enrolled at Chulalongkorn University where, as noted, there were also 68 female students. At the same time, however, a larger number of young men were also studying in institutions of advanced learning attached to various government ministries, for example, the Military Training College run by the Ministry of Defense and the Law College operated by the Ministry of Justice. *Statistical Year Book* (1933–1935), 28–29.

10. Some 191 new periodicals appeared in the decade after 1916. Matthew Copeland, "Contested Nationalism and the 1932 Overthrow of the Absolute Monarchy in Siam," Ph.D. Diss., Australian National University, Canberra, 1993, 54.

11. Suwadee notes the existence of *Nari chaleng* but tells us next to nothing about the paper in her study. Suwadee Tanaprasitpatana, "Thai Society's Expectations of Women, 1851–1935," Ph.D. diss., Sydney University, 1989, 210.

12. While I was unable to locate the last two of this list of publications during my research in Thailand they are mentioned in Suwadee, "Thai Society's Expectations," 210.

13. The proprietor, manager, and editor of *Satri-sap* was Miss Pha-'ob Phongsichan (*Satri sap*, 22 September 1922). *Satri thai* (also referred to in English as *The Ladies Friend Classic Weekly* on its masthead) was owned and edited by Miss Chalaem Chirasuk, managed by Mrs. Phat Phaophaet, with a Miss S'ongsi employed as an adviser (*Satri thai*, 1 March 1926). *Nari kasem* was owned and edited by M'om Luang-ying Wanida Chumsai na Ayuthaya and managed by M'om Ratchawong-ying Ch'unchit Nanthisak na Ayuthaya, with Miss Wichian Chupanya employed as the paper's secretary (*Nari kasem*, 1 October 1926). *Nari nithet* was owned, managed, and edited by (Mrs./Miss) Sut Thammasan with a Miss Niam Nathachira as her assistant editor (*Nari nithet*, 1 May 1926). No details are available regarding the owner or staff at the daily *Ying sao*. The owner and editor of *Sayam yuphadi* was Mrs. Tangkui Limmongkhon; the paper was managed by Miss Pradap Emkamon (*Sayam yuphadi*, 27 October 1928). *Suphap nari* was owned by Mrs. Chan Tiawbunl'u. The principal members of staff included her daughter, Miss Chom Tiawbunl'u (editor), Miss Th'ongdam Singth'ong (secretary), and Miss Ari Asakit (manager) (*Suphap nari*, 14 March 1930). Both the owner and the editor of *Ying sayam* were men, Wong L'owichit and Sanan Phakdiwong (*Ying sayam*, 3 October 1930).

14. *Satri thai*, 1 March 1926.

15. *Satri thai*, 5, 12, 26 July 1926; 2, 9, 16, 22, 30 August 1926.

16. *Nari kasem*, 1 October 1926.

17. See Scot Barmé, *Luang Wichit Wathakan and the Creation of a Thai National Identity* (Singapore: Institute of Southeast Asian Studies, 1993).

18. *Luang* Wichit Wathakan, "Phuying" [Women], text of radio broadcast by Wichit on 3 November 1930, in *Pathakatha lae kham banyai* [Lectures and Talks, vol. 2] (Bangkok: Soemwit Bannakhan, 1973), 91.

19. *Luang* Wichit Wathakan, "Phuying," 94.

20. Copeland, "Contested Nationalism," 145–58.

21. *Sayam rat*, 16 December 1920.

22. At the same time, however, as noted above, a small number of women were permitted to study medicine at Chulalongkorn University.

23. *Satri thai*, 20 June 1927. As things turned out, it was not until the 1930s that Siamese women were permitted to study law locally. In the latter 1920s, however, a handful of women went to the Philippines to pursue legal studies.

24. B. J. Terwiel, *Monks and Magic: An Analysis of Religious Ceremonies in Central Thailand* (London: Curzon Press, 1979), 93, 274.

25. *Sikrung*, 9 March 1929.

26. *Satri thai*, 20 June 1927.

27. *Satri niphon*, September 1915, 152–57.

28. *Satri niphon*, September 1915, 157.

29. *Satri sap*, 15 September 1922.

30. *Satri sap*, 15 September 1922.

31. *Sayam sakkhi*, 26 June 1922.

32. *Sayam sakkhi*, 26 June 1922.

33. *Kammak'on*, 19 January 1924.

34. *Satri thai*, 5 July 1926.

35. *Satri thai*, 3 May 1926.

36. "If a man attains strength, property, wisdom and knowledge, and if he can additionally acquire a capable wife as his companion, she can be compared with a useful fertilizer which will help a good plant to flourish, extend its trunk, and produce flowers and fruits." Quoted in Suwadee, "Thai Society's Expectations," 117.

37. *Sikrung*, 1 January 1930.

38. *Sikrung*, 1 January 1930.

39. *Sikrung*, 1 January 1930.

40. *Sikrung*, 1 January 1930.

41. *Sikrung*, 10 January 1930.

42. *Sikrung*, 10 January 1930.

43. *Sikrung*, 14 January 1930.

44. *Sikrung*, 14 January 1930.

45. *Sikrung*, 7 January 1930.

46. *Sikrung*, 7 January 1930.

47. *Sikrung*, 6 January 1930.

48. *Sikrung*, 9 January 1930.

49. *Sikrung*, 9 January 1930.

50. *Sikrung*, 9 January 1930. Two hundred to 300 baht represented a considerable salary at the time, equivalent to that earned by an upper-middle-level bureaucrat.

51. *Sikrung*, 9 January 1930.
52. *Sikrung*, 9 January 1930.
53. *Sikrung*, 21 January 1930.
54. *Sikrung*, 21 January 1930.
55. *Sikrung*, 18 January 1930.
56. *Sikrung*, 18 January 1930.

6

❧

A Question of Polygamy

A nyone with more than a passing interest in contemporary Thailand knows that talk about major and minor wives (*mia luang mia n'oi*) is one of the most common and avidly discussed topics in informal conversation and gossip; indeed, interest in the intimate goings-on of other people's lives, whether they be high-profile figures (politicians, business people, those in the entertainment industry, and even royalty) or more ordinary folk, is—like talk about food— something of a national obsession. This particular fascination is reflected in the countless films, novels, short stories, and television soap operas that incorporate themes dealing with the complex and difficult relations between major and minor wives and the men in their lives. In 1999, for example, a TV adaptation of Kritsana Asokesin's 1960s novel *Major Wife* (*Mia luang*), was one of the most watched programs of the year. Kritsana's story about the trials and tribulations of Dr. Wikanda Phanphak'on in coping with the philandering behavior of her husband, Dr. Anirit Sanlawit, was of such appeal that, although the TV series was produced three decades after the original, the relevance of the topic was, if anything, greater than ever.[1]

The present chapter focuses on an earlier age—the 1920s—when the question of polygamy and multiple wives emerged as the most passionately discussed issue in the national debate about equality between the sexes. While equal access to education and paid employment primarily concerned women from the middle and upper classes, the question of marriage and the existing laws which sanc- tioned polygamy affected women across the social spectrum. Polygamy, a practice closely identified with the royal-noble elite, came to be seen by its opponents not only as fundamentally unjust but also as a symbol of Siam's backwardness. In examining various critiques of polygamy, or more specifically the law which allowed a man to have more than one wife, it will be shown that critics viewed it not only as iniquitous, archaic and uncivilized, but also as something which

157

was at the root of various social problems, in particular the spread of prostitution and venereal disease.

SOCIOCULTURAL MORES AND VALUES: THE SEXUAL DOUBLE STANDARD

In premodern Siam subordination of women to men was enshrined in law and religious ideology. As *Chaophraya* Thiphak'orawong pointedly noted in his late-nineteenth-century tract "Defence of Polygamy," women were also regarded as being subordinate to men sexually. Thiphak'orawong drew a sharp distinction between normative male and female behavior, asserting that it was the role of a man to initiate sexual contact while the role of a women was to passively acquiesce.[2] In other words, the right to have sex was regarded as a wholly male prerogative.

Specific sociocultural values with respect to male and female sexuality were also encoded in common expressions used to refer to women's and men's first experience of sexual intercourse. Traditionally, great importance was placed on an unmarried female's virginity, sometimes referred to as her "treasure" or "wealth" (*sombat*). As noted earlier, the *Law of the Three Seals* specified that if an unmarried woman was physically violated, and this included touching (any part of the body), hugging, or kissing, her parents were to be financially compensated in line with the nature of the particular offense. A woman's loss of virginity—her *khwam-borisut* or "purity"—was referred to by the expression *sia tua* (a term that remains in contemporary usage), which, when translated literally, means "spoiled body" (or perhaps to have *lost* one's body to another's love/lust). Clearly, a woman's loss of virginity outside of matrimony was seen to have negative connotations.

A man's loss of virginity, by contrast, was conceived of rather differently. In having his first experience of intercourse a man was said to *kh'un khru* (another expression that remains in contemporary usage) meaning "to go up to or approach the teacher" or "get onto the teacher," a figure of speech which suggests that it was the norm for a man to be on top of a woman when having sex. It also implies that men commonly were initiated into sex by a woman practiced in the art of lovemaking, that is, a prostitute. Thus, unlike women, men's extramarital loss of virginity was viewed as an educational experience rather than an act that polluted their bodies.

Here it may be noted that there were apparently graphic sex manuals produced in the Ayuthayan period (perhaps something akin to the *Kama Sutra*) to provide young men with guidance; these texts, however, were presumably of limited circulation among the elite.[3] Moving forward in time to the early twentieth century we learn from the rather frank (at least by the standards of modern Thai public discourse) personal memoirs by the late film actor S'o Atsanachinda that during the 1920s and 1930s information about sex was not readily available. "In the past," he wrote, "morality was strict and the 'matter of sex' was generally regarded as being 'top secret' " (*thi m'uang thai samai k'on khreng nai silatham— pokati 'r'uang phet' pen 'khwam-lap sut y'ot'*).[4] Consequently young men learned next to nothing about sexuality from their elders until they were fully grown. By this time, S'o noted, it was too late as they had already found out by experimenting with masturbation and visiting prostitutes.[5]

In summary, a clearly defined sexual double standard operated in premodern Siam as in so many other societies. Leaving aside the question of homosexuality, a man's promiscuous sexual activity was not condemned or punished unless he slept with an unmarried woman or committed adultery with the wife of another man. The expression of a woman's heterosexuality, on the other hand, was legally and culturally limited to one man within the confines of marriage. One may presume that, given the social value placed on female virtue, women's understanding of their own sexuality was far less developed than that of men, and it seems likely that in general they had little knowledge about heterosexual intimacy until they were married.

THE GOVERNMENT DEBATES POLYGAMY

Polygamy, it will be recalled, first became an issue of public concern in Siam during the latter part of the nineteenth century as the kingdom entered into closer relations with the West. In the process members of the elite developed a keen awareness of European sensibilities and morality. Responding to early Western criticism of polygamy, *Chaophraya* Thiphak'orawong, arguing from a Buddhist perspective, insisted that the practice was in no way immoral and therefore perfectly acceptable within the context of Siamese society.[6] From this point it appears that the matter was not subject to further consideration until the early twentieth century when the government, anxious to reassert full authority in judicial matters within its borders, began a process to reform the legal system along Western lines.[7]

The first stage of legal reform was completed in 1908 with the promulgation of a new Criminal Law Code. This was subsequently followed by preliminary discussions about a proposed Civil and Commercial Code. One of the elements to be included in the code was a family law that, among other things, necessitated a consideration of indigenous marriage customs. In order to facilitate the discussion Mr. L'Evesque, a French legal adviser employed by the Siamese government, was asked to compile all the existing laws relating to the family and marriage. Over the following two years L'Evesque diligently collected a diverse range of materials that were then surveyed by a commission of European jurists headed by Mr. G. Padoux, another French legal adviser engaged by the government.[8]

In December 1910, Padoux presented a memorandum based on the investigations of the committee to Prince Charoon, the acting minister of justice. Padoux's report provides a remarkable picture of the contemporary legal situation regarding marriage in Siam. Indeed, one can do no better than quote him directly.

> The [current law on marriage, dating from 1805] disposes of a list of particular cases, which are of course the commonest, but which leave a large ground uncovered. In most of the sections, several different legal questions are mixed up. The text is therefore not easy to understand, and it is still less easy to discern for which reasons and under which general rule each case is decided.
>
> A great number of points concerning marriage are not decided at all in the [1805 law], nor in the other laws and decrees [the committee has examined]. On the majority of these points we have been unable to find out how the Siamese custom exactly stands. The information collected by us [was at] times inconsistent and contradictory. On several occasions our informants said that there was no law or custom on the point, or that they could not commit themselves so far as to give the point a definite opinion. The lectures delivered by H.R.H. Prince Rabi [one of the sources consulted] have greatly helped us. But Prince Rabi himself states in several parts of his lectures that there are points where law and custom differ, or where the law is insufficient or abstruse, or where there is no law at all.[9]

In concluding his memorandum the French jurist, seemingly overwhelmed by the daunting nature of his commission, suggested that Siamese legal specialists needed to be more directly involved in the process of drafting a new marriage-family law if it was to succeed. The government accepted Padoux's advice and a joint Siamese-European committee, under his leadership, was appointed to further investigate the question of legal reform. By mid-1912 the committee had been able to produce what Prince Charoon considered to be a workable preliminary draft law, one that allowed for the continued practice of polygamy.

A year later, in May 1913, Prince Svasti Sobhon (Sawat), one of Chulalongkorn's brothers, circulated a memorandum in which he criticized the inequities between men and women under the existing Siamese marriage laws. The prince, who had studied law at Oxford University, argued that monogamy should be the central principle in drafting new legislation. His stance, however, was not based on notions of social equality or moral concerns about polygamy, but rather on the image it presented to the outside world. For him the practice gave foreigners the means to "criticize our morality by saying that our law is not of the same standard as the Western laws, thereby bringing disgrace to our country."[10]

The prince's memorandum, in turn, provoked a detailed rejoinder from King Vajiravudh. The king's response, which stressed his impartiality in the matter, began with what appears to be a thinly veiled allusion to his own homosexuality (or perhaps the fact that he was unmarried). "I shall neither gain nor lose by the adoption of either the system of monogamy or polygamy, so I feel that I am competent to state a disinterested opinion on the subject."[11] Unlike the prince, Vajiravudh evinced little concern about disapproving Western attitudes toward polygamy and said that to enshrine monogamy in law while men continued to take numerous wives would amount "to deceiving the world at large" while doing nothing "to enhance the dignity of either the King or the Nation."[12] He also rejected the prince's view that if polygamy ·were permitted by the new law it would indicate that Siam was "on a lower moral plane than that of the Western Nations."[13] Vajiravudh, like Thiphak'orawong over forty years earlier in his "Defense of Polygamy," invoked the notion of cultural relativity, insisting that "our moral plane and that of the Europeans [cannot] . . . be compared with fairness, because they are so different, and it is most difficult to judge who is on the higher plane and who on the lower."[14] The institution of polygamy, Vajiravudh emphasized, was "deep-rooted" in Siamese society, and he suggested that if monogamy were introduced by law the concept would not be understood in the European sense since "minor wives would still consider themselves to be 'wives' . . . even though they may have ceased to entertain any affection for the men."[15] Furthermore, he argued that the introduction of monogamy would create serious problems with regard to the legal status of children. While admitting that many children were "not acknowledged by their fathers" under the present system, he claimed that "a law requiring monogamy would only worsen the situation as *any* children born outside such a union would not be recognized by law." By contrast, he indicated that the existing system was somewhat more equitable since it allowed for offspring born to minor wives to be accorded formal recognition by their fathers.[16]

At the same time, Vajiravudh was not blind to the personal misery often associated with polygamy, noting that "in general, women who become minor wives . . . or secret wives . . . are very unhappy."[17] He was also well aware that such women were frequently abandoned by their husbands, with "many of them turning to prostitution out of necessity."[18] Yet despite acknowledging some of the negative consequences of polygamy, Vajiravudh, supported by most of his ministers, expressed the view that the practice should continue. However, he believed the present situation could be improved and suggested that a system requiring men to register their wives be introduced. This proposed initiative was based on the modest hope that it "would serve in a small measure to protect girls from being deceived (and forced into prostitution), for at least a girl would always have the means of proving the seriousness of a man's intentions toward herself, and whether he really meant to give her the status of a wife or not."[19]

Ultimately the king's suggestion did not come to much, although it seems that some form of marriage registration was eventually introduced for members of the palace staff and military officers.[20] Official debate on reforming the legislation more generally went unresolved and discussion of the matter, which it should be emphasized was conducted in private high-level meetings, appears to have lapsed completely, and the existing laws (as collated by Padoux), continued in force. While the question of polygamy was taken up again for debate by high-ranking officials during Prajadhipok's reign, resistance to change among members of the old elite remained strong and no substantive reforms were instituted by the absolutist administration.[21] Given that men dominated the official debate, this was perhaps hardly surprising.

THE POPULAR DEBATE ON POLYGAMY

Women's Views

> A major factor in determining whether a particular country will flourish and become civilized is the question of peace and harmony. . . . The family [khr'op-khrua] represents one part of the nation. If there is no peace and harmony in the family, it is unlikely that there will be any peace in the nation.[22]

The above passage, taken from a letter by a woman referring to herself as Th'ong Ch'ua, was published in the newspaper Kammak'on (The Laborer) during the latter part of 1923. In advancing this view the writer voiced an idea similar to that expressed almost ten years earlier by the anonymous author of "Why are Siamese Women so Jealous?" published in Satri niphon (see chapter 1), albeit in a rather more concrete, coherent form. Th'ong Ch'ua drew a metaphorical connection between the home and the nation and, in doing so, questioned the notion of male dominance implicit in this type of formulation (i.e., the father as head of the household analogous to the king as the ruler of the nation). She was of the view that it was the responsibility of both husbands and wives to maintain peace in the home.

> For a husband and wife to be happy and live in contentment there must be love, a sense of unity [khwam samakkhi], and mutual respect. If, however, one party simply thinks of their own interests it is extremely difficult to achieve a peaceful atmosphere in the family. Although love is an intangible thing a woman is unwilling to allow her husband to share his affections with other women. It is unlikely that a man with many wives can give evenly of his love. Indeed, it is hard to imagine that the love of such a man is equal to that of a man in a monogamous marriage.
> [In Siam] a husband will not tolerate another man touching his wife. Women, too have feelings, and they think the same way. [I put it to you that] jealousy leads to arguments and disputes; it threatens the unity of the family. This, in turn, causes growing turbulence which undermines peace and harmony more generally.[23]

While presenting a critical view of men in general for the way they treated their spouses, Th'ong Ch'ua singled out "men of wealth and rank" as being the worst offenders by far. Such men, she claimed, commonly "abused and demeaned their wives as if they were slaves [that]."²⁴ In saying this she denounced the practice of polygamy in class terms, adding another voice to the growing popular nationalist critique of the existing order by portraying the behavior of Siam's rich and powerful men toward their wives as inimical to the country's progress.

A similar theme was also developed, although somewhat differently, by the editor of the women's magazine *Satri thai* early in 1926. According to the editor, the way in which a man acted in his home was an indicator of his true character and how he would behave at work.²⁵ She claimed, for example, that if *Chaokhun K'o* (i.e., *Chaokhun* So and So), a hypothetical member of the male elite, was an even-tempered, reasonable individual at home, in all probability he would also display the same qualities at work. If, on the other hand, he was a mean-spirited fellow who treated his wives, children, or young female servants in a "beastly" fashion, he would most likely be a tyrant at work.²⁶ Love of the nation, she insisted, came from a prior love of the home. In other words, the two spheres were seen as intimately related, with the state of the domestic realm regarded as being of fundamental importance. By way of conclusion the author suggested that men who abused their wives and families should not be permitted to work in government service, claiming that they were the type of people who would "cause the nation to regress rather than progress."²⁷ By choosing to focus her argument on a hypothetical member of the Siamese elite, the editor of the magazine was making what amounted to an overt political statement. In effect, her comments suggested that there were serious problems at the upper levels of the nation's administration and that this could be more fully appreciated when one considered the domestic lives of men from the ruling elite, in particular their treatment of women.

Apart from this type of commentary on male-female relations *Satri thai* regularly featured a cartoon graphic on its cover. These images were nearly always concerned with relations between the sexes, invariably from a perspective highly critical of men. The following cartoon (fig. 6.1), for example, is typical. This particular image focuses on behavior closely associated with members of the urban male elite. Here the cartoonist portrays such men as having "two hearts" (*s'ong chai*), as philanderers with a sexual interest in numerous women. That the man depicted in the graphic is a *phu-yai* is signified not only by the size of his head in relation to the women but also by his domineering, aloof countenance. Beneath the picture the caption serves as a warning to readers, offering young women the following advice: "You must take great care and watch out for men who lack sincerity and are unable to commit themselves." The consequences of entering into a relationship with men of this sort, although unstated by the cartoonist, were devastating, commonly leading to a woman's abandonment and ruin. This type of visual commentary was not only confined to women's publications such as *Satri thai*, however. Consider the cartoon (fig. 6.2) that appeared in the popular daily *Sayam rat* in the early 1920s.

Fig. 6.1. *Satri thai,* 21 June 1926

This graphic, consisting of two scenes, represents a pithy observation about elite male attitudes toward women or, more precisely, young women. In scene one, on the left, a shapely woman stands proudly before a group of enchanted male admirers; the caption beneath reads simply "The beginning." In the second frame we see what is presumably the same woman holding a tiny baby in her arms looking on at a well-dressed, obviously well-to-do, man (the father of the child) as he casually walks off into the distance. The caption below says "later on" (*luang laew*). Here the image of a forlorn young mother signifies the fate of many such women, the cartoon providing a blunt critique of the propensity of upper-class men to regard women as little more than sexual playthings to be cast off at will.

Women commentators commonly saw such behavior on the part of men as a

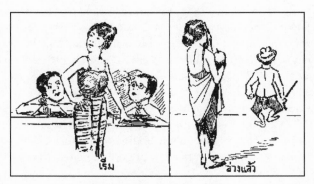

Fig. 6.2. *Sayam rat,* 5 June 1923

consequence of the country's marriage laws. In 1922 one observer, writing under the pseudonym Anrachun, published a two-part essay entitled "The Condition of Thai Women" (*Saphap satri thai*) in the feminist newspaper *Satri sap*. She claimed that "it has now reached the stage where men and women should be accorded equal rights [*sit samoe kan*],"[28] and by "rights" here she meant those concerning marriage. Anrachun noted that while women only had the right to one husband, the law permitted a man to marry as many women as he liked "without the slightest hint of embarrassment." She asked readers to reflect on this situation and then went on to say:

> Who gave men this right? It was the government, wasn't it? Dear sirs in government, don't say that I'm making things up. . . . Why don't you promulgate a law forbidding men who have already married from taking another wife? And if a married man then went and broke the law he should be suitably punished. But you in government [*than ratthaban*] have allowed men to oppress women. . . . This is a fact that can be discerned by anyone with eyes to see.
>
> In civilized countries [*araya prathet*] I know that men and women have equal rights. When a man marries he is not permitted to take another wife. Similarly, a woman is not allowed to be unfaithful to her husband.
>
> Has our government ever considered these principles? If those of you in power have not done so, it must be because you regard yourselves as a government of men for men who take advantage of the opposite sex.[29]

By negatively contrasting the form of marriage in Siam with that in the West the author implied that the royal-noble ruling elite was both uncivilized and oppressive. Further, by characterizing political authority as wholly masculine, geared to serving male (and in particular elite male) interests, Anrachun implied that the government, by sanctioning inequality between the sexes, did not truly represent the national community. By reserving her harshest criticism for upper-class men, Anrachun made a bold political statement expressed both in class (commoner versus elite) and gender (female versus male) terms. In doing so she called the legitimacy of authority into question.

The emphasis in the second part of Anrachun's essay was, by contrast, less overtly political. She sought to develop a critique of the existing law on marriage, the type of male behavior it fostered, and its social costs. She put forward the view that perhaps the greatest evil of the present law was that it allowed men to abandon their wives with impunity and take up with younger women in their place.[30] In such cases, she claimed, men completely forgot about their former wives and left any children from the union to their own fate. She expressed her indignation with this state of affairs in the following terms:

> The dire consequences of what I am talking about are there for all you men to see, both day and night. But then again, maybe you don't notice that the droves of young, wayward boys who hang around outside the cinemas and playhouses are *your*

own sons—do you? And what about the young thirteen- or fourteen-year-old girls
you go off and embrace and fondle in private homes. Perhaps you don't even realise
that they're *your own daughters*—do you?[31]

Drawing attention to the question of such young girls, Anrachun said that the
reason they could be found prostituting themselves was the poverty of their
mothers along with the fact that their fathers had done nothing to provide for
them since they were children.

None of the young girls you find working as prostitutes have fathers who look after
them or provide support. For women in our country the ways of earning a living are
very limited. Should the government do nothing to rectify the situation the numbers of girls going to ruin will increase by a thousand a year and Bangkok will
become [a brothel] like Paris.[32]

This observation is particularly revealing for the way in which the author uses
the "West" as a reference point in developing her critique. Here the "West,"
embodied by the French capital, is characterized in highly negative terms. Earlier
in the same essay, however, it will be recalled that Anrachun had praised the
"West" for its system of monogamous marriage while denouncing Siamese marital practices. This rhetorical strategy of employing various idealized constructions of the "West" in popular debate is what the Chinese scholar Xiaomei Chen
refers to as "occidentalism." Broadly defined, "orientalism" represents "a discursive practice that, by constructing its Western Other, has allowed the Orient to
participate actively and with indigenous creativity in the process of self-appro-
priation."[33] More specifically, Chen notes, "occidentalism is primarily a discourse that has been invoked by various and competing groups within . . . society
for a variety of different ends, largely . . . within domestic . . . politics."[34] While
this observation was made with reference to contemporary Chinese sociopolitical realities, it is a view that is equally applicable to Anrachun's intervention
and the 1920s Siamese popular debate on the status of women and social equality
more generally.

As a vocal advocate for an improvement in the status of women Anrachun
was nonetheless rather pessimistic about the possibility of bringing this about,
suggesting that men tended to be "very thick-skinned and resistant to change."[35]
Indeed, as popular debate and discussion about polygamy intensified during the
1920s, her characterization of men as being firmly set in their ways was often
reflected in the observations and comments they made in the press. At the same
time, however, other men expressed more negative attitudes toward polygamy.
To better appreciate male opinion about the practice it is useful to look in some
detail at a range of views published during 1926 in *Sayam rat*, one of Bangkok's
most popular daily newspapers.

Men on Polygamy

While many women argued that there was an urgent need to reform the kingdom's marriage laws, men often took a more equivocal view by suggesting that
the relationship between the law and marriage was largely irrelevant. According
to "Krasai," the author of an article published in *Sayam rat* entitled "Marriage
Partners" (*khu somrot*), the important thing was that a man and woman were
suitably matched and that both had a similar level of education.[36] He claimed
that if a husband and wife had the same degree of schooling, the woman could
influence her husband in such a way that he would be satisfied with having just
one wife. Another contributor to the debate who used the pseudonym "Cupid"
also believed that reforming the law would not necessarily make for more stable,
durable marriages. While he reproached men who abandoned their wives in favor
of other women, he believed that the notion of personal responsibility rather
than an emphasis on legal reform was the best way of dealing with the problem.
To make his point he quoted what an upper-class female (*than satri*) acquaintance had once told him: "I have no objection to my husband having other
wives; all I ask is that he provides for my needs. If not, there is no way I'd let
him take another woman."[37]

"Upakan," another commentator, expressed a similar view to that of the
authors above but put it in a broader national perspective.

> In my opinion it is beside the point if a man has many wives or just one wife. Rather,
> the whole issue revolves around the individual male and his understanding of the
> value of marriage. If a man has sufficient wealth and authority to prevent trouble in
> his household and maintains a sense of justice in dealing with his wives, I believe
> the system of polygamy has positive benefits in increasing the population. . . . On
> the other hand, if a man has many wives simply for the purpose of self-gratification
> this is of no benefit whatsoever to the nation. And when women find no happiness
> in their husbands they are likely to turn to prostitution.
>
>   I am of the view that the benefit of having many wives is related to one's under-
> standing of what is suitable for the times and what is not. At this stage it is unneces-
> sary for us to rush off and change our customs and traditions when the law does not
> require it and when fortune allows men to have many wives.[38]

This nativist defense of long-standing male practice parallels, in part, the sentiments voiced by Vajiravudh on the matter during the early stages of his reign.

An even stronger endorsement of polygamy came from the writer of a piece
entitled "How Many Wives Should One Have?" (*khuan mi phanraya ki khon*).[39]
The author, who wrote under the pseudonym "King kaew," began by noting that
he was well aware that polygamy had been strongly condemned in both the Thai
and English-language press. Most local commentators, he claimed, were of the
view that the practice reflected badly on Siam's public image. "The continued
existence of polygamy was held to not only to lower the esteem of Thai women

in the eyes of foreigners, but also to make it appear that there was an inordinate amount of sexual desire in Siam." Furthermore, he noted that maintaining a polygamous household was expensive and frequently caused the women involved a great deal of misery. However, notwithstanding these problems, he argued vigorously in favor of polygamy.

> If a country is to progress it first needs to have an extensive population and a certain degree of technological sophistication. The second stage is for a government to make efforts to ensure that the population is well behaved, and not to allow confusion and chaos to develop as has been the case in China. If the first condition is not met, however, that is if a country's population is small, it will only advance slowly. . . . What is really important is that a country has a large population and does not allow foreigners to build up their numbers to such an extent that the local people become marginalized.
>
> At this point Siam is underpopulated in terms of its geographical size. Consequently the practice of polygamy should be seen as something positive since it contributes toward increasing the population and is in accord with government policy.[40]

Although he conceded that polygamy did pose various problems, "King kaew" was of the view that these were of secondary importance and that the practice should be seen as contributing toward the greater good of the Siamese nation.[41] His thinking represents a curious combination of elements. In essence he sought to marry a nativist conception of women's subordination to men to a form of popular ethnic nationalism that was on the rise as Thai anxiety about Chinese immigration and economic power grew.[42] Unlike those who saw polygamy as inhibiting progress, King kaew asserted that the practice served to bolster the nation against encroachments by other ethnic groups as well as facilitating its future development.

Other contributors to the debate derided the view that polygamy was a factor in increasing the nation's population. One such critic, S. Niti, dismissed King kaew's ideas as fanciful. "After all, Siamese men have had the opportunity to have numerous wives for a very long time, yet we still have not achieved the same sort of growth as Japan."[43] In his view the retention of polygamy would do nothing to increase the population in future. On the contrary, he insisted, it was a practice which "instilled ever-increasing sexual excess" among the male population. And like many other observers he was of the view that it was a contributing factor in the growth of the commercial sex trade.[44]

Further criticism of the practice was voiced by "Theri" in an article entitled "Siam, It's Time" (m'uang thai th'ung wela thi khuan laew). Supportive of the idea of equality (khwam samoe-phak) between men and women in marriage, Theri said the widespread instance of men deserting their wives was directly related to the kingdom's marriages laws. He noted that under the existing legislation "if a man tires of a wife he drives her away" and added, "the situation is particularly bad when it came to wealthy, ruthless men who, unconstrained by the law, have limitless opportunities to use women as their playthings."[45] However, while stating that the introduction of a new law instituting monogamy in place of polygamous marriage would be desirable in preventing such behavior, he was of the opinion that it was still not feasible to institute such a change. In saying this he argued that there were various reasons that militated against the introduction of monogamy. First of all he asserted that there was a lack of educated women in society and claimed that only three out of every hundred females had had a formal schooling. Echoing a view similar to that expressed by Krasai and Cupid, he wrote that "if a man was compelled to have but one wife it would be extremely difficult for him to find a woman that would both please him and meet his [intellectual] needs." The second objection he raised to the introduction of monogamy was based on unspecified population statistics which, he said, showed that there were more women in Siam than men. He inferred that, given such a disparity between the numbers of males and females, a law that limited a man to a single wife would prevent some women from ever finding a husband. In addition, he claimed that a change to compulsory monogamy would lead those men who "liked to have lots of wives" to marry one woman then divorce her, take another woman as his wife, and then do the same thing over and over again. This type of wanton behavior, he concluded, would be made all the easier by the fact that an uneducated or poorly educated woman lacked the requisite knowledge to fight any divorce case a husband may initiate against her.[46] As we have already seen, the existing laws were not always readily understood, even by learned jurists.

Recognizing the social value of monogamy in theory yet rejecting its immediate practical implementation, Theri proposed that the existing law should be reformed by requiring men to register each of their wives officially. Unlike Vajiravudh's formulation on registration, however, which maintained the traditional distinctions between major and minor wives, Theri was of the view that *all* registered wives should be regarded as equal under the law. To make the point he wrote that "there should be no exceptions and no limit on the number of wives who could be registered." The effect of introducing legislation along these lines, he suggested, was twofold. First, it "would bring greater justice to women if they were not properly supported or abandoned. A woman in this position could cite the registration of her marriage in any legal proceedings and subsequent property settlements."[47] More generally, he believed that such a change would have the effect of "dissuading lust-crazed men from daring to go around ravaging the future mothers of our children." If this happened, he noted in conclusion, "our beloved country would no longer have such a proliferation in the number of prostitutes as is presently the case."[48]

In addition to being widely discussed and debated in the press, the question of polygamy also came under critical scrutiny in prose fiction, a medium which provided writers with greater opportunities to personalize and humanize the issue. One typical work of this type was a 1930 short story entitled "Mia n'oi" (Minor Wife) by "Kulap khao" (White Rose—K'opkan Wisitthasi) published in the literary magazine *Suphapburut* (The Gentleman).[49]

Luang Sisombunsak, the lone male character in the story, is a thirty-year-old government official from a well-to-do background. He has lost sexual interest in his wife Wipha and begins a liaison with a young lower-class woman named Ranchuan. However, rather than keep the affair a secret, *Luang* Si urges Ranchuan to become his minor wife and live with him and Wipha under the same roof. Although Ranchuan is infatuated with him she is reluctant to agree to his proposal and says, "The life of a minor wife is the most wretched thing of all; they are usually poor and likely to sacrifice their virginity for momentary happiness and comfort." She also tells him that she would feel a great sense of embarrassment if she were "to snatch away the happiness of a member of the same sex," adding that "all women feel the same way—they don't want others to steal their men."[50] Notwithstanding Ranchuan's reservations, and a nagging feeling she had that their relationship was one of "impure love" (*rak kan doi mai borisut*), *Luang* Si is able to convince her to become his minor wife.

When Ranchuan first moves into *Luang* Si's house, both women try hard to adjust to the new arrangement, in particular Ranchuan, who is acutely aware of her humble origins. Unsurprisingly, this state of affairs does not last very long. After catching her husband and Ranchuan embracing one another, Wipha becomes embittered and develops a great hatred for the younger woman, whom she likens to a "low-class bandit" (*chon phrai*) who has made off with her man. All the while, however, she keeps her feelings well hidden from *Luang* Si, as does Ranchuan, in the hope that things will somehow change for the better. As for the man of the house, he has not the slightest inkling of his first wife's loathing for Ranchuan and, at one point after the threesome have finished eating dinner, says to both of them:

> I've got to laugh at those men who complain that having two wives is a misery. Right now, I've got the two of you and I feel what they say is completely misplaced. They simply don't know how to choose women, and they know nothing of the right timing [*kalathetsa*]. Consequently, they suffer. If, on the other hand, they had found angels [*thepthida*] who could live together like you, it would be as if they were in heaven.[51]

Over the following months *Luang* Si becomes no wiser as to the animosity Wipha feels toward Rachuan, since both women continue to maintain a facade of conviviality in his presence. Subsequently Rachuan falls pregnant and Wipha, who is unable to bear children, becomes even more resentful. During her fifth month of pregnancy Rachuan, fearing that Wipha wants to kill her, decides to quietly slip out of the house and leave for good without telling anyone. For a time she finds work as a nanny and is later admitted into a public hospital when she goes into labor. This proves to be rather difficult and following the delivery of a healthy baby boy complications set in. In a painfully drawn-out, tear-drenched scene that prefigures the type of portentous melodrama screened nightly on contemporary Thai television, *Luang* Si and Wipha appear at her bedside where he begs her to cling to life and return home with them. Ranchuan, however, unmoved by his entreaties, says "I don't want your love any more. The whole world shows its compassion for me, but not you." He insists that she is still his wife, to which Rachuan feebly replies, "I'm not anyone's wife . . . now I'm free in body and soul, and in any case you've already got a wife."[52] She then goes on to tell him how terribly she had suffered at the hands of Wipha and cries out deliriously for her child before passing away.

"Minor Wife" is noteworthy in that while written by a man it was told from a female perspective. Clearly the author, Kulap khao, whose short fictional work "Mia klang wan" (Daytime Wife) was discussed in chapter 4, had a sympathetic view toward women, with "Minor Wife" providing another sharply drawn critique of elite male attitudes toward the opposite sex.[53] Indeed, the critique of male behavior developed in this story is underscored by the fact that Ranchuan, the lower-class heroine, is ultimately destroyed by *Luang* Si's insistent desire to possess her. In short, "Minor Wife," apart from its entertainment value, served as a critical commentary which linked the suffering and misery associated with polygamous marriage with the dominant male elite.

From the discussion above it can be seen that views about polygamy were largely (although not wholly) differentiated along gender lines, with women generally opposed to the practice while men either supported it or adopted something of an equivocal stance on the issue. There was one thing, however, which all commentators tended to agree on—that the continuance of polygamy was a factor in the contemporary growth of prostitution.

POLYGAMY, PROSTITUTION, AND DISEASE

In premodern Siam polygamy was a privilege enjoyed exclusively, it would seem, by upper-class males. Admittedly there were no legal prohibitions against men from the lower orders taking more than one woman as a wife, but a lack of wealth would certainly have been a strong factor militating against them doing so. In the context of a developing market economy and the freeing-up of the population through the formal abolition of debt bondage and slavery from the late nineteenth century, however, this particular distinction between elite and commoner males was to change dramatically. While the country was undergoing a range of major transformations, in particular increased spatial and social mobility, new opportunities for contact between the sexes, and the emergence of new urban middle and working classes, the ancient laws on marriage remained unchanged.

What this meant in practical terms was that in addition to men from the noble-aristocratic-business elite, new generations of commoners had increased opportunities, sanctioned by law, to enter into polygamous relationships.

This phenomenon was often remarked upon by press commentators. In 1926, for example, one observer noted that there were many men of modest means who had two or three wives.[54] Furthermore, while a man was legally entitled to have more than one wife (*mia*), which in the Thai context often meant (and continues to mean) little more than having an ongoing sexual relationship with a woman, the law did not require any genuine commitment on the man's part toward his spouse. As a contributor to the daily press in the mid-1920s wrote, "Under the present law it is as easy for a man to cast off a wife as it is to throw a stone into the water."[55]

This way of thinking was exacerbated by the continuing development of the market economy and the avid embrace of consumerism among the urban population referred to earlier. In this environment it became increasingly difficult for upper-class men to meet the material wants and needs of their extensive polygamous households. Should such a man tire of a particular wife and be unwilling to support her, there was little to stop him from ending the relationship.[56] The same type of behavior was also prevalent among the ranks of less well-off sections of the urban male population. Indeed, newspaper reports of the period suggest that this was particularly common among adolescent men who, after having had sexual relationships with young women, often abandoned them when they fell pregnant or became too expensive to keep.

Given the high social value placed on female virtue, it was hardly surprising that many abandoned wives, now regarded as soiled women, were unable to enter into new stable relationships with other men. And it seems that those women who had already been married more than once were at an even greater disadvantage in finding a reliable partner.[57] This reality, in conjunction with the general lack of employment opportunities for women, saw many abandoned wives, especially the young and attractive, turning to prostitution to support themselves. One also finds instances in which men, unwilling or uninterested in regular employment, forced their wives to provide for them by working as prostitutes. The following cartoon (fig. 6.3) from *Satri thai* encapsulates, in dramatic form, this type of behavior—a fearsome-looking man bellows at the woman cowering on the ground (his wife) demanding that she go off and earn him some money.

That there was a strong connection between the kingdom's marriage laws and the growth of prostitution in the early decades of the twentieth century should be clear. Men not only had the legal right to have more than one wife, but they could also cast them off with virtual impunity, a woman having little legal recourse in such cases. The law, in conjunction with the sexual double standard which served to stigmatize unmarried or divorced women who had lost their virginity, and a lack of suitable employment opportunities, meant that prostitution

Fig. 6.3. *Satri thai*, 26 July 1926

was often the only viable alternative for abandoned wives or girlfriends to maintain themselves. And just as critiques of polygamy were part of the popular
nationalist assault of the ancien régime, so was the issue of prostitution. As will
be recalled, newspaper cartoonists frequently accused members of the upper class
of being directly involved in the business side of prostitution or of frequenting
prostitutes themselves. Another equally significant form of criticism related to
prostitution was that concerned with the issue of venereal disease and its impact
on the vitality and health of the nation.

Venereal diseases had been in evidence in Siam since Ayuthayan times and
were said to be "quite common" in Bangkok during the mid-nineteenth century.[58] With the growth of prostitution from this time there was a rapid increase
in the number of cases of venereal disease, often referred to euphemistically as
"men's disease" (*rok burut*). In the period from 1914 to 1920, for example, infection rates of between 60 and 80 percent for the male population aged nineteen
years old and above were reported.[59] As for the situation with regard to the
women who serviced these men, one observer writing in 1927 claimed that "at
least 90 percent of prostitutes have VD."[60] Indeed, the threat of sexually transmitted diseases was such that by the early 1920s various VD treatments, many of
which were highly dubious herbal remedies, had become the largest selling type
of medication to be found in the country.[61] And for those who could afford
them, modern prophylactics were also available, including the reassuringly
named "Never Rip" condom imported from Germany.[62]

Prostitution was repeatedly equated with danger in the popular press. As Ch'o. ch'o ch'o, the author of an article entitled "The Government should be Deeply Concerned about the Threat of Prostitution" (*phai haeng ying nakh'on sopheni rathaban khuan r'on-chai*) wrote, "Prostitution impedes national progress and poses a serious threat not only to the family but also to the country's independence and the wealth of the people." He pointed out that as a result of the rapid spread of venereal disease fewer men would be able to reproduce, limiting the growth of Siam's future population. Furthermore, he stressed that infected parents transmitted the disease to their offspring whose life expectancy was sharply reduced. These infected children, he added, had "pus-filled eyes and bodies covered in sores" while those who contracted syphilis "also suffered from shortsightedness and weak nerves."[63]

The author of another account entitled "Something of Real Concern to the Thai Race" (*sing thi na witok samrap ph'ut phan thai*)[64] sought to quantify the effects of venereal disease on children. He claimed that 80 percent of the babies born to parents infected with VD died shortly thereafter, and that the surviving 20 percent suffered the ill effects of the disease in some way or other for the rest of their lives. If the authorities continued to ignore the problem, he warned, it would reach catastrophic proportions and place the entire population under the threat of contracting venereal disease.[65] Yet another newspaper commentator, a Doctor Phlong (*m'o phlong*), expressed similar concerns.

> In Siam the government is not interested in the question of prostitution and therefore the business just thrives. . . . Prostitutes can be compared to noxious flowers. If we embrace them and look at their color and complexion we assume they pose no danger, but if we pluck them and sniff them or put them in a vase we will discover just how dangerous they are. Indeed, they are worse than deadly snakes. For while the venom from a snakebite cannot be transmitted to our offspring, the poison given off by prostitutes is inevitably passed on to our wives and children.[66]

Dr. Phlong, like many other contributors to the press, was dismayed by the health problems associated with prostitution and feared that the spread of sexually transmitted diseases imperiled the future of the nation.[67] By addressing their concerns in such broad terms these commentators drew attention to what they considered to be a serious failing on the part of the government to act in the best interests of the people. Here, as in other critiques of the status quo, it was suggested that the absolutist regime was incapable of coping with the contemporary demands of governance. Yet again its authority and legitimacy were called into question.

The debate on equality between the sexes discussed in this and the previous chapter was an integral part of a broader discursive process that began to unfold in earnest during the 1920s when existing social beliefs, practices, and forms were increasingly called into question by members of the emergent middle class.

The idea of equality in marriage, one man-one wife, for example, paralleled the drive for the establishment of a more egalitarian representative political system in place of royal absolutism. As we have seen, women were largely united in their opposition to polygamy, and their critiques of the practice (which tended to focus on elite male behavior) were commonly framed in class terms. By contrast, male opinion on the issue was more varied. While there was a class element in some of the views expressed by men, the diffuse nature of opinion indicated that male power tended to operate in a domain that crossed class boundaries. At the same time polygamy, or rather the law that permitted it, was seen as contributing to the spread of prostitution and venereal disease, problems which were seen to endanger the nation. Over time, mounting criticisms of the government for its failure to deal with these issues were significant in that they, together with those of a more political and economic nature, contributed toward a gradual diminution of royal authority and legitimacy, paving the way for the overthrow of the absolute monarchy in June 1932.

The critical debate on the status and position of women in Siamese society discussed above went hand in hand with efforts to redefine or redraw relations between the sexes, to create a new morality as it were, a morality more in keeping with the changing times. This process of redefining interpersonal behavior is taken up in the following chapter.

NOTES

1. The novel was originally written in 1969 and serialized in the weekly magazine *Sakun thai* during 1969. First published in book form shortly afterward, it has gone through numerous reprintings, most recently in 1998. See Kritsana Asokesin, *Mia luang* [Major Wife] (Bangkok: Double Night Printing), 1998.

2. C. J. Reynolds, "A Nineteenth-Century Thai Buddhist Defense of Polygamy and Some Remarks on the Social History of Women in Thailand," paper prepared for the Seventh Conference, International Association of Historians of Asia, Chulalongkorn University, Bangkok, 22–26 August 1977.

3. I have been reliably informed by members of staff at the National Library of Thailand that such materials are held by the library. They are not, however, readily accessible.

4. S'o Atsanachinda, *Phrung-ni cha rot nam sop* [Tomorrow They'll Consecrate My Corpse] (Bangkok: Na Ban Wannakam, 1993 [3rd printing]), 59.

5. S'o Atsanachinda, *Tomorrow*, 60.

6. Reynolds, "A Nineteenth-Century Thai Buddhist Defense."

7. Under the various treaties concluded with foreign powers in the mid-nineteenth century, Siam was compelled to forfeit a degree of her legal autonomy. These treaties contained clauses on extraterritoriality which meant that legal cases involving foreign nationals were to be heard in consular courts outside Siamese jurisdiction.

8. The material compiled by L'Evesque included the 1805 "Law on Husbands and Wives," extracts from a range of laws such as those relating to inheritance, slavery, kid-

napping, and the settling of debts. In addition, notices on abduction and the payment of dowries, together with various court decisions and lectures given by Prince Rabi at the law school in 1900, were also consulted. National Archives R.6 Y (*Krasuang yuttitham*, Ministry of Justice] 2/2 [*r'uang kot-mai laksana phua mia*, Concerning the Law on Husbands and Wives], 8–9.

9. National Archives R.6 Y, 9–10.

10. Quoted in Adul Wichiencharoen and *Luang* Chamroon Netisastra, 1968, 97.

11. Memorandum dated 3 June 1913, *National Archives* R.6 Y [*Krasuang yuttitham* - Ministry of Justice] 2/2 National Archives R.6 Y [*Krasuang yuttitham*, Ministry of Justice] 2/2, 38.

12. 2/2 National Archives R.6, 39.

13. 2/2 National Archives R.6, 41.

14. 2/2 National Archives R.6, 43.

15. 2/2 National Archives R.6, 40.

16. 2/2 National Archives R.6, 43–45.

17. 2/2 National Archives R.6, 39.

18. 2/2 National Archives R.6.

19. 2/2 National Archives R.6.

20. Nanthira Khamphiban, "Nayobai kiaw-kap phuying thai nai samai sang chat kh'ong ch'om phon p'o phibun songkhram, 2481–2487" [Policies toward Thai Women during the Nation-Building Era of Field Marshall Phibun Songkhram, 1938–1944], M.A. thesis, Thammasat University, Bangkok, 1987, 44.

21. Suwadee Tanaprasitpatana, "Thai Society's Expectations of Women, 1851–1935," Ph.D. diss., Sydney University, 1989, 225.

22. *Kammak'on*, 13 October 1923.

23. *Kammak'on*, 13 October 1923.

24. *Kammak'on*, 13 October 1923.

25. *Satri thai*, 22 March 1926.

26. The Thai word used here was *deratchan*, commonly used to refer to a wild, savage animal (e.g., *sat deratchan*). When applied to a person it is a highly derogatory term signifying unrestrained disgust and loathing.

27. *Satri thai*, 22 March 1922.

28. *Satri sap*, 19 September 1922.

29. *Satri sap*, 19 September 1922.

30. *Satri sap*, 22 September 1922.

31. *Satri sap*, 22 September 1922. Emphasis added.

32. *Satri sap*, 22 September 1922. The polemical nature of Anrachun's statement "Bangkok will become like Paris" here is underlined by the fact that in the first part of her essay she talked admiringly of the marriage laws in civilized countries. France, along with Great Britain, was commonly held to be the very epitome of "civilization."

33. Xiaomei Chen, *Occidentalism: A Theory of Counter-discourse in Post-Mao China* (New York: Oxford University Press, 1995), 4–5.

34. Xiaomei Chen, *Occidentalism*, 5.

35. *Satri sap*, 22 September 1922.

36. *Sayam rat*, 11 April 1926.

37. *Sayam rat*, 11 April 1926.

38. *Sayam rat*, 5 June 1926.

39. *Sayam rat*, 16 May 1926.

40. *Sayam rat*, 16 May 1926.

41. It should be mentioned that during the mid-nineteenth century King Mongkut, in defending the practice of polygamy, advanced the idea that polygamy served to increase the available workforce. Suwadee, "Thai Society's Expectations," 86–87.

42. Even a partial survey of the vernacular press during the 1920s gives a clear indication of such anxieties on the part of Thai commentators. Indeed, ethnic tensions between Thais and Chinese in the early decades of the twentieth century represents a major field of study in its own right.

43. *Sayam rat*, 20 May 1926.

44. *Sayam rat*, 20 May 1926.

45. *Sayam rat*, 19 January 1926.

46. *Sayam rat*, 19 January 1926.

47. *Sayam rat*, 19 January 1926.

48. *Sayam rat*, 19 January 1926.

49. K'opkan Wisitthasi, "Mia n'oi" [Minor Wife], *Suphapburut* [The Gentleman] 15 February 1930: 3266–310.

50. K'opkan Wisitthasi, "Mia n'oi," 3270.

51. K'opkan Wisitthasi, "Mia n'oi," 3284.

52. K'opkan Wisitthasi, "Mia n'oi," 3305.

53. Although *Luang* Sisombunsak only held the second lowest of officially conferred titles in government service, his membership of the upper classes is implied by his ownership of a substantial home and a large American automobile (a green Chrysler).

It is also interesting to note that he was not depicted as an overtly villainous character. Nonetheless, the author's deft portrayal of his various qualities (self-indulgence, insensitivity, and an remarkable degree of self-delusion) ensure that this is precisely how he must have come across to readers.

54. *Sayam rat*, 16 May 1926.

55. *Sayam rat*, 27 March 1926.

56. At times this type of behavior became the subject of court action. In 1922, for example, *Phra* Phamnak Natchanik'on, a government official, initiated legal proceedings to divorce his wife Wankosum. *Phra* Phamnak claimed that Wankosum, whom he paid an allowance of 40 baht a month (approximately twice the salary of a base-level government clerk), had taken a lover. He brought in witnesses to support his claim, including the alleged lover himself. As things turned out, however, it seems that *Phra* Phamnak had fabricated the whole story so as to get rid of Wankosum and allow him to take on another woman in her place. *Satri sap*, 22 September 1922.

57. *Sayam rat*, 19 January 1925.

58. Scott Bamber, Kevin Hewison, and Peter Underwood, "A History of Sexually Transmitted Diseases in Thailand: Politics, Policy, and Control," *Genitourinary Medicine* 69 (1993): 148–57.

59. *Chino sayam warasap*, April 1920.

60. *Pakka thai*, 22 January 1927. Here it is interesting to note that the general medical term for venereal disease, *kamarok* (literally, "sexual disease"), was used in a particular sense with regard to prostitutes, who were often known as *tua kamarok* (VD bodies), a

derogatory expression which implied that women alone were responsible for making men ill. *Krungthep deli me* [Krungthep Daily Mail], 4 September 1932.

61. *Chino sayam warasap*, 7 April 1920. For some the available treatments were to no avail, as in the case of a Chinese man who committed suicide after the various remedies he tried failed to cure him. *Sayam rat*, 19 June 1922.

62. This product was regularly advertised in the pages of *Siam Cinema* movie magazine. Elsewhere in the world of advertising, the seriousness of venereal disease was underscored. For example, one advertisement for a VD treatment remedy referred to the disease as "the mysterious killer" (*khathakam l'uk-lap*). The text of the advertisement—which interestingly absolves men from acting responsibly—reads as follows:

> A husband who goes out and mixes with other women secretly murders his wife without leaving any evidence admissible in a court of law. Whenever a man comes to visit the city he seeks leisure and relaxation at a house of easy virtue and when he returns home the murder takes place. However, you can't blame him because he went and fraternized with prostitutes and brought the disease home to his wife without knowing it. (*Pakka thai*, 27 January 1926)

63. *Sikrung*, 7 March 1927.

64. The term *ph'ut phan*, used here to denote "race," carries a strong connotation of "fertility." Indeed, *ph'ut phan* is a plant propagated for its seeds or capacity to reproduce.

65. *Pakka thai*, 22 January 1927.

66. *Sikrung*, 19 July 1927.

67. One finds similar expressions of concern in contemporary Thailand over the continuing impact of the HIV/AIDS pandemic.

7

꧁

Bourgeois Love and Morality: Gender Relations Redefined

The world we live in is a world of relationships.

—*Suphap-burut*, 15 June 1929

The critiques of upper-class society discussed in the preceding chapters were part of the complex and diffuse process of sociopolitical transformation associated with the rise of the middle class. In addition to the critical assaults on the ancien régime, middle-class commentators also sought to develop and define a range of new social understandings and conceptions more in keeping with contemporary realities, including those concerned with gender roles and relations between the sexes. Among other things, this involved the public articulation of what may be described as a bourgeois notion of romantic love and the development of corresponding codes of sexual morality, a new morality that was seen by its proponents as being fundamental to the progress and well-being of Siam as a nation. The media, in particular newspapers and journals, played a crucial role in popularizing concepts of love and creating a discursive environment for the process of social redefinition. In this chapter I examine some key texts published during the 1920s and early 1930s which were in large part informed or inspired by Western influences and notions of rationality (*het-phon*) and in which authors discuss such things as love in marriage, the selection of suitable marriage partners, the emergent bourgeois notion of the "gentleman," and the more intimate side of interpersonal relations between the sexes. It is through this body of material that we will be able to discern how "modern love" was being formulated by and for the reading public.

TOWARD MODERN IDEAS OF
MARRIAGE AND THE FAMILY

In March 1926, the feminist magazine *Satri thai* published the first in a series of articles on marriage and the family by a writer who used the pseudonym *Nai* Y'ot Rak Yao (literally, Mr. Supreme Love of the Home). Interestingly, *Nai* Y'ot described himself as a farmer (*chao rai*) from Pathumthani, north of Bangkok, yet he displayed a remarkable degree of learning and erudition not usually associated with such a livelihood. The fact that he claimed to be a man of the land and was contributing to social debate nonetheless underscores a point emphasized throughout this study, that the 1920s was a period during which educated commoners were increasingly involved in setting the agenda of Siamese public life.[1]

Nai Y'ot's contribution took the form of a series of letters providing advice to his younger brother and sister. In the first of these missives he said that the question of marriage and the family (*khr'op khrua*) was of utmost importance for young men and women. Yet, as he pointed out, there was a lack of suitable material available to guide the young in these matters; those works that were available only provided readers with very general moral principles expressed in arcane poetic language that most people found extremely difficult to understand.[2] In seeking to address such problems *Nai* Y'ot said that he would take a more focused approach and write about marriage and the family in plain, readily comprehensible prose. The topics he proposed to discuss were:

1. Marriage in a historical perspective from past to present, and the selection of suitable marriage partners;
2. The scientific (*pen witthayasat*) investigation of sexual desire. The purpose of this is to illuminate the nature of such desire and the need to counter inappropriate sexual behavior;
3. The type of moral and ethical behavior necessary for married couples to be happy, avoid conflict and stay together; and,
4. How to raise intelligent, capable children for the benefit of the nation.[3]

Nai Y'ot noted that although "knowledge, the state of the roads, and forms of dress" had improved immeasurably in Siam during the present era of "civilization," such progress was not evident in the case of marital relationships.

These days we hear of people marrying one minute then divorcing the next; otherwise the couple quietly go their separate ways. The number of divorced women [*mae mai*] is increasing daily and most of them are young. Generally they have little or insufficient education to earn a living. As a result they turn to selling sex [*kha praweni*]. And while it might seem that this situation favors men, the reverse is in fact the case, for it is their own morality that suffers.[4]

The author argued that the reason for this particular state of affairs was that the married lives of men and women remained a subject shrouded in secrecy and mystery.

Anyone who writes about these things seriously is condemned, while anyone who tries to talk about them in public is ignored. The reason for this is that the subject of sexual intimacy is regarded as crude and unseemly. Indeed, we're only likely to hear about this sort of thing from comedians who play around with the meanings of words. Fathers won't dare explain such matters to their sons, and mothers are the same with their daughters. Consequently, young men and women learn about sex from their own experiences, often with the most unfortunate results.[5]

Nai Y'ot said that in order to address the marital problems experienced by young men and women it was necessary for them to develop a thorough understanding of the concept *mi r'uan* (literally, to "have a home.") According to him the expression *mi r'uan* did not simply refer to a couple setting up house together; rather, it meant marriage in the deepest sense of the word. As he pointed out, the term was now used in place of the old expression *mi phua mi mia* (literally, "have husband, have wife," or to be sleeping with a partner on a regular basis) which had come to assume negative connotations in the present age as new notions of politeness and respectability were articulated. In developing his ideas about marriage, *Nai* Y'ot said that "love" (*khwam-rak*), as opposed to "desire" (*tanha*), was the thing that drew men and women together; "love," he added, was "the source of all things, from art and science [*witthayasat*], to strategy [*yutthasat*] and political thought [*ratthasat*]." Exhibiting an impressive degree of learning for a Siamese farmer at the time, the author then went on to quote Goethe who, he said, had once written, "love and marriage represent the basis and the highest expression of progress."[6] "Love," according to *Nai* Y'ot, was not simply an abstract ideal, however, but something closely associated with "the idea of setting up a home"—a relationship, he added, that was formally recognized in "civilized countries" (*araya prathet*) where a "fundamental element of government policy [*ratprasat-nayobai*] was to create the conditions necessary for love and marriage to flourish and take root." A love of one's home, he insisted, was the only real basis for a genuine love of the nation.[7]

In subsequent articles *Nai* Y'ot emphasized that there was a pressing need to adopt a more formal, structured approach to marriage than was generally the case in Siam at the time. He envisaged this as being a three-stage process: first, a man and woman were to be formally engaged; next, they would be married in a public ceremony; and finally, they would live together as husband and wife.[8] To a degree this process of betrothal, marriage, and union under the same roof may appear to be a reaffirmation of traditional practices associated with elite families (marriage among commoners, by contrast, tended to be rather more informal). Yet, when considered in the broader context of his overall argument, this formulation was far more suggestive of an emergent new sensibility than of a backward-looking call to embrace traditional elite practices such as arranged marriages and polygamy. As we have noted, Nai Y'ot was interested in Western notions of civilization and he advocated a fundamentally modernist position, arguing that the present chaotic and ambiguous situation in Siam could be overcome by following the lead of Western countries where formalized, publicly sanctioned marriage was the norm. Moreover, in the West, instructional texts (*tamra*) which provided young men and women with information about all aspects of conjugal life were readily available. These materials, he stressed, were written in refined, dignified language and the ideas they contained were based on rational (*mi het-phon*) scientific ways of thinking. In other words, such texts were to be seen as socially acceptable, modern forms of knowledge.

Regrettably, while talking about the need for taking a reasoned, scientifically based approach to the vexed issue of marital relations in 1920s Siam, Nai Y'ot did not elaborate any further upon the subject. Indeed, the author's ambitious plans to provide the readers of *Satri thai* with detailed information about the various topics he had proposed at the outset appear to have gone unrealized, and as far as I have been able to determine the magazine did not publish any more of his writings. Even so, despite the partial, undeveloped nature of Nai Y'ot's contribution, his work was significant in that it represented an early attempt to advance modern, rational ideas with regard to marital relations.

SUPHAP-BURUT (THE GENTLEMAN)

Other writers of the period addressed similar themes in a range of publications, including the important middle-class literary journal *Suphap-burut* (The Gentleman) launched in 1929 by the noted journalist and novelist Kulap Saipradit. In the introduction to the inaugural issue of the journal Kulap wrote an editorial in which he said:

> We understand the word "gentlemen" in many different ways, yet to say that all of these interpretations are correct is not true. Some people see a smartly attired man and say to themselves "There, that's a gentleman." In point of fact, clothing does nothing whatsoever to make a man a gentleman. Dress is merely an outward symbol. Indeed, one finds gentlemen who are not interested in such symbols, symbols that can be easily copied or imitated. As a result one needs to take care when forming opinions about other people—on the surface a man might appear to be a gentlemen when in fact he is not.[9]

Kulap said that a gentleman was essentially a modern type of man quite distinct from the older *phu-di*, a term traditionally used to refer to members of the upper classes. The hallmarks of the *phu-di* male, he noted, were good manners and polite speech. By contrast, the gentleman, or rather the "true gentleman" (*suphap-burut thae-ching*) was a more substantial, purposeful figure. According to Kulap the defining feature of a gentleman was the idea of sacrifice which, he stressed, represented "the well-spring of virtue and goodness in its manifold forms."[10] Above all a gentleman was unselfish, an individual who made personal sacrifices for the benefit of others.

In making these observations Kulap sought to define the ethos of the new journal and that of its young, largely male, contributors. More generally, his remarks suggested that a new generation and class of socially aware males was emerging in Siam. It is in this context that the work discussed below is to be understood.

LILASAT (THE SCIENCE OF LOVE)

"Lilasat" (The Science of Love),[11] a lengthy essay by Sanit Charoenrat, was serialized in the first four issues of *Suphap-burut*. Like *Nai Y'ot*, Sanit looked to the West for inspiration. He said that since there was little practical information about love available in Thai it was necessary to consult foreign texts to develop an understanding about the subject (in all likelihood, the image in figure 7.1 which accompanied the article was drawn from one of these works). Indeed, in the introductory section to his essay Sanit admitted that he was something of a novice in the field and had consulted the writings of various Western authors such as "Walter McCallaghan" and "Eleanor Klin" [*sic*].[12] At the same time, however, he also drew on ideas which had deep local roots, in particular the view that men and women did not understand each other's "true nature" (*thammachat thae ching*); the idea of a fundamentally different male and female nature, it will be recalled, had been expounded by *Chaophraya* Thiphak'orawong in his nine-

Fig. 7.1.

teenth-century defense of polygamy.[13] Sanit argued that this lack of understanding had led to all types of conflicts and tensions between the sexes. In the present age of "burgeoning knowledge" (yuk thi witthayakan rung-rot), however, he believed that such misunderstandings had begun to diminish as people started to think in more logical and rational ways than before.[14] Thus, while not rejecting the notion of fundamental differences between men and women, the author was of the view that such differences could be managed in such a way as to benefit society at large.

According to Sanit, most philosophers and thinkers (nak-prat) regarded humans as quintessentially social beings who depended on one another in order to survive. "The world we live in," he stressed, "is a world of relationships."[15] As a consequence, one of the most crucial things in life was to have friends. And the most important type of friend, he stressed, was a member of the opposite sex (pen ph'uan tang phet). Here it may be added that although he made no direct reference to homosexuality, Sanit was dismissive of the idea of love between male friends, which, he claimed, was always bland and insipid (he did not, however, say anything about same sex friendships between females).[16] In his opinion a relationship with a member of the opposite sex was crucial in that it helped an individual cope with the rigors of working life and achieve peace of mind. A relationship in this context, it needs to be emphasized, meant marriage and, by extension, the raising of a family.

In Sanit's opinion the question of finding a suitable marriage partner was paramount and love was crucial to the process. Genuine love between a man and woman, he emphasized, was not to be confused with desire. Instead, it involved sacrifice, mutual respect, and a sincere wish to do whatever one could for one's partner.[17] Like Nai Y'ot, Sanit saw love as a profound force central to the human experience; uncivilized peoples, he said, used sorcery and witchcraft to stimulate it while those in more advanced, civilized societies promoted love through various literary forms such as poetry, plays, and "sensual" novels (niyai an kiaw pai nai thang loki).[18] Sanit believed that a reasoned, rational approach to the subject was required and claimed that "as the world progresses people are becoming more interested in the condition and the characteristics of love than ever before—so much so, in fact, that increasing efforts are being made to gather together information in order to create a specific branch of knowledge."[19] He further suggested that love had certain "laws" or "principles" (kot-ken) and that those who were familiar with these laws would be more successful in matters of the heart than those who lacked such knowledge.

Unfortunately, Sanit did not expand upon this particular idea; instead, he turned his attention to what he termed "traditional beliefs" (prapeni boran). He noted that according to ancient custom (as exemplified in the writing of Chao-phraya Thiphak'orawong), it was the man who played the active role in establishing a relationship while a woman had the duty (na thi) of remaining passive and waiting for love to come to her. By contrast a woman who displayed an overt interest in a particular man was regarded as "highly deviant" (*pen khon uttari yang raeng*) and a threat to the social order.[20] Sanit took strong exception to such beliefs. He said that in being duty-bound to assume a wholly passive role in relation to men, women were "particularly unfortunate" (*pen khon khr'o rai thi sut*) in that they had no opportunity of selecting a husband of their own choosing and were commonly obliged to wed the first man who asked for their hand in marriage.[21] This, he argued, was a totally unsatisfactory state of affairs as it often resulted in great personal misery and a whole range of associated problems. For similar reasons he was also critical of the traditional elite practice of arranged marriages. As a means of improving relations between the sexes he suggested that women should be allowed to socialize with a range of different men in order to assess their sincerity and worthiness before deciding on which one to take as a husband.

Sanit pointed out that the idea of socializing between the sexes (*kan khop kha samakhom rawang chai kap ying*) was something new to Siam. In certain quarters this type of thinking was viewed with alarm, those holding such opinions believing that socializing posed a danger to both men and women alike. According to Sanit, however, such concerns reflected a superficial outlook and lacked a "rational basis" (*mai mi het-phon*). While admitting that there were potential problems in allowing men and women to mix with one another, he reasoned that if certain conditions were met much was to be gained by greater contact between the sexes. Sanit said that increased social intercourse should not be taken to mean that all constraints be cast aside and women be allowed to establish relations with men on their own accord. Rather, he proposed that if a woman was to meet a range of men it was necessary for her to expand her circle of female friends and acquaintances. By doing this a woman had the opportunity of meeting the male relatives and friends of one of the women she knew, thereby increasing her chances of finding a suitable marriage partner.

This was just the first step, however. To take the fullest advantage of her network of friends and acquaintances, Sanit suggested that a young woman should host a party (*pati*) at her home, if permitted by her parents, and invite her female friends along with their brothers, cousins, and male friends. On such occasions the woman organizing the party should do everything she could to present herself as an able homemaker, a good cook, and a convivial host. In short, what the author sought to do was to promote a bourgeois vision of womanhood in which domestic skills were combined with social graces. Sanit then went on to say that a woman's manners, her speech, and the way in which she dressed were the key factors in attracting male interest. For their part women were said to be attracted to men on similar grounds, although ideally a man should also be educated and knowledgeable. While briefly noting what made men attractive to women, the emphasis of the article was very much on the way a woman should behave and act in order to win a man's favor. The manner in which women related to one another, Sanit pointed out, was entirely different from the way they should act in the company of men. When socializing with men he advised that a woman "should be neither too bold nor too shy and withdrawn."[22] In order to do this it was necessary for a woman to feel relaxed in male company, something he believed required women to understand that men were also human beings who "possessed the same sort of brain and the same abilities [as themselves]." Once this idea had been fully grasped, he added, "a woman should be able to talk to ten men at the same time."[23] In contrast to traditional notions of femininity with their emphasis on passivity and deference, Sanit expressed a view that in the present era it was the "duty" of a woman to initiate a conversation, claiming that men were not particularly good at doing this sort of thing. The best way for a woman to begin a conversation with a man was for her to talk about what books she had been reading or what films or plays she had seen, or to discuss travel. These were the types of topics a man might easily respond to so that the conversation could continue. However, adding a note of caution, the author advised women to be "rational" and "sensible" in what they said; "meaningless chatter," he stressed, "only served to annoy male listeners."[24]

In providing this kind of practical advice Sanit contributed toward the discursive process of delineating and extending the notion of what it was to be "modern" (*samai*). As he pointed out, "modernity" was not simply a matter of adopting particular styles of clothing and fashion, as many people believed, but rather was a much more profound, complex phenomenon that encompassed such things as forms of human behavior and interaction.[25] A crucial aspect of becoming modern, Sanit argued, was to foster greater understanding between the sexes, a new degree of understanding that would lead to happier, more stable marriages than was presently the case. The creation of harmonious relations in the home, he wrote in conclusion, were of fundamental importance in that they underpinned the future progress and prosperity of the nation more generally.

The works of Sanit and *Nai* Y'ot were representative of an emergent trend in which writers articulated a type of bourgeois view of interpersonal relations. For the most part, however, these writings tended to avoid a more candid discussion of the more intimate, sexual side of male-female relationships. While *Nai* Y'ot had made it clear that this was indeed a very delicate subject and intimated that he would be addressing the issue in the pages of *Satri thai*, his views and ideas were, for whatever reason, never published. At the same time, however, there were other authors whose writing on sexuality did appear in print. One such text from the late 1920s is examined in detail below. Before looking at this particular work, however, it is instructive to consider a rare and fascinating text about sex and sexuality from earlier in the century.

THE *VAGINA MANUAL*

The work in question was entitled the *Vagina Manual* (*Phra tamrap yoni*), an eighty-page pocket-sized booklet published in 1908. According to information provided by the publisher, only 200 copies were produced, an indication that it was aimed at an exclusive, elite readership. In the introductory section to the text proper, the editor noted that the material used in the manual was drawn from other older works not generally available in the public domain. This material, or at least some of it, originally came from an Indic source, as indicated by a reference early in the work to two Thai princes who were said to have traveled to India to study the "science" of physiognomy. The nature of the physiognomic system they learned about is briefly discussed in relation to various physical characteristics typically associated with individuals blessed with good fortune (i.e., a disquisition on the shape and size of the face, hands, legs, and so on). The greater part of the text, however, is given over to the female genitalia, and what differently shaped sex organs signified. For our purposes a few typical instances will suffice.

It was noted, for example, that if a "woman had a vagina shaped like a betel leaf" (*ying dai yoni dang bai phlu*) and her clitoris (*daet*) was not visible even when her legs were spread wide apart, she would be very wealthy.[26] As for a woman with a "vagina shaped like a skull" (*ying dai yoni dang kraban*), it was said she would find it difficult to find a man she could rely on.[27] Elsewhere, the manual included advice to men on various lovemaking techniques, this being related to the shape of a woman's vagina. For example,

A woman with a vagina like a buffalo's cunt [*hi khwai*] is sensitive around the hips. A man who has intercourse with this type of woman should hold her around the waist, press down on her and enter. Let him pound her heavily [*krataek hai nak*] for this is what pleases her. If she does not respond the man should withdraw his penis then stab [*thim*] it in and out of her three times before entering deep inside. This is what such a woman really likes.[28]

As for the male genitals, the text states that if a man had a penis (*l'ung*) which remained permanently erect he was "cursed and would have a short life, most probably dying a violent death."[29] A man who did not suffer this problem and whose penis was well proportioned and "nicely rounded" (*klom di*) was regarded, by contrast, as being favored with wealth and worldly success.[30] Penis length, if not thickness, was also an issue. Men with "short cocks" (*khuay san*), defined here as between four and five inches (*niw*) in length, were said to be reviled by women. However, a five and a half inch long penis was seen as an acceptable size, while a six-inch penis was regarded as superlative (*pen ek*). If a man had a longer member (seven inches and over) he was advised that he should only make love to plump women; such penile length, the author suggested, posed dangers to thin females.

One of the most striking aspects of the manual is the language used to refer to the male and female genitals. The words *hi* (cunt) and *khuay* (cock) are used throughout the text, together with their Sanskrit equivalents *yoni* (vagina) and *l'ung* (penis). In contemporary Thailand the terms *hi* and *khuay* are the crudest of swear words (there are a number of euphemistic terms commonly used as alternatives); textually their use is limited to pornographic magazines and comic books. However, it would appear that this was not the case in early-twentieth-century Siam. One may speculate that these terms, like the old expression for marriage, mi phua mi mia (mentioned above), only began to acquire their present negative connotations during the Vajiravudh era as Western-derived notions of social propriety and civilization, largely originating in Victorian England, were embraced.

With its emphasis on physiognomic relations between sexuality and the physical qualities of the sex organs, the Vagina Manual embodied a premodern, prescientific form of knowledge. It presented sexuality in wholly carnal, male-focused terms, devoid of any moral or social dimension. This aspect of the text is significant in that it says something about the times in which the booklet appeared, an age when relationships between sexual behavior, morality, and society had yet to become an issue, a problematic area of intense interest and debate. Within two decades, however, the situation had changed markedly as is demonstrated in the following work from the late 1920s which addresses the issue of sexuality in a very different manner.

THE PRACTICE OF SEX

Over a month-long period at the end of 1928 the popular daily Ratsad'on (known in English as The Citizen's Paper) published a series of articles entitled "The Practice of Sex" (Kama-pathibat).[31] According to the author, Nai Chalat Nanthayobon, the purpose of the series was to increase readers' awareness of the "dangers posed by sex" as well as providing them with information about the "science of sex" (kamasat). Like Nai Y'ot and Sanit before him, Chalat believed that love was fundamental to successful marriage; indeed, it represented "the very basis of personal happiness." While there were many different types of love, he said that among the young the idea was often confused with lust and sexual desire. This sort of "love," he argued, was temporary and thoughtless and generally evaporated just as quickly as it appeared. By contrast, genuine love, the basis for a lasting marriage, was born of familiarity and emotional closeness between a man and a woman or, alternatively, developed out of a couple's kindness and compassion toward one another. Curiously, having said this, Chalat then went on to complicate the issue by advancing a metaphysical view of love. Referring to the Buddhist concept of reincarnation he claimed that a man and woman could also fall in true love instantly if they had had a close, intimate relationship in a previous lifetime. In other words, notwithstanding his remarks on the necessity for a high degree of empathy between a couple, Chalat offered the view that genuine love was mysterious, unfathomable, and possibly fated.

Although he stressed the importance of love to successful and happy marriage,

Chalat's primary focus was sex. He was at pains to emphasize the centrality of sex to human experience saying that sexual stimulation was "something which no person, except for religious ascetics, could do without." Indeed, the subject was so important that "philosophers learned in the science of mankind [*manu-sat*]" had produced texts (*tamra*) concerned exclusively with the question of sexuality.[32] While it is clear that Chalat drew on such material in his work, he provided no information as to the particular text, or texts, he used. However, given the paucity of indigenous writings on the subject, as noted by *Nai Y'ot*, it is reasonable to assume that Chalat's ideas were largely based on Western sources.

In saying that sexuality was a fundamental aspect of human nature (*sandan manut*), Chalat argued it was necessary to recognize that sex was something that had both positive and negative aspects. With respect to the latter the author was particularly concerned about the behavior of the young. In his view, young men and women tended to give little thought or consideration to their actions, noting that "as their bodies begin to mature a sexual stirring develops within which incites them to have intercourse with one another."[33] He said this situation was much more pronounced in the urban environment of Bangkok where the sexes had the opportunity to fraternize with each other to a far greater extent than in rural areas. Based on his own observations, Chalat claimed that in the rapidly changing life of the capital sexual feelings among the young were becoming manifest at an earlier age than ever before.

> In the past young people did not begin to feel the urge to have sex until they were seventeen or eighteen. Once upon a time, for example, young women did not notice a change in their breasts before they were fifteen years old. Nowadays, however, as soon as girls reach the age of twelve their breasts fill out, clearly testifying to their womanhood; this also becomes evident in their movements and behavior. As for boys, when they reach fourteen they begin to show signs of the rowdiness and excitability common among young men.[34]

This growing sexual precocity among urban youth, Chalat argued, posed a range of dangers with major social ramifications. Early marriage, by which he meant sexual relations between adolescents, was seen to have a debilitating effect in that it caused young couples to be afflicted with "all types of serious illness." Furthermore, he claimed that children born from such liaisons were generally unhealthy and in some cases died prematurely. The subtext to this was that sex among adolescents had the potential to weaken Siam's population, a worrying prospect in a nation where the vigor of the populace was seen as fundamental to the nation's future progress and prosperity. As a consequence he advised parents to pay close attention to their children's behavior as they began to mature, and to ensure that they were not exposed to materials that could arouse or awaken sexual desire. Chalat believed that the greatest danger to the young in this regard was the type of licentious plays and films commonly staged and screened in Bangkok. He claimed that when adolescent boys were exposed to these particular forms of entertainment they became sexually excited, which, in turn, led them to seek out prostitutes—"the source of dreadful diseases"—as an outlet.[35] Alternatively, the author suggested that adolescent males "under the influence of books, plays, and films" would turn to masturbation (*kan lang nam kam duay ton eng*) which, he added, was highly deleterious to their health. Consequently, he advised parents to be mindful of this and alert their sons to the harm caused by masturbation. He even went so far as to warn parents that when it became evident that their sons were masturbating they needed to act immediately and not allow the practice to become chronic (*r'ua rang*).[36] Precisely what they should do to remedy the situation, however, was not spelled out.

In making these observations Chalat echoed a view that had originated in Europe toward the end of the eighteenth century. As George L. Mosse notes, it was at this time that masturbation came to be regarded as "the root cause of all loss of control, indeed, of abnormal passion in general. It was said to reflect an over-heated imagination, inimical to bourgeois sobriety, and was supposed to induce nervousness and loss of energy."[37]

While Chalat made no mention of female masturbation, he nevertheless stressed the need for parental control over daughters' sexuality. This particular duty, he said, lay with the mother, who had the responsibility of advising and instructing her adolescent daughter(s). Chalat advised mothers to tell their daughters that having sex was not "all fun and games as popular belief had it," but rather something fraught with danger (the threat of venereal disease) and suffering (the pain of childbirth). In other words, he advocated cultivating a fear of sex, or the consequences of sex, in the hearts of young women. At the same time, he insisted it was vital that mothers, in educating their daughters, emphasize the need to maintain one's dignity and honor.

In essence Chalat argued that countering the dangers inherent in adolescent sexuality rested squarely with parents. For him it was crucial that they instill the idea of respectability in their daughters while encouraging their sons to develop self-control rather than be at the mercy of the "demon rider," rampant physical desire. This notion of parental involvement was underscored by his view that, in the contemporary era, one should put the interests of one's immediate family above those of one's other relatives.[38] In saying this he was advocating the primacy of the nuclear as opposed to the extended family, yet another notion that reflected an emergent bourgeois sensibility.

Apart from discussing the dangers of sex with regard to the young, Chalat also had words of caution for more mature married couples. Here it should be mentioned that the author was, in general, a supporter of monogamy and promoted a bourgeois ideal of marriage with the husband going off to work while the wife maintained the home. There was one caveat to this, however, in that he believed that if a married woman was incapable of having sexual relations with her husband he should be permitted to take a minor wife (at the same time, implicitly endorsing the existing sexual double standard, he had nothing to say about the physical needs or wants of a woman with an impotent or inattentive husband). The important thing, Chalat emphasized, was for the major wife not to be jealous and to accept the new situation gracefully; to do otherwise, he said, would incur the husband's wrath and destroy the marriage.[39]

While recognizing that humans were sexual beings, Chalat asserted that if mature couples had too much sex it would damage or impair their health. Male vigor, he suggested, was directly related to sperm, seen as being comparable to a highly concentrated form of blood, the basic and most tangible manifestation of the human life force. Excessive sex on the part of a husband, he asserted, was debilitating and would prevent him from living to an old age.[40] As for women, too much sex was said to lead to "chronic illness" and similarly reduce their lifespan. According to the author, some women desired to have intercourse only four or five times a month while others wanted it every day. The latter, in his opinion, were intemperate, and he suggested that it was "sufficient for a caring and considerate husband to sleep with his wife twice a week."[41] He further advised men against having intercourse with their wives when they were having their periods, intimating that male contact with menstrual blood could cause health problems in later life. Similarly, he said that it was inadvisable for a husband to sleep with his wife after she had given birth and was breast-feeding the infant child. Should a man be incapable of restraining himself, however, Chalat recommended that he wear a condom (*thung yang*) during intercourse. The reason for this, he said, citing "unnamed expert opinion," was that "sperm was a danger to babies who were still being breast-fed."[42] Chalat's ideas about the negative aspects of sex are fascinating in that they represent a curious amalgam of foreign ideas and local Siamese belief, the latter drawing on metaphysical conceptions concerning menstrual blood which was regarded as "dangerous, polluting, and diametrically opposed to beneficial [male] power."[43]

At the same time, however, the author also drew the reader's attention to the positive side of sex. As mentioned earlier, Chalat emphasized that sexual relations were an intrinsic element of human nature and could be the source of great pleasure and happiness. Indeed, he argued that total abstinence could be just as harmful as excessive sexual indulgence: "People who are denied sex are prone to disease and an early death. Although the human body is strengthened and energized by other means, if it is denied sex it will not be able to achieve its full potential."[44] In talking about the positive aspects of sex he advised couples that they should not be shy or embarrassed about intercourse. On the contrary, he argued "the best thing for a couple to do is to let themselves go and hold nothing back when making love."[45] Chalat said that intense, all-embracing sexual contact was the most satisfying of all, and claimed that if each partner gave completely of themselves "one bout of lovemaking would suffice for a long time."

Furthermore, he claimed not only that a total physical release was good for the body but also that if the woman fell pregnant the baby would be stronger and healthier than those born to couples who indulged their passions too frequently.[46]

One important, if somewhat contradictory, facet of Chalat's discussion was his advice to men on how they should treat their wives sexually. As we have seen, he suggested that a man should seek to control his wife's sexuality by determining the frequency of intercourse. At the same time, however, Chalat said that it was necessary for men to recognize that women also possessed a sex drive and that it was of crucial importance that women's sexual needs were met. "All women crave sex to a greater or lesser degree, yet they are shy about their bodies. Even when they have a desire for sex they won't dare let their husbands know unless he asks them. Therefore, it is the duty of the husband to learn about his wife's feelings and how to satisfy her."[47] A failure to do so, the author cautioned, could have unfortunate consequences. A woman who had unsatisfactory sexual relations with her husband, he suggested, would, in all probability, seek physical gratification elsewhere, ultimately leading to a breakdown in the marriage.

In promoting the idea that men should make serious efforts to please their wives and not simply treat them as sexual objects without desires or wants of their own, Chalat's work reflected, in its own particular way, the changing nature of gender relations in the 1920s, a change which saw women (or rather more accurately, upper- and middle-class women) accorded greater recognition and social value than in the past. Indeed, this was further underlined by the author's views on various other aspects of male-female relations. For example, he was extremely critical of married men who visited prostitutes. The chances of contracting venereal disease and passing it on to one's spouse and children, he pointed out, were very high; moreover, he condemned men who went to prostitutes as totally irresponsible for frittering away money which could have been used more profitably on their families, in particular the education of their children.[48] On similar grounds he was opposed to the widespread male penchant for going out on drinking bouts, taking aphrodisiacs (*ya kamlang*) to enhance their sex drive, and then going to visit a brothel. Women, Chalat said, loathed men who behaved in such a self-indulgent, destructive fashion and, in the interests of greater marital harmony, he urged men to behave in a more socially responsible manner. Furthermore, he condemned those men who were of the view that "having sex with thirteen- or fourteen-year-old girls was the source of the most exquisite pleasure." He regarded this type of thinking to be "totally wrong" and said that these young girls were irreparably damaged by the experience.[49] Significantly, he identified men of "rank and position" as those who were most actively engaged in this type of abusive behavior. In making this observation Chalat added yet another voice to the burgeoning middle-class critique of the sexual mores of the ruling male elite.

The writings of the authors considered above embodied a range of new social perceptions and beliefs associated with the emergent middle class in Bangkok during the 1920s. Broadly speaking, these writers articulated a new, essentially bourgeois, form of romantic love and sexual morality. Indeed, the idea of romantic love was seen as a fundamental element in creating lasting and meaningful relations between men and women, a view in marked contrast with the long-standing elite tradition of arranged marriages in which family interests prevailed and love had little or no place. It is particularly noteworthy that the new type of sexual morality proposed in the works examined here was of an expressly secular nature, lacking explicit religious overtones. Moreover, this emergent morality was, for the most part, grounded in notions of reason and rationality. Indeed, reason and what passed for scientifically based rational behavior between the sexes were promoted as ideals suited to the contemporary age, modern ideals which were regarded as being of fundamental importance to the future progress of Siam as a nation.

NOTES

1. Then again, it may be imagined that *Nai* Y'ot may have been an educated urbanite who had assumed a rustic identity so as to give readers the impression that he was somehow untainted by the immorality which presumably characterized city life.

2. *Satri thai*, 15 March 1926.

3. *Satri thai*, 15 March 1926.

4. *Satri thai*, 22 March 1926.

5. *Satri thai*, 22 March 1926.

6. *Satri thai*, 22 March 1926.

7. *Satri thai*, 15 March 1926.

8. *Satri thai*, 5 April 1926.

9. *Suphap-burut*, 1 June 1929.

10. *Suphap-burut*, 1 June 1929.

11. While the title *"Lilasat"* defies an exact translation, a gloss along the lines of "The Art of Love" is adequate.

12. *Suphap-burut*, 1 June 1929, 197–98. A number of even more obscure authors were also referred to in the article. However, I hesitate to transcribe their names in English since even their approximate spellings cannot be readily discerned from the way Sanit has rendered them in Thai.

13. C. J. Reynolds, "A Nineteenth-Century Thai Buddhist Defense of Polygamy and Some Remarks on the Social History of Women in Thailand," paper prepared for the Seventh Conference, International Association of Historians of Asia, Chulalongkorn University, Bangkok, 22–26 August 1977.

14. *Suphap-burut*, 1 June 1929, 150.

15. *Suphap-burut*, 15 June 1929, 231.

16. *Suphap-burut*, 15 July 1929, 629.

17. *Suphap-burut*, 15 July 1929, 632.

18. *Suphap-burut*, 1 June 1929, 143.

19. *Suphap-burut*, 1 June 1929, 143.

20. *Suphap-burut*, 15 June 1929, 234.

21. *Suphap-burut*, 15 June 1929, 234.

22. *Suphap-burut*, 15 June 1929, 242.

23. *Suphap-burut*, 1 July 1929, 460.

24. *Suphap-burut*, 1 July 1929, 460.

25. *Suphap-burut*, 1 July 1929, 464.

26. *Phra tamrap yoni* [*Vagina Manual*] (Bangkok: n.p., 1908), 37.

27. *Vagina Manual*, 33.

28. *Vagina Manual*, 34.

29. *Vagina Manual*, 54.

30. *Vagina Manual*, 53.

31. *Ratsad'on*, 31 December 1928.

32. *Ratsad'on*, 31 December 1928.

33. *Ratsad'on*, 4 January 1929.

34. *Ratsad'on*, 1 January 1929.

35. *Ratsad'on*, 15 January 1929.

36. *Ratsad'on*, 16 January 1929.

37. George L. Mosse, *Nationalism and Sexuality: Respectability and Abnormal Sexuality in Modern Europe* (New York: Howard Fertig, 1985), 11. According to Mosse (12) "[few] had paid attention to masturbation before 1760, when Dr. Simon André Tissot's *L'Onanisme* pointed out its supposed dangers. Voltaire popularised Tissot, and Rousseau joined in the chorus."

38. *Ratsad'on*, 15 January 1929. As Chalat wrote, "If a husband or wife devotes his or her energies to the needs of those outside the home . . . their own family will not flourish and progress."

39. *Ratsad'on*, 11 January 1929.

40. *Ratsad'on*, 11 January 1929.

41. *Ratsad'on*, 9 January 1929.

42. *Ratsad'on*, 14 January 1929.

43. B. J. Terwiel, *Monks and Magic: An Analysis of Religious Ceremonies in Central Thailand*, Scandinavian Institute of Asian Studies Monograph Series no. 24 (London: Curzon Press, 1979), 93–94.

44. *Ratsad'on*, 11 January 1929.

45. *Ratsad'on*, 24 January 1929.

46. *Ratsad'on*, 20, 25 January 1929.

47. *Ratsad'on*, 21 January 1929. Continuing to develop this theme he offered the following advice: "A woman's breasts require gentle, loving care. Her nipples, for example, are very sensitive, one of the sources of sexual arousal. A man should be alert to this fact and not neglect to stimulate his wife and thereby greatly increase her pleasure."

48. *Ratsad'on*, 18 January 1929.

49. *Ratsad'on*, 28 January 1929.

8

❦

Romance and Desire in Film and Fiction

In Thai [film] drama the conflicts and confusions of modernity are represented in the relations between the sexes and the generations: typically through a dynamic of love, error, guilt, reparation and redemption as the individual struggles with the consequences of pre-modern gender, social and familial relations.

—Annette Hamilton, 1992[1]

The growing commodification of culture, as witnessed by the development of commercial publishing and indigenous filmmaking, has already been discussed in general terms. At this point I would like to look more closely at a range of popular works produced during the 1920s and early 1930s, including a number of short stories, novels, and films, most of which incorporate a strong romantic element. This discussion moves from an examination of conventional romantic stories, which promoted traditional notions about marriage and choice of romantic partners, to those projecting ideas of assertive womanhood and independent love. In addition a number of works that were primarily concerned with conveying moral messages to young men and women about the pitfalls of romance and sexual intimacy are considered. Broadly speaking these works can be seen to complement the press commentaries and cartoon graphics examined earlier and provide us with a more nuanced view of questions concerning the position of women and relations between the sexes in the latter years of absolutist rule. In part, I am taking my cue from an article on Thai film drama by Annette Hamilton, from which the above quote is taken. Here it should be mentioned that Hamilton's observation, suggestive as it is of a key relationship between Thai popular culture and modernity, was made with reference to late-twentieth-century Thai film drama. As we shall see, however, the dilemmas of modernity she identifies were also intrinsic to much Siamese prose fiction writing and filmmaking from the latter 1920s, the period in which indigenous popular commercial culture first came into its own.

CONVENTIONAL ROMANTIC TALES

In the following section a number of romantic works representative of the dominant trend in popular fiction and film during the latter 1920s and early 1930s are considered. While these works were invariably set in the contemporary world of Bangkok, an environment that presented unattached young men and women with unprecedented opportunities to fraternize and form relationships with one another, they tended to be socially conformist in the way in which they were resolved. Although projecting images of modernity and the promise of youthful independence in matters of the heart, such narratives reaffirmed certain long-standing elite social practices and values, in particular that of the arranged marriage and the idea that romance and marriage were only acceptable between men and women from the same social class.

Arranged Marriage

The long-standing elite practice of arranged marriage was a common element in many of the romantic confections produced during the period under discussion. It was, for example, central to one of the first Siamese films, *Mai khit loei* (Well, I Never Imagined), an action-romance feature, made in 1927 by *Luang* Sunth'on Atsaworarat's Thai Film Company.[2]

Prapha Sethakun, the central female character in the story, is the only child of *Phra* Sethakit Wibun, a fabulously wealthy Bangkok widower and prominent race-horse owner. *Phra* Sethakit has made plans for his daughter to marry Kalong Bunchup, the scion of an even wealthier family. However, despite her father's wishes, Prapha has no interest in marrying Kalong, whom she sees as an uninspiring if earnest fellow, hardly enticing husband material. Indeed, she is far more attracted to Amnuay, another young man whom she met by chance when he came to her aid following a minor horse-riding accident. Meanwhile, yet another young man, Prasoet Sakloet, a cousin of Prapha, has his eye on her and makes a number of unsuccessful attempts to win her affections. Later, when Prasoet becomes aware of Prapha's fondness for Amnuay, he begins to plot with some of his criminal cohorts to eliminate this potential rival. An opportunity arises when Amnuay is chosen to ride one of *Phra* Sethakit's horses in an upcoming race. Prasoet instructs his men to tamper with the girth strap hoping that Amnuay will fall from his mount at speed and be seriously injured or, even better, killed. At the last minute, however, Amnuay is prevented from taking his mount after inadvertently hurting himself and the eager but inexperienced Kalong is called on to take his place. Notwithstanding his lack of riding ability the novice jockey somehow manages to stay in the saddle and win the race. Prapha is greatly impressed by this feat and begins to warm to him. At this point, however, she is kidnapped by the vengeful Prasoet and his gang. Emboldened by his success on the track, Kalong rises to the occasion once again and single-handedly rescues the young woman from the villain's den before Prasoet can have his way with her. Now that he has proved himself a hero in her eyes, Prapha realizes she's in love with him rather than with Amnuay who, rather conveniently, suddenly disappears from the scene. With the various complications, such as they are, having been resolved, the film concludes with Prapha and Kalong being joined in matrimony. Thus, despite Prapha's initial disinclination to wed the man of her father's choosing, she ultimately does what is expected of her, the film reaffirming, with a gesture toward romance, the appropriateness of arranged marriage and the underlying wisdom of elite tradition and custom.

A similar theme was also taken up in the 1929 novel *Her Foe* (*Sattru kh'ong chao l'on*) by D'ok Mai Sot, Siam's most renowned early female author.[3] However, whereas Prapha in *Well, I Never Imagined* was little more than a cipher who simply functioned as an object of competing male desire, Mayuri, the heroine of *Her Foe*, in common with most of D'ok Mai Sot's female characters, was a thoughtfully constructed figure who combined intelligence, femininity, and a sense of purpose.

Mayuri is the feisty daughter of *Phraya* Maitriphitak, a former Siamese ambassador to the United States who now operates a textile factory in Bangkok. While Mayuri was still a teenager, *Phraya* Maitriphitak had arranged for her to marry one of her cousins, Prasong Wibunsak, the foreign-educated son of a retired high-ranking government official. Having spent a number of years in America during her father's posting, Mayuri has become decidedly "Westernized" in that she smokes, drinks, and goes out to the cinema unchaperoned.[4] Most important, she is strongly opposed to the idea of arranged marriage and has absolutely no interest in becoming involved with Prasong. Once these details have been established the story, somewhat predictably, concerns the drawn-out process whereby Prasong, with the connivance of his father and Mayuri's, gradually wins the affections of his betrothed. In the beginning Prasong, disguised with the aid of a moustache and posing as a young man by the name of Prasom, continually runs afoul of Mayuri who loathes him with a vengeance. Not to be put off, he pursues her assiduously and, at one point, fearlessly defends her honor by administering a beating to two impetuous men who openly cast aspersions on her character and morality at a dinner-dance party in a glitzy Bangkok mansion. Shortly afterward he comes to her aid once again and saves her from being raped by another man who had initially sought to court her. As a result Mayuri develops an affection for Prasom which ultimately blossoms into love when he reveals his true identity as Prasong.

In *Her Foe* the complex and multifaceted issue of tradition versus Western notions of modernity is simplified and personalized in a romantic context. Briefly put, D'ok Mai Sot was articulating a fundamentally traditionalist perspective in the face of change, thereby affirming customary forms of behavior rather than questioning or challenging them. Here the dilemmas and confusions of modernity referred to by Hamilton earlier are highlighted yet neatly resolved with little sense of ambiguity or conflict. Overcoming her foreign ideas of independent action and behavior, Mayuri ultimately embraces the long-standing indigenous practice of arranged marriage. With her acceptance of the man chosen by her father, Mayuri's independence of thought is, in effect, shown to be an illusion. While she may exhibit modern, Western traits, the author seeks to emphasize that the heroine is, at heart, a traditionally minded Siamese. Indeed, to do otherwise would reflect a deep and powerful sense of cultural alienation that was perhaps too disturbing to contemplate.

Interestingly, while the question of cultural alienation and the slavish embrace of the West was critically discussed in the press, most notably by King Vajiravudh,[5] a fervent nationalist on the one hand and an avid Anglophile on the other, novelists of the period tended to express similar views to those of D'ok Mai Sot. Cultural dissonance, for example, was the central theme taken up in the novels of M. C. (Prince) Akat Damkoeng Raphiphat.[6] Despite Akat's deep appreciation of and admiration for much to be found in the West, his characters—notwithstanding their foreign learning—ultimately come to identify themselves, in the deepest sense, as Thai. This suggests that notions regarding Thai identity exerted an extremely powerful if not hegemonic influence on the writers and thinkers of the time.

Conforming to Class: Poor? Rich? Boy Meets Rich Girl

Another socially confirming theme common to both early film and prose fiction was that involving romance and social class. This theme, for example, was incorporated in *Survarna of Siam* (*Nangsao suwan*), the American-Thai feature film referred to in chapter 2. A contemporary story primarily set in Bangkok, the film traces the vexatious romance of *Nangsao* Suwan and *Nai* Kla Han, or Mr. Bravery.[7] The problem lies in the fact that whereas Suwan comes from a wealthy background, Kla Han, a lowly clerk at the National Library, grew up in an ordinary lower-class family. The two first meet when Kla Han rescues Suwan after she has accidentally fallen into the Chaophraya River while on a boat trip. Kla Han is immediately smitten by the young woman and begins thinking about her night and day. While grateful to Kla Han for saving his daughter's life, Suwan's father is firmly opposed to any relationship between the pair owing to Kla Han's lower-class origins. Indeed, he is planning for his daughter to marry *Nai* K'ong Kaew, a well-born young man who has been courting her.

Despite these obstacles Kla Han and Suwan meet by chance on a number of occasions and soon develop a close rapport with one another. Seeing the two enjoying themselves together during one such encounter, K'ong Kaew becomes jealous and, later, after she rejects his proposal of marriage, hatches a plan to have his rival murdered. The action then moves to the northern city of Chiang Mai where K'ong Kaew has made arrangements for Kla Han to get work in a timber business operated by his family and where he believes it will be easier for the assassination to be carried out. But K'ong Kaew's plan goes awry, and he and his accomplices are arrested by the police. Meanwhile, it is revealed that Kla Han is not really a member of the lower classes after all, but rather comes from an illustrious northern lineage. What had transpired was that as a child Kla Han had accompanied his father on a trip to Bangkok. Shortly after arriving in the city, however, his father died suddenly, leaving the boy to fend for himself. As it turned out, he was discovered by a lower-class couple who took him in and raised him as their own son. When this becomes known and Kla Han's real social origins are established, Suwan's father immediately drops his objections to the young man taking up with his daughter and the film ends with the happy couple getting married.

The method of resolving class differences between the lovers found in *Survarna of Siam* (the discovery that the hero was not really from a lower order but actually came from the same social stratum as the heroine) was, as suggested earlier, a common element in many popular cultural works of the time.[8] The idea of an enduring relationship across class lines, particularly between a lower-class man and a higher-class woman, was virtually inconceivable. Indeed, it reflected the continuing, and pervasive, influence of traditional elite thought and practice which was rigidly opposed to such unions.[9] Even that most progressive and idealistic of writers, Kulap Saipradit, confirmed the status quo in his work. In Kulap's 1932 novel *Songkhram chiwit* (The War of Life),[10] for example, Raphin Yuthasin, the lower-class protagonist of the story, is ultimately rejected by Phloen (the poor young woman he is enamored with) when she is discovered by a filmmaker and becomes a movie star. In brushing Raphin aside Phloen reveals to him the long-kept secret that she originally came from a wealthy upper-class family. While her sudden change in fortune in becoming an actress was a factor in the termination of their relationship, it is clear that their love was actually doomed from the start by the fact that they came from vastly different social worlds. The underlying message was clear enough: romantic relationships across class lines were untenable, particularly between well-born women and lower-class men, and individual feelings and desires were of secondary importance to the social imperative of maintaining class boundaries.

Dynamic Women, Independent Love

With the appearance of a rash of new literary magazines and journals during the last decade of absolute rule, aspiring young authors (both male and female) had unprecedented opportunities to have their work published. In concert with the rigorous national debate on the social position of women, dynamic new images of womanhood were also increasingly manifest in the less overtly political realm of prose fiction writing. A notable example of this particular phenomenon was "The Female Bandit Leader" (*Ch'om chori*), a simple yet intriguing 1931 short story serialized in the weekly women's paper *Suphap nari* (Genteel Lady).

The story, by a female writer referred to as "Miss Sichan" (*Nangsao Sichan*), is set in contemporary Bangkok and describes one night in the working life of a female gang boss who, incidentally, is also named Sichan. In a preface to the story proper, Sichan is described as an "unflappable aristocratic criminal boss" (*ch'om chon phu-di mi nisai y'uak yen*) who was well known throughout Siam for her brazen exploits. She was tough, decisive, and fearless, something of a female "godfather" (*Nang phaya s'ua tua kwaen*), ruthless in her criminal pursuits.[11]

The image which accompanied the story (fig. 8.1) shows a couple in a speeding automobile pursued by a masked figure of indeterminate sex on a horse, the chase set against a mountain backdrop. While the graphic does not bear a direct relationship to the story as such, it would not be out of place in one of the popular Western action-adventure films screened in the Bangkok cinemas at the time. Indeed, a relationship between this particular narrative and film is underlined elsewhere in the same issue of *Suphap nari* when the magazine's editor, discussing its literary offerings to readers, likens Sichan, the female bandit leader, to the screen character "Asaenglupaeng," a Parisian gang boss well known to local cinema-going audiences.[12]

In *Ch'om chori* Sichan carries out a daring theft at the celebrated nightclub on the seventh floor of what was then Bangkok's tallest modern structure, commonly referred to by the city's inhabitants as the "seven-story building" (*t'uk chet chan*).[13] Sichan and her gang go to the nightclub with the intention of stealing a

Fig. 8.1.

valuable necklace from *Nangsao* Pradap (Miss Adornment), the daughter of a local millionaire. Pradap is seated at a table together with her boyfriend, Police Captain San'o, and her younger sister. Sichan walks up to Captain San'o as if to greet him. The policeman is somewhat taken aback and says he does not know her. She smiles and wipes her face with a handkerchief, a prearranged signal for a member of her gang to throw the lights for a fraction of a second, in which time she steals Pradap's prized necklace. When the lights come back on moments later Sichan, on hearing that San'o is a police captain, says, "It doesn't matter who you are, I'm not afraid of anything" and dangles Pradap's necklace contemptuously in front of him, before vanishing as the lights go out again. Although San'o manages to arrest Sichan shortly afterward, she escapes with the help of her gang, takes the policeman and the two sisters prisoner, and relieves them of their remaining valuables. Having robbed her victims, in a further act of mockery, Sichan orders her men to release the captives. For his part, San'o is devastated by what has occurred and the story ends with him walking away in bewildered silence, totally outfoxed by his female nemesis.

Cho'm chori represents an early, if crude, attempt to portray a Siamese (as opposed to a Western) female character in marked contrast to the stereotypical indigenous view of women as the "weaker sex" (*phet 'on ae*) who lacked courage and decisiveness. Moreover, the story incorporates, in its own way, a degree of social comment. In the context of the broader movement for female equality at the time, *Ch'om chori* offered an insouciant critique of male authority. The hapless Police Captain San'o, a symbol of this authority, is outwitted by Sichan at every turn. He is made to look foolish and incompetent. More generally, the way in which the efforts of San'o are ridiculed can be read as an oblique commentary on the failings of the police, something that was well documented in the contemporary press,[14] and, by extension, the law itself, a central instrument of state authority.

The bold, self-confident, and flamboyant image of womanhood projected in *Ch'om chori* was also found in other types of women's writing of the period. For example, at the same time as *Ch'om chori* appeared, *Suphap nari* began to serialize two fascinating historical works: "*Phra* Suriyothai phadet s'uk" (Suriyothai Ends the War) by "Charoensuk," which dealt with the martial exploits of Queen Suriyothai during the Ayuthaya period, and "*Thao* Thepkasatri" (Lady Thepkasatri) by 'O R'o Asakit, the story of Thepkasatri's role in organizing Siamese resistance to a Burmese invasion of Thalang (Phuket) in the late eighteenth century.[15] These historical figures, it will be recalled, had been briefly discussed in the early women's magazines *Kunlasatri* and *Satri niphon*. When the stories of Queen Suriyothai and *Thao* Thepkasatri appeared in *Suphap nari*, however, there was a significant difference: they were published in the form of chronicle-style historical adventure-romances, similar to the immensely popular Chinese chronicle-style histories featured in the leading Bangkok dailies during the 1920s.[16] Simply put, what the authors of "*Phra* Suriyothai phadet s'uk" and "*Thao* Thepkasatri" had done was to incorporate a nationalist-feminist discourse, in which women were portrayed as no less courageous or significant than men in "national" struggles of the past, into a popular genre of writing that was both familiar and appealing to readers.

These popular historical representations of the "national Thai woman" (a term Reynolds uses in his discussion of gender and Thai history)[17] are significant in that they not only promoted a new, assertive image of womanhood but also prefigured various developments in the realm of state-sanctioned culture during the post-1932 period. A notable example of this was the 1936 historical dance-drama, *L'uat Suphan* (Blood of Suphan) written by *Luang* Wichit Wathakan, director of the Department of Fine Arts (see chapter 9). As mentioned earlier Wichit was a member of a new generation of Thai men who believed in greater equality between the sexes. This view, expressed in his 1930 radio talk on women, was also articulated in some of his earliest prose fiction works, including "Sam'on" which is discussed.

INDEPENDENT LOVE AND ROMANCE

Everyone in the world wants to be independent/free [*thai*]. Nobody likes to be ruled over by a coercive, oppressive master [*nai*]. . . . In certain cases, however, it is necessary to have a master or leader. For example countries need leaders and different types of work require bosses. In other instances this is not the case. Women, for example, don't necessarily always need a husband to watch over them.[18]

The above passage comes from an article published in the woman's magazine *Satri thai*. While the article was primarily concerned with the question of female independence and freedom in relation to employment, its underlying message was to affirm the idea of liberty for women more generally, including the notion of greater female independence and freedom with regard to love and romance.

The idea of female independence in love has been remarked on by Reynolds. Discussing the issues of gender and pre-1932 popular culture he suggests a particular relationship between romantic prose fiction and nationalism. In his view characters in romantic works "were portrayed as being in control of their own fate and making their own choices in matters of the heart." From this he hypothesizes a type of parallelism or congruence between romantic fiction and nationalism, claiming that "just as nationalists were arguing about self-rule in the public sphere so the characters in [romantic works] sought self-rule in the private domain."[19] This is an interesting notion, although it is contradicted by the type of romantic works discussed above that endorse, as we have seen, the idea of arranged marriages. Even so this is not to say that Reynolds's formulation is without merit. In fact it relates to other literary texts which challenged or went against the dominant trend in popular cultural representations of love and romance.

One such work was "Sam'on" (Beautiful and Beloved Woman), a short story by *Luang* Wichit Wathakan published in 1929.[20] Sam'on, the central character in the story, comes from a middle-class provincial family. Her parents, who had socially progressive views for the times, taught her from a young age to be self-reliant and to think for herself. She is highly intelligent and in the hope of realizing her full potential they send her to a school in the capital where she receives a good education. On graduating, Sam'on is employed as the personal assistant of *Luang* Banchong, a well-to-do government official who has made a name for himself as a writer of romantic fiction. Although Banchong is married to a young woman, simply referred to as Madam (*khun nai*) rather than by name, the story centers on an evolving relationship between himself and Sam'on, a relationship that evinces little evident concern or jealousy in Madam, whose primary motivations in life are money and material comforts.

In working together Banchong takes on the role of Sam'on's mentor and introduces her to the notion of "pure love" (*khwam-rak an borisut*), a concept at the very heart of the story. He tells her that such love is like a force of nature, immensely powerful, uncontrollable, and beyond the laws of man. Indeed, Banchong believes that pure love is the most wondrous thing of all and claims that anyone who experienced such love, no matter how poor or wretched they happened to be materially, were infinitely more fortunate than a wealthy person who knew nothing of it.[21]

Sam'on becomes intrigued with Banchong's ideas and tells him that she has begun writing a fictional biography of a young woman, entitled *Pure Love*. Some months later, when Banchong asks Sam'on how the book is going, she tells him she is having problems developing the plot. The crux of the matter is this: the female protagonist is deeply in love with a married man who seems unaware of her affections; meanwhile, the young woman's mother has arranged for her to marry a rich man without bothering to get her daughter's consent. Sam'on tells Banchong that an arranged marriage is an "impure" form of love (*khwam-rak mai borisut*) and asks him what the young woman should do. To this, Banchong responds that the young woman should defer to her mother's wishes and go ahead with the marriage.[22] On hearing this Sam'on casts all pretence aside and reveals that she is not really writing a book at all and that she is madly in love with him. Banchong, while taken aback by her frank admission, quickly regathers his composure and reaffirms what he has just said, that she should do as her mother wishes. He even offers to sponsor the wedding himself.

With great reluctance Sam'on agrees to his proposal, and plans are made for the wedding to take place in her home province. Notwithstanding what he had told her, Banchong has strongly mixed feelings about the planned marriage. On the morning of the wedding he thinks to himself that it would probably bring her "security and happiness," while ruefully musing, "Alas, this wonderful fresh rose will be bruised tonight and henceforth there will be one less virgin to contribute to the beauty and splendor of this world."[23] However, Sam'on has plans of her own and, after going through with the marriage ceremony, disappears without a trace, leaving her new husband to spend their wedding night alone.

A few days later, Banchong, who has returned to Bangkok, receives a letter from Sam'on in which she writes:

> All over the world women are greatly undervalued. The way things are it is as if women are simply objects to be bought and sold. . . . I was born with a soul . . . I've got a heart and feelings. I don't want my life to be like a water hyacinth [*phak top chawa*] swept along willy-nilly in a flowing river. I want to have the right to do what I want to do. My love is far more valuable than a mere commodity. I want to have the right to choose the person I love, not to be handed over to a rich man who has money in his wallet and uses it to buy whatever he takes a fancy to.[24]

In a dramatic flourish she declares that she is going to leave the city for the country, where she can assert her independence away from the disapproving gaze of others. Finally, in closing, she says that if he ever wants to see her again she will be on a train leaving for the northeastern region the following day. Banchong deliberates over her ultimatum long and hard, unsure as to what to do. Ultimately, however, he decides to sacrifice everything—his job, his wealth, and his wife—to be with Sam'on, to become (as he puts it) her "slave" (*that*).[25]

They meet on the train, leave the city behind and, with the help of local villagers, establish a home in the mountains leading up to the Khorat plateau. Together in their lofty redoubt, far from civilization, the couple feels as if they are a Thai Adam and Eve, the only two people on earth. Banchong is well satisfied with their new life, while Sam'on, feeling "happier than a queen," is inspired to begin work on a novel that she plans to call *Pure Love*.[26]

Meanwhile news of the couple filters back to Bangkok, where their flight becomes the talk of the town. They are roundly condemned in many quarters; lawyers refer to the matter as a case of adultery, while parents warn their children not to follow Sam'on's lead. The only people to come to the couple's defense are writers (*nak-praphan*). Writers, according to Wichit in an authorial interjection, "knew all about the power of love; they understood the pair, their motivations and feelings. . . . [In their view] seeking freedom of the heart [*ha itsaraphap kae hua-chai*] was in no way as evil as accepting bribes or cheating the public . . . [therefore] they willingly wrote in support of the lovers and defended them against their critics."[27]

At the same time the "husband" Sam'on had left behind, having closely followed the gossip surrounding the pair, discovers where they are living and prepares to avenge himself. One night, as Banchong and Sam'on are asleep in their idyllic if crude abode (she three months pregnant), the "husband," with the help of friends, carts a large quantity of kerosene up into the hills, douses the dense bush surrounding their dwelling with fuel, and sets it alight. An inferno ensues, incinerating the house and the couple inside; the villagers later find the charred remains of the two corpses, one lying on top of the other.

The passing of the lovers is mourned by few people at the time. But as Wichit predicts, in a reflective aside which concludes the story, this would be but a temporary aberration. "We are born, and who among us doesn't die? Sam'on has passed away, but her name lives on. One day the bad associations that presently surround it will vanish and all just people will recognize the good in her."[28]

In "Sam'on" Wichit gave full expression to the ideal of independence in romantic love, the supreme value of this being emphasized by the lovers' sacrifice of material comfort and security in order to be together. Such a love, however, was sharply at odds with reigning social beliefs and practices, this being underlined by the couple's flight from the city in an attempt to create a new, better world of their own. Clearly, "Sam'on" can be seen as an allegory in the sense suggested by Reynolds: a romance with a popular nationalist resonance. Indeed, viewed in this light it is a story which speaks of a complex reality. On the one hand, it gives voice to a sense of frustration and pessimism with regard to the possibility for independent love and, by extension, political—albeit crudely utopic—independence. But, on the other, it holds out the hope that, despite powerful forces opposed to change, the struggle for greater freedom in the realm of the personal—as well as the political—was something that would ultimately be realized. In writing "Sam'on" Wichit revealed himself as a leading proponent of a new type of thinking among the rising generation of young middle-class men. This thinking is further evidenced by the moral subtext of the story, which may be summarized as follows: the practice of arranged marriages was taken to be unconscionable; the idea of having a minor wife was eschewed (after all, there was no legal impediment preventing Banchong from taking Sam'on as a second wife); and the practice of monogamy was projected as the ideal form of marriage.

The theme of assertive womanhood and independent love was also developed by Wichit's contemporary D'ok Mai Sot in her 1930 short story-cum novella entitled "Romance s'on r'uang ching" (Romance Concealed in a True Story), although in a somewhat more muted form.[29] This work offers something of a counterpoint to the ideas D'ok Mai Sot advanced in her novel *Her Foe*, discussed earlier, and reminds us that it is mistaken to assume that authors project a wholly consistent, singular view of the world in their writings.

Chawi, the central character in the story, is the daughter of a high-ranking official, *Phraya* Worakanphamrung, and one of his minor wives. Following her father's premature death Chawi is left in the care of her paternal uncle, *Phra* Norarat, who ensures that she receives a well-rounded education. Over time she develops into a virtuous, thoughtful young woman. At this point Wat Purinsuang, a thirty-eight-year-old government official from a prosperous Bangkok fam-

ily, arrives on the scene and is strongly attracted to her. For all of his wealth Wat
is portrayed as a "shallow thinker" given to easy pleasures, a man with a desul-
tory, casual attitude to work. Moreover, he has a wife and two young children
and suffers from something of a drinking problem. Not surprisingly, Chawi, half
his age and religiously inclined, shows little interest in him, although her opinion of the man gradually begins to soften slightly when she learns that his wife
has left him and his children are being raised by another member of the family.
Even so, in a heart-to-heart talk with Chamnong, an elder sister, Chawi is dismissive of Wat for his lack of ambition, and says, "He doesn't even make the
slightest effort to be a good citizen of the nation, his birthplace."[30]

 At this point the author breaks into the narrative and interjects:

> When the nation was mentioned in relation to individuals in such a way, Cham-
> nong, like most women—who never consider what the nation actually means—
> became confused. When Chawi uttered the words "good citizen" [phonlam'uang di]
> and "nation" they made no sense to her. Chamnong simply could not understand
> what her sister was talking about when she spoke of the "nation" and the "people."

Here the authorial voice drops away and the passage continues as an interior
monologue by Chamnong who thinks to herself, "What have women got to do
with the nation? It's inappropriate for women to concern themselves with being
good or bad citizens, or with the nation for that matter."[31]

But Chawi is depicted as a modern Siamese woman, vitally interested in and
concerned with national issues. And this is what puts her at odds with Wat. In
her view Wat, while rich and good looking, is a vain, self-centered individual,
unworthy of respect or love and, worst of all, blind to the needs of the nation.
In order to redeem himself Chawi urges Wat to abandon his frivolous obsession
with fine clothes and horse racing and to lend a hand to "the poor farmers who
are so ruthlessly exploited by Chinese merchants and other foreigners."[32]

At this point the pair go their separate ways. Several years later, however, they
happen to meet again when Chawi is holidaying with her stepparents in Phetburi
province, to the southwest of Bangkok. We learn that Wat is now a changed
man; having resigned from the bureaucracy and abandoned his profligate ways,
he has begun a purposeful new life in Phetburi, where he raises cattle and has
established a sugar factory employing local Siamese workers. Initially, Chawi
does not know what to make of Wat's transformation and is unsure of her feelings toward him. On returning to Bangkok, however, she gradually realizes that
she loves him and willingly accepts his offer of marriage conveyed to her family
by one of his uncles.

We subsequently learn more about Wat's dramatic transformation. He tells his
young bride:

> After my widowed mother passed away I was depressed and lonely. I traveled to
> Malaya and later on to Java. When I visited these colonies I saw people who were

enslaved by other nations, yet at the same time I saw the material progress Europeans had brought about. This experience gave me a greater sense of perspective and, in turn, made me think more about my own country. . . . I felt both love and pity for Siam and worried for its future. When I returned from Malaya I traveled up through the south and saw it was fertile but sparsely populated. What is more, I found that the people were woefully ignorant, they simply didn't know what was going on. I felt the need to help in some way yet didn't know what to do. Then I thought about what you'd said and how you'd reproached me for not being of use to anyone, even to myself.[33]

Wat then goes on to admit, with some embarrassment, that she was right—that he was indeed a "worthless, good-for-nothing." Having confessed to his past follies he sings Chawi's praises and says that with her as his confidante he now has the inspiration and perseverance needed to succeed in business.[34]

In "Romance Concealed in a True Story" D'ok Mai Sot presented her readers with an idealized image of contemporary womanhood, and manhood. It was an image that not only incorporated the bourgeois notion of "wife as partner" (similar to that articulated by Thianwan in the early 1900s) but also stressed the importance of committing oneself to working for the good of the nation. The story is also interesting for other reasons. As the title of the work suggests, the romance was fictional while other elements of the text were concerned with real life. When Chawi goes to Phetburi on holiday, for example, we learn about various aspects of local life such as the intricacies of the sugar-making process. Of more interest, however, are the author's observations about the female population of Phetburi. "The women of Phetburi do not regard themselves as inferior to men; indeed some of them play a more prominent role than that of the men." This was reflected in the economic life of the provincial capital where women had traditionally dominated small-scale marketing activities. With the growth of the money economy, women had come even more to the fore and a new type of female entrepreneur had begun to emerge. The author mentions two such women, apparently bitter rivals, one who owned a local market and the other who operated a small fleet of taxis. Described as "middle class" (*chan klang*), these women were members of a "new social stratum . . . following the modern way of people in Bangkok" (*chan mai-mai . . . tam samai chao krung-thep*). D'ok Mai Sot also notes that there were women in Nakhorn Pathom (a province to the west of Bangkok) even more modern (*samai mai mak kwa*) than those in Phetburi, in that they dressed more stylishly, played sports, and raced bicycles. These developments are fascinating and illustrate that social change affecting women was not confined to the capital. At the same time, this type of "reporting from the provinces" complemented the fictive aspect of the story by giving both substance and credence to the author's idea of the modern, dynamic woman.[35]

Another category of popular cultural works from the same period were those concerned with sexual morality and propriety, issues that increasingly came to

the fore in the freer, more fluid social environment of Bangkok during the final
years of absolute rule.

MORAL MESSAGES: WARNINGS
TO YOUNG WOMEN

The cartoon graphic depicted in figure 8.2, featured on the cover of the feminist
magazine *Satri thai*, provides a pointed commentary on relations between the
sexes. To the left of the picture is a notice board that refers to three kinds of
news story commonly found in the press of the day. These stories (from left to
right) concern "divorce cases," "husbands beating their wives," and "wives running away from their husbands." In front of the board stands a figure identified
as *Kamathep*, the Siamese equivalent of Cupid, the Roman god of love. Dejected
by the reality of the daily news reports, a tearful *Kamathep* breaks his bow and
arrow in two. Women's intimate relations with men, the cartoonist implies, were
a source of heartbreak and sorrow, this being one of the major and recurrent
themes addressed in the magazine as it sought to provide its readers with a sense
of purpose and moral guidance.

While such guidance generally took the form of editorial comment and exhor-
tation, from time to time *Satri thai* also published literary works conveying moral
messages, essentially cautionary tales about the pitfalls of adolescent love. One
such tale, indeed the first fictional work to be published by the magazine, was
entitled "Mistaken Love or Free Marriage" [*thalam rak r'u somrot doi itsara*].[36] The
story, credited to a woman writer who used the pseudonym "Atsawanon," was

Fig. 8.2. *Satri thai*, 27 December 1926

putatively based on "The Free Marriage of the Headstrong Young Mary Woodson," the work of an unnamed American author. As an adaptation (*pen r'uang riap riang*) rather than translation (*r'uang plae*) of a foreign text, the story represents something of a transitional form of Siamese prose fiction, transitional in the sense that it was neither a direct translation nor an original piece of indigenous prose fiction, a form that was still very much at an embryonic stage.

Set in the United States during the early 1920s, the story is about the wayward life of Mary Woodson, the teenage heiress to a substantial fortune in Washington, D.C. A comely beauty, Mary thinks that a woman's life is primarily concerned with finding a man and stubbornly holds to the view that "good-looking men only marry good-looking women." For her, appearances are everything, so much so in fact that she is deaf to her widowed mother's repeated warnings that an evil man, no matter how handsome, would always remain a villain. Unlike her mother, however, Mary believes in the possibility of redemption, a view that was crucially influenced by a film she had seen in which a notorious criminal was transformed into a respectable, upstanding citizen through the power of a woman's love.

Aged sixteen, Mary is ready to assert her independence; she drops out of school and disappears from home without warning. Her anguished mother, fearful that Mary has been kidnapped or even murdered, engages a private detective to track her daughter down. As a result of the detective's investigations Mrs. Woodson discovers that Mary has run off and married a handsome thirty-year-old man by the name of Jack and has moved to Brooklyn with him. With some trepidation the mother travels to Brooklyn in the hope of making her daughter come to her senses and return home. On arriving in the city she learns that Jack, who works as a humble bread van driver, is actually "Maurice Shelkhovitz," a Russian émigré with a criminal background. This news comes as a great shock to Mrs. Woodson; Mary, in an attempt to assuage her fears, says that she knows all about his past and is convinced he is now a changed man.

However, Mary's trust proves to be misplaced. Rather than forsaking his criminal ways, Jack has become rather more adept at concealing them. Moreover, it is revealed that he is a bigamist (a criminal offense in the West) having already married a number of other women before taking Mary as his wife. As this comes to light Jack is arrested and sent to court, where the judge orders him deported to his native Russia. At this point the narrative proper breaks off and the author, that is the author of the original story, concludes the tale by making the following observation: "to believe that there is no one as silly or stupid as an old person is simply not true. Young men and women are no less foolish than the old. Indeed, sometimes they are far more so."[37]

Interestingly, the Thai version of the story includes a number of further observations. For example Atsawanon, the writer who adapted the work, bemoaned the fact Mary had lost her virginity (*sia khwam-borisut*) and was at pains to emphasize that this happened because she had willfully disregarded her mother's warnings. No longer chaste and now husbandless, Mary was described as "irredeemably tarnished" (*pen monthin yu mai ru hai*). In saying this, the author reaffirmed traditional social values concerning women and the sexual double standard. She also pointed out that Mary's case was in no way unique and that nowadays most women—including those in Siam—were prone to making similar errors of judgment. But this was not inevitable, she intimated, and told readers that if they wished to avoid such misfortunes they should reflect on the advice of the renowned nineteenth-century Siamese poet Sunthorn Phu, contained in his "Sayings for the Teaching of Women" (*Suphasit s'on ying*): "If a man really loves you, ask him to go and seek your mother's permission to marry. Don't think about running away with him just because he's handsome. If he fails to take care of you and casts you aside it will be the cause of much shame and embarrassment. You'll simply become a divorced woman stuck at home, a humiliation to yourself."[38]

Here Atsawanon drew the past and present together by citing native wisdom as the way of overcoming what was seen as a serious contemporary problem—that increasing social interaction between the sexes posed dangers to the young, especially young middle- and upper-class women. In other words, the answer to a modern dilemma was to be found in traditional Siamese culture.

Apart from being a cautionary moral tale, the story—despite its foreign origins—had a number of other local resonances. As mentioned above Mary's belief in redemption for the wicked was crucially shaped by her exposure to a film about a villain reformed by the power of love. In Siam film had come to be regarded as an extremely potent medium, and its influence on the values and behavior of the young was frequently discussed in the daily press (not to mention by essayists such as Chalat, whose work was examined in the previous chapter).[39] More often than not, writers were of the view that the cinema, or more specifically films with themes that involved crime or sex, had a harmful effect on the nation's youth by filling their minds with all manner of sensational and salacious ideas. Mary's credulity in accepting what she saw in the cinema as true only served to confirm such critical views.

There was also an ethnic dimension to the story that would have struck a chord of familiarity in readers. Indeed, the ethnic element of the story is intriguing. That Jack, the scoundrel of the piece, happened to be a Russian was surely not coincidental. Coming from an atheistic communist state can only have served to amplify his wickedness among American readers. And just as the evils of communist Russia were familiar to those in the United States, so they were to the Thai reading public who were kept abreast of international events through the daily press. In other words, Jack's ethnic origins, and the fact that he was deported back to his homeland as punishment, signified his villainy not only to readers of the English-language original but also to those of the Thai adaptation of the story.

Another typical cautionary tale from the period was an original short story entitled "Lom rak" (Windy Words of Love) published by the women's newspaper *Suphap nari* in April 1930. Written by a female author using the pseudonym "Atsawayut," the story was prefaced by the following observation: "The life of a poor young orphaned woman is a life surrounded by danger; the life of such a girl is like that of a small boat adrift in the middle of the ocean."

The central figure in the story is Saman, a poor young orphaned woman with little formal education. She is employed as a servant in the home of *Chao khun* Phakriangyot, a wealthy noble. On returning to Siam after studying in England, Phitsawong, the *Chao khun's* only son, is immediately attracted to the eighteen-year-old Saman and begins to flirt with her. Although she initially resists his advances, Saman finally succumbs to Phitsawong's sophisticated manner and honeyed words of love.[40] While the couple's affair goes unnoticed at first, it can no longer be kept a secret when Saman becomes visibly pregnant. Phitsawong's parents are enraged when they discover what has been going on and banish her to a small shack far away from the main residence. At the same time they arrange for Phitsawong to marry one of his cousins. Phitsawong makes no attempt to oppose their plan and tells Saman that he had no choice but to accede to his parent's wishes. To do otherwise, he argues, would be to "betray" them and cause them a huge loss of face. Saman, appalled by Phitsawong's failure to stand by her, condemns him bitterly, saying that for all his foreign education and charm he is nothing more than a cruel, heartless beast. At this point Phitsawong's mother appears on the scene and verbally abuses the young woman, referring to her as *Nang* Wan Th'ong, the ill-fated lead female character in the classical Siamese poem "Khun Chang Khun Phaen" (*Khun* Chang and *Khun* Phaen are the two male protagonists involved in a love triangle with *Nang* Wan Th'ong), whose name signifies female promiscuity and wanton behavior. She then demands that Saman collect her things and leave the house immediately. No one raises a finger to help her and Saman is left to fend for herself as best she can in the cruel city. She somehow manages to survive and months later gives birth to a stillborn baby boy. Exhausted and weakened by the birth, however, she too passes away. The author concludes the story by telling readers that the only way for young, innocent women to avoid suffering a similar fate to that of Saman was to "hold back and carefully ponder things" before entering into an intimate relationship with a man.

Apart from its overt didactic purpose, "Windy Words of Love" is notable for the way in which it incorporates a critique of the type of gender and class oppression commonly discussed in the popular press of the day. As a young woman from the lower classes, Saman, possessing little social, cultural, or economic capital, represented the essence of female vulnerability. Her seduction and abandonment by an upper-class man only confirmed her powerlessness. More generally her tragic story, a tale that surely had many parallels in real life, was yet another

critique of elite Siamese society in which hierarchical, exploitative social relations were the norm.

MORAL MESSAGES TO MEN

In addition to the type of cautionary moral tales aimed at young women discussed above, there were also popular works that addressed moral dilemmas commonly faced by young men. One such work was *Long thang* (Gone Astray),
Siam's first talking film released in early 1932. With a script by the celebrated
writer *Khun* Wichit Matra [Sanga Kanchanakhaphan], *Gone Astray* relates a dramatic episode in the life of *Nai* Sawaeng Ph'utphon (literally, Mr. Seeker of
Agricultural Produce), a young university graduate.[41] On completing his studies
in Bangkok, Sawaeng moves to the country were he establishes his own farm and
marries a local woman, Y'ot Ming, with whom he has a child. Sawaeng adores
his wife and infant son and makes a good start in becoming a successful farmer.
However, in order to build on this achievement he has to travel to Bangkok to
buy new agricultural equipment. Promising his wife that he will only be away for
a week Sawaeng goes to stay at the home of an old friend, Chamnong Suknak-
h'on (Aiming for City Pleasures), who, it turns out, has become a hardened
drinker and avid womanizer. In the company of Chamnong, Sawaeng visits a
swanky bar-cum-nightclub where he meets eighteen-year-old F'ong Sawat
(Foaming Love), a high-class prostitute of great renown. He is swept off his feet

Fig. 8.3. Scene from *Gone Astray*

by the modish young femme fatale and they strike up an intimate relationship. The photograph shown in figure 8.3, a still from the film, shows the couple kissing in the bar—the first screen kiss in Thai cinema history[42]—while a drunken Chamnong and a fellow reveler are entertained by another prostitute.

Over the following days Sawaeng spends most of his time in an alcoholic haze carousing around the capital with F'ong before finally returning home to his wife. But he soon grows tired of country life and urges Y'ot Ming to go with him and live in Bangkok. Reluctantly his wife agrees and they move to the city. Despite Y'ot Ming's efforts to please him, Sawaeng is indifferent to her and spends most of his time in hotels and dance halls drinking and gallivanting about with F'ong. As a result the relationship between Sawaeng and Y'ot Ming breaks down and she returns to their farm. Meanwhile he sets up house with F'ong in Bangkok. As it turns out, however, Sawaeng's new "wife" proves to be very expensive to maintain, costing him 500 to 600 baht a month (a sum equivalent to the salary of a high-ranking government official), money which he borrows from Chamnong. Eventually Sawaeng's credit with his friend runs dry and when he is no longer able to meet F'ong's endless demands for money she walks out on him. Reduced to penury Sawaeng wanders forlornly through the streets of Bangkok reflecting on what has happened. He realizes he has made a grievous mistake and, poorer but wiser, decides to leave the city and go back to the country in search of Y'ot Ming. On meeting up with his wife again, Sawaeng implores her to take him back, to which she willingly agrees, and the couple are reconciled in a shower of tears.

In offering such a conclusion *Gone Astray*, like "The Headstrong Young Mary Woodson" and "Windy Words of Love," was profoundly conventional in the manner in which it reaffirmed the traditional sexual double standard. Whereas a female character such as Saman was ruined as a result of her dalliance with Phitsawong, Sawaeng suffered no such fate for his affair with F'ong. On the contrary, he is absolved for his transgressions and emerges as a laudable fellow who was able to learn from the error of his ways. Thus, while a man could be forgiven his sexual indiscretions, a woman who made a false step was not so fortunate.

Notwithstanding its traditionalist approach to sexual mores, *Gone Astray* embodied a new trend in the way that the moral dimension of the story was amplified by the contrast it drew between the country and the city. While both "Romance Concealed in a True Story" and "Sam'on" also highlighted this contrast, the makers of *Gone Astray* framed the rural-urban dichotomy in considerably bolder terms. Life in the country was represented as pristine, virtuous, and wholesome. Bangkok, on the other hand, was depicted as a den of iniquity, a sensual realm of decadence and immorality. This was a very different way of portraying the city than had once been the case. In the classical poetry of the past, the royal capital was represented as the center of refinement and civility, a repository of all things good and desirable, while the country was seen in diametrically opposed terms, as backward, sinister, and frightening.[43] However with the growing development and urbanization of Bangkok, the Siamese hinterlands now began to be idealized in a way not dissimilar to that which had occurred in Europe with the onset of the Industrial Revolution and the rise of the romantic tradition associated with such figures as Jean-Jacques Rousseau. This new idealization of the countryside in Siam spoke of shifting perceptions among sections of the urban populace, in particular a feeling that life in the capital had a corrupting, debilitating quality, that contemporary urban society was in the throes of a deep and prolonged malaise.

It was against this backdrop of festering social and moral decay that the old absolutist order was, as we have seen, increasingly challenged before eventually being toppled in the bloodless revolution of 24 June 1932.

NOTES

1. Annette Hamilton, "Family Dramas: Film and Modernity in Thailand," *Screen* 33, no. 3 (1992): 261.

2. Details of the film's plot are taken from the August 1927 issue of the monthly magazine *Phaphayon* [Cinema], 1685–711. According to the magazine, *Luang* Sunthorn Atsaworarat wrote the film script himself.

3. Do'k Mai Sot, *Sattru kh'ong chao l'on* [Her Foe] (Bangkok: Bannakhan, 1971).

4. D'ok Mai Sot, *Her Foe*, 37–38.

5. Matthew Copeland, "Contested Nationalism and the 1932 Overthrow of the Absolute Monarchy, in Sian," Ph.D. diss., Australian National University, Canberra, 1993, 36.

6. M. C. Akat Damkoeng Raphiphat, *Lak'on haeng chiwit* [The Circus of Life] (Bangkok: Phrae Phitaya, 1974); *Phiw luang phiw khaw* [East and West] (Bangkok: Phrae Phitaya, 1962).

7. Details of the story outlined here are taken from *Phaphayon sayam*, 29 June 1923.

8. It should perhaps be noted that in real life such scenarios were not wholly fanciful. Elite men frequently had clandestine affairs with lower-class women who bore them children. If a child from such a union became aware of their parentage they could make a legitimate claim to being well born. A typical fictional example of this was *Watsana kammak'on* (The Laborer's Good Fortune), a popular novella by S'o P'o D'o Kulap from 1924 (Bangkok: n.p.). Bunchoet, the "laborer" hero, is actually a chauffeur in the employ of a wealthy Bangkok family. Despite his lowly social status he falls in love with his employer's daughter, Chaloem, but his affections seem doomed. Ultimately, however, he discovers that his late father was a member of the upper classes, a fact that ensures his love for Chaloem can be realized.

9. Tamara Loos, "Gender Adjudicated: Translating Modern Legal Subjects in Siam," Ph.D. diss., Cornell University, 1999, 30.

10. Kulap Saipradit, *Songkhram chiwit* [The War of Life], (Bangkok: Kh'o Phai, 1979).

11. *Suphap nari*, 14 March 1931, 31. The figure of the audacious female criminal was not entirely unknown in Siam. In 1901, for example, when the *Bangkok Times* reported

that there were some 1,500 prisoners in the Central Bangkok Jail, it noted there were also some sixty women inmates, "the doyenne [of these] being the notorious Me Law [most likely not a real name but rather *Mae lao*, the generic term for a female brothel keeper], leader of the 1889 riots." Me Law, described as "a comely young woman," was serving a fifteen-year prison sentence after admitting she "had assisted her lover to dispose of an encumbrance in the way of a husband." *Bangkok Times*, 6 April 1901.

12. *Suphap nari*, 14 March 1930.

13. For further details about this building and other early tall structures in Bangkok (and the type of facilities and entertainment they housed), see Thepchu Thapth'ong "7–9 lae 41 chan" [Seven, Nine, and Forty-one Storeys] in *Lao r'uang thai* [Thai Stories], vol. 2, (Bangkok: S'ong rao, 1992).

14. For example, see editorial comments in *Bangkok kan-m'uang*, 12 March 1923; *Pakka thai*, 30 July 1927; *Sikrung*, 3 August 1927.

15. The first instalment of *"Phra* Suriyothai phadet s'uk" was published in *Suphap nari*, 14 March 1931, while *"Thao* Thepkasatri" appeared two weeks later on 28 March 1931.

16. Sukanya Tirawanit, *Prawatikan nangs'uphim nai prathet thai phai tai rab'op sombura-nayasitthirat* [Newspapers in Thailand under the Absolute Monarchy] (Bangkok: Thai Watana Panit, 1977), 101.

17. C. J. Reynolds, "Predicaments of Modern Thai History," *Southeast Asian Research* 12, no. 1 (March 1994): 66.

18. *Satri thai*, 1 March 1927.

19. Reynolds, "Predicaments," 66.

20. *Luang* Wichit Wathakan, "Sam'on" [Samorn] in *Ammata niyai chut phua hai* [Classic Stories, the "Disappearing Husband" Series] (Bangkok: Khlang-Samo'ng media fokat, 1992).

21. *Luang* Wichit Wathakan, "Sam'on," 13.

22. *Luang* Wichit Wathakan, "Sam'on," 20.

23. *Luang* Wichit Wathakan, "Sam'on," 24.

24. *Luang* Wichit Wathakan, "Sam'on," 30.

25. *Luang* Wichit Wathakan, "Sam'on," 35.

26. *Luang* Wichit Wathakan, "Sam'on," 41–49.

27. *Luang* Wichit Wathakan, "Sam'on," 48.

28. *Luang* Wichit Wathakan, "Sam'on," 56.

29. D'ok Mai Sot, "Romance s'on r'uang ching" [Romance Concealed in a True Story] in *Phu klin* [The Scented Tassel], a collection of D'ok Mai Sot's shorter writings (Bangkok: Phrae Phitthaya, 1971), 1–193.

30. D'ok Mai Sot, "Romance s'on r'uang ching," 44.

31. D'ok Mai Sot, "Romance s'on r'uang ching," 45.

32. D'ok Mai Sot, "Romance s'on r'uang ching," 47.

33. D'ok Mai Sot, "Romance s'on r'uang ching," 186. This passage referring to Wat's travels abroad recalls similar observations made by Chulalongkorn during his 1896 trip to Java. I thank Craig Reynolds for bringing this correspondence to my attention.

34. D'ok Mai Sot, "Romance s'on r'uang ching," 187. A similar theme, that of a dissolute young man from the elite being influenced by a socially conscious woman to change his ways for the good of the nation, was taken up by Kulap Saipradit in his 1950 novella *Until We Meet Again* [*Chon kwa rao cha phop kan ik*]. An English-language translation of this work appears in Barmé, *Kulap in Oz*, 1995, 113–80.

35. D'ok Mai Sot, "Romance s'on r'uang ching," 132, 137.

36. The first installment of the story was published in the 16 August 1926 issue of *Satri thai*.

37. *Satri thai*, 6 September 1926.

38. *Satri thai*, 6 September 1926.

39. For example see *Sayam rat*, 30 March 1922, 13 October 1923.

40. When Phitsawong has his way with her, their coupling is described in the meta-phoric language of "wind and rain" similar to that of the erotic *bot atsachan* (extraordi-nary scenes) in traditional Siamese verse.

41. Details of the film are taken from a special supplement (a magazine with text and photographs) included with the 29 March 1932 issue of the daily newspaper *Sikrung*. My thanks to Dome Sukwong for making this extremely rare document available to me.

42. Dome Sukwong, *Long thang lae khadi long thang* [*Gone Astray*, the Film: *Gone Astray*, the Legal Case] (Bangkok: Film House, 1996), 88.

43. This particular distinction between city and country was drawn in the work of vari-ous novelists such as S'o Bunsanoe in *Kiat thahan* (Soldier's Honor, 1929), and Yot Watcharasathian in *Mitraphap* (Friendship, 1934), the city being equated with "heaven" while rural life was conceived of as a form of purgatory. However, since the contrast between the rural and urban worlds in these novels was framed wholly in material (as opposed to moral) terms, it was hardly surprising that the city seemed to be eminently more desirable. Em'on Niranrat, "Thatsana thang sangkhom nai nawaniyai thai samai ratchakan thi 7" [Social Perspectives in Thai Novels during the Seventh Reign], M.A. thesis, Chulalongkorn University, 1978, 73.

9

❧

Gender, Class, and Popular Culture in Post-absolutist Siam, 1932–1940

In response to long-standing popular disenchantment with the royal-noble ruling elite and, particularly, the inability of the absolutist state to address the economic hardship wrought by the Great Depression, the military-civilian coalition known as the People's Party (Khana ratsad'on) overthrew the monarchy on June 24, 1932, and seized power. Announcing the change in government, Siam's new rulers issued a strongly worded statement in which they espoused both a powerful nationalist and democratic ethos. Excoriating the old elite for its failings, the People's Party pledged that "[Henceforth] the nation will be independent, the people will be safe from danger, everyone will have work, everyone will have equal privilege and none will be servants or slaves."[1]

This emphasis on freedom and equality signified a major conceptual transformation at the national level: whereas the commoner population had largely been ignored under the absolute monarchy, the new regime was at pains to recognize the needs and interests of the people (ratsad'on), at least in principle. Whatever the talk of freedom and equality, however, a chauvinistic state-centered nationalism and not democracy emerged as the dominant ideological force in the post-1932 period, a development crucially influenced by the political divisions and behind-the-scenes infighting endemic to the early constitutional era.[2] Broadly speaking the decade after the overthrow of the absolute monarchy can be seen as comprising two distinct periods: a brief, relatively open, democratic interlude characterized by a heightened sense of optimism and vociferous public debate (which lasted from the change in government until roughly the latter part of 1933), followed by an increasingly coercive era in which the new state stifled all forms of dissent and sought to regulate and direct society to an unprecedented degree. This process reached its apogee with the hypernationalism of the Phibun

Songkhram regime that came to power in 1938.³ The present chapter examines questions concerning women, class, and relations between the sexes in this tumultuous environment.

EARLY DAYS: 1932–1933

Following the change from absolutism to constitutionalism, a raft of new daily newspapers appeared on the market including such titles as *24 Mithuna* (24 June), *Satcha* (Truth), *Khwam-hen ratsad'on* (Public Opinion), *10 thanwa* (10 December), *Chaloem ratthathammanun* (Celebrating the Constitution), *Seriphap* (Freedom), and *Ying thai* (Thai Woman).⁴ Drawing inspiration from the change in government these new publications had a strongly democratic political orientation and emphasized the need for active public participation in national life.

Ying thai is of particular interest from the perspective of the present study in that its editorial approach incorporated not only a political but also a feminist dimension. Indeed, *Ying thai* together with *Sao sayam* (Young Siamese Woman [1933]), another women's publication of the era,⁵ represented the last feminist-type newspaper to appear in Siam during the pre–World War II period. Owned and managed by *Nang* (Mrs.) Sap Angkinan, with an all-female editorial staff including Anong Amatayakun and Chaliaw Serirat,⁶ *Ying thai* had the same type of format as most other contemporary Bangkok dailies. It featured local and international news items often, though not exclusively, concerned with women, together with a range of serialized fiction, including "*Khatiya nari*" (Warrior Woman), an historical chronicle-style work similar to those published in *Suphap nari* a few years earlier (see chapter 8).⁷ The paper also featured a general advice column for young men and women (in which such issues as "The Selection of an Appropriate Marriage Partner" were discussed), as well as a smattering of cartoon satire and a regular didactic cartoon strip.

In common with virtually all of the new dailies that appeared after 24 June, *Ying thai* was strongly supportive of the change in government. This was regularly affirmed in the paper's editorial column where writers were given free rein to voice their opinions. The views of one writer who used the pseudonym "*Nat*" (supporter, protector) were typical. *Nat* said that the announcement of the provisional constitution on 27 June 1932, represented a major turning point for Siam in that it erased the "heavy-heartedness and misery which had afflicted the Thai people for hundreds of years."⁸ In discussing the absolute monarchy *Nat* condemned the use of personal connections in place of merit and more generally its indifference toward the populace at large who were seen as little more than slaves. But with the announcement of the constitution the writer enthused "freedom is ours; now we have our rights; from that day [27 June] the desires of the people were finally realized."⁹

At the same time, however, this optimism was tinged with reservations about the future. For one thing, *Nat* wrote that if the change in government was really to usher in a new era in Siam, it was essential that state officials function as "honest servants of the people" (*khon chai thi s'u sat kh'ong ratsad'on*) and not their masters (*nai*), as had been the case in the past.[10] Furthermore, the author voiced concerns about the ability of members of the public to express their opinions freely, noting that several newspapers had already suffered the wrath of the government censor (see below). Other writers expressed similar views. For example, in September 1932 one contributor, while also strongly supportive of the change in government, expressed disquiet about the way members of the new National Assembly had been chosen without any popular mandate, intimating that this did not portend well for the future of representative democratic politics in Siam.[11]

Apart from such concerns, various correspondents (both members of the *Ying thai* staff and contributors from the general public) availed themselves of the opinions page to offer advice and suggestions for Siam's advancement. Given the continuing impact of the Great Depression, the economy was one area that elicited a good deal of comment and discussion. Economic nationalism was a recurrent theme that had been regularly taken up in the popular press since the 1920s. One of the more striking *Ying thai* editorials on this subject appeared under the title "Civilization—Old and New" (*Arayatham kao kap mai*).[12] The author of this piece wrote that the idea of civilization was historically variable and claimed that in the present age it was primarily concerned with money, which had become the measure of all things. In contemporary Siam, people had begun to "worship money" (*bucha ngoen*), a practice, the writer claimed, that had been imported from the West. This obsession with money developed because the Siamese were not sufficiently nationalist in outlook. As a result the local economy had become enmeshed in the global marketplace, a transformation which had devastating consequences, particularly for the country's peasant farmers whose livelihoods were now determined by the forces of international capital. In order to reverse this trend the writer argued that Siam should emulate the Japanese, whose enthusiastic embrace of an assertive nationalism was seen as fundamental to their continued economic independence.[13]

In another editorial taking up the theme of economic nationalism, *Ying thai* lent its support to the idea (circulating in the capital at the time) of establishing an association for the promotion of Thai products.[14] If this went ahead, so the argument went, more money would stay in the country which could be used to build up local industry and provide Siamese laborers with a livelihood. In addition, the editors called on the government to increase taxes on luxury foreign goods and those wealthy enough to afford them, as well as to impose a levy on the remittances Chinese workers in Siam sent back home.[15] Such ideas, which were in no way unique to the pages of *Ying thai*, were subsequently taken up by the state when it actively embarked on a policy of economic nationalism, a process that began in the mid-1930s and intensified during the first Phibun era (1938–1944).[16] At the same time, the issue of labor, or more specifically Siamese labor, was a major preoccupation of *Ying thai* and a subject of frequent editorial

comment. In one such editorial the paper called for greater recognition and support for poor Thai laborers (*phuak kammak'on yak chon kh'ong thai*), a group who
was seen as "representing a vitally important part of the nation."[17] Significantly,
while *Ying thai* was strongly supportive of and sympathetic toward Siamese laborers in general,[18] the paper's primary focus was with the female members of the
working class. This concern is of particular interest in that it leads us to a consideration of the feminist dimension of *Ying thai*—a publication, it should be said,
that was unique in its commitment to advancing the cause of two historically
subordinate social groups in Siam, women and workers.

In September 1932 the paper celebrated the establishment of the Tramwaymen's Association (Siam's first officially recognized labor organization)[19] and the
formation of a Taxi Drivers' Association. These initiatives were seen as important developments heralding the beginning of a new "age of associations or organized labor."[20] At the same time, while acknowledging the significance of the
establishment of these bodies, the editor of *Ying thai* said that it was time that a
similar type of union be created for women workers. Pointing out that most of
the laborers employed in Bangkok's cigarette, match, and textile factories were
female, the paper noted many people were in favor of the idea and claimed that
the establishment of such a body "would raise the status of these women and give
them hope."[21] This idea was developed further by a contributor to the editorial
column who wrote under the name Angkhana (woman, maiden). According to
her, the establishment of a "Trades union" (she used the English term as well as
rendering it in Thai as *sahakan kammak'on*), would "bring unity and a sense of
purpose to women workers and enable them to fight injustice from employers
and raise funds to help fellow members when they became sick or too old to
work."[22] Interestingly, her conception of a union was somewhat different from
that found in the West, where conflict between organized labor and capital was
endemic. "Unions," she wrote, "should not be established as the enemy of
employers; instead they should serve the mutual benefits of both workers and
bosses." Having said this, however, she went on to express her doubts about the
possibility of setting up a women's union in Siam at the time, a prediction that
proved to be all too true.[23] Indeed, the promise of improved working and living
conditions for laborers in the new "age of associations" was short-lived. In the
wake of the Boworadej Rebellion in October 1933 and a major strike which shut
down Bangkok's rice mills a few months later, those workers' organizations
which had been established (such as the Tramwaymen's Association mentioned
above) collapsed as the state, loathe to tolerate any form of dissent, sought to
monopolize power and proscribed the formation of independent collective organizations that could challenge its authority.[24]

Apart from expressing its support for working-class women and promoting the
idea of establishing a union for female workers, *Ying thai* focused on the same
issues concerned with women that had been taken up in the press during the
latter absolute period. However, there was one major difference. The notions of

equality and freedom articulated by the new regime when it came to power now had a greater salience and were repeatedly invoked in discussions about improving the status of women. Drawing inspiration from the administration's egalitarian rhetoric, various writers argued that for the nation to progress it was imperative for the authorities to provide girls and young women with the same level of education as that available to men.[25] Similarly, the newfound emphasis on equality gave added impetus to the debate on polygamy which now, more than ever, was conceived by its critics as an archaic, unjust practice. This perspective was encapsulated in an editorial by Ratsami, a trenchant critic of polygamy. Proclaiming that the present era was "the age of equality in which everyone wants to have the same rights and be equal with one another," she called on the government to live up to its rhetoric, and asked how much longer it would allow the existing laws on marriage, which allowed "sex-crazed" men to treat women in a "coarse and uncouth" manner, to continue.[26]

Such louche behavior was also condemned in graphic form by a cartoonist whose work appeared in *Ying Thai*.

Entitled "An Old Man's Lust" (*kae tanha*), the four scenes that make up the

Fig. 9.1. *Ying thai*, 5 September 1932

cartoon (fig. 9.1) focus on an elderly man and the various women in his life. Beginning at the top left corner and moving from left to right, the captions to the pictures read: (1) "[I'm] fed up with my old wives. I actively seek out . . . (2) young women and prepare them to become mine, (3) so they can lavish and pamper me; (4) I'm sick and tired of the old ones; I'll get some new faces; there's no need for me to suffer." As in some of the graphic images from the absolute period examined earlier, the cartoonist here targets wealthy elite males and lambastes them for their propensity to regard women in a contemptuous, self-serving manner. In focusing specifically on elite behavior, the cartoon was part of a broader phenomenon manifest during the months immediately following the overthrow of the monarchy whereby the popular press, which had constituted and promoted itself as the voice of the public at large, mounted a sustained attack on members of the old princely-noble class for egregiously flaunting their wealth and sexual appetites.[27]

Mae Sim'uang, another contributor to the editorial page, also wrote about the question of equality between the sexes. She condemned the unfairness of the existing laws governing marriage and divorce property settlements.[28] The main thrust of her argument, however, was to advance another, rather novel, type of equality ostensibly aimed at furthering the public good. She began by noting that when Chulalongkorn was king his numerous wives (Chao ch'om) received varying levels of financial support (Chulalongkorn, it should be recalled, was the last Siamese monarch to publicly maintain a harem). The most favored wives (Chao ch'om manda, those who had given birth to children with senior royal titles) had an allowance of 20,000 baht a year (in addition to income they received from rentier and money-lending activities). Other wives, in particular those who had not borne the king children, were variously allotted lesser sums, the lowest paid of these receiving an annual stipend of 240 baht, equivalent to the yearly salary of a junior government clerk.

Mae Sim'uang pointed out that although state-funded payments to the deceased monarch's wives and consorts had been reduced by varying amounts, they were still receiving substantial sums of money each year. She also pointed out that, in contrast to the laboring masses, these women were extremely privileged and, in the name of equality, suggested that in future they should all receive exactly the same amount of money—2,400 baht per annum. The money saved by this measure, she argued, should be put into a charitable fund to be used for the benefit of the needy.[29] Such a discussion of the financial arrangements of members of the royal family in public—particularly women associated with King Chulalongkorn, the most revered of Siamese monarchs—would have been hard to imagine during the absolutist period. Under the new political dispensation, however, at least in its early days, expressing such opinions was not unusual and well reflected the tenor of times in which everything and anything seemed to be open to public scrutiny and debate.

Mae Sim'uang's sympathetic attitude toward the underprivileged along with the calls for the establishment of a union for female workers (referred to above) were typical of the views aired in *Ying thai* and underline the fundamentally egalitarian, humanist ethos of the paper. This was further underscored by a contributor's letter published in the editorial column that concerned prostitutes, the most déclassé category of women in Siamese society. Written by Lawan Phancharoen, the letter was addressed to the committee of the Thai Women's Association of Siam (*Samakhom satri thai haeng krung sayam*), a new organization founded with the broad aim of improving the status of women.[30] Noting that the draft charter of the new organization specified that potential members should be "well behaved and of unblemished reputation" (*t'ong pen phu mi khwam-praphr'ut di mai sia ch'u siang*), Lawan suggested that the association could best achieve its objectives if it drew its membership from "every class and every type of woman" (*thuk chan bukhon lae thuk chanit kh'ong bukhon thi pen satri*). By this she meant that the association should allow women who worked as prostitutes to become members. Her rationale was premised on a belief that prostitutes could be redeemed if given the appropriate moral support and guidance, something that would, in turn, allow them to reform themselves and become upright, respectable mothers. Admittedly, while this may be seen as a deeply patronizing attitude, particularly from a contemporary Western perspective, in early 1930s Siam Lawan's views were undeniably progressive, especially given the fact that up until then educated women had commonly sought to distance themselves from prostitutes and condemned them in the harshest of terms. As we saw in "A Conversation between Ladies" published by *Satri niphon* in 1915 (chapter 1), "respectable" women tended to view prostitutes as "whores" and "creatures from hell," while a contributor to the feminist magazine *Satri thai* during the mid-1920s wrote, "we [respectable women] detest those showy, filthy women who clutter up the city. Ladies [*suphap-satri*] loathe prostitutes [*ying th'uan*] so much, but we don't know how to disassociate ourselves from them. Whatever we do, they always copy us."[31] In publishing the letter, *Ying thai* rejected such prejudices, something emphasized by the fact that the editor of the paper lauded Lawan's ideas and urged readers to give careful consideration to what she had to say.[32]

As to the fate of the Thai Women's Association of Siam, the available sources suggest that, despite whatever good intentions were behind its formation, the fledgling body did not amount to anything at the time.[33] Indeed, the lack of tangible success on the part of the association may well have been due to the fact that it was difficult for educated women to reach any consensus on what actually constituted an improvement of the position of women in Siamese society. As Worasai, a writer in another of the newspaper's editorials, pointed out, contemporary educated women held widely divergent views as to their own status and the nature of the society in which they lived.[34] Some wanted complete equality with men in all respects, most specifically in the area of employment.

Others advocated distinct gendered spheres of activity, men working in paid employment as providers while women were responsible for domestic matters—maintaining the home and raising children. A third category of women were those who fell somewhere in between, embracing the idea of a certain degree of equality with men, particularly in terms of education and legal status, while at the same time accepting the notion of distinct male and female spheres of activity.[35] These differences in viewpoint, it would seem militated against the development of a formal, organized Siamese "women's movement" as such. Alternatively, what we find during the 1920s and early 1930s was the development, facilitated by the spread of female literacy and print, of a somewhat diffuse feminist consciousness as increasing numbers of educated women from the middle and upper classes came to participate in a vigorous public debate on various issues that directly affected them.

PROSTITUTION IN PRINT

The egalitarian views commonly expressed in *Ying thai* reflected a broader popular trend in which the existence of ordinary, less-privileged members of society (such as farmers and laborers) were recognized to a far greater degree than had ever been the case during the absolutist era. Apart from the inclusive, democratic rhetoric of state leaders and the establishment of collective organizations such as the Tramwaymen's Association, this development was manifest in the appearance of various works which portrayed common people in a sympathetic light as human beings. For example, the vigor and tenacity of the working classes was celebrated in a musical drama entitled *A Laborer's Life* (*Chiwit kammak'on*),[36] while the human face of prostitution was presented in "Men Made Me Bad" (*Chan chua phr'o chai*), the story of a sex worker serialized in the daily newspaper (*10 thanwa*) *phanuak khaw rew.* As we have seen earlier, although the issue of prostitution was frequently debated in the press, this discussion seldom conveyed any sense of who the women involved in the business were or the nature of their experience. It is for this reason that this work is of particular interest.

Written by a woman author using the pseudonym, *"Loi lom"* (Floating on the Breeze), "Men Made Me Bad" was the "biography" of a prostitute named Keyun Phaksaneh. Whether it was indeed a genuine biography, however, is impossible to say. The decidedly voyeuristic, raunchy tone of the story suggests that it may have been a fictional work which the publishers of (*10 thanwa*) *phanuak khaw rew* hoped would appeal to the prurient interests of readers and thereby help boost sales in the cutthroat world of the newspaper industry. Moreover, the biographical nature of the work is called into question by the fact that at one point in the narrative, when the protagonist contracts venereal disease, she seeks treatment at a VD clinic which regularly advertised its services on the very same page on which the story appeared. Yet, despite the problematic nature of "Men Made Me

Bad," much of the material contained in the story has the unmistakable ring of truth about it, a view I base on personal observations and lived experience in Thailand over a period of many years.

The work charts the life of Keyun from the age of fourteen to her mid-twenties. An only child, Keyun came from a provincial middle-class family and was raised by her widowed father *Khun* (the lowest rank of conferred nobility) Sutha Kekha, a government official stationed in the town of Ratburi to the southwest of Bangkok. Apart from noting that *Khun* Sutha was a doting parent, however, the account does not provide any additional information about Keyun's early life or educational background. At the beginning of the first installment of the story she is described as an attractive physically mature, yet sexually naive, fourteen-year-old who cannot understand the inordinate amount of attention she receives from local young men whenever she goes out in public. Shortly afterward, however, things begin to change.[37]

One evening Keyun, accompanied by a female servant, goes to the Siriwathana cinema for a night's entertainment. As she wanders through the theater Keyun's eyes meet the gaze of a handsome young man standing nearby, an experience that sets her heart aflutter for the first time in her life. On returning home she cannot stop thinking about the stranger and thereafter begins going to the Siriwathana almost nightly in the hope of seeing the "man with the sweet eyes" again. She soon learns that the fellow's name is Sanitwong Lert and that he had come from Bangkok to manage the cinema for the Phathanakorn Company, which operated theaters in various provincial centers. Keyun is charmed by his sophisticated city manner and becomes totally infatuated with him. Less than a month later, convinced of his sincerity and love for her, she secretly leaves her father's house and they spend the night together. This, her first sexual encounter, proves to be a torrid affair in which the insatiable Sanit makes love to her over and over again. The next morning Keyun, sore, stiff, and bruised, makes it clear to him that if he genuinely cares for her he should be more tender in bed. He accedes to her wishes and they begin to live together as husband and wife, a development that results in her father disowning her. After they have lived for a few months in lustful bliss, however, the Phathanakorn Company goes bankrupt, leaving Sanit without a job. The couple moves to Bangkok, where Keyun uses money obtained from selling her gold jewelry to support both of them. For his part Sanit makes little attempt to find work, and as their finances dwindle, the relationship sours and he abandons her. At this point Keyun is almost destitute and is taken in by a kindly neighbor, Mr. Sai, who provides her with food, lodgings, and a small allowance. She then meets another young man, Lamyong, an acquaintance of Sanit, who shows a keen interest in her. Shortly after, they begin living together. As it turns out, however, Lamyong is an inveterate gambler who regularly loses large sums of money playing cards and punting on the horses. When Keyun tries to get him to change his ways he becomes enraged, beats her up, and throws her out on the street.

By chance she had befriended another woman from Ratburi, named Sut-chai, who now takes her into her home which, unbeknown to Keyun, also happens to double as a covert brothel. Having found a new place to live Keyun is hopeful of being reconciled with Lamyong, whom she still loves and misses greatly. Her romantic illusions about him are dashed, however, when she goes to visit his house only to find him in bed with a prostitute. Making no apologies for his behavior, Lamyong, hardly missing a beat, simply turns and smiles at her contemptuously before continuing to have sex with the other woman.[38]

Following this unfortunate turn of events Keyun falls into another relationship with a male friend of Sut-chai's husband. Again this is a short-lived affair that ends after the man loses interest in her and goes his own way. Without a job and dependent on Sut-chai for support Keyun feels increasingly uneasy and vulnerable. A Sikh man who patronizes the brothel from time to time begins to show an interest in her and helps pay off some of her debts. Although she finds him physically repellent Keyun gradually develops a sense of gratitude for his kindness, a feeling that is shattered one day when he shows up at the house and rapes her. As it turns out the Sikh had conspired with Sut-chai by paying her to allow him into Keyun's room when she was asleep and have his way with her. In an effort to compensate Keyun for the assault Sut-chai gives her some of the money put up by the Sikh. Then, not long after this incident, Keyun is raped again after accepting an invitation to go for a drive with another man known to Sut-chai; once again she is financially compensated by her "friend" who had arranged the outing in the first place.

These experiences have a profound influence on Keyun, who feels that she has little alternative but to trade on her sexual allure and become a prostitute in order to survive. Indeed, she comes to the view that "receiving money for sleeping with a man is better than any other sort of work; not only do you get paid for it but you also get taken out on the town for a good time." From this point she begins having sex with "lots of men," young and old, Siamese and Chinese as well as "strange-looking Europeans" who take her out "for a good time at various local hotels." Working at the upper end of the market she makes in excess of 1,000 baht during a three-month period, a considerable amount of money equivalent to four times the annual salary of a junior government official. Her financial good fortune abruptly comes to an end shortly afterward, however, when she falls ill with a stomach infection and has to stop working temporarily. During this time she meets Thongdam Netkham, a taxi driver, who nurses her back to health and they begin living together as husband and wife. Once more this relationship proves no more durable than those with the previous men in her life and she goes back to working as a prostitute in a brothel near Phan Fa bridge operated by a ruthless madam, Mae 'Ob. Thongdam learns that she is making good money, pays her a visit, roughs her up, and steals her gold jewelry. A month later he returns, threatens her life, and again strips her of a set of jewelry that she has just purchased. Reduced to penury Keyun is forced to work harder than ever and contracts venereal disease in the process. While seeking medical treatment and recuperating she comes to dread the thought of continuing to work as a prostitute. Meanwhile Thongdam suddenly reappears on the scene and asks her forgiveness. Ever the optimist, she agrees to take him back and they begin living together again. He then loses his job and urges her to go back to her old profession. Terrified of contracting another bout of venereal disease she refuses; he responds by bashing her. She begins working in Mae 'Ob's brothel once more, with the madam taking her earnings and giving them to Thongdam who spends them all. Whenever she tries to avoid work she is thrashed and forced to sleep with all sorts of men including "big Indians with unkempt beards," customers whom she particularly loathes. Despite being infected with venereal disease for a second time Thongdam insists she keep on working. Finally, unable to endure the situation any longer, she is able to escape the clutches of Thongdam and Mae 'Ob and finds refuge in the house of another madam, Mae Som-si in the Thonburi area on the west bank of the Chao Phraya River. By contrast Mae Som-si is a kind-hearted woman who takes Keyun in and allows her to recover and play a managerial role in running the brothel. During this time she meets Ken, another somewhat older man, a bank teller, with whom she has an affair that lasts for five months before he, too, loses interest. Keyun then discovers she is pregnant by him, but suffers a miscarriage and goes back to work once more. This time, however, she bands together with a handful of other women who have previously been working under Mae Som-si and opens a new brothel that operates under the protection of a high-ranking police officer favorably disposed toward her. This arrangement, in which Keyun provides the officer in question with sexual favors, proves to be highly lucrative and she is able to accumulate a large amount of cash (8,000 baht in less than a year), enabling her to buy a car and a substantial amount of gold jewelry (most of which she deposits in a bank for safekeeping). Yet despite her newfound wealth Keyun, who at twenty-five-years-old describes herself as being "middle-aged," longs for a stable, long-term relationship—in short, to have a husband. A number of seemingly ideal men show a keen interest in her but once again she chooses a suitor who, as a result of his passion for drink and gambling, ultimately causes her nothing but grief. In the process she loses virtually all of her assets and, in order to save her skin, is forced to abandon the illicit brothel that had provided her with such a handsome income. Although now living in much reduced circumstances Keyun still attracts men "as ants are attracted to sugar"[39] and falls into a number of short-term relationships with a series of lovers.

After contracting yet another bout of venereal disease during one of these affairs, for which she seeks treatment at the Yokhi sathan (Yogi Institute) Clinic (which regularly advertised its services on the same page on which the story appeared each day), Keyun makes contact with a distant and rather elderly male relative who employs her as a housekeeper. At the outset nothing untoward happens, and then one day the man asks her to massage him and then proceeds to rape her. Although Keyun is revolted by the experience she realizes that things could be even worse and comes to accept that occasionally sleeping with her uncle, who otherwise treats her kindly, was preferable to living in total impoverishment on the street.

Some four months after Keyun comes to live in the house her uncle's eldest son, Chamnong, a police captain stationed in the provinces, is reassigned to work in the capital and moves into his father's home. Keyun is immediately attracted to the young man and soon she is sleeping not only with the father but also with the son. Chamnong, however, finds the duplicitous nature of this arrangement intolerable and, fearing that their relationship will be exposed and bring shame on the family, decides to end the affair and leave the house. For her part Keyun is deeply saddened by his departure and, unable to stomach her uncle any longer, also leaves the house after finding accommodation at the house of a new female acquaintance, Mae Anong, in return for doing the housekeeping. As it happens though, little more than a month later Mae Anong is taken ill and dies. After a period of obligatory mourning, her widowed husband, Phirom, an official who works at the Ministry of Justice, begins to pressure Keyun to have sex with him. Ultimately she relents and discovers that he is a passionate lover. She is enamored with his lovemaking and they begin living together as husband and wife. At this point Phirom is informed by his superiors that he is going to be transferred to Nong Khai in northeastern Siam. Keyun tells him in no uncertain terms that if he goes she would not be accompanying him. Rather than ending the relationship he decides to resign from the public service and seek work in Bangkok. While Phirom finds employment as a laborer, toiling from dawn till dusk, his earnings are very meager and the couple is reduced to living in ever more straightened circumstances.

When he suddenly falls ill and is unable to continue working, Keyun sees little alternative but to go back to her old profession to earn a living. Late one night not long after resuming work in an illicit brothel (operated by an accommodating madam, Mae Yun), Keyun, desperate for money, agrees to go off to entertain a group of six drunken but well-dressed men who happened to visit the house. Much to her surprise, however, they are anything but gentlemen. She is taken to a house where the men repeatedly have sex with her until she falls unconscious. In the morning when Keyun comes to her senses she finds herself alone, unpaid, bruised, and very sore. As she later recounts, "my intestines felt as if they had been torn to shreds . . . even a horse is treated with more kindness by its rider than customers treat a person like me."[40]

Despite this harrowing experience, mounting financial pressures leave Keyun with little choice but to go back to work as soon as she is well enough. Over the following month her fortunes improve somewhat as she begins to develop a regular, well-paying clientele. One of these men, Eng Seng, the portly but kind son of a wealthy Chinese merchant, becomes infatuated with her and beseeches her to stop working and marry him. Meanwhile Phirom, who has regained his health, reappears on the scene and starts sleeping with her again. This situation does not last long, however, for Eng Seng is dispatched to Hong Kong by his father and Phirom goes off with another woman who has won his heart. As for Keyun, she is courted by an elderly but well-to-do noble gentleman and becomes his wife. However, while he provides her with emotional and financial support, he is unable to give her the same type of physical gratification as that which she experienced with younger lovers. In order to meet this need she slips out of her husband's house from time to time and visits Mae Yun's sly brothel for a bit of fun. At this point the tale of Keyun Phaksaneh comes to an end.

In the context of early 1930s Siam it may well be imagined that "Men Made Me Bad" would have been regarded by many among the reading public as a work of pornography (*r'uang po*). After all, this was how K'o Surangkhanang's 1937 novel *The Prostitute* (*Ying khon chua*) (see below), a far more coy, reserved piece of writing than Loi Lom's racy biography, was viewed in some quarters.[41] And, in a sense "Men Made Me Bad" was indeed pornography, if one recalls that the original Greek cognate for the term—*pornographos*—meant the "description of the life, manners, etc. of prostitutes and their patrons."[42] This is precisely what makes the story so fascinating.

While in all likelihood other similar works were produced at the time, "Men Made Me Bad" represents what is perhaps the only extant, readily accessible text which deals with the issue of prostitution from the perspective of a woman actually engaged in the trade. Significantly, Keyun's story, at least that aspect concerned with how she became a sex worker, was in no way unique. In fact going by accounts which frequently appeared in the contemporary press her experience (being seduced and subsequently abandoned to fend for herself) was all too common, with many young women consigned to the murky world of prostitution as a result of their romantic infatuations and indiscretions. Indeed, the ubiquity of this downward trajectory perhaps served as an inspiration for K'o Surangkhanang when she wrote *Ying khon chua*. Like Keyun, R'un, the female protagonist of Surangkhanang's work, is an attractive young provincial woman who falls for the charms of a sophisticated fellow from Bangkok and accompanies him to the capital, where she is abandoned and left with little alternative but to sell her body in order to survive. However, in contrast to Loi Lom's biography, the novel was fundamentally melodramatic in tone with R'un going to an early grave after suffering one humiliation and misfortune after another. Notably, despite its lack of literary merit, "Men Made Me Bad" does not convey the same sense of predictability as this novel, a work underpinned by conventional notions of morality in which unleavened misery and sorrow was the inevitable fate of the fallen woman. Despite Keyun's apparent good fortune in entering into a relationship with the geriatric *Khun Phra*, what we know of her life up to this point makes the very idea of closure, in the sense of a "happy ending" or "timely death," seem far too simple and contrived. If anything, her experience is testimony to the capricious, contingent nature of human existence itself. For all one knows, Keyun's new life of comfort and leisure may have been as transitory as the halcyon days when she worked for herself with the aid of police protection. Or then again she may have continued to prosper and thrive.

That Loi Lom chose to call the story "Men Made Me Bad" is in itself telling. Indeed, the title was a pithy affirmation of the moral critiques of men's behavior toward women with which we have become familiar over the course of this study. In its own way the story served as yet another indictment of the traditional sexual double standard that gave license, if not encouragement, to male carnality. For the most part the men who figure in Keyun's account are portrayed as self-centered, lustful creatures; a number of them are depicted as predatory, violent individuals who commonly resort to physical force and intimidation to achieve the object of their desires. But there are also some men who demonstrate a degree of consideration and tenderness in their relationships with Keyun, such as her Chinese lover Eng Seng, who not only acted in a respectful, gentlemanly fashion but also treated her to the pleasures of cunnilingus (a practice, one suspects, that may not at the time have been common among Thai men who held to traditional notions of the sanctity of the head in relation to other parts of the body, and particularly those of the female body).[43]

While most of the men referred to in the biography are unabashedly odious characters, the same could also be said of a number of Keyun's female acquaintances. For example, not long after she was abandoned in Bangkok it will be recalled that she was raped on two occasions, her "friend" Sut-chai being instrumental in facilitating both these sexual assaults for personal financial gain. Subsequently Keyun is abused mercilessly by the madam Mae 'Ob during the time she works in her brothel. This type of exploitation among women was in no way unusual in the Siamese demimonde. Indeed, the occupation of brothel keeper was, if anything, a predominately female one and had been so since at least the mid-nineteenth century when the most renowned houses in the capital were owned and operated by women.[44] At the same time, women commonly functioned as procurers who actively sought out new recruits to service the large and diverse male clientele that made prostitution, for those who controlled the flow of money, such an attractive business.

Apart from providing unflattering portraits of the men in Keyun's life, her customers and some of the women she associated with, "Men Made Me Bad" is interesting for a number of reasons. Among other things it underscores the fluid and rather ambiguous nature of the concepts "prostitute," "husband," and "wife" as well as the notion of "marriage" itself. Following Keyun's abandonment by her first love (Sanit) she enters into a succession of ongoing relationships with men she refers to as her "husbands" (*sami*); in between these "married" interludes, and in certain instances at the same time as living with a particular spouse, she sells her sexual services in order for both herself and her husband to survive. Furthermore, in some of these unions she feels little love for the man involved and is essentially a kept woman, yet from her perspective such a relationship also constitutes a "marriage." To a degree, the ambiguity conveyed by the story may be seen as reflecting a marked difference in meaning between formal, legalistic notions of "husband," "wife," and "marriage" as espoused among those in polite, upper-class society, and the way in which ordinary individuals actually conceived of interpersonal relationships.

At the same time, the account is also notable for the way in which Keyun is portrayed. The title of the story aside, nowhere is it suggested that she is indeed a "bad" woman. In contrast to conventional notions of Siamese womanhood which idealized demure, restrained, and chaste behavior, Keyun was represented as a sensual, physically desirable woman who, notwithstanding her particular line of work and often sour relationships with boyfriends and husbands, had an unabashed love of sex. For some, this characteristic may have only served to confirm her "wickedness," her fundamentally "whorish nature," although perhaps it would be more accurate to see this depiction of robust sexuality as recognizing the force of female desire, a phenomenon briefly discussed by Chalat Nanthayobon in "The Practice of Sex" (*Kama-pathibat*) (see chapter 7), but generally suppressed or elided in local constructions of femininity and womanhood. The fact that the story passed no moral judgment on Keyun's uninhibited sex drive is significant, for in so doing it allowed readers to draw their own conclusions from the story independent of authorial interjection. To this extent "Men Made Me Bad" represented a small yet bold example of the egalitarian spirit of the times.

A NARROWING OF THE PUBLIC SPHERE

Despite hopes that the change in government would usher in a new democratic age, less than a year and a half after the People's Party seized power in June 1932 the once vibrant realm of critical public debate had contracted sharply. This development was related to a number of factors, in particular the continuing effects of the Great Depression on the local economy (notably on the publishing business and other commercial enterprises) and increasing government control and regulation of the print media. Press censorship, which had been implemented in an ad hoc and often capricious fashion in the pre-1932 period (reflecting the highly personal nature of the absolutist state), was far more strictly enforced and unforgiving under the rule of the People's Party. While formal censorship was briefly abolished in July 1932, the press continued to be closely monitored by the authorities and a number of papers deemed to be critical of, or opposed to, the government were temporarily closed down.[45] In September 1932, a new press law superseding the existing 1927 edict was announced, the first in a series of measures instituted by the state over the next few years to curb public debate and expression.[46] Indeed, government sensitivity to controversy and criticism was such that in the first year of constitutional rule a total of fourteen separate orders were issued, closing down a range of newspapers from across the political spectrum for varying periods of time. Among those publications to suffer the government's wrath was *Ying thai*, which was temporarily shut down in November 1932 for publishing remarks that were deemed to endanger public order.[47] Although it recommenced publication shortly afterward, the newspaper was to survive only a few more months before disappearing altogether.

Following the demise of *Ying thai* in early 1933, discussion of issues concerning women and their relations with men, while not disappearing entirely from the print media, was largely depoliticized. With the muzzling of the critical press, those newspapers and magazines which catered to the reading public tended to promote views supportive of the government and increasingly focused on the sensational, the exotic, and the titillating.[48] By the mid-1930s, for example, pictures of scantily clad and sometimes totally naked European (or other non-Siamese) women had become a staple feature of various popular dailies.[49] And when questions relating to women in society or relations between the sexes were discussed in print it was invariably in personal terms, embodied by the appearance of personal advice columns, rather than in an overtly collective political or national sense.[50]

In addition to economic factors and the growing attempts on the part of the government to stifle critical and oppositional voices, there was perhaps also a generational factor at work in the weakening of the critical environment. Indeed, with the passage of time it may be imagined that many of those who had been so vociferous in their condemnation of the old order in their younger years no longer viewed the world they inhabited in simple black-white oppositions, but rather as a far more complex reality than they had once imagined. In the process the critical activism of the 1920s and early 1930s was replaced to a large extent by a growing pragmatism toward and acceptance of the new sociopolitical order.

SIAM'S NEW AUTHORITIES TAKE THE LEAD

While public expression came under increasing state control, various ideas that had long been debated in the popular press, including those promoting greater equality between the sexes, were gradually embraced by the constitutional regime. Toward the end of 1932, for example, it was announced that women were to enjoy the same voting rights as men in the country's first elections planned for the following year, and similarly the same rights as men to run for office in the National Assembly.[51] Siam's new rulers also began to promote female education—together with that for males—to an unprecedented degree.[52] And in 1935, following lengthy debate in the National Assembly, the existing law allowing for polygamous marriage was replaced by new legislation, contained in the Commercial and Civil Code, instituting the practice of monogamy and requiring that all marriages henceforth be registered.[53]

Yet however laudable these various initiatives may have been, with the possible exception of the expansion of the education system for girls, they primarily benefited middle- and upper-class females. Indeed, with regard to the new law on marriage it seems that only the most educated women had any understanding of the changes. By contrast, the government's initiatives were of little immediate significance for lower-class women whose social position remained largely unaltered. Although there was now greater formal equality in marriage, men were still favored in a number of ways. For example, the law stipulated that a man had the right to initiate divorce proceedings if his wife committed adultery. If, on the other hand, a husband committed adultery his wife had no legal grounds to sue for divorce. Thus the new legislation, while providing for a greater degree of equality in marriage than was previously the case, continued to affirm the traditional sexual double standard.[54] Law or no law, many men continued to engage in the practice of maintaining minor wives and mistresses.

At the same time as legal and institutional changes were being introduced, the constitutional regime was also actively involved in establishing its own legitimacy, a complex process by which it sought to foster a heightened sense of national consciousness among the populace. Among other things the government, in an attempt to develop and promote a vision of the Siamese nation in keeping with its populist, egalitarian rhetoric, sought to project certain images of Thai womanhood to the public.

WOMEN IN THE NATIONAL IMAGINARY:
BEAUTY AND BRAVERY

Miss Siam

In seeking to consolidate its authority, the new government made strenuous efforts to promote the constitution, if not exactly the idea of constitutionalism itself, among the population at large.[55] The tenth of December 1933 (the first anniversary of the day in 1932 when King Prajadhipok had formally granted a constitution to the Siamese people) was proclaimed as Constitution Day and the following year the occasion was promoted as a major public event celebrated by a range of officially organized and sanctioned festivities held over a number of days. At the heart of these festivities was the Miss Siam (*Nang-sao sayam*) contest, a national beauty pageant staged under the auspices of the Interior Ministry.

In her extensive study of the history of the Miss Siam and subsequent Miss Thailand beauty competitions, Suphatra K'opkitsuksakun has little to say about exactly how the idea of staging a national beauty pageant in Siam came to be embraced by officialdom. She does point out, however, that from the 1920s the urban population was increasingly exposed to modern—that is, Western— images and ideas of beauty and fashion through both the press and film. This, together with the fact that the number of beauty parlors, hairdressing salons, and dressmaking shops was rapidly increasing and that middle- and upper-class women were taking on an ever more public role helped create the conditions necessary for the beauty pageant to emerge.[56] Indeed, clear signs of this were evident in the twelve months prior to the inaugural Miss Siam contest when the Silom Association (*Samos'on silom*), a group of Bangkok entrepreneurs, orga nized Siam's first women's fashion competition. The contest entrants, sponsored by a range of local enterprises, modeled a range of clothing from daywear to eve ningwear and lingerie to beachwear before a panel of judges.[57] Shortly thereafter a series of other women's beauty-cum-fashion competitions took place: some held in conjunction with the annual temple fairs in Nakhon Pathom and Phet buri, while in the northern Siamese capital, Chiang Mai, a number of local stores sponsored young women to appear in a clothing-beauty contest as a part of the yearly cool season festivities.[58]

These events proved to be extremely popular. Moreover, they were imbued with an aura of respectability, something that could not always be said for another popular form of public female display, the women's dance troupes that had performed in Bangkok's cinemas and theaters during the 1920s (see chapter 2). It seems that this contrast was not lost on members of the government who came to view the staging a national beauty competition that had the potential to enhance its own standing with the public. Indeed, considering the politically fractious environment of the times, the idea of holding such an event was an inspired strategy, a public occasion which people from all points along the socio political spectrum could readily appreciate and support, whatever their feelings may have been about other aspects of the new regime. Unlike the competitions organized by the Silom Association and businesses in Chiang Mai, however, the authorities eschewed the notion of commercialization in staging the Miss Siam pageant.[59] Instead of endorsing particular products or business interests, female beauty was recruited in the service of the nation. As one patriotic journalist was led to write: "we have genuine beauty in Siam and this should be seen to symbol ize the goodness of 'our race' (*chat-phan kh'ong rao*)."[60]

The first two years of the competition (1934 and 1935) were carefully con trolled by the state with Interior Ministry officials responsible for selecting all the entrants. In 1936, however, the event was opened up to private sector partic ipation with a number of the capital's newspapers taking a leading role.[61] The entry requirements for the pageant were as follows: a contestant had to be a Thai national, over fifteen years of age (this was raised to sixteen following the 1935 competition), a respectable member of society, and not in any form of paid employment.[62] Significantly, the event emphasized natural, unadorned beauty, with the use of make-up and body-enhancing undergarments (such as padded or uplifting brassieres) strictly prohibited. A panel composed of distinguished members of the public (primarily members of the nobility and wives of prominent business figures) together with a number of recognized experts in particular fields (for example, health, photography, and the performing arts) was appointed to judge the competition.[63] As for the judging process itself, the members of the panel were provided with a detailed checklist which specified a range of attributes held to be undesirable in a woman.[64] The contestants were evaluated with reference to the list, the winner being adjudged as being the woman with the fewest number of officially defined flaws or blemishes. Somewhat ironically, the ideal of female beauty projected by the contest was defined in negative terms.

From its inception the Miss Siam beauty pageant was enormously popular and, over time, came to serve as a potent means of presenting the regime in a favorable light. It was also used as a vehicle to promote particular "State Conventions" or "Cultural Mandates" (*Rathaniyom*) launched by the government of Phibun Songkhram (1938–1944).[65] With the exception of the inaugural Miss Siam competition, in which most contestants wore Western-style evening dresses, traditional Thai female attire—the *pha-thung* (a sarong-like dress), *sabai chiang* (a type of shawl or wrap), and bare feet—was de rigueur in the years leading up to the Phibun era.[66] Following Phibun's elevation to power, however, it was decided that entrants should only wear Western-style clothing (that is, dresses, high-heeled shoes, hats, and gloves), this being given much greater emphasis in 1941 when the newly proclaimed "State Convention" required that, in the name of "civilization" and national progress, the Thai public was to adopt European modes of dress. In addition to popularizing modern Western-style fashion among women, the pageant was also used to promote another "State Convention" which exhorted the public to use Thai-made goods instead of imported wares. As a consequence it was stipulated that all contestants wear garments made from Thai-produced cloth. At the same time, in an effort to extend the popular appeal of the pageant, members of the public were called on to develop their own occidental-inspired designs for a fashion competition held in conjunction with the beauty contest itself.[67]

The Miss Thailand competition, as it came to be known in 1939 when the name of the country was officially changed, was a multifaceted event in which female beauty, the promotion of the constitution, dress reform, and economic nationalism were combined in a new form of popular mass display. The competition emphasized natural beauty and youthful good health. In celebrating wholesome, vital specimens of Siamese womanhood—exemplary procreators of the future—the state, by means of the competition, sought to project a sense of national vigor and strength to the public at large. Indeed, given Phibun's admiration for the fascist regimes of Europe, it would not be out of place to think of the Miss Thailand competition of the late 1930s and early 1940s as a popular expression of the "fitness of the [Thai] race." At the same time, however, it also needs to be borne in mind that the ideal of Siamese womanhood promoted by the competition was essentially framed in terms of social class and looks. While the entry requirements for the contest made no mention of educational attainment or intellectual ability, they did stipulate that participants were not to be engaged in paid employment. In effect this limited entrants to Siam's more privileged young women such as high school students, or the idle daughters of the rich. The emphasis on a woman's looks, something which, it will be recalled, Thianwan had identified at the turn of the century as a long-standing male obsession that devalued women and impeded the progress and development of the nation, came to be a defining element in the formation of female identity in contemporary Siam. To put this another way, through its intimate involvement with the competition the state came to endorse what Lois Banner refers to as the "Cinderella mythology."[68] A counterpart to the notion of the self-made man, the "Cinderella mythology" promoted a view that female beauty was fundamental to a woman's social advancement and success, the pursuit of beauty being held to be her primary goal. Further, in a related discussion of the beauty pageant in early-twentieth-century America, Banner claims that this development represented a major triumph of what she terms "fashion culture" over feminism.[69] While her observation was made in relation to the United States, the phenomenon she refers to was in no way unique, for it clearly parallels what was happening in Siam as the state, while placing strict limits on critical expression and debate, sought to promote the beauty contest as an event of major national significance. In the process feminine beauty became an officially endorsed national ideal that remains very much in evidence to this day.

Martial Women: The *Thao* Suranari Monument

Print-mediated representations of martial women had circulated in Siam since the early twentieth century. In 1915, it will be recalled, the women's magazine *Satri niphon* had featured a section which extolled a number of historical female figures for their bravery in war. One of these women was *Than phu-ying* Mo (Lady Mo, popularly known as *Ya* Mo or Grandmother Mo), later given the more illustrious title *Thao* Suranari (Dame Gallant Lady) by King Rama III, who, it was claimed, played a key role in the defeat of an invading Lao force during the early nineteenth century.[70] For the author writing in *Satri niphon*, the actions of *Thao* Suranari were seen as a part of an unfolding Siamese national narrative.

It was not until the period following the abortive royalist Boworadej Rebellion in October 1933,[71] however, that *Thao* Suranari emerged as an official national icon. It was at this time that the constitutional regime sanctioned the erection of a statue of the historic heroine in Khorat, the capital of her native province, Nakhon Ratchasima. This initiative, it should be noted, was related to the fact that troops stationed in Khorat formed the core of Prince Boworadej's forces arrayed against the government in Bangkok. As Saiphin Kaew-ngamprasoet points out in her book on *Thao* Suranari, the defeat of the royalist rebellion fueled grave concerns among the people of Nakhon Ratchasima that they would be perceived by other Siamese as traitors who had betrayed the nation.[72] In order to combat such fears two high-ranking, locally based state officials, the newly appointed governor of Khorat (*Phraya* Kamth'onphayapthit), and the region's military commander (Lieutenant Colonel *Phra* Roengrukpatchamit) responding to requests by a number of local people, sought the permission of the central government to erect a statue of *Thao* Suranari as a symbol of local loyalty to the Siamese state.[73] For their part the authorities in Bangkok were strongly supportive of the proposal and, using funds contributed by members of the Khorat community, commissioned the Italian sculptor Corrado Feroci (known in Thai as Sin Phirasi) to make a statue of *Thao* Suranari. Feroci, who was employed by the Department of Fine Arts, quickly set to work and within the space of two months produced an impressive metal statue which was unveiled to the public in January 1935.[74] This event, the centerpiece of five days of celebrations, was widely publicized and promoted by the state. Among other things, the authorities sought to entice the members of the public to attend the unveiling ceremony by offering half-price railway fares to Khorat as well as staging a beauty competition, boxing matches, and organizing an exhibition of local produce. The extent to which officialdom wished to encourage popular participation in the festivities was further underlined by the fact that, for the duration of the event, gambling, an otherwise illegal activity, was permitted.[75] In addition a book about the life of *Thao* Suranari was specially produced for the occasion by Major *Luang* Si-yotha and offered for sale during the celebrations.[76] Written in the style of a popular novel, the eponymously titled work portrayed *Thao* Suranari as a heroine (*wirasatri*) possessed of great bravery, intelligence, and cunning, an image somewhat at odds with that found in the *Third Reign Chronicles*, the first known text to mention her (see below).

The monument created in honor of *Thao* Suranari is of particular significance in that it was not only the first public statue erected during the constitutional era but also the first ever state-sponsored statue of a commoner, who also happened to be a woman. While, as Charles Keyes notes, the monument embodied notions of "militant patriotism" and "regional loyalty,"[77] it also gave expression to the democratic, egalitarian rhetoric of the new order. Broadly speaking, the monument honored the actions of a commoner (*samanchon*) who fought for the country's territorial integrity in the face of an enemy, something that had been associated solely with royalty in the past. At the same time, the monument also

served to celebrate female heroism in time of war, a domain traditionally identified with men. In a sense, then, the *Thao* Suranari monument may be seen as
representing a form of official endorsement for the ideal of equality between the
sexes that had been so widely debated and discussed over the previous decades.

Not surprisingly, perhaps, the manner in which *Thao* Suranari came to be celebrated as a figure of national significance was seen among some of the leading
members of the old order as unnerving. On learning that the exploits of Suranari
were to be commemorated in the form of a public monument, Prince Naris wrote
to Prince Damrong telling him that he could not understand why such a fuss was
being made about her. He told Damrong that the *Third Reign Chronicles* simply
noted that she was in charge of local women in the Nakhon Ratchasima area
when Lao forces arrived on the scene and not directly involved in any hostilities—no more, no less. In other words he questioned the validity of her being
feted as a national heroine. For his part, Damrong responded by writing that the
idea of having a monument commemorating *Thao* Suranari was just "one more
example of how present-day thinking is totally at odds with that of the past."[78]
Indeed, this was precisely what was occurring as the new regime sought to promote a revisionist agenda in which it reconceptualized history for the sake of
furthering its own legitimacy and popular support at the expense of the royal-
aristocratic elite.

Martial Women on Stage: *The Blood of Suphan*, *The Battle of Thalang*

In addition to the *Thao* Suranari monument female valor was celebrated in various historical operas/dance-dramas written and produced by *Luang* Wichit
Wathakan during the mid to late 1930s. As director of the newly restructured
Department of Fine Arts his artistic contributions bore the official imprimatur
of the state. The best known of these works was his 1936 dance drama *The Blood
of Suphan* (*L'uat Suphan*), one of the most durable and influential cultural arti-
facts from the early constitutional era. Set at some unspecified time during the
Ayuthaya period (1350–1767), the play focuses on a Burmese invasion of the
Suphan (Suphanburi) area of central Siam.

Following their victory the Burmese put the local population to work as slave
laborers. However, Mangrai, one of the Burmese military commanders, is a man
of compassion and tries to treat the subjugated Thai villagers fairly. At one point
he comes to the aid of an attractive young woman, Duangchan, and her parents
when they are being terrorized by Mangratho, one of his fellow officers. After he
has saved her life a bond of affection develops between Mangrai and Duangchan.
He offers to free her and her parents but she refuses and tells him that she could
not abandon her people in order to save her own skin. Eventually, he decides to
allow all the captives to escape, an act for which he is sentenced to death by his

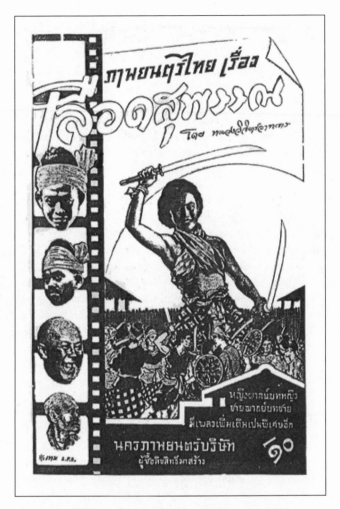

Fig. 9.2. Cover of film booklet for *The Blood of Suphan*

superiors. Meanwhile the Burmese commanders learn of Mangratho's mistreatment of Duangchan and her parents, and he is summarily executed. Just before this Mangrai is facing the same fate; Duangchan returns to plead for his life but her appeal is turned down and he too is put to the sword. Duangchan is given her freedom and goes in search of the other villagers who have fled into the jungle. Along the way she comes across the bodies of her parents, who have been slain by Mangratho's men keen to avenge his death. Enraged by what has happened, Duangchan meets up with the surviving villagers and beseeches them to join her and launch an attack on the Burmese. The people, emboldened by

Duangchan's fearlessness, follow her into battle where they fight valiantly before they are overwhelmed and slaughtered by their merciless foe. With this ending Wichit sought to portray Duangchan, above all, as the epitome of personal hero-ism and sacrifice in defense of the nation, a female martyr figure in no way infe-rior to men.

With its mixture of rousing martial music, ill-fated romance (between Duang-chan and Mangra), and bloodshed, *The Blood of Suphan* was designed to elicit a strong emotional response in audiences. And it was eminently successful in doing so, playing to packed houses in the Department of Fine Arts theater for months on end. At the same time, great efforts were made to ensure that the play reached as wide an audience as possible. Shortly after its premiere in Bang-kok, for example, *The Blood of Suphan* was broadcast in serial form over Siam's rapidly expanding state radio network, and the military and police authorities made it compulsory viewing for all young cadets. For its part the Ministry of Education also played a key role in disseminating the work by sending copies of the play to government schools throughout the country where it was studied in class.[79] The campaign to promote *The Blood of Suphan* continued into 1937 when an officially endorsed cinematic version of the play was produced by the Nakhon Film Company and released for general exhibition.[80] The role of Duangchan was given to an inexperienced young actress Somchit Inthusophon (shown in the graphic in figure 9.2) who would not have been out of place as a contestant in the Miss Siam competition. In the emergent image-driven mass media age, glam-our and heroism were combined in powerful and enticing new ways.

The idea of the martial Siamese woman was also developed in *S'uk Thalang* (The Battle of Thalang), another of Wichit's historical dramas of the mid-1930s.[81] *S'uk Thalang* was based on one of his early, if not earliest, plays, a 1934 spoken drama entitled *Luk Ratthathammanun* (Children of the Constitution).[82] This production, "a thinly disguised account of the Boworadej Rebellion,"[83] was an overtly partisan work, and thus tended to limit its popular appeal, especially to those who were less than enamored with the new regime. Moreover, it lacked the simple but stirring songs and dances that were to become a hallmark of his subsequent plays. In contrast to the contemporariness of *Luk Rathathammanun*, *S'uk Thalang* was set in the Early Bangkok period (late eighteenth century), a distant and far less contentious age. The play also included numerous songs and dance performances to enhance its entertainment value.

The two central characters in *S'uk Thalang* are N'uang and her brother N'om, orphaned commoners who were raised in the home of *Khun* Phimon, a wealthy Thalang noble. Phimon also has a son of his own, Sutchit, born to his wife, Sutchai. Over time Sutchit and N'uang fall in love, much to the annoyance of Sutchai who has plans for her son to marry a woman from another well-to-do family. Ultimately, as a result of their stepmother's incessant carping and ill-disguised resentment toward them, N'uang and N'om decide to leave their adoptive home and take to working the land as farmers. Sutchit is heartbroken but can do nothing to change his mother's hostility toward N'uang and her brother.

A few years later Thalang is threatened by a Burmese invasion force. *Khunying* Chan (the widow of the local ruler *Phraya* Thalang) and her younger sister, Muk, call on the local farming population to join forces and resist the invaders. In the process N'uang is given command of the female militia while N'om is appointed as the leader of the men's force. At this point Sutchit appears on the scene and volunteers for the male troop. However, his request is turned down and he goes to see N'uang and pleads with her to join the women fighters. Again he is rejected, with N'uang bluntly telling him, "It's only the poor who go off to battle; the rich [*phuak mang mi*] don't involve themselves in actually fighting wars."[84] Denied the opportunity for active service, Sutchit is relegated to the supply corps away from hostilities. Finally, after he continues to plead his case with N'uang, she relents and he goes into battle only to be taken prisoner by the Burmese. Meanwhile both N'uang and N'om play a decisive role in crushing the Burmese invaders and cover themselves in glory. On vanquishing their foe the assembled Siamese forces come together to perform a dance accompanied by a typical Wichit martial tune, the rousing *Kraw thalang*, or "Thalang Symphony," extolling the valor of the common folk.

> In times of peace they live simple day-to-day lives, but if there's war they won't shrink from battle.
> Should any nation [*chat*] dare to attack, each is willing to die for the country [*ban-m'uang*];
> Come fellow Thais, both men and women, let the world know of Siam's honor, let it be known far and wide.[85]

From this point the various romantic and familial dilemmas set in train before the war with the Burmese are quickly resolved. Following his escape from capture, Sutchit is reunited with N'uang, now convinced of his bravery and worthiness; at the same time, Sutchai expresses remorse for her harsh treatment of N'uang and N'om, gives her blessings to a union between Sutchit and N'uang, and promises to find N'om a wealthy Chinese girl to marry. As for her great wealth, which she had kept very much for her own pleasure, Sutchai plans to donate it to the government for the purpose of building warships to repel any further Burmese encroachments on Thai territory.

In comparison to the bloody theatrics of *L'uat Suphan*, in which Duangchan and her fellow villagers sacrifice themselves in defense of the homeland, *S'uk Thalang* had little in the way of out-and-out gore, none of the principal characters lost their lives in battle, and closure was achieved with a classic "happy ending." Even so, despite the difference in tenor between the two plays, the theme of female valor in time of war was underlined in both. In the case of *S'uk Thalang* while two upper-class women (*Khunying* Chan and her sister) were responsible

for the overall leadership of the Siamese forces, N'uang, an ordinary but courageous commoner, was portrayed as the real heroine of the piece with her brother,
N'om, cast in a similar if lesser role as hero. More generally the subtext of the
play was to accord recognition to the efforts of the common people, rather than
those of their social superiors. In this way S'uk Thalang echoed the egalitarian
rhetoric of the constitutional regime which acknowledged both men *and* women
from across the social spectrum. The play also projected the idea of unity at both
the communal and the familial level. The former, for example, was underscored
by the way the people of Thalang readily coalesce into fighting units at the urg-
ing of Khunying Chan and Muk to defeat the Burmese, while as a direct consequence of the battle the rupture between N'uang and N'om and their adoptive
stepmother is healed and peace and harmony in the family established. Here the
implication seems to have been that to demonstrate one's worth in battle was a
means not only for achieving honor but also of overcoming social difference.
This was a notion very much in line with the attempts to promote and popularize
militarism among the Siamese public by the defense minster, Phibun Songkhram, and his cohorts in the armed forces from the mid-1930s onward.

As we have seen, the martial woman and the beauty queen were two feminine
constructs that were avidly promoted by the military-dominated government.
There was, however, a significant difference between the two. The former, for
example, while acknowledging the heroic actions of women, was, in essence,
backward looking, a new addition to the collective memory of the nation.
Admittedly, there was one contemporary development in which women were
cast in a military, or rather a quasi-military, role. As a part of the state program
to popularize militarism, Phibun, inspired by developments in Hitler's Germany,
launched what was known as the *yuwachon* or military youth movement.[86] At its
inception this was designed to provide military training for schoolboys, although
a female section of the movement (referred to as the *yuwanari*) was subsequently
established. Drawn from the educated upper ranks of society, the women and
girls who formed the membership of the *yuwanari* were not given any military
training as such; rather, they were seen as having an ancillary role to provide
nursing care and clerical services to the armed forces.[87] Women warriors, it
seems, were regarded as an historical phenomenon to be remembered and celebrated, not individuals with any place in contemporary affairs. Thus, notwithstanding the public recognition of Thai heroines of the past, both real and
imagined, the gendered notion of the military as a quintessentially male bastion
remained intact.[88] In contrast to the martial woman, the figure of the beauty
queen, whose youthful good looks were objectified and associated with the
nation-state, represented a potent model for shaping notions of Siamese female
identity. Indeed, this particular association between women and the broader polity proved to be a great success and has continued, albeit with an ever-increasing
commercial aspect, in the present age during which an overriding fascination

with beauty queens and female glamour has become an integral feature of the contemporary Thai national persona.[89]

STATE-SPONSORED FILMMAKING: NATIONALIZING ROMANCE, HISTORICIZING MONOGAMY

As Charnvit and Wani point out in an essay entitled "Thai Films and 'Nation Building': *Blood of the Thai Military, The King of the White Elephant,* and *Our Farms and Fields*" (*Phaphayon thai kap kan 'sang chat': l'uat thahan thai, phrachao chang ph'uak, ban rai na rao*), the promoters of the People's Party were members of the first generation of Siamese to grow up familiar with the cinema.[90] It was therefore not surprising that such dominant personalities in the constitutional regime as Phibun Songkhram and Pridi Phanomyong made use of film as a means of promoting certain ideas to the broader public.

We have already noted that, as minister of defense in the mid-1930s, Phibun was involved in a program aimed at popularizing the military among the populace at large. One notable aspect of this endeavor was the production of two big-budget motion pictures by Siam's premier movie-making business, the Sikrung Film Company. This enterprise, it will be recalled, was owned and operated by Manit Wasuwat, a canny businessman and media entrepreneur who had come to enjoy close links with members of the new government. The first of these films was the 1935 production *Blood of the Thai Military* (*L'uat thahan thai*); the second, *The Heart of the Navy* (*Kaen Kalasi*), dates from early 1937.

Blood of the Thai Military was an extravagantly staged film made with the cooperation of the three armed services together with the police force. However, it was not, as Charnvit and Wani have suggested, wholly concerned with military activity.[91] While it did feature Siam's armed forces in action, including massed battle scenes in which the army, navy, and air force expended prodigious amounts of live ammunition, this activity was developed within a broader narrative context. Indeed, notwithstanding its propagandistic overtones, *Blood of the Thai Military* was a highly eclectic work, a romantic action adventure film which incorporated a strong musical element in the form of both popular love songs and stirring martial tunes.[92] In many respects, then, it was similar to various commercial Hollywood-inspired features produced by the Sikrung Film Company during the 1930s. As for *The Heart of the Navy*, a similar eclecticism was evident in that it combined romance, adventure, comedy, contemporary popular music, and military propaganda, in this case focusing specifically on the Siamese navy. In fact, much of the film's "action" footage was taken in 1935 when Thai naval officers sailed to Italy to take delivery of a number of new torpedo boats that had been ordered from Mussolini's fascist regime.[93]

Rather than go into detail about the plot of either film, my concern here is simply with the romantic aspect of these works. In *Blood of the Thai Military* the

central male characters are two young officers from different branches of the services who were often bitterly at odds with each other during the early constitutional era: Lieutenant-Commander *Luang* Saha Nawin, a navy man, and his close
friend from the army, Colonel *Luang* Kritsana Songkhram. The female lead is
Phani Norakun, the daughter of Lieutenant-General *Phraya* Norakun, a high-
ranking military official. These three characters, representatives of the new elite,
affect a modern international style: they dress in modish Western fashions, dance
the foxtrot, and drink champagne. There are also two central male characters
and one major female character in *The Heart of the Navy*, all representatives of a
distinctly lower social order than their counterparts in *Blood of the Thai Military*.
The men in question are from the noncommissioned ranks, Second Petty Officer
(*Cha-tho*) W'ong and Second Petty Officer U'am, while the female lead, Sisawat,
is an attractive young woman who works as a hostess in a Bangkok dance hall.

In each film relations between the men and women take the form of a classic
romantic triangle. In *Blood of the Thai Military* Saha and Kritsana are strongly
attracted to Phani and, despite their friendship, the men become rivals for her
affection; as for *Kaen kalasi*, a similar romantic rivalry over Sisawat develops
between W'ong and U'am, although in this case the pair are not friends but
bitter enemies. Ultimately, however, the rivalry between the male protagonists
is not sustained. In *Blood of the Thai Military*, as the struggle for Phani's affections
begins to unfold, Siam is confronted by an unnamed foreign power and the
armed forces are hurriedly mobilized to meet the threat. In the process, Saha and
Kritsana, urged on by Phani, bury their differences and rush to the defense of
the homeland—a rapprochement that perhaps reflected the hopes that the military and navy could bury their differences and develop a united sense of purpose
(tensions between these two branches of the armed forces was particularly
marked during the first few years of constitutional rule). Meanwhile, in *The
Heart of the Navy*, volunteers are called to make the sea voyage to Italy to take
delivery of the torpedo boats. W'ong decides to volunteer, but U'am, who has
entered into an intimate relationship with Sisawat (*pen phua mia kan*), is reluctant to give up the woman he has pursued so assiduously. At this point U'am is
shown pondering his situation and an image of Sisawat appears in his mind.
However, as he fondly contemplates her smiling visage it is suddenly replaced by
another image, the naval ensign for which he, as a military man, has the greatest
respect. This experience has a profound effect on him and he decides to forsake
Sisawat and volunteer for the long voyage to Europe where he works alongside
W'ong, the pair becoming firm friends in the process.

The overriding message conveyed by both films was that the most important
thing in life was to be able to sacrifice one's own personal interests for the collective good of the nation. While romance and intimacy represented an enormously
powerful force, the emotions needed to be denied or sublimated for the sake of
a higher calling, to serve the nation, the ultimate source of one's identity and

well-being. In effect, both *Blood of the Thai Military* and *The Heart of the Navy* sought to project the type of portentous nationalist mythology which was so wickedly mocked in the humorous sketch featured at the beginning of this study (see page 1).

PEACE NOT WAR: PRIDI AND
THE KING OF THE WHITE ELEPHANT

While Phibun supported the making of films extolling militarism and chauvinistic nationalism, Pridi Phanomyong, his long-term associate and sometimes rival, was involved with a cinematic project of a very different nature: *The King of the White Elephant* (*Phrachao chang ph'uak*), a 1940 full-length sound feature film based on a short historical novel of the same name which he had written during his time as finance minister.[94] Significantly, the book was produced in English, as was the soundtrack to the film, a language that gave Pridi the opportunity to present his pacifist views to the broader international community, apparently with an eye to winning the Nobel Peace Prize.[95] Given that war had already broken out in Europe and conflict was threatening to engulf much of Asia, Pridi may have imagined (somewhat naively, one would suppose) that his filmic contribution could secure him the prestigious award and thereby enhance his political standing.

Set in the Ayuthaya period, the story of *The King of the White Elephant* draws a sharp contrast between a refined peace-loving Thai monarch, King Cakra, and his arch-enemy, King Hongsa, a licentious, warmongering tyrant from Burma. While the theme of peace (which may also be read as a critique of the chauvinistic militarism embraced by Phibun) is discussed at length by Charnvit in a 1980 article about the film,[96] he gives scant attention to the significance of another key element of the work, that concerning the issue of polygamy. At the very beginning of the film, King Cakra condemns the practice in no uncertain terms, much to the annoyance of his lord chamberlain who insists that the monarch, according to royal custom, is to have a different wife for each day of the year. Finally, however, the views of the king prevail and at the close of the film he is shown to take just one wife, the woman of his choosing.

Here we may ask: what did Pridi have in mind by making the hero of his work, King Cakra, a fervent advocate of monogamy? On one level, if we recall earlier critiques of polygamy that identified the practice as a primary source of friction and disharmony in the home (the nation writ small), the idea of monogamy resonated powerfully with the film's central theme of peace. At the same time, given that *The King of the White Elephant* was largely created with an international English-speaking audience in mind, it would seem that Pridi, in disavowing polygamous marriage, was actually attempting to influence Western perceptions about the type of sexual morality that operated in contemporary

Thailand. The film's monogamous hero, King Cakra, was an exemplary figure, a representative of a civilized nation, albeit in premodern guise, which embraced the same type of moral values—concerning women—as those espoused in the West. This, it should be emphasized, represented a marked shift in the type of official stance taken in an earlier age when *Chaophraya* Thipkh'orawong vigorously defended polygamy against its Western critics. By means of the cinema, the most modern and powerful form of cultural expression at the time, Pridi sought to project an image of Siam to the wider world as a progressive highminded, peace-loving nation.

With the overthrow of the absolute monarchy in June 1932 Siam entered a new era, one characterized from the start by a burgeoning populism and widespread hope that a more egalitarian, representative sociopolitical order would develop. The appearance of *Ying thai*, the last feminist type newspaper in the pre–World War II period, was one manifestation of this newfound optimism. Less than eighteen months after the change in government, however, the situation had changed radically. The print-mediated public sphere, the site of popular debate and discussion, grew increasingly narrow as the state, in seeking to assert its authority, assumed the dominant role in setting the public agenda. And while the new regime was responsive to populist sentiment it responded only on its own terms. Indeed, the egalitarian, representative ethos expressed when the People's Party came to power was not invoked to further the development of a democratic system of government; instead, it was incorporated into the nationalist rhetoric of successive regimes. In the process the state formally recognized women as an integral part of the nation by means of beauty competitions, public statuary, and dramatic works. On the ideological level, at least, women were seen as being the equal of men.

NOTES

1. Kenneth P. Landon. *Siam in Transition* (Westport, Conn.: Greenwood, 1968), 12.

2. See Scot Barmé, *Luang Wichit Wathakan and the Creation of a Thai National Identity*, (Singapore: Institute of Southeast Asian Studies, 1993), chapter 5.

3. Barmé, *Luang Wichit Wathakan*, chapter 6.

4. Suphaphan Bunsa-at, *Prawat nangs'uphim nai prathet thai* [A History of the Press in Thailand] (Bangkok: Bannakit, 1974), 82–83.

5. As far as I have been able to ascertain, the National Library of Thailand in Bangkok has no copies of *Sao Sayam* in its collection although it is listed in the library's general newspaper-magazine catalogue.

6. *Ying thai*, 3 August 1932 (premier issue).

7. At the same time, the 1930s labor newspaper *Kammak'on* (not to be confused with a paper of the same name published in the early 1920s) was serializing another chronicle-style work about martial Siamese women in the past entitled *Lup khom dap* [Stroke the Sharp Sword], *Kammak'on*, 18 October 1932.

8. *Ying thai*, 5 August 1932.

9. *Ying thai*, 5 August 1932.

10. *Ying thai*, 5 August 1932. A similar idea was expressed by Neti, another contributor, who said that under the new constitutional regime state officials should be regarded as the employees (*luk-chang*) of the people. See *Ying thai*, 13 September 1932.

11. *Ying thai*, 20 September 1932.

12. *Ying thai*, 22 October 1932.

13. *Ying thai*, 25 October 1932.

14. *Ying thai*, 11 August 1932.

15. *Ying thai*, 20 August 1932.

16. Barmé, *Luang Wichit Wathakan*, 87, 141, 152–54.

17. *Ying thai*, 1 October 1932.

18. This sensitivity toward the difficulties faced by Siamese workers was reflected in the paper's publication of a letter by N'om Siwong, the leader of a group of unemployed Thai laborers. N'om wrote that he and his associates had been looking long and hard for work but without success since virtually all the building contractors in Bangkok were Chinese who only employed their fellow nationals. He urged the new government to stamp out this practice and compel Chinese contractors to start using local Thai labor. *Ying thai*, 17 August 1932.

19. The tramway workers had begun to organize themselves during the absolutist period. This was most apparent in 1923 when they engaged in a bitter struggle with their employers, the Siam Electric Company, to win improved working conditions and wages. See Andrew Brown, "Locating Working-Class Power" in *Political Change in Thailand: Democracy and Participation*, ed. Kevin Hewison (London: Routledge, 1997), 166–67.

20. *Ying thai*, 29 September 1932.

21. *Ying thai*, 29 September 1932.

22. *Ying thai*, 19 October 1932.

23. *Ying thai*, 19 October 1932.

24. Barmé, *Luang Wichit Wathakan*, 106–107. Pasuk Phongphaichit and Chris Baker, *Thailand: Economy and Politics* (Kuala Lumpur: Oxford University Press, 1999), 181, 256.

25. *Ying thai*, 10 August 1932.

26. *Ying thai*, 9 September 1932.

27. Barmé, *Luang Wichit Wathakan*, 69; Virginia Thompson, *Thailand: The New Siam* (New York: Paragon Book Reprint, 1967), 795.

28. *Ying thai*, 18 October 1932.

29. *Ying thai*, 18 October 1932.

30. *Ying thai*, 10 January 1933. This organization was formed in December 1932. Its leading members included Miss Yai Khunadilok, who had completed a bachelor of arts in the Philippines and received a medical diploma from New York University; Miss Raem Phrommobon, a qualified lawyer, and various other well-educated women such as Mrs. Niwettiban (Anong Amatayakun), a former staff member of *Ying thai*, Mrs. Lamai Bunya-thamik and Mrs. Arun Angsulayothin. *Prachathai*, 25 December 1932.

31. *Satri thai*, 14 June 1926.

32. *Ying thai*, 10 January 1933.

33. Apparently, however, this association reemerged in the public arena during the Phibun era in the late 1930s. Nanthira Khamphiban, "Nayobai kiaw-kap phuying thai

nai samai sang chat kho'ng ch'om phon p'o phibun songkhram, ph'o s'o 2481–2487" [Policies toward Thai Women during the Nation-Building Era of Field Marshall Phibun Songkhram, 1938–44], M.A. thesis, Thammasat University, Bangkok, 1987, 63.

34. *Ying thai,* 2 September 1932.

35. *Ying thai,* 2 September 1932.

36. *Kammak'on,* 18–19 February 1933.

37. *(10 thanwa) phanuak khaw rew,* 12 June 1933.

38. *(10 thanwa) phanuak khaw rew,* 13,14,15,17 June 1933.

39. *(10 thanwa) phanuak khaw rew,* 4 July 1933.

40. *(10 thanwa) phanuak khaw rew,* 21 July 1933.

41. See Prince Chulachakrabongse's introduction to the original edition of the novel. K'o Surangkhanang, *Ying khon chua* [The Prostitute] (Bangkok: Chiraphanit, 1937, n.p.) Recently David Smyth has produced a fine English-language translation of this work, *The Prostitute* (Kuala Lumpur: Oxford University Press, 1994).

42. *The Shorter Oxford Dictionary,* vol. 2 (Oxford: Clarendon Press, 1973), 1631.

43. *(10 thanwa) phanuak khaw rew,* 23 July 1933.

44. Dararat Mettarikanon, "Sopheni kap naiyobai rathaban thai ph'o s'o 2411–2503" [Prostitution and Thai Government Policy 1868–1960], M.A. thesis, Chulalongkorn University, Bangkok, 1983, 45.

45. Virginia Thompson, *Thailand: The New Siam,* 795.

46. Thompson, *Thailand: The New Siam,* 795–98.

47. Suphaphan, *A History of the Press in Thailand,* 104–108.

48. See various issues of the dailies *Sayam nik'on* and *Pramuan wan* in the mid to late 1930s. A typical example is a story on teenage sex in Bali accompanied by a picture of a pubescent Balinese girl baring her breasts. *Pramuan wan,* 16 September 1936.

49. See, for example, *Pramuan phap,* 8 January 1936, which featured a large photograph of a young, totally nude European woman, pubic hair and all.

50. For example, see the regular "Love Problems" [*panha khwam-rak*] column in *Pramuan wan,* June 1936–March 1938.

51. *Ying thai,* 7 December 1932.

52. Between 1932 and 1935, for example, the number of girls receiving primary education increased from 290,572 to just under 400,000 (the corresponding figures for primary age boys rose from 423,779 to 516,945); at the secondary level the increase in the number of females during this period rose from 4,358 to 11,540 (boys, from 18,210 to 33,186), and at the tertiary level 175 to 387 (the comparable male figures showing a rise from 298 to 9,152). This increase in numbers at the tertiary level was directly related to the opening of Siam's second tertiary institution, Thammasat University, in 1934. *The Statistical Yearbook of Siam* (1933–1935), 28–29.

53. Landon, *Siam in Transition,* 157–58; Thompson, *Thailand: The New Siam,* 684.

54. Suwadee Tanaprasitpatana, "Thai Society's Expectations of Women, 1851–1935," Ph.D. diss., Sydney University, 1989, 232.

55. See Barmé, *Luang Wichit Wathakan,* 107–13.

56. Suphatra Ko'pkitsuksakun, *Sen thang nang ngam* [A History of Beauty Contests (in Thailand)] (Bangkok: D'ok bia, 1993), 17–19.

57. Suphatra, *A History of Beauty Contests,* 35.

58. Suphatra, *A History of Beauty Contests,* 47–48.

59. Suphatra, *A History of Beauty Contests*, 74. In the United States, the home of the beauty pageant as we know it, such contests had their roots in the nineteenth century and were driven wholly by commercial imperatives. See A. R. Riverol, *Live from Atlantic City: The History of the Miss America Pageant before, after, and in Spite of Television* (Bowling Green, Ohio: Bowling Green State University Popular Press, 1992), 7–25.

60. *Sayam riwiw*, 7 December 1935. Here we find an affirmation of an old concept found in the Western tradition and perhaps the Siamese tradition as well, the association of beauty with virtue.

61. Suphatra, *A History of Beauty Contests*, 727–33.

62. *Pramuanwan*, 27 October 1936.

63. Suphatra, *A History of Beauty Contests*, 93.

64. *Sayam riwiw*, 7 December 1935. With regard to a contestant's facial appearance, for example, each component was considered separately (i.e., the mouth, eyes, ears, chin, nose, tongue, neck, face, teeth, and shape of the head). In assessing a woman's nose she would be marked down if it was flat and broad, or if it was too narrow, if her nostrils were large, if there was mucus visible or if she had a profusion of hairs growing from her nostrils. Similarly with regard to her head she would lose marks if it was not in proportion with the rest of her body, if her hair was falling out or she had small bald patches, or if the skin on her head was dirty. As for the contestant's figure, each woman was evaluated in terms of the appearance of her chest, back, hips, arms and hands, stomach, and so on. A woman whose breasts were unequal in size or malformed (however this was adjudged), for example, would be marked down, as would a woman whose ribs were clearly visible.

65. Barmé, *Luang Wichit Wathakan*, 144–60.

66. Suphatra, *A History of Beauty Contests*, 83.

67. Suphatra, *A History of Beauty Contests*, 83.

68. Lois W. Banner, *American Beauty* (Chicago: University of Chicago Press, 1984), 14.

69. Banner, *American Beauty*, 15.

70. Exactly where the author of this piece obtained her information about *Than phu-ying* Mo is not entirely clear, although it is probable that it was drawn from the Third Reign chronicles written by *Chaophraya* Thiphak'orawong in 1869, but not made available to the public until 1901. For details about Thiphak'orawong's work and other early writing on *Thao* Suranari, see Saiphin Kaew-ngamprasoet, *Kan-m'uang nai anusawari thao suranari* [The Politics of the Monument of Thao Suranari] (Bangkok: Matichon/Silapa-Wattanatham, 1995), chapter 4 (268–71 in particular).

71. See Barmé, *Luang Wichit Wathakan*, chapter 4.

72. Saiphin Kaew-ngamprasoet, *Kan-m'uang nai anusawari thao suranari* [The Politics of the Monument of *Thao* Suranari] (Bangkok: Matichon/Silapa-Wattanatham, 1995), 61–62.

73. Saiphin, *The Politics of the Monument*, 60.

74. Saiphin, *The Politics of the Monument*, 58.

75. Saiphin, *The Politics of the Monument*, 78.

76. Saiphin, *The Politics of the Monument*, 158–59.

77. Charles Keyes, "National Heroine or Local Spirit? The Struggle over Memory in the Case of Thao Suranari of Nakhon Ratchasima," paper presented at the Sixth International Thai Studies Conference, Chiang Mai, October 1996.

78. Saiphin, *The Politics of the Monument*, 88–89.

79. Barmé, *Luang Wichit Wathakan*, 122.

80. The company published some 20,000 copies of a booklet containing photographs taken on the set and interviews with the director, Chaem Sukhumalachan, and a number of his actors as part of the promotional campaign which accompanied the release of the film.

81. Thalang is an old name for the island of Phuket in southern Thailand.

82. See the introduction (written 23 June 1937) to (*Luang*) Wichit Wathakan, *S'uk thalang kap nanchao* [The Battle of Thalang and Nanchao (Two plays)], published in the *Cremation Volume* for (Mrs.) Bunsong Khunakasem, 10 March 1963.

83. Barmé, *Luang Wichit Wathakan*, 111.

84. Wichit, *The Battle of Thalang*, 12.

85. Wichit, *The Battle of Thalang*, 18.

86. Thompson, *Thailand: The New Siam*, 308–309.

87. Nanthira, "Policies toward Thai Women," 76.

88. Perhaps this idea of the gendered nature of the military sphere was no more unequivocally stated than in a 1921 speech by Princess Vallabha Devi, Vajiravudh's official consort at the time, to the paramilitary organization the Wild Tigers when she voiced her regrets about being unable to become a soldier: "Woman that I am, I would, no less than you, like to be a fighter. . . . It is a matter of regret and pity that I should have been unlucky enough to be born a woman." *Bangkok Times Weekly Mail*, 14 February 1921.

89. Penny Van Esterik, "The Politics of Beauty in Thailand" in *Beauty Queens on the Global Stage: Gender, Contests, and Power*, eds. Colleen Cohen, Richard Wilk, and Beverly Stoeltje (New York: Routledge, 1996), 206.

90. Charnvit Kasetsiri and Wani Samranwet, "Phaphayon thai kap kan 'sang chat': l'uat thahan thai, phrachao chang ph'uak, ban rai na rao" [Thai Films and "Nation Building": *Blood of the Thai Military*, *The King of the White Elephant*, and *Our Farms and Fields*], *Warasan Thammasat* 19, no.2 (May–August 1993): 96.

91. *Khun* Wichit Matra wrote the script to the film and also directed it, although the original plot was apparently conceived of by Phibun himself. Charnvit and Wani, "Thai Films and 'Nation Building,' " 97.

92. Details about the film used in this section are primarily drawn from a seventy-six-page booklet entitled *L'uat thahan thai*, by Kaew Kanchana [Wibun Rongkhasuwan, 1899–1963], n.d., n.p.

93. Details about *Kaen kalasi* are taken from a booklet put out by the Sikrung Film Company at the time of the film's release in January 1937.

94. Pridi Banonyong, *The King of the White Elephant* [in English] (Los Angeles: The Thammasat Association, 1990).

95. Charnvit and Wani, "Thai Films and 'Nation Building,' " 100. Notwithstanding such pretensions on the part of Pridi the film was seen as something of a joke by reviewers in the United States. In April 1941, for example, *Variety Film Review*'s correspondent wrote, "Despite a certain quaintness the picture is so badly done that it will do negligible business (and that on curiosity value alone) and have little propaganda effect. . . . The incredible determination and energy involved is admirable, of course, but the finished product seems merely rather childish and not a little pathetic. . . . Instead of basing the picture on authentic Thai traditions, legends or customs, producer Pridi Banomyong

chose to do a kind of jingoistic Western, with elephants substituted for horses. The story is agonisingly hokey, the dialogue is crammed with bombastic propaganda and the acting is doubtless the most exaggerated in all screen history. . . . On the whole it's a lengthy 66 minutes." Bosley Crowther, the *New York Times* reviewer, was similarly unimpressed: "An amusing cinematic oddity . . . in its primitive quality lies a certain amount of charm and, indeed, of unintentional humour deriving from its juvenilities. *The King of the White Elephant* is, except for sound, about twenty-five years behind the times. . . . Aside from the elephant pictures and the highly exotic costumes, this film is really in a class with a home-made movie turned out by a bunch of precocious kids."

96. Charnvit Kasetsiri. "Kae r'oi phrachao chang ph'uak" [Picking Up on the Trail of the King of the White Elephant] *Sinlapawathanatham* 2, no. 14 (1980): 26–33.

Conclusion

This study has addressed a range of questions concerning women, relations between the sexes, the rise of the middle class, and the concomitant development of popular commercial culture during the early decades of the twentieth century, a crucial period in the formation of the modern Thai nation. It was at the beginning of the century that the issue of the social position of women first became a focus of public debate and discussion, this being manifest in the work of the commoner-intellectual Thianwan and in the various female contributors to the early women's magazines *Kunlasatri* and *Satri niphon*. While much of this emergent discussion, in particular opinions voiced in these latter publications, was narrowly focused on the situation of elite women, it also incorporated elements of broader national significance by suggesting that Siam's future progress demanded greater social equality between the sexes.

However, it was not until the early 1920s, a time when the emergent middle class (created through the interrelated processes of economic change and administrative reform) reached a critical mass that the idea of social equality, including equality between the sexes, began to gain general currency. This type of social egalitarianism was central to a wide-ranging public debate on the state of the nation carried on in the popular press, a debate in which the old absolutist order was characterized as being anachronistic, oppressive, and corrupt—in other words, inimical to the good of the nation. Much of this study has been devoted to examining interrelated gender and class aspects of this popular debate. In particular, emphasis has been given to middle-class criticisms of the ancien régime for failing to provide women with educational and employment opportunities equal to those enjoyed by males, and for maintaining inequality between the sexes in the interpersonal sphere by upholding ancient laws and the practice of polygamy. Apart from being regarded as an uncivilized, immoral practice, polygamy was also seen by its critics as contributing to the growth of prostitution and the spread of venereal disease, a presumed threat to the vitality of the nation.

These gender-related critiques, in conjunction with those of a more political and economic nature, were the most tangible manifestations of a deep-seated frustration and anger among the commoner population with the existing socio-political order. For its part, the royal-noble elite was largely unmoved by such criticisms and made little effort to appease the public and initiate any substantive popular reforms. This increasingly tense situation constituted a growing crisis in the Siamese polity from the early 1920s onward—a crisis, to cite an apposite remark from Gramsci, which "consist[ed] precisely in the fact that the old [was] dying and the new [could] not be born."[1]

Here it may be noted that some readers may regard my examination of the press debates on women and relations between the sexes during the absolutist period as incomplete in that I have not discussed King Vajiravudh's ideas on these matters, except in passing. In the work of such scholars as Nanthira and Suphatra, for example, the king's writings on women from the late 1910s and early 1920s are seen as significantly contributing to the process of female emancipation in Siam.[2] This view, I would suggest, is misleading. The fact is that the king's work barely figured, if indeed it figured at all, in the press debates of the 1920s, either by direct quotation or indirectly through citation.

That Vajiravudh's writings on women have been accorded such importance in academic studies to date says a good deal more about the type of restrictive, socially confirming intellectual environment in which contemporary Thai historiography operates, not to mention the fact that the king's writings remain readily available in print, than it does about the period in which he wrote his essays. Whereas the newspapers and magazines used as source material in this study were ephemeral publications (quickly produced, and just as quickly read and discarded) Vajiravudh's works have been edited and republished by the Vajiravudh Foundation over the years and continue to circulate freely in the public realm. In contrast, the task of working one's way through the disorganized and poorly maintained newspaper and magazine holdings of the National Library in Bangkok (the only institution at which these materials are held in Thailand, in their rapidly decaying original form as well as on microfilm) is a rather more daunting and difficult prospect, something which has doubtless dissuaded many researchers from exploring these sources. By investing the king's work with a wholly unwarranted degree of significance, the scholarly contributions of Nanthira and Suphatra promote a highly selective view of the past, one that dovetails neatly with official royal-centered history while obscuring the far more complex, innovative, and contentious realities of the period.

The present study, on the other hand, has sought to provide an alternative to such narrowly conceived elite histories and develop an understanding of the dynamics of this complex reality as manifest within the urban context. By the early 1920s signs abounded that Bangkok was becoming a more cosmopolitan city in which the middle class came to play a crucial defining role. Indeed, by that time the Thai capital had emerged as the locus of what amounted to a new hybrid culture that invites comparison with, albeit on a far smaller scale, Republican Shanghai. Wen-hsin Yeh has described Shanghai as:

the scene of a unique urban middlebrow culture of department-store consumerism, cafes, night clubs, casinos, movie houses, amusement halls, racecourses, charity balls, and other forms of activities inspired by Western examples on the one hand, and, on the other, of popular films, dramas, fiction, newspapers, and magazines that contained adaptations of traditional motifs.[3]

Among other things this study has attempted to chart, in part, the rise of the middle class to a central position in the cultural life of the nation, a role formerly monopolized by the royal-noble elite. The confluence of the expanding market economy and the growth of the literate, wage-earning middle class created the conditions for the development of popular commercial culture in its various forms: newspapers, magazines, cartoons, novels and short stories, films, recorded music, and so on. The middle class provided not only a market for these new commodities but also the majority of entrepreneurs behind this new industry, as well as the cultural producers themselves—writers, journalists, graphic artists, and filmmakers.

It was by means of the new mass cultural media—in particular, the daily press—that members of the Bangkok middle class mounted their critiques of various elite practices and behavior such as polygamy, the use of prostitutes, and so on. At the same time, the new cultural forms of the short story, the novel, and film served as potent means to represent imaginatively the social world and moral values of the middle class and urban elite (and, in doing so, to make Bangkok life of the period recognizable to the twenty-first-century observer with an immediacy that was not possible in the earlier pre–mass culture era). As we have seen, the type of popular romantic works produced during this period were diffuse in nature and conveyed the changing dynamics of interpersonal behavior in middle-class and elite urban society. In a broad sense these works embodied key dilemmas, contradictions, and tensions between traditional notions (e.g., arranged marriage) and those of a more modern variety (e.g., independent love). The expression of conflicting values and ideals in the cultural realm can be seen as representing another dimension of the aforementioned crisis gripping Siamese society during the late absolutist period.

The sociopolitical malaise of the times (as embodied in the various press critiques of the existing order) in conjunction with the onset of the effects of the Great Depression from 1930 provided the broader context and cultural ambience in which the events of June 1932 are to be understood. By this I mean to say that the overthrow of the monarchy by the People's Party was not simply a naked grab for power by a small group of disenchanted military and civilian officials, as suggested in conventional interpretations of the event by such writers as Thawatt and Wilson,[4] but rather a response to long-term public antipathy toward the existing order of things. To put this another way, 24 June 1932 should not be seen as merely the first in a series of successful coups d'état which have been such a marked feature of Thai political life over the following half-century or so, but rather as the political manifestation of a nationalist revolution that ushered in a new populist era.

In contrast to the absolute monarchy, which had ruled the country in an ad hoc, highly personal, and remote fashion, the post-1932 state played a far more direct interventionist role, seeking to reorder and redefine Siamese society on the one hand, while attempting to instill a heightened sense of national unity and purpose among the populace at large on the other. Under this new political dispensation, with its incorporative, reformist ethos, women were accorded far greater recognition and support than in the past. Among other things, women's educational and employment opportunities were enhanced, they were given the same political rights as men, and the legal (if not actual) introduction of monogamy in place of polygamy formalized the idea of equality between the sexes in marriage. At the same time, women were prominently featured in the nation-building ideology of the state. As we saw, female heroism and sacrifice for the nation in the premodern era was celebrated both in public statuary and in various historical dance dramas staged by the Department of Fine Arts. Paralleling these initiatives the state in its own ways also celebrated and honored contemporary womanhood, this being embodied by the Miss Siam (and later Miss Thailand) competition, begun in 1934, and the inauguration of Mother's Day (*wan mae*) by the Phibun regime in 1943 as a part of its hypernationalist agenda.[5]

In a broad sense these various developments represented a significant change in the social status of women from what it had been at the turn of the century. Indeed, one can talk of a growing process of female emancipation as one of the key, yet little recognized, areas of transformation that accompanied Siam's emergence as a modern nation-state. Even so, it needs to be emphasized that this process was primarily one which benefited middle- and upper-class women, who were best placed to take advantage of the increased social, educational, and vocational opportunities that became available with the growth of the market-based economy. In many ways, then, such women gained greater social parity with members of the male population.

At the same time, however, in at least one important area, little changed: the sexual double standard has continued to be a central defining element in gender relations and identity across the social spectrum, even though equality in marriage was enshrined in law. In contemporary Thailand, for example, heterosexual male identity continues to be closely associated with the idea of being a *chai chatri*, or womanizer; the more conquests or sexual liaisons an individual can claim, the more masculine he is deemed to be.[6] Meanwhile female identity, with respect to unmarried women, remains closely bound up with the maintenance of virtue, not to mention the cultivation of physical beauty, an obsession that is endlessly reaffirmed through the plethora of beauty contests that are such a prominent feature of modern Thai life. In the case of married women, notions of identity are similarly limited, revolving for the most part around the role of motherhood and the sphere of domesticity more generally.

Significantly, the persistence of these distinct gendered social values concerning masculinity and femininity is seen as problematic by many Thais. In the early 1980s, for example, a vociferous public debate was sparked by proposed amendments to the law on abortion.[7] Many of those involved in the debate expressed deep concern about what they perceived to be the rampant lasciviousness and carnality engulfing Thai society, views that were not unlike those expressed by middle-class critics of the absolutist sociopolitical order back in the 1920s. A number of participants in the 1980s debate insisted that new social values relating to the defining of gender identity were desperately needed if the nation was to survive and prosper.[8] In conclusion, it can be seen that many of the debates and issues current today have a much longer history than is suggested in simplistic and superficial accounts which promote the view that American influence during the Vietnam War era marked a watershed in Thai sociocultural life.[9] As this study has demonstrated, Thailand's "modernity" is, in fact, far older than generally claimed, and is much more of an indigenous phenomenon, albeit one that evolved in response to European models, than the result of post–World War II political and cultural impositions from the West.

NOTES

1. Antonio Gramsci, *Selections from the Prison Notebooks of Antonio Gramsci*, edited and translated by Q. Hoare and G. Nowell Smith (London: Lawrence and Wishart, 1971), 276.
2. Nanthira Khamphiban, "Nayobai kiaw-kap phuying thai nai samai sang chat kh'ong ch'om phon p'o phibun songkhram, ph'o s'o 2481–2487" [Policies toward Thai Women during the Nation-Building Era of Field Marshall Phibun Songkhram, 1938–44], M.A. thesis, Thammasat University, Bangkok, 1987, 41–42; Suphatra K'opkitsuksakun, *Sen thang nang ngam* [A History of Beauty Contests] (Bangkok: D'ok bia, 1993), 27–28.
3. Wen-Hsin Yeh, *The Alienated Academy: Culture and Politics in Republican China 1919–1937* (Cambridge, Mass.: Council on East Asian Studies, Harvard University, 1990), 56.
4. See, for example, Thawatt Mokarapong, *History of the Thai Revolution* (Bangkok: Chalermnit, 1972); David A. Wilson, *Politics in Thailand* (Ithaca, N.Y.: Cornell University Press, 1962).
5. Nanthira, "Policies toward Thai Women," 125.
6. Interestingly, while this behavior often appears to be tolerated by women, at other times it frequently leads to crimes of passion, perhaps none more dramatic than the spate of penile severings by jealous wives which have been widely reported over the last two decades.
7. *Chuay sangkhom dai: kae-khai kot-mai kan tham-thaeng* [You Can Help Society: Amend the Law on Abortion]. From the proceedings of a seminar on abortion, organized by the Family Planning Association of Thailand [*Samakhom wang phaen kr'op-khrua haeng prathet-thai*], held 2 August 1980 at the National Women's Council, 36–37.

8. Family Planning Association of Thailand, *You Can Help Society*, 36–39.

9. Thanh-Dam Truong. *Sex, Money, and Morality: Prostitution and Tourism in Southeast Asia* (London: Zed Books, 1990). Also see Heather Montgomery, "Pattaya and Child Prostitution as a Form of Cultural Crisis," Proceedings of the 6th International Conference on Thai Studies, vol. 1, 207. Chiang Mai, Thailand, 14–17 October 1996.

Bibliography

SERIALS (ENGLISH AND THAI)

Bangk'ok kan-m'uang, 1922–1927
Bangkok Post
Bangkok Times, 1897–1930
Bangkok Times Weekly Mail, 1918–1930
Chaloem prathet, 1933
Chino sayam warasap, 1914–1923
Chum-num phaphayon, 1941
Kammak'on, 1923–1924
Khao phaphayon, 1927
Krungthep Daily Mail, 1914–1929
Kulasatri, 1906
Nari kasem, 1926
Nari nithet, 1926
Pakka thai, 1926–1928
Phaphayon, 1927

Phaphayon sayam, 1922–1924
Prachathai, 1932
Pramuan wan, 1936

Ratsad'on, 1928–1929

Satri niphon, 1914
Satri sap, 1922
Satri thai, 1924–1926
Sayam nik'on, 1936–1937
Sayam rat, 1923–1925
Sayam riwiw, 1926–1927, 1935
Sayam sakki, 1922–1924
Sayam yuphadi, 1928
Sikrung, 1926–1932
Suphap-burut, 1929–1931
Suphap nari, 1930
Thai thae, 1931
(10 thanwa) phanuak khaw rew, 1932
The Nation
Ying sayam, 1930
Ying thai, 1932–1933

BOOKS, THESES, AND ARTICLES
(IN ENGLISH AND THAI)

Adul Wichiencharoen, and *Luang* Chamroon Netisastra. "Some Main Features of Modernization of Ancient Family Law in Thailand." In *Family Law and Customary Law in Asia: A Contemporary Legal Perspective*, ed. David C. Buxbaum, 89–106. The Hague: Martinus Nijhoff, 1968.
Akat Damkoeng Raphiphat, M. C. [Prince]. *Lakh'on haeng chiwit* [The Circus of Life]. Bangkok: Phrae Phithaya, 1974.

259

―――. *Wiman thalai* [Crumbling Mansion (a collection of short stories)]. Bangkok: Phrae Phithaya, 1972.

―――. *Phiw l'uang phiw khaw* [East and West]. Bangkok: Phrae Phithaya, 1962.

Akin Rabibhadana. *The Organization of Thai Society in the Early Bangkok Period, 1782–1873.* Ithaca, N.Y.: Southeast Asia Program, Cornell University, 1969.

Anake Nawigamune. *Khosana thai samai raek* [Advertising in Thailand: The First Era]. Bangkok: Saeng-daet, 1990.

Anderson, Benedict R. O'G. *Imagined Communities: Reflections on the Origin and Spread of Nationalism.* London: Verso, 1991.

Apinan Poshyananda. *Modern Art in Thailand, Nineteenth and Twentieth Centuries.* Singapore: Oxford University Press, 1992.

―――. Modern Art in Thailand in the Nineteenth and Twentieth Centuries. Part 1, Ph.D. diss., Cornell University, 1990.

Bamber, Scott, Kevin Hewison, and Peter Underwood. "A History of Sexually Transmitted Diseases in Thailand: Politics, Policy, and Control." *Genitourinary Medicine* 69 (1993): 148–57.

Banner, Lois W. *American Beauty.* Chicago: University of Chicago Press, 1984.

Barbu, Zev. "Popular Culture: A Sociological Approach." In *Approaches to Popular Culture,* ed. C. W. E. Bigsby, 39–68. London: Edward Arnold, 1976.

Barmé, Scot. *Luang Wichit Wathakan and the Creation of a Thai National Identity.* Singapore: Institute of Southeast Asian Studies, 1993.

―――. *Kulap in Oz: A Thai View of Australian Life and Society in the Late 1940s.* Melbourne: Monash Asia Institute, 1995.

―――. "Early Thai Cinema and Filmmaking." *Film History* 11, no. 3 (1999): 308–18.

―――. "Protofeminist Discourses in Early Twentieth-Century Siam." In *Genders and Sexualities in Modern Thailand,* eds. Peter A. Jackson and Nerida M. Cook, 134–53. Chiang Mai: Silkworm Books, 1999.

Barnouw, Erik, and S. Krishnaswamy. *Indian Film.* 2nd ed. New York: Oxford University Press, 1980.

Basu, Amrita, ed. *The Challenge of Local Feminisms: Women's Movements in Global Perspective.* Boulder, Colo.: Westview, 1995.

Batson, Benjamin A. *The End of the Absolute Monarchy in Siam.* Singapore: Oxford University Press, 1984.

Benjamin, Walter. "The Work of Art in the Age of Mechanical Reproduction." In *Mass Communication and Society,* eds. James Curran, Michael Gurevitch, and Janet Woollacott, 384–408. London: Edward Arnold, 1977.

Bennett, Tony. "Theories of the Media, Theories of Society." In *Culture, Society, and the Media,* eds. Michael Gurvevitch, Tony Bennett, James Curran, and Janet Woollacott, 30–55. London: Methuen, 1982.

Berger, Peter L. *Facing Up to Modernity.* New York: Basic, 1977.

Bigsby, C. W. E. "The Politics of Popular Culture." In *Approaches to Popular Culture,* ed. C. W. E. Bigsby, 3–25. London: Edward Arnold, 1976.

Bishop, Ryan, and Lillian S. Robinson, *Night Market: Sexual Cultures and the Thai Economic Miracle.* New York: Routledge, 1998.

Boonrak Boonyaketmala. "The Rise and Fall of the Film Industry in Thailand, 1897–1992." *East-West Film Journal* 6, no. 2 (1992): 62–98.

Boxer, Marilyn J. " 'First Wave' Feminism in Nineteenth-Century France: Class, Family, and Religion." In *Reassessments of 'First Wave' Feminism*, ed. Elizabeth Sarah, 551–59. Oxford: Pergamon Press, 1982.

Brandon, James R. *Theatre in Southeast Asia*. Cambridge, Mass.: Harvard University Press, 1967.

Brown, Andrew. "Locating Working-Class Power." In *Political Change in Thailand: Democracy and Participation*, ed. Kevin Hewison, 163–78. London: Routledge, 1997.

Brown, Ian. *The Elite and the Economy in Siam, 1890–1920*. Singapore: Oxford University Press, 1988.

Bulbeck, Chilla. *One World Women's Movement*. London: Pluto Press, 1988.

Buls, Charles. *Siamese Sketches*. Trans., illus., and annotated Walter E. J. Tips. Bangkok: White Lotus, 1994.

Burgess, Jacquelin, and John R. Gold. "Introduction: Place, the Media, and Popular Culture." In *Geography: The Media and Popular Culture*, eds. Jacquelin Burgess and John R. Gold, 1–32. London: Croom Helm, 1985.

Burke, Peter. "The Discovery of Popular Culture." In *People's History and Socialist Theory*, ed. Raphael Samuel, 216–26. London: Routledge and Kegan Paul, 1981.

Callahan, William A. "The Ideology of Miss Thailand in National, Consumerist, and Transnational Space." *Alternatives* 23 (1998): 29–61.

Campbell, J. G. D. *Siam in the Twentieth Century*. London: Edward Arnold, 1902.

Chai-anan Samudawanich. *Chiwit lae ngan kh'ong thianwan lae ko s'or'o kulap* [The Life and Work of Thianwan and K. S. R. Kulap]. Bangkok: Bannakit, 1981.

Charnvit Kasetsiri. "Kae r'oi phrachao chang ph'uak" [Picking Up on the Trail of the King of the White Elephant]. *Sinlapawathanatham* 2, no. 14 (1980): 26–33.

Charnvit Kasetsiri, and Wani Samranwet. "Phaphayon thai kap kan 'sang chat': l'uat thahan thai, phrachao chang ph'uak, ban rai na rao" [Thai Films and 'Nation Building': Blood of the Thai Military, The King of the White Elephant, and Our Home and Fields]. *Warasan Thammasat* 19, no.2 (May–August 1993): 89–112.

Copeland, Matthew Phillip. "Contested Nationalism and the 1932 Overthrow of the Absolute Monarchy in Siam." Ph.D. diss., Australian National University, Canberra, 1993.

Corelli, Marie. *Vendetta* [*The Story of One Forgotten*]. Leipzig: Berhard de Lauretis, Tauchnitz, 1887.

Dal Lago, Francesca. "Crossed Legs in 1930s Shanghai: How 'Modern' the Modern Woman?" *East Asian History*, no. 19 (June 2000): 103–44.

Dararat Mettarikanon. "Sopheni kap naiyobai rathaban thai ph'o s'o 2411–2503" [Prostitution and Thai Government Policy 1868–1960]. M.A. thesis, Chulalongkorn University, Bangkok, 1983.

Darunee Tantiwiramanond, and Shashi Pandey. "The Status and Role of Thai Women in the Pre-modern Period: A Historical and Cultural Perspective." *Sojourn* 2, no.1 (February 1987): 125–49.

de la Loubere, Simon. *The Kingdom of Siam*. Singapore: Oxford University Press, 1969.

Department of Fine Arts. *Nithan kh'ong lung r'uang 'waen wiset' phaphayon fi phrahat phrabat somdet phra pokklao chao yu hae lae phaphayon phuthaprawat 'burapha prathip'* [Uncle's Folk Tale 'The Magic Ring': A Film by His Majesty King Prajadhipok, and a Historical Film on Buddhism, 'The Light of Asia']. Bangkok: Department of Fine Arts, The Thai Film Foundation, and the National Film Archives, 1987.

D'ok Mai Sot. *Sattru kh'ong cao l'on* [Her Foe]. Bangkok: Bannakhan, 1971.

———. *"Romance s'on r'uang cing"* [Romance Concealed in a True Story]. In *Phu klin* (collected short stories and articles), 4–193. Bangkok: Phrae Phitthaya, 1971.

———. *"N'ua khu"* [The Perfect Couple]. In *Phu klin*, 197–267. Bangkok: Phrae Phitthaya, 1971.

———. *Kam kaw* [Past Karma]. Bangkok: KhlangWithaya, 1971.

Dome Sukwong. "Khut kru nang kaw kh'ong krom rot-fay luang" [Unearthing Old Films Made by the Royal Railway Department]. *Sinlapawatthanatham* 2, no. 12 (October 1981): 51–61.

———. "85 pi phaphayon nai prathet thai" [Eighty-five Years of Cinema in Thailand]. *Sinlapawatthanatham* 3, no. 8 (June 1982): 7–29.

———. "Kamnoet kham phayphayon" [Origins of the Word "Film"]. *Sinlapawatthanatham* 3, no. 12 (October 1982): 46–61.

———. "Manit Wasuwat kap phaphayon siang sikrung" [Manit Wasuwat and the Sikrung Talkies]. *Sinlapawathanatham* 4, no. 7 (May 1983): 90–97.

———. "R'uang kh'ong rong yipun" [The Japanese Cinema in Bangkok]. *Silapak'on*, no. 28 (5 May 1984): 70–94.

———. *Prawat phaphayon thai* [The History of Thai Film]. Bangkok: Ongkan kha kh'ong khurusapha, 1990.

———. "Phrabat somdet phra pok klao kap phaphayon" [King Pradjadhipok and Film]. Unpublished paper, Bangkok, 1993.

———. *Long thang lae khadi long thang* [*Gone Astray*, the Film: *Gone Astray*, the Legal Case]. Bangkok: Film House, 1996.

Dunn, Tony. "The Evolution of Cultural Studies." In *Introduction to Contemporary Cultural Studies*, ed. David Punter, 71–91. London: Longman, 1986.

Eagleton, Terry. *The Illusions of Postmodernism*. Oxford: Blackwell, 1996.

Em'on Niranrat. "Thatsana thang sangkhom nai nawaniyai thai samai ratchakan thi cet" [Social Perspectives in the Thai Novel during the Seventh Reign]. M.A. thesis, Chulalongkorn University, 1978.

Family Planning Association of Thailand. *Chuay sangkhom dai: kae-khai kot-mai kan thamthaeng* [You Can Help Society: Amend the Law on Abortion]. From the proceedings of a seminar on abortion held 2 August 1980 at the National Women's Council in Bangkok.

Field, Audrey. *Picture Palace: A Social History of the Cinema*. London: Gentry, 1974.

Fiske, John. *Understanding Popular Culture*. Boston: Unwin Hyman, 1989.

Frisby, David. *Fragments of Modernity: Theories of Modernity in the Work of Simmel, Kracauer, and Benjamin*. Cambridge: Polity Press, 1985.

Graham, W. A. *Siam*, 2 vols. London: Alexander Moring Limited, 1924.

Gramsci, Antonio. *Selections from the Prison Notebooks of Antonio Gramsci*, ed. and trans. Q. Hoare and G. Nowell Smith. London: Lawrence and Wishart, 1971.

Gronewold, Sue. *Beautiful Merchandise: Prostitution in China, 1860–1936*. New York: Haworth Press, 1982.

Hamilton, Annette. "Rumours, Foul Calumnies, and the Safety of the State: Mass Media and National Identity in Thailand." In *National Identity and Its Defenders: Thailand 1939–1989*, edited by Craig J. Reynolds, 341–79. Melbourne: Monash Papers on Southeast Asia no. 25, 1991.

———. "Family Dramas: Film and Modernity in Thailand." *Screen* 33, no.3 (1992): 259–73.

Heider, K. G. *Indonesian Cinema: National Culture on Screen.* Honolulu: University of Hawaii Press, 1991.

Holm, David Frederick. "The Role of the State Railways in Thai History, 1892–1932." Ph.D. diss., Yale University, 1977; Ann Arbor, Mich.: University Microfilms.

Hong Lysa, "Palace Women at the Margins of Social Change: An Aspect of the Politics of Social History in the Reign of King Chulalongkorn." *Journal of Southeast Asian Studies* 30, no. 20 (September 1999): 310–24.

Inglis, Fred. *Popular Culture and Political Power.* New York: Harvester-Wheatsheaf, 1988.

Ingram, J. C. *Economic Change in Thailand 1850–1970.* Stanford, Calif.: Stanford University Press, 1971.

Jackson, Peter A., and Nerida M. Cook, eds. *Genders and Sexualities in Modern Thailand.* Chiang Mai: Silkworm Books, 1999.

Kaew Kanchana [Wibun Rongkhasuwan]. *L'uat thahan thai,* n.d., n.p.

Keyes, Charles. "National Heroine or Local Spirit? The Struggle over Memory in the Case of Thao Suranari of Nakhon Ratchasima." Paper presented at the Sixth International Thai Studies Conference, Chiang Mai, October 1996.

Khun Wichit Matra [Sa-nga Kanchanakhaphan]. "80 pi nai chiwit khaphachao" [Eighty Years of My Life]. Bangkok: *Anus'on* (Cremation Volume), 1980.

"Khun Wichit Matra kap wongkan nang thai" [*Khun* Wichit Matra and the World of Thai Film], *Siam nik'on* 4, no. 166 (1980): 34.

K'o Surangkhanang. *Ying khon chua* [The Prostitute]. Bangkok: Chiraphanit, 1937.

K'opkan Wisitthasi. "Mia n'oi" [Minor Wife]. *Suphapburut* [The Gentleman], 15 February 1930: 3266–310.

Kritsana Asokesin. *Mia luang* [Major Wife]. Bangkok: Double Night Printing, 1998.

Kulap Saipradit. *Saen rak saen khaen* [So Much Love, So Much Revenge]. Bangkok: San Muanchon, 1986.

———. *Songkhram chiwit* [The War of Life]. Bangkok: K'o Phai, 1979.

Lan, Hua R., and Vanessa Fong, eds. *Women in Republican China: A Sourcebook.* New York: M. E. Sharpe, 1999.

Landon, Kenneth Perry. *Siam in Transition.* New York: Greenwood Press, 1968.

League of Nations. *Commission of Enquiry into Traffic in Women and Children in the East* (Report to the Council). Geneva: Series of League of Nations Publications, 1933.

Lent, John A. *The Asian Film Industry.* London: Christopher Helm, 1990.

Leyda, Jay. *Dian Ying: Electric Shadows: An Account of Films and the Film Audience in China.* Boston: MIT Press, 1972.

Loos, Tamara. "Gender Adjudicated: Translating Modern Legal Subjects in Siam." Ph.D. diss., Cornell University, 1999.

Lyttleton, Chris. "Changing the Rules: Shifting Bounds of Adolescent Sexuality in Northeastern Thailand." In *Genders and Sexualities in Modern Thailand,* eds. Peter A. Jackson and Nerida M. Cook, 28–42. Silkworm Books: Chiang Mai, Thailand, 1999.

Macrae, Henry, *Film Daily Yearbook.* New York and Hollywood, 1924.

Manun Wathanakomen. "Narirom: manda haeng nangs'u-phim phuying" [*Narirom:* The Mother of Women's Newspapers]. *D'ok nangs'u,* vol. 22, 1996: 43–54.

Marr, David G. *Vietnamese Tradition on Trial 1920–1945.* Berkeley: University of California Press, 1981.

Mattani Rutnin. "Modern Thai Literature: The Process of Modernization and the Transformation of Values." *East Asian Cultural Studies*, vol. 17, nos. 1–4 (March 1978); Tokyo: The Centre for East Asian Cultural Studies.

————. *Modern Thai Literature: The Process of Modernization and the Transformation of Values*. Bangkok: Thammasat University Press, 1988.

McCoy, Alfred, and Alfredo Roces. *Philippine Cartoons: Political Caricature of the American Era, 1900–1941*. Quezon City, Philippines: Vera-Reyes, 1985.

Montgomery, Heather. "Pattaya and Child Prostitution as a Form of Cultural Crisis." Proceedings of the 6th International Conference on Thai Studies, vol. 1. Chiang Mai, Thailand, 14–17 October 1996, 205–15.

Mosse, George L. *Nationalism and Sexuality: Respectability and Abnormal Sexuality in Modern Europe*. New York: Howard Fertig, 1985.

Nakkharin Mektrairat. *Kan-pathiwat sayam ph'o s'o 2475* [The Siamese Revolution of 1932]. Bangkok: The Foundation for the Social Sciences and Humanities [*Muliniti sangkhomsat lae manutsat*], 1992.

Nanthira Khamphiban. "Nayobai kiaw-kap phuying thai nai samai sang chat kh'ong ch'om phon p'o phibun songkhram, ph'o s'o 2481–2487" [Policies towards Thai Women during the Nation-Building Era of Field Marshall Phibun Songkhram, 1938–44]. M.A. thesis, Thammasat University, Bangkok, 1987.

Nithi Aeusrivongse, "Lok kh'ong nang nophamat" [The World of *Nang* Nophamat]. In *Pak kai lae bai r'ua* [Pen and Sail], ed. Nithi Aeusrivongse. Bangkok: Amarin, 1984.

Norden, Hermann. *From Golden Gate to Golden Sun: A Record of Travel, Sport, and Observation in Siam and Malaya*. London: H. F. and G. Witherby, 1923.

Nuttanee Ratanapat. "King Vajiravudh's Nationalism and Its Impact on Political Development in Thailand." Ph.D. diss., Northern Illinois University, 1990; Ann Arbor, Mich.: University Microfilms.

Pasuk Phongphaichit. *From Peasant Girls to Bangkok Masseuses*. Geneva: International Labor Organization, 1982.

Pasuk Phongpaichit and Chris Baker. *Thailand: Economy and Politics*. Kuala Lumpur: Oxford University Press, 1995.

Phongdeit Jiangphattanarkit and Marcel Barang, trans. and eds. *The Circus of Life* [English translation of M. C. Akat Damkoeng's 1929 novel *Lakh'on haeng chiwit*]. Bangkok: Thai Modern Classics, Chaiyong Limthongkun Foundation, 1994.

Ph'onphirom Iamtham. *Bot bat thang kan m'uang kh'ong nangs'uphim thai (2475–2488)* [The Political Role of Thai Newspapers from 1932 to 1945]. Bangkok: Thai Watana Panich Press, 1977.

Phra tamrap yoni [*Vagina Manual*]. Bangkok: n.p., 1908.

Phra-aiyakan laksana phua mia [The Royal Code concerning Husbands and Wives]. In *Kotmai tra sam duang* [Law of the Three Seals], vol. 2. Bangkok: Khurusapha, 1962.

Phunphit Amatayakun. "Phaen siang phleng thai nai adit" [Thai Records in the Past]. *Sinlapawatthanatham* 2, no. 14 (1980): 8–24.

Pilbeam, Pamela M. *The Middle Classes in Europe, 1789–1914: France, Germany, Italy, and Russia*. London: Macmillan, 1990.

Pridi Banonyong. *The King of the White Elephant*. Los Angeles: Thammasat Association, 1990.

Quaritch Wales, H. G. *Siamese State Ceremonies: Their History and Function*. London: Bernard Quaritch, 1931.

Reid, Anthony. *Southeast Asia in the Age of Commerce, 1450–1680*. New Haven, Conn.: Yale University Press, 1988.

Reynolds, C. J. "Predicaments of Modern Thai History." *Southeast Asian Research* 12, no. 1 (March 1994): 64–90.

———. "A Nineteenth-Century Thai Buddhist Defense of Polygamy and Some Remarks on the Social History of Women in Thailand." Paper prepared at the Seventh Conference, International Association of Historians of Asia, Chulalongkorn University, Bangkok, 22–26 August 1977.

Rhode, Eric. *A History of the Cinema from Its Origins to 1970*. Hamondsworth, Eng.: Pelican Books, 1978.

Riverol, A. R. *Live from Atlantic City: The History of the Miss America Pageant before, after, and in Spite of Television*. Bowling Green, Ohio: Bowling Green State University Popular Press, 1992.

Saiphin Kaew-ngamprasoet. *Kan-m'uang nai anusawari thao suranari* [The Politics of the Monument of Thao Suranari]. Bangkok: Matichon/Silapa-Wattanatham, 1995.

Sakdina Chatrakul na Ayudhya. "Direction Unknown." *Cinema* (summer 1989): 58–62.

———. "Phaphayon kap kan t'o-su thang chon-chan nai huang wela haeng phlat phaendin" [Film and Class Struggle in a Time of Turmoil in the Kingdom]. *Sethasat kan-m'uang* 7, no. 1–2 (1989): 15–32.

Sa-nga Kanchanakhaphan (*Khun* Wichit Matra). *Yuk phleng nang lae lakon nai adit* [The Past Era of Song, Film, and Drama]. Bangkok: R'uangsin, 1975.

Santiago, Lilia Quindoza. "Rebirthing Babaye: The Women's Movement in the Philippines." In *The Challenge of Local Feminisms: Women's Movements in Global Perspective*, 110–28. Boulder, Colo.: Westview, 1995.

Sarah, Elizabeth, ed. *Reassessments of "First Wave" Feminism*. Oxford: Pergamon Press, 1982.

Scott, J. W. *Gender and the Politics of History*. New York: Columbia University Press, 1988.

Seabrook, Jeremy. *Travels in the Skin Trade: Tourism and the Sex Industry*. London: Pluto Press, 1996.

Shorter Oxford English Dictionary, The, vol. 2. Oxford: Clarendon Press, 1973.

Siaw (Sieow) S'onguan Sibunr'uang. Cremation Volume, Bangkok: Phathanakorn Printery, 1928.

Siffin, W. J. *The Thai Bureaucracy: Institutional Change and Development*. Honolulu: East-West Center Press, 1966.

Siriphorn Sakhrobanek. "Kan riak-r'ong sithi-satri kh'ong ying thai (2398–2475)" [Thai Women Call for Their Rights, 1855–1932]. *Satrithat* (August–October 1983): 28–35.

Skinner, G. W. *Chinese Society in Thailand: An Analytical History*. Ithaca, N.Y.: Cornell University Press, 1957.

Sklar, Robert. *Movie-made America*. New York: Random House, 1971.

Smith, Malcolm. *A Physician at the Court of Siam*. Kuala Lumpur: Oxford University Press, 1982.

Smyth, David. *The Prostitute* [English language translation of K. Surangkhanang's novel, *Ying khon chua*]. Kuala Lumpur: Oxford University Press, 1994.

S'o Atsanachinda. *Phrung-ni cha rot nam sop* [Tomorrow They'll Consecrate My Corpse]. Bangkok: Na Ban Wannakam, 1993.

Somer, Doris. "Irresistible Romance: The Foundational Fictions of Latin America." In *Nation and Narration*, ed. Homi K. Bhabha, 71–98. London: Routledge, 1990.

Sukanya Tirawanit. *Prawatikan nangs'uphim nai prathet thai phai tai rab'op somburanasithirat* [Newspapers in Thailand under the Absolute Monarchy]. Bangkok: Thai Watana Panich Press, 1977.

———. *Nangs'uphim chak pathiwat 2475 su pathiwat 2516* [The Thai Press from the Revolution of 1932 to the Revolution of 1973]. Bangkok: Thai Watana Panich Press, 1983.

Sumalee Bumroongsook. *Love and Marriage: Mate Selection in Twentieth-Century Central Thailand.* Bangkok: Chulalongkorn University Press, 1995.

Suphaphan Bunsa-at. *Prawat nangs'uphim nai prathet thai* [A History of the Press in Thailand]. Bangkok: Bannakit, 1974.

Suphatra K'opkitsuksakun. *Sen thang nang ngam* [A History of Beauty Contests]. Bangkok: D'ok bia, 1993.

Suwadee Tanaprasitpatana. "Thai Society's Expectations of Women, 1851–1935." Ph.D. diss., Sydney University, 1989.

Terwiel, B. J. *Monks and Magic: An Analysis of Religious Ceremonies in Central Thailand.* Scandinavian Institute of Asian Studies Monograph Series no. 24. London: Curzon Press, 1979.

Thamkiat Kanari. "Mae wan kap khwam phayabat" [Mae Wan and the Novel "Vendetta"]. *Sinlapawathanatham* 5, no. 9 (July 1984): 102–105.

Thanh-Dam Truong. *Sex, Money, and Morality: Prostitution and Tourism in Southeast Asia.* London: Zed Books, 1990.

Thawatt Mokarapong. *History of the Thai Revolution.* Bangkok: Chalermnit, 1972.

Thepchu Thapth'ong. "Nakleng to nakleng khon keng" [Bigtime Gangsters]. In *Lao r'uang thai-thai* [Thai Stories], vol. 1, 189–95. Bangkok: S'ong rao, 1992.

———. "7–9 lae 41 chan" [Seven, Nine, and Forty-one Storeys]. In *Lao r'uang thai* [Thai Stories], vol. 2. 67–72. Bangkok: S'ong rao, 1992.

Thompson, Virginia. *Thailand: The New Siam.* New York: Paragon Book Reprint, 1967.

Thongchai Winichakul. *Siam Mapped: A History of the Geo-Body of a Nation.* Honolulu: University of Hawaii Press, 1994.

Turner, Bryan S. *Max Weber: From History to Modernity.* London: Routledge, 1992.

Van Esterik, Penny. "Gender and Development in Thailand: Deconstructing Display." In *Women, Feminism, and Development,* eds. Huguette Dagenais and Denise Piché, 264–79. Montreal: McGill-Queen's University Press, 1994.

———. "The Politics of Beauty in Thailand." In *Beauty Queens on the Global Stage: Gender, Contests, and Power,* eds. Colleen Cohen, Richard Wilk, and Beverly Stoeltje, 203–16. New York: Routledge, 1996.

———. "Repositioning Gender, Sexuality, and Power in Thai Studies." In *Genders and Sexualities in Modern Thailand,* eds. Peter A. Jackson and Nerida M. Cook, 275–89. Chiang Mai: Silkworm Books, 1999.

Vella, Walter F. *Chaiyo! King Vajiravudh and the Development of Thai Nationalism.* Honolulu: University of Hawaii Press, 1978.

Walkowitz, Judith R. *City of Dreadful Delight: Narratives of Sexual Danger in Late-Victorian London.* Chicago: University of Chicago Press, 1992.

Warren, J. F. *Ah Khu and Karayuki-san: Prostitution in Singapore, 1870–1940.* Singapore: Oxford University Press, 1993.

Wathinee Boonchalaksi, and Philip Guest. *Prostitution in Thailand.* Bangkok: Institute for Population and Social Research, Mahidol University, 1994.

Wender Zak, Michelle, and Patricia A. Moots. *Women and the Politics of Culture.* New York: Longman, 1983.

Wen-Hsin Yeh. *The Alienated Academy: Culture and Politics in Republican China, 1919–1937.* Cambridge, Mass.: Council on East Asian Studies, Harvard University, 1990.

Wichit Wathakan, *Luang.* "*Sam'on*" [Samorn]. In *Ammata niyai chut phua hai* [Classic Stories: The "The Disappeared Husband" Series]. Bangkok: Khlang-sam'ong- media fokat, 1992: 1–56.

———. "*Phua hai*" [The Disappeared Husband], *Ammata niyai chut phua hai* [Classic Stories: The "The Disappeared Husband" series]. Bangkok: Khlang-sam'ong- media fokat, 1992: 59–60.

———. "*Phuying*" [Women], text of radio broadcast by Wichit on 3 November 1930. In *Pathakatha lae kham banyai* [Lectures and Talks], vol. 2, 84–97. Bangkok: Soemwit Bannakhan, 1973.

———. *S'uk talang kap nanchao* [The Battle of Talang and Nan Chao (Two plays)]. *Cremation Volume*, Mrs. Bunsong Khunakasem, 10 March 1963.

Wipha Senanan. *The Genesis of the Thai Novel.* Bangkok: Thai Watana Panich Press, 1975.

Wilson, David A. *Politics in Thailand.* Ithaca, N.Y.: Cornell University Press, 1962.

Wyatt, D.K. *The Politics of Reform in Thailand: Education in the Reign of King Chulalongkorn.* New Haven, Conn.: Yale University Press, 1969.

Xiaomei Chen. *Occidentalism: A Theory of Counter-discourse in Post-Mao China.* New York: Oxford University Press, 1995.

Yoneo Ishi, and Toshiharu Yoshikawa. *Khwam samphan thai—yipun 600 pi* [600 Years of Thai-Japanese Relations]. Bangkok: Mulinithi khr'ong-kan tam-ra sangkhomsat lae manutsat, 1987.

Yingjin Zhang. *The City in Modern Chinese Literature and Film: Configurations of Space, Time, and Gender.* Stanford, Calif.: Stanford University Press, 1996.

Yuphaphorn Chaengchemchit. "Kans'uksa kh'ong satri thai: s'uksa korani chaph'o kh'ong rong-rian rachini (ph'o. s'o 2447–2503)" [Thai Women's Education: The Case of the Rachini School, 1904–60]. M.A. thesis, Thammasat University, Bangkok, 1987.

Index

About the Author

Scot Barmé first traveled to Thailand in the early 1970s and has subsequently lived, worked, and conducted research in the country over a period of many years. His previous works include *Luang Wichit Wathakan and the Creation of a Thai National Identity* (1993) and *Kulap in Oz: A Thai View of Australian Life and Society in the Late 1940s* (1995). He is presently a visiting fellow at the Australian National University in Canberra, a restaurateur, and also involved in various translation projects.